The 100 Worst Military Disasters in History

The 100 Worst Military Disasters in History

John T. Kuehn with David W. Holden

An Imprint of ABC-CLIO, LLC

Santa Barbara, California • Denver, Colorado

Library of Congress Cataloging-in-Publication Data

Names: Kuehn, John T., author. | Holden, David W., author.
Title: The 100 worst military disasters in history / John T. Kuehn with David W. Holden.
Other titles: One hundred worst military disasters in history
Description: Santa Barbara, California : ABC-CLIO, [2020] | Includes bibliographical references and index.
Identifiers: LCCN 2019029148 (print) | LCCN 2019029149 (ebook) | ISBN 9781440862687 (hardback) | ISBN 9781440862694 (ebook)
Subjects: LCSH: Battles. | Military history.
Classification: LCC D25.5 .K84 2020 (print) | LCC D25.5 (ebook) | DDC 355.4/8—dc23
LC record available at https://lccn.loc.gov/2019029148
LC ebook record available at https://lccn.loc.gov/2019029149

ISBN: 978-1-4408-6268-7 (print)
     978-1-4408-6269-4 (ebook)

24 23 22 21 20   1 2 3 4 5

This book is also available as an eBook.

ABC-CLIO
An Imprint of ABC-CLIO, LLC

ABC-CLIO, LLC
147 Castilian Drive
Santa Barbara, California 93117
www.abc-clio.com

This book is printed on acid-free paper ∞

Manufactured in the United States of America

Contents

Part VI. Recent Military Disasters

Introduction

THE DYNAMICS OF MILITARY DISASTERS

What are military disasters? What are their dynamics? Are there common threads that link them? These are the sorts of questions that we hope to address in this book. Military disasters are not related only to battles, but in some cases campaigns, or even entire, disastrous wars. Their commonality is that they occur in human conflict, mostly among larger entities such as empires, states, and nations, or any permutation therein. In categorizing them as *military*, we have decided not to limit ourselves to military disasters on land, but also to include sea and air disasters, as well as what one might call *multidomain environments*—those that encompass conflict in its broadest sense, such as the campaign of Gallipoli in 1915.[1]

We also strove to prevent this being a work that stresses warfare in Western Europe, but rather encompasses the entire globe. However, because we are writing this in English, the authors' common language, we could not avoid a bias toward picking Western military disasters, especially those of the last 300 years. We do go back millennia, but choosing a majority of recent disasters is more the result of actually knowing so much more about the circumstances of these conflicts and engagements, rather than deliberate bias. There are undoubtedly major military disasters from human history that could be covered but are either poorly chronicled, lost to history, or have yet to be more fully discovered and articulated.

One of our criteria for picking the disasters that we did, other than our effort not to limit ourselves to land battles, comes from the work of Carl von Clausewitz—namely, that the disaster has some sort of political result. One could argue, semantically and tendentiously we suppose, that when people are killed, maimed, or captured, as well as held hostage for ransom (which used to be a common practice in most wars), a political consequence of some measure results. True, but we are talking about major political or operational results—destruction of an army, leading to a diplomatic outreach or outright capitulation; ceding of a province or trading privilege; and other things of this nature. This does not mean that the obverse is true. Not all political circumstances flowing from war come from military disaster; they often are the result of steady or artful application of force and diplomacy over time. Another feature of military disasters in this work is that they are dramatic: they have the shape and form of what evolutionary biologists call "punctuated equilibrium"—large amounts of violent change in a relatively short period of time.

As for the patterns that one might discern from this study, we might say something about what we anticipate based on other accounts of military disaster. First, but listed by no means in any priority, we might look at the *hubris* of the defeated party, sometimes categorized as "overconfidence." This relates to tragedy, in that the fall is great for the proud and vain. Related to this is an underestimation of the enemy, a failure to fight the enemy as they actually are rather than one's conception, and misperception, of that enemy. In military circles, this is often captured by the motto, "The enemy gets a vote." Neither of these is always found in military disasters—there have been unconfident losers (e.g., Pompey at Pharsalus), as well as protagonists who had a good understanding of their opponent and still lost disastrously.

Another feature of military disasters is leadership. It is rare that a professional or well-trained army, navy, or air force prevails when its senior leadership is incompetent or just plain bad compared to the enemy. Associated with this idea are those disasters where two highly successful risk takers meet, and one simply outperforms the other. The other side of this coin, of course, is the role of military institutions, how well trained and organized they are, and their morale when considering a military defeat. Sometimes good armies (e.g., the Army of the Potomac) are failed by their leaders; more rarely, poor armies are less likely to be committed to all-out war, battle, or operations by competent leaders. Then there are organizations that seem very resilient but collapse with overuse or are used for a purpose they are not designed for, such as Napoleon's army at Waterloo.

Finally, one cannot help but account for the role that chance plays in military disaster. Clausewitz famously wrote: "War is the realm of chance. No other human activity gives it greater scope: no other has such incessant and varied dealings with this intruder."[2] Thus, the issue of a battle or campaign may turn on one chance event, or many. This is the idea that for the want of a horse, the battle is lost (see the account of the Battle of Bosworth, later in this work). Thus, contingency plays its role. More often, that role is seen in the *scale* of disaster, not the underlying *cause*, but occasionally a series of accidents or coincidences add up to become a primary factor. Or they combine with the beneficial form of contingency, serendipity, where one side's bad luck is augmented by the other side's lucky breaks. Further, as the reader will find, military disaster often gives to both sides, to the nominal winner as well as to the loser.

This work owes something of a debt of gratitude for some of its approach, albeit a greatly constrained one (by virtue of the number and words allotted to each case), to the work of Eliot A. Cohen and John Gooch entitled *Military Misfortunes*.[3] However, this work is not an attempt to either revise or replace that still valuable analysis and taxonomy of failure. If the book has any overall objective, it is to emphasize patterns in military disasters that, in addition to being interesting, might help provide wisdom and insight into the genesis of failure. We often learn more from failure than we do from success, especially when that failure occurs in the most unforgiving human activity of all—war.

The number of disasters that we have chosen to focus on, 100, is entirely arbitrary and not related to any comprehensive review of military catastrophes in human history. This is not the top 100 disasters, but rather a survey of 100 military disasters that occurred, which we believe have significance.

NOTES

1. For a discussion of the concept of multidomain battle, see David Perkins, "Multi-Domain Battle: Driving Change to Win the Future," August 2017; accessed May 7, 2019, from https://www.armyupress.army.mil/Journals/Military-Review/English-Edition-Archives/July-August-2017/Perkins-Multi-Domain-Battle.

2. Carl von Clausewitz, *On War,* trans. Peter Paret and Michael Howard (Princeton, NJ: Princeton University Press, 1986), 101.

3. Eliot A. Cohen and John Gooch, *Military Misfortunes: The Anatomy of Failure* (New York: Free Press, 1990).

PART I

Ancient Military Disasters

1. Megiddo

Date: April 16, 1457 BCE
Location: Megiddo, Canaan

OPPONENTS

1. Egyptian Empire
    Commander: Thutmose III
2. Kingdoms of Canaan
    Commander: The king of Kadesh

BACKGROUND

The battle of Megiddo is one of the first for which there is a relatively accurate account. It is primarily from the Egyptian point of view and is based on hieroglyphic writings, and most of it was also recorded by Thutmose III's scribe, Thaneni. The date for the battle is open to debate. Based on the Egyptian calendar, the battle took place on the twenty-first day of the twenty-third year of Thutmose's reign, which had been roughly interpreted to be April 16, 1457, though some accounts claim the year was as early as 1482 BC or 1479 BC.

When Thutmose II died, Thutmose III was only eight, and his mother, Hatshepsut, ruled as regent. Breaking with tradition, Hatshepsut elevated herself to pharoah. Her reign saw Egypt continue to prosper as her son studied and prepared himself to take the throne. When he was twenty-one, Hatshepsut passed away, and Thutmose III ascended. Using the inherent confusion during a change of rulers, some of the kingdoms of Canaan decide to test the young pharoah. They allied with the king of Kadesh to break free of Egyptian rule.

The king of Megiddo offered the fortress city and his capital, Megiddo, as the base for the revolt. It was not only a strong fortress, but it also sat on the main supply route, near the Jezreel Valley. Blocking this route would hamper the Egyptians' ability to trade and could provide the rebels leverage over Thutmose III. The rebel alliance assembled 10,000–15,000 soldiers and 1,000 chariots to block the passes into the Jezreel Valley and waited for Thutmose III to react. They would not have long to wait.

When word of the revolt reached the pharoah, he wasted no time in assembling a force of 10,000–20,000 infantry and 1,000 chariots of his own. His army moved rapidly, covering the 150 miles from Tjaru to Gaza in ten days. From there, the Egyptian army marched to Yehem, southwest of Megiddo, to prepare for battle. As his army rested, Thutmose III held a council of his generals about the upcoming battle.

THE BATTLE

There were three passes into the Jezreel Valley. Two of them, one on the north and one on the south, were wide enough for the Egyptian army to get through quickly. The third was in the center, along the Wadi Ara, and came out at the village of Aruna. However, that path was narrow, and Thutmose's soldiers would have had to pass through it in a single file. Not only would this route be slower, but it also would put the army at risk of being destroyed piecemeal as they exited. Thutmose's generals advised that the wisest course of action was to take either the northern or southern pass. Thutmose disagreed, reasoning that his opponents would be thinking like his generals and would not be defending the center pass. It was a calculated risk that could cost Thutmose his young reign. To reassure his generals, Thutmose said he would be in the first chariot through the pass.

Standing in his golden chariot, Thutmose, as promised, led his soldiers through the narrow defile near Aruna. After defeating a small contingent of Canaanites, left to defend the pass, the Egyptians exited unopposed. Thutmose had been correct—the king of Kadesh had assumed that Thutmose would take one of the more accessible routes and left the Aruna pass unguarded. Thutmose took the rest of the day to get the rest of his troops through the pass and deployed for battle the next day. He would command the center, with his wings positioned on high ground to the north and south.

The king of Kadesh belatedly realized his mistake, but Thutmose's surprise created a crisis in command among the Canaanites. They squabbled among themselves as to the best action to take to counter the Egyptians. The king eventually prevailed and began shifting his forces from the other passes to Megiddo. However, they were still in the process of moving when Thutmose struck the next morning.

On the morning of April 16, both sides were about equal in size, roughly 10,000 infantry and 1,000 chariots, as they faced each other. Thutmose struck first, launching his left wing against the Canaanite right wing. The Egyptians caught the Canaanites as they were still getting into position and quickly routed them. Thutmose saw his chance and led his chariots into the mass of the Canaanite army. The broken rebels hastily retreated to the safety of Megiddo's walls. Once inside, they closed the gate before pulling up other survivors, including the king of Megiddo and king of Kadesh, over the walls with ropes. Unfortunately for Thutmose, his soldiers began plundering the Canaanite camp rather than pursuing them to Megiddo. However, they did capture 200 suits of armor and 924 chariots.

Nonetheless, Thutmose was now forced to lay siege to Megiddo. He built a moat around the fortress and a palisade around the moat. For seven months, the Egyptians kept anything or anyone from leaving or entering Megiddo before the Canaanites surrendered, ending the rebellion.

CONCLUSION

After the surrender, among the things Thutmose and his army took back to Egypt were 340 prisoners, almost 2,000 head of cattle, 2,000 horses, and over 22,000 sheep, along with the chariot and armor of the king of Megiddo. The king of Kadesh was able to slip away, but Thutmose required the Canaan kings to provide him with one of their sons to take back to Egypt. These children were well treated and educated in Egyptian ways, making them ready and loyal allies of Egypt when they returned to rule their lands. For Thutmose III, Megiddo was the first and most significant of his many victories, as he went on to spread Egyptian influence and hegemony throughout the Levant and beyond.

Further Reading

Cline, Eric H., and David O'Connor. *Thutmose III: A New Biography.* Ann Arbor: University of Michigan Press, 2006.

Gabriel, Richard A. *Thutmose III: A Military Biography of Egypt's Greatest Warrior King.* Washington, DC: Potomac Books, 2009.

Gabriel, Richard A. *Warrior Pharoah: A Chronicle of the Life and Deeds of Thutmose III, Great Lion of Egypt, Told in His Own Words to Thaneni the Scribe.* Lincoln, NE: iUniverse.com, 2001.

Spalinger, Anthony John. *War in Ancient Egypt: The New Kingdom.* Malden, MA: Blackwell Publishing, 2005.

2. Marathon

Date: September 490 BCE
Location: Marathon, Greece

OPPONENTS

1. Athens and Allies
    Commander: Miltiades
2. Persian Empire
    Commander: Datis

BACKGROUND

The Battle of Marathon, which checked Persian expansion into the Greek city-states, had its roots in the Ionian Rebellion. The city-states of Athens and Eretria sided with the Ionians in their fight to overthrow the Persians. Athens and Eretria scored a minor success when they captured Sardis, but they were forced to retreat when the Persians counterattacked. With a naval victory during the Battle of Lade, the Ionian Rebellion was put down. Nonetheless, despite their limited support and success during the rebellion, the Persian king, Darius, vowed to seek revenge on Athens and Eretria, especially Athens.

BATTLE OF MARATHON, 490 BCE

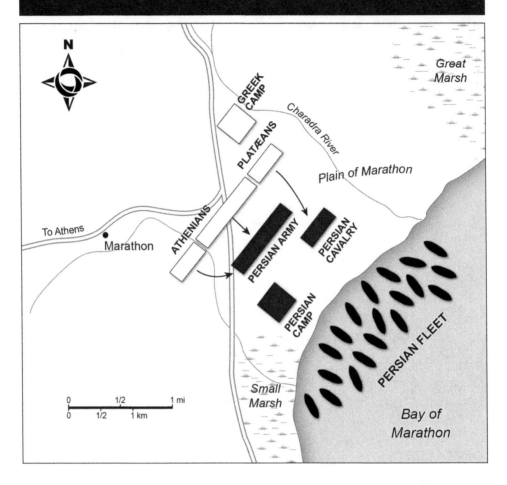

In 492 BC, Darius sent a fleet under the command of his son-in-law, Mardonius, to Greece to bring the restive Greek city-states back into line. Mardonius was successful in bringing Thrace and Macedonia back into the Persian fold. However, Mardonius's fleet ran into a violent storm that destroyed most of the ships and cut his campaign short. Still determined to bring Athens and Eretria to heel, Darius prepared another force under the command of the Median admiral Datis in 490 BC. This new army contained roughly 25,000 infantry and 2,000 cavalry that were loaded onto 600 large ships. Datis's mission was threefold: subjugate the Cyclades, punish Naxos for resisting Persian rule, and force Athens and Eretria to submit to Persian rule or else be destroyed.

Datis's first action was to raid Naxos and make it pay for its impertinence. After Naxos, Datis moved his fleet to Euboea in order to lay siege to Eretria. Having captured and burned Eretria, Datis and his fleet moved down the coast to Athens. Datis disembarked his force at Marathon, approximately twenty-five miles northwest of Athens. Rather than march directly on Athens, Datis chose to make camp on the plain of Marathon and await the Athenians. The plain was only ten miles deep and three miles wide, but Datis hoped it was large enough to give his cavalry the advantage they would need to defeat the Athenian infantry.

Hearing of the Persian landing, the Athenians assembled an army of approximately 9,000 hoplites (heavy infantry), along with 1,000 more hoplites from Plataea. The combined force, under the command of Miltiades, marched quickly to Marathon. At the same time, they sent a runner to Sparta to enlist their aid in the fight against the Persians. They hoped that the presence of the Spartans, who had a reputation as fierce warriors, would help convince the Persians to give up their cause and go home. Unfortunately, the Spartans were in the middle of the sacred Carneia festival and sent back word that they could not march until the festival was over, in approximately ten days. For several days, the Athenian and Persian armies watched each other across the plain at Marathon. The Persians assumed that time was on their side and they could outwait the Greeks. The Athenians knew that every day they postponed the battle brought them one day closer to the arrival of the Spartans. However, for some unknown reason, the Persian cavalry departed. Some historians suggest that Miltiades, having fought with the Persians, knew that without their cavalry, they would be at a disadvantage; and therefore he decided to attack. Whatever the reason, the Greeks made the first move.

THE BATTLE

Marathon was not only a battle between competing cultures; it was also between two different styles of warfare. The Persians preferred to use their archers to weaken and demoralize an enemy at a distance before sending in their cavalry to finish the engagement. Typically, the lightly armed Persian infantry would form a shield wall to protect the archers as they fired, and at the right moment, the Persian commander would send in his cavalry. This tactic supports the theory that the missing Persian cavalry encouraged Miltiades to attack. Meanwhile, Miltiades had the Greek hoplites at his disposal. Each hoplite was armed with a long spear and sword and carried a bronze shield for protection. The hoplites were organized into an eight-man by eight-man square called a *phalanx*. The phalanx marched toward the enemy, closing in to defeat them in brutal, hand-to-hand combat. Against the lightly armed infantry of the Persians, all the advantages would be with the Greeks—if they could get close enough.

Approximately 1,500 meters separated the armies as they formed for the battle. The Greeks were outnumbered roughly two-to-one. Datis, in typical Persian manner, placed his best infantry in the center and his weaker units on the wings. Seeing the broader frontage of the Persian army, Militiades thinned out his center to extend his line and prevent the Persians from outflanking him. Some modern historians conjecture that this was a deliberate tactic by Militiades to strengthen his wings, which he knew would be facing the weaker Persian formations. Regardless, his action would prove decisive during the battle.

It is not clear what initiated the battle, but the ancient historian Herodotus claims the Greeks ran the entire 1,500 meters. However, this seems unlikely, given the weight that each hoplite carried. Some suggest the Greeks ran to within several hundred meters of the Persians before reforming their phalanxes to close with them. Others believe that the Greeks marched in formation toward the Persians before charging the last few hundred meters.

Whatever the exact sequence, it is clear that at some point, the Greeks charged the Persians at a run. This action caught the Persians by surprise as the two sides crashed together. Initially, the Persians gained the upper hand in the center, where their better soldiers pushed back the thinner part of the Greek formation. However, on the flanks, the Athenians and Plataeans easily defeated the weaker Persian infantry and began closing in on the Persian center. As the Greeks approached, the Persians broke and fled back to their ships, with the Greeks in hot pursuit. Most of the Persian ships were able to escape; however, the Greeks managed to capture seven of them. Herodotus claims that Persian casualties totaled 6,400, as opposed to 192 Greeks. Some historians believe this might be an exaggeration. Regardless of the exact numbers, the Persians fled, ceding the battlefield altogether to the Greeks.

Datis sailed what was left of his army to attack Athens directly while the Greek army was recovering from the battle. Realizing what was happening, Miltiades ordered his army back to Athens on the double. Surprised to see the Greek army waiting on shore, Datis elected to sail back home. Militiades's action saved Athens, and the Battle of Marathon was over.

CONCLUSION

The Greco-Persian War was far from over; Darius's successor, Xerxes, would continue the fight until he was defeated at sea at Salamis and on land at Plataea in 480 BC. Nonetheless, the Athenian victory at Marathon boosted the morale of all Greeks and established Athens as a leading power. The battle also gave its name to the modern marathon race. In 1896, the first modern Olympic committee, to commemorate the ancient Olympic Games, instituted a long-distance race that would cover 26 miles, the same distance as between Athens and Marathon.

Further Reading

Bardunias, Paul M., and Fred Eugene Ray Jr. *Hoplites at War: A Comprehensive Analysis of Heavy Infantry Combat in the Greek World, 750–100 BCE.* Jefferson, NC: McFarland & Company, 2016.

Billows, Richard A. *Marathon: The Battle That Changed Western Civilization.* New York: Overlook Press, 2010.

Green, Peter. *The Greco-Persian Wars.* Berkeley: University of California Press, 1996.

Krentz, Peter. *The Battle of Marathon.* New Haven, CT: Yale University Press, 2010.

3. Salamis

Date: circa late September, 480 BCE
Location: Aegean Littoral

OPPONENTS

1. Athens and allied Greek states

Commanders: Themistocles (Athens)/Eurybaides (Sparta)

2. Persian Empire

Commanders: Xerxes (overall), and four admirals, including Queen Artemisia of Halicarnassus and Xerxes's half-brother Ariabignes (Ariaramnes)

BACKGROUND

The Battle of Salamis occurred during the campaign of the Persian king Xerxes against the Greeks in 480 BCE. Initially, the Persians had an overwhelming advantage—perhaps up to three times as many ships as the Allied Greek fleet. Also, the Persian ships tended to be more maneuverable and were all captained by veteran mariners and admirals from Persia's Greek, Phoenician, Egyptian, and Ionian allies. In the days preceding the arrival over land of Xerxes's huge army opposite Thermopylae, the Persian fleet suffered a number of setbacks that reduced its size. First, it divided, sending a squadron south and east of Euboea to intercept any reinforcements from Athens because the Greek fleet guarded the seaward passage west of the isle of Euboea. Second, the main fleet was badly damaged and scattered by a storm as it proceeded south from the coastal waters of Thessaly toward its rendezvous through the narrow passage of Artemisium to the army at Thermopylae.

Just as the Spartan force under King Leonidas held the pass at Thermopylae, the Allied Greek fleet held off the Persian fleet from Artemisium for three successive days. After Xerxes forced the famous pass at Thermopylae and other points against the Spartan-led defenders, the leaders of the Greek fleet, Themistocles (Athens) and Eurybaides (Sparta), realized that they too must retreat. Under the cover of darkness, they fell back down the western side of Euboea to Athens, right past Xerxes's army celebrating its recent victory. Once there, the Athenians scattered to the hills, their ships, and the island of Salamis during the last days of summer in 480.

THE PLAN

The decision of the Greeks to remain in the vicinity of Athens at Salamis was important, and most of the credit for it must go to Themistocles. However, Eurybaides provided the critical support of the Spartans for this course of action, which swayed all the other allies to accede; otherwise, the Greek fleet might have

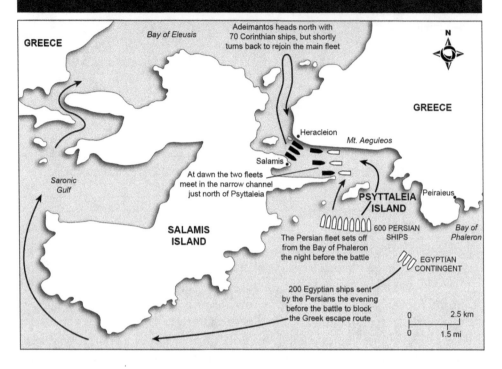

BATTLE OF SALAMIS, 480 BCE

scattered to its various ports and been destroyed in detail, or even off Corinth. It seems clear that they decided beforehand to evacuate to an island they controlled, from which they could feed their large fleet, and near waters they were familiar with. Now they had decided to fight there as well—no more retreat.

Themistocles was banking on Xerxes pursuing them to complete his chastisement of the Greeks. The Persians would have to control the seas before they could cross the narrow sound of water that separated the island from the mainland and complete their campaign. If the Greek fleet could prevent the Persian fleet from gaining command of the sea long enough, eventually the poor winter weather and storms might force the latter to return to safer waters for the winter.

Much has been written about Themistocles's plan for the battle, and most recent accounts now agree that his plan was to negate the superiority of the Persian fleet by limiting its ability to deploy en masse and encircle the Greek fleet with its greater numbers. To do this, the narrow waters of the sound between Salamis and Attica were ideal—they prevented full deployment of the Persian fleet, much as Thermopylae had prevented full deployment of the Persian army. The key was to get the Persian admirals to enter the strait and fight there. To do that, the Athenians, either accidentally or through a deliberate ruse, gave the Persians the impression that they had decided to fall back once again, as they did after Artemisium, possibly to Corinth. There was even the chance that the Athenian citizens might switch sides to gain back their city. This caused the Persian admirals, aware that the Greek fleet had given them the slip once already, to pursue what they thought was a disunited,

retreating force. When informed that the Persian admirals recommended an immediate attack, Xerxes approved the plan.

The second part of the plan involved using a flanking force made up of the very
capable trireme squadron of the Aeginatans, plus the small Spartan squadron on
the left (i.e., west) side of the Persian fleet, to both restrict and lessen the main body
as it sailed up the sound toward the main Allied fleet that contested the narrows
across which the Persian army must cross to attack the Athenians now sheltering
on Salamis. This flanking force would be relatively obscured as the Persian fleet
approached the entrance to the strait. Because the fleets would be spread along a
lengthy shore in narrow waters, the Persians would be unable to surround the Greek
fleet, nor could they deploy their entire force.

THE BATTLE

The Persian fleet ended up fighting the battle a day later than anticipated. After
deciding to attack, it hastily gathered outside the eastern entrance to the strait and
waited. However, the Greek fleet remained in the strait, and the Persians returned
to their anchorage southeast of Athens at Phaleron. The Persians were not finished,
though; it remained manned and ready while Xerxes consulted with his admirals.
They decided to deploy the fleet that night, with one squadron to plug any Greek
escape from the narrow strait in western Salamis opposite Megara, and the main
body of the fleet to enter the eastern strait from the south. Morale in the Persian
fleet was high—they expected a quick victory in anticipation of the defection of
the Athenian portion of the fleet. However, the rowers and marines had been at their
oars and stations all day and most of the night.

On the Greek side, most of the men in the fleet were rested. The numbers are
not certain, but estimates put the Persian fleet (including the detached squadron) at
three times the size of the Greek fleet (which numbered somewhere between 330
and 360 triremes). During the night, a lone trireme from Tenos, impressed into
Xerxes's fleet, wore away from the main body and scurried into the harbor of the
town of Salamis to warn their fellow Greeks. This was when Themistocles and the
nominal commander, Eurybaides, learned that their plan to lure the Persians into
battle in the strait had worked. The Greek mariners were roused from their sleep
and given last-minute pep talks by their commanders. They then manned their vessels, sterns already pointing into the strait, per the plan. On the tactical level, each
squadron was awaiting the moment it judged right to sally from the shallows into
the Persian fleet and begin ramming and fighting their opposite numbers. Vice
Admiral Horatio Nelson would have approved this "melee" approach for the combat, which relied on each commander's individual judgment.

As with all melees, then, Salamis was a series of battles based on an overall master plan that gave the Greeks a positional advantage. The flanking force (commanded by Eurybaides) performed its role to perfection, tying down the excellent
Ionian contingent of the Persian fleet so it could not deploy at full strength in the
constricted waters. The Athenian navy confronted the other most dangerous element of Xerxes's fleet: the veteran Phoenician component.

Now the heat of the battle and the positional advantage of the Greeks combined to cause the ranks of Persian ships behind the front line of ships to press against their comrades from the rear all up and down the line against the Greek defenders. This caused the front lines of Persian ships on all fronts to lose both their maneuverability and cohesion, while their Greek counterparts had sea space behind them to backrow and make repeated ramming attacks.

It was this mechanism that turned the Persian advantage in numbers against Xerxes and led to the incredible slaughter that ensued. The Phoenician flank against the Athenians began to waver and then rolled back out into the open sea of the strait. The Athenians followed and flanked the Phoenicians, pushing them down the strait. Imagine an upside-down *L* being pushed down the strait, bunching the large, wavering Persian fleet in on itself, now not from one side, but two. This occurred about midday, and it was the tipping point of the battle, as the Persians began to flee with the Greeks in pursuit. The Ionians, now pressed on two sides and with their cohesion disrupted by retreating ships from farther up the strait, also broke, and the Aeginetan-Spartan squadron now flanked the Persians from the southeast.

The battle became a pursuit in open water, and this was where most of the Greek losses occurred in individual ship actions against Phoenician or Ionian crews, which now had more room to fight. But it was too little too late. Xerxes's half-brother, one of his admirals, was killed, and the final act involved the slaughter by an Athenian landing party of Xerxes's 400 elite troops, left on the island of Psyttaleia to kill Greek marines as they swam ashore from the expected defeat. Instead, they were the ones who were slaughtered.

CONCLUSION

In terms of the numbers of ships captured or sunk and men killed (surviving wounded not being kept close track of in the accounts), the Athenians suffered extremely light casualties, perhaps in the hundreds, if not less; and the Persians certainly lost thousands, perhaps even tens of thousands, of men. We do know that after that battle, though, that the Persian fleet in anchor at Phaleron still outnumbered the remaining ships of the Greek fleet. However, it was a defeated fleet, and after the Phoenician fleet—its largest contingent—sailed away to its home ports, Xerxes made the wise decision to bring the rest of the fleet back to the Hellespont (i.e., the Dardanelles) for the winter. His army remained in Greece, but it was finally decided, especially after revolts among the Ionians and threats elsewhere in the empire, to abandon Greece. Thus, Salamis represents the high tide of the Persians in Greece and a political disaster for Xerxes and the prestige of his empire.

Why did Xerxes lose at Salamis? Historian Barry Strauss boils it down to three words: "shock, command, and geography": shock at the presence of a strong Greek fleet in good order as day broke, ready to fight. The Greek commanders employed a command philosophy of individual initiative, fed by a centralized plan informed by the genius of Themistocles. This system is known as *mission command* today, but in their lighter more maneuverable ships, its execution by the Greeks was synergistic with that of the shock. Geography again can be attributed to wise commandership—credit Themistocles for having the idea of forcing a fight that

---

Trireme

The Trireme was a galley type of warship, with banks of openings for oarsmen. They could either be open-deck or closed-deck (with the oar banks divided by complete fore-to-aft decks). To get a lighter design, the Athenians chose to build mostly open-deck triremes. The trireme made its debut in warfare in the ancient world around the time of the birth of the later Navarch (admiral) Themistocles (ca. 524 BCE). It relied on speed and a ram as the primary means to disable enemy vessels, rather than having soldiers board and engage in hand-to-hand combat. The vessels were shallow draft and could thus be beached and used for amphibious operations, but because of their sleek design and shallow draft, they were not suited to open ocean navigation and often limited to sailing or rowing within sight of land. They represented the coin of Athenian naval power at battles like Salamis, and later in the various naval battles of the Peloponnesian Wars. At the time of the Peloponnesian Wars, it cost Athens about 480 talents (a talent was roughly equal to one working man's wages for a year) to maintain sixty triremes for the sailing season of seven to nine months.

---

annulled the Persian numbers and Eurybaides for having the good sense to support the Athenians in taking the stand at Salamis.

We might add one other factor—fatigue. The Persians were tired, if not exhausted, before the battle began. Once the adrenaline wore off, their well-rested Greek foes simply had more stamina and the mental acuity that rest brings. The final act of the disaster, though, would have to wait 150 years when another Greek—Alexander the Great—finally defeated the Persian armies once and for all. Salamis marked the beginning of the end of the Persian Empire.

Further Reading

Delbrück, Hans. *Warfare in Antiquity,* Volume I. translated by Walter J. Renfroe, Jr. Lincoln: University of Nebraska Press, 1990.

Herodotus. *The History of Herodotus.* Translated by George Rawlinson, ed. Manuel Komroff. New York, Tudor Publishing, 1928.

Strauss, Barry. *The Battle of Salamis: The Naval Encounter That Saved Greece—and Western Civilization.* New York: Simon and Schuster, 2004.

4. Syracuse Expedition

Date: 415–413 BCE
Location: Sicily

OPPONENTS

1. Syracuse
    Commander: Hermocrates
2. Sparta
    Commander: Gylippus

3. Corinth

   Commander: Gongylus

4. Athens

   Commanders: Nicias, Alcibiades (later defects to Sparta), Lamachus Demosthenes, and Eurymedon

BACKGROUND

The war between Athens and Sparta had entered its sixteenth year when an envoy
arrived at Athens from the city of Egesta, located on the island of Sicily. The
Egestaians were engaged in a war against the Selinuntines and Syracusans, and
losing. The Egestan envoy invoked an alliance made with Athens in 418–417, calling them to assist. Thucydides observed that man is motivated by the triumvirate
of fear, honor, and profit. The Egestan envoy played on all three: For honor, as the
Athenians had to abide by the alliance; for fear that should the Syracusans win,
they would lend their support to Sparta; and for profit from the riches to be gained
by the conquest of Syracuse and the greater island.

Athens dispatched envoys to ascertain the validity of the statement made by the
Egestaians—primarily that they had enough wealth to support the cost of Athenian military operations. The following year, the envoys returned, affirming the
claims. In reality, the Egestaians had duped the Athenian envoys. The abundance
of silver that the Athenians observed was merely the same silver, recirculated.

Athens selected Nicias, Alcibiades, and Lamacus to lead the expedition to Syracuse. However, Nicias counseled the Athenians to abandon their imperial designs
on Sicily and to examine the costs both in men and material should they fail. The
expedition represented a strategic-level gamble, and yet it did not receive the req-
uisite level of analysis. To bolster his argument, Nicias listed the massive logistical
requirements for such an undertaking, hoping to dissuade the Athenians. It had the
opposite effect. The scale of the operation inspired the Athenians, and Alicibiades
fanned the flames. On a midsummer day, the largest military force yet assembled
by Athens sallied forth under fair winds. The fleet contained over 150 triremes and
supporting vessels, 4,000 hoplites, 300 cavalry, and auxiliary forces.

THE PLAN

The Athenians arrived in Italy only to discover that the Egestaians had tricked
them—they did not have the vast sums of wealth that had been touted, and they
lacked the fiscal means to support military operations for any length of time. In
light of this unwelcome news, the Athenian commanders developed three courses
of action. Nicias suggested they provide the Egestaians with the sixty ships that
they could pay for and try to settle the issue between the cities of Egesta and Seli-
nus. This plan of action preserved Athenian power, but it meant returning to Athens empty-handed. Furthermore, the Spartans might perceive it as a sign of
weakness. Nicias's plan appeared the most prudent of the three.

Alcibiades, ever the opportunist, proffered a more involved plan. First, they must win over the cities in Sicily to be allies against Syracuse. Second, they convince those cities to actively aid in the attack. The Syracusans, faced with this overwhelming force, could choose peace or destruction. Either way, the Athenians would return home victorious. Alcibiades risked more than Nicias, but his plan was not unreasonable. The scheme offered a rational and logical process to reduce the power of Syracuse, while also achieving Athenian objectives. Alcibiades struck a political chord rather than just a military one, and this sets his plan apart from the others.

Lamachus put forth the most ambitious plan. However, from a purely military perspective, it also made the most sense. If Nicias suggested a modest military solution, and Alcibiades a more prolonged political campaign, Lamachus sought to settle the question by using a direct naval assault. Rather the a laborious siege, Lamachus advocated sailing right into the harbor and taking the city by storm before the defenders had time to marshal their forces. Sieges frequently failed in this era, and Lamachus's plan skirted this likely outcome. The circumference of Syracuse measured around three to four miles on the landward side—no small undertaking. It should be remembered that the Spartans, whose military prowess was unquestioned on the battlefield, failed to penetrate the walls of Athens. Furthermore, the fiscal and logistical costs of a long siege only increased with time. A prolonged campaign also gave outside hostile forces a chance to make their presence felt. Lamachus set aside caution in favor of boldness. In this respect, he was in good company; centuries later, Napoleon thought boldness the better purchase.

Nevertheless, Alcibiades's plan was adopted, but without Alcibiades.

Shortly after the decision, Alcibiades was recalled back to Athens. Political intrigue took precedent over Athenian imperial policy, and their most capable commander was removed from the field.

THE BATTLE

In 415 BCE, the Athenians made several limited incursions against smaller cities in Sicily, meeting with limited success and were repulsed outright at Hybla. Without Alcibiades's silver tongue, the Athenians were unable to secure additional allies; with his summon to Athens, the expedition lost its architect and diplomat.

The Athenians employed their navy and occasional ruses to good effect. Their navy provided superior mobility, allowing the Athenians to move to the north and south of Syracuse with surprising speed. However, the Athenians were prevented from conducting a siege on the landward side because of the Syracusan cavalry. The Athenian army, composed primarily of hoplites, lacked the mobility to engage the Syracusan cavalry. The cavalry could harass the Athenian army at will, and largely without risk. The asymmetric advantage forced the Athenians to retire and await cavalry reinforcements from Athens the following year.

Following the battle, both forces retired for the winter, with only minor scrimmages until spring. One can only speculate on how Lamachus's plan of storming the city from the water might have played out, but it would have skirted the cavalry problem, and Athenian losses may have been curtailed.

Syracuse used the closing months of the winter of 415 to improve the fortifications and defenses around the city. Envoys were dispatched to Sparta and Corinth in a bid for aid. After some internal debate, Sparta responded by sending Gylippus to take command of the defenses of Syracuse, but he would not arrive in Syracuse before Athens invested the city.

Athens renewed its campaign in the summer of 414. Cavalry had arrived from Athens, neutralizing the Syracusan cavalry, which had largely impeded Athenian forces the previous year. The Athenian forces immediately began to invest Syracuse by building a wall of circumvallation. The Syracusans responded by building counterwalls to divide Athenian forces and impede their construction—but the effort failed. Suffering numerous losses at the hands of the Athenians, the Syracusans began to discuss terms of surrender.

Nicias heard of the approach of Gylippus, a Spartan general, but discounted any effect that he might have on the situation and gave it little heed. However, never underestimate the effect of sound leadership. Gylippus made landfall at Himera and convinced the city to join in the attack. He now marched overland with his allies toward Syracuse, with a force numbering several thousand men, including 100 cavalrymen. The fortunes of Syracuse improved under Spartan leadership, albeit with occasional setbacks. As winter approached in 414, Gylippus canvased Sicily for more allies and petitioned Sparta and Corinth for more support. Meanwhile Nicias informed Athens of the deteriorating situation in Sicily and that, without further reinforcements, the expedition would be forced to retire.

In the summer of 413, Demosthenes arrived in Sicily with reinforcements. Nearly 5,000 hoplites and a large number of allied troops filled the hulls of seventy-three ships. Demosthenes achieved initial successes against Syracusan forces, but the winds of fortune had shifted. Shortly thereafter, Gylippus returned from the Peloponnesian with a large hoplite force. The Athenians were now forced on the defensive. The noose closed around Athenian forces from both land and sea. A desperate naval battle ensued, with the Syracusans and Spartans fighting for revenge and the Athenians for survival. Revenge carried the day. The remaining Athenian forces attempted to escape by land to an allied city, but the Syracusan cavalry again frustrated them. Defeated, cornered, and low on supplies, the Athenians surrendered under a hail of arrows. Nicias and Demosthenes were executed, and the remaining Athenian forces were forced to work in the mines before being sold as slaves.

CONCLUSION

Thucydides's driving narrative was not that of military failure, but of a failure in political leadership. The decision to go was a poor one, but the battle might have been winnable. The ultimate failure rested with a political leadership that lacked the fortitude and integrity to restrain the vagaries of Athenian democracy.

Syracuse is exceptional in the annuals of military disasters not for being a colossal failure (though it was), but because it was entirely unnecessary. Athens staked the balance of her imperial power, political credit, military, and financial resources to achieve an objective that in no way justified the risk. And war—if it is anything—is always a gamble. Nicias inflated the initial requirements of the expedition in hopes of convincing the Athenians that the risks outweighed the benefits. The gambit backfired. In the end, Athenian contributions exceeded the wildest claims of Nicias. Athens gambled and lost. Every empire has a tipping point, and Syracuse marked the beginning of the end of Athens.

Further Reading

Liebeschuetz, W. "Thucydides and the Sicilian Expedition." *Historia: Zeitschrift für Alte Geschichte*, Bd. 17 H.3 (July 1968).

Strassler, Robert B. *The Landmark Thucydides: A Comprehensive Guide to the Peloponnesian War*. New York: Simon & Schuster, 1996.

5. Gaugamela

Date: October 1, 331 BCE
Location: Gaugamela (near modern-day Erbil, Kurdistan)

OPPONENTS

1. Macedonia
    Commander: Alexander the Great
2. Achaemenid
    Commander: Darius III

BACKGROUND

After ascending to the throne of Macedonia following the assassination of his father in 336 BCE, Alexander set out to conquer Persia. In his first two battles, he easily defeated the Persians and spent a year refitting before continuing his campaign. He next met the Persians at Issus, and once more defeated them. However, this time, Alexander added to his victory by capturing Darius's mother, wife, and daughters. Alexander refused Darius's request to negotiate the release of his family and instead moved on to lay siege to the island port of Tyre. After a seven-month siege, the port fell, and Darius, once again asked to negotiate; once again, Alexander refused; he continued his march down the coast to Egypt.

In the face of little opposition, Alexander completed his occupation of Egypt by March 331 BCE. While deliberating his next move, Alexander oversaw the plans for the city of Alexandria. Some time in the spring, with a force of around 50,000, the Macedonian general marched to the city of Thapascus, on the Euphrates. Reaching the city, Alexander linked up with an advance party that was preparing to cross sites. Darius received word of Alexander's movement and dispatched a force of 6,000 to prevent the crossing. However, upon seeing Alexander's superior force, the Persians withdrew back to Babylon.

Once across the Euphrates, Darius expected Alexander to take the most direct route to Babylon; however, Alexander led his army north through an area that provided better forage for his soldiers. Darius knew that Alexander would eventually have to cross the Tigris, and he sent out another force to shadow the Macedonians while he led his main army north to Arbela. The Tigris River's strong current temporarily delayed Alexander, but with great difficulty, his troops eventually crossed and continued south along the Tigris. Along the way, they captured several of Darius's scouts, who told Alexander that the Persian army was encamped near Gaugemela. After four days of marching, the Macedonian army reached the high ground around the plain of Gaugamela. From this vantage point, Alexander had an excellent view of the field of battle and the Persian army's preparations.

Darius chose Gaugemela because it was large enough for him to deploy his approximately 100,000-man army to capitalize on his tactical advantages. Darius may have had 40,000 infantry, 40,000 cavalry, and 200 scythed chariots, along with more than 20,000 auxiliaries or mercenaries. To accommodate his scythe-armed chariots, he had the plain flattened and cleared of rocks and brush.

Alexander's force amounted to roughly 50,000, broken into 31,000 heavy infantry of hoplites and mercenaries, 9,000 light infantry with a few archers mixed in, and 7,000 cavalry. Alexander prized his cavalry above all but was going into this battle outnumbered roughly five to one in cavalry. Undaunted by these odds, Alexander planned to attack Darius on the morning of October 1.

THE BATTLE

Darius and his Persians were already on the plain of Gaugamela on the morning of October 1. They spent the previous night in their positions expecting an attack by Alexander that never came. Darius arrayed his forces in the typical manner of the day, with infantry in the middle and cavalry on the flanks. He was with his best heavy infantry in the middle, along with his archers and Indian cavalry. Behind this line was his main force of heavy infantry. He placed the bulk of his cavalry on the flanks. The scythed chariots were in front of the entire formation. With his larger force, Darius planned to outflank the Macedonians and then roll them up with his cavalry.

Alexander divided his army in two. He commanded the right flank with his Companion cavalry. Parmenion, Alexander's most trusted subordinate, commanded the left flank with the Thracian cavalry. In the middle, Alexander placed his heavy infantry and Greek archers. Behind the main line was a smaller phalanx of infantry and other auxiliaries to intercept any Persians that penetrated the front lines. Alexander intended for Parmenion to hold the left flank while he led the right flank to defeat the Persians. Expecting Darius to outflank him, Alexander placed his units on the far right in an echelon formation to "deny" this flank to the Persians.

The battle opened with Alexander advancing his infantry. Darius countered by using his cavalry to attack the Macedonian left flank. Trusting Parmenion to do his part, Alexander began extending his right flank, hoping to draw the Persian cavalry away from the main line. If the Persians followed his movement, it would create a gap in Darius's formation that Alexander could exploit. He also wanted to goad Darius into attacking by moving the battle away from the ground that the latter had prepared.

As Alexander expected, the Persians kept moving farther to the flank until Darius was forced to attack. Darius launched all of his left-flank cavalry toward the

Macedonians. Alexander's men were outnumbered, but they were skillfully commanded and resolutely met the Persians' attacks and were able to ward them off. Next, Darius sent in his scythed chariots, hoping that the shock would turn the battle. Instead, they met a hail of javelins that broke up their attack. A few chariots made it past the javelin barrage and were allowed to pass through the Macedonian ranks to be dispatched by the second Macedonian line. Nonetheless, the battle was developing as Alexander envisioned, and a gap was opening up in the Persian lines.

Seeing his chance, Alexander took a chance by disengaging his Companion cavalry from the desperate fight on the right flank to exploit this opportunity. Organizing his nearby phalanx into a wedge formation, Alexander led them, with his Companion cavalry in the lead, toward the Persian mainline. The Persian infantry, weakened by the nonstop battle, was no match for Alexander's new attack, and they began to give way. Darius sent in his Royal Guard to fill the gap and stop Alexander, but they were no match for the highly motivated Macedonians. Darius, fearing capture, fled the battlefield, followed by the majority of his army. Alexander was prepared to pursue Darius hoping to end the war by capturing and killing him. However, Alexander received word that Parmenion was in dire straits and needed his assistance. Alexander, torn between pursuing Darius and the risk of losing a portion of his army or ending the war, chose to end the war and save his army.

Ironically, Alexander's attack into the gap in the Persian lines created a similar gap in his lines. A portion of Persian and Indian cavalry tried to exploit this gap; however, instead of attacking into the exposed Macedonian flank, they continued on the Macedonian baggage train, hoping to loot the trains or save Darius's family. Instead, they were eventually cut off by Alexander's rear line. In the meantime. Alexander returned to engage the main force of the Persian cavalry attacking Parmenion. The mixed force of Persians, Indians, and Parthians fought a desperate battle to escape. However, Alexander and his men eventually won out, though suffering heavy losses in the process. The remaining Macedonian cavalry began running down the fleeing Persians, while Alexander gathered small force to begin his pursuit of Darius.

CONCLUSION

The Battle of Gaugamela was an unmitigated disaster for the Persians. Alexander claimed that he lost 500 men, as well as seeing roughly 5,000 wounded. The battle cost Darius approximately 40,000 men; however, the loss at Guagemela cost Darius far more personally.

Eventually, the remnants of his army linked back up with Darius. Darius assured them that he was going to form another army to deal with Alexander. Unfortunately for him, his subordinates had other plans, and they murdered him, leaving his body behind as they continued east. Alexander was shocked to find his most worthy opponent murdered like that and, out of respect, gave him a ceremonial burial. When he caught up with the Persian fugitives, Alexander had Darius's murderer, his subordinate and relative Bessus, executed. The majority of the Persian satraps acknowledged Alexander's sovereignty, effectively ending the Achaemenid Persian Empire and giving Alexander control of western Asia.

Darius III (380–330 BCE)

Darius, a cousin of the Persian king Artaxerxes III, ascended to the Persian throne in 336 BCE after a court eunuch, Bagoas, assassinated Artaxerxes and his heir, Arses. Never a popular or effective monarch, Darius eventually turned on his benefactor and murdered Bagoas. However, a resurgence by the Greeks under Philip II of Macedon soon overshadowed the intrigue in the Persian court.

Darius did not rate Alexander much of a threat and was not present for the first engagement between Persians and Greeks at Granicus in 334 BCE. After the Persian defeat at Granicus, Darius personally led the Persian army at the Battle of Issus in 333 BCE. Even with a two-to-one advantage, Darius proved an even less effectual commander than he was a monarch. Alexander outgeneraled Darius and forced the Persian army to flee. In his haste to get away, Darius let his family fall into Alexander's hands.

Two years later, Darius and Alexander met again, in the Battle of Gaugemela (also known as the Battle of Arbela). Once again, all the advantages rested with Darius. He not only outnumbered Alexander, but the terrain was better suited for Darius to employ his chariots. However, once again, Alexander proved the better general, and the Greeks routed the Persians. This time, however, after the Persians stopped to regroup, Darius's subordinates suggested that he relinquish command of the army. Darius refused. His frustrated subordinates eventually murdered him, leaving his body for the Greeks to find. After he saw the body, Alexander gave Darius a funeral befitting his station.

Further Reading

Billows, Richard A. *Before and After Alexander: The Legend and Legacy of Alexander the Great.* New York: Overlook Duckworth, 2018.

Freeman, Philip. *Alexander the Great.* New York: Simon and Schuster, 2011.

Martin, Thomas R. *Ancient Greece: From Prehistoric to Hellenistic Times.* New Haven, CT: Yale University Press, 1996.

6. Chang-Ping

Date: 260 BCE
Location: China

OPPONENTS

1. State of Qin
   Commanders: General Wang He and General Bai Qi
2. State of Zhao
   Commanders: Generals Lian Poh, Zhao Chieh, and Zhao Gua

BACKGROUND

The modern state in Europe, as it is known today, came into being in the seventeenth century. Kings moved to unify the desperate and independent principalities into geographically homogenous states. The European inclination to centralize power and bureaucratic functions followed a similar trajectory and timeline. China developed a long and parallel path—only it happened 1,800 years earlier.

Traditionally, battles constituted engagements between elites with small retainers to gain honor, prove bravery, and assert regional hegemony. Slowly, these limited means gave way to greater objectives and larger armies. The pastime of the aristocracy eventually expanded to include peasants. War naturally escalated, and so did the ravages. If peasants made up part of the army, then farms and villages—civilian targets—became legitimate aims. Battles frequently had over 100,000 soldiers, numbers rarely attained in the West until the eighteenth century. During the Spring-and-Autumn period (722–481 BCE), there were nearly 200 small states. Slowly, stronger and more capable states subsumed weaker ones. As the Spring-and-Autumn era came to a close, and that of the Warring States (403–221 BCE) began, only seven states remained.

If geography has blessed some and cursed others, then fate smiled warmly on the state of Qin. The most westward of the seven remaining kingdoms, it was securely nestled against a mountain range that opened to the east. Geographically secure, the Qin state confidently concentrated its forces, with little concern for the other three cardinal directions.

The Qin population hailed largely from the steppes; they were a virile and primitive people. Seen as barbarians by greater China, the Qin were fierce warriors, and their reputation for terror aided in their conquests. Additionally, the Qin had reformed tax codes and instituted bureaucratic reforms to increase revenue and produce a new and loyal elite. The Qin reforms, combined with the use of infantry armed and protected by iron and bronze, made them the premier military state.

However, the other states were not without advantages. The Chu state possessed the greatest population and geographical boundaries. The Qin state maintained a long shoreline that provided for prosperous trade and fishing. And the Zhao state instituted military reforms that transitioned to a cavalry heavy force that provided a distinct advantage over competing states, and it appeared to be one of the best states positioned to resist Qin.

In 262 BCE, General Wang invaded the Han state with an army that numbered between 200,000 and 300,000 soldiers. Militarily, the Han kingdom found itself inferior in nearly every important metric. With a significantly smaller population and geographically disadvantaged position between no fewer than four of the warring states, the Han state turned to the Zhao kingdom. Rather than cede the Shang Dang region to the Qin, the Han state offered it to Zhao. The Zhao kingdom accepted the territory, and with it, war with the Qin state. The battle lines were drawn for one of the single greatest losses of human life in antiquity between two armies—the Battle of Chang-Ping.

THE PLAN

General Lian Poh marched the Zhao army of over 200,000 soldiers to meet the threat. The first engagement between the lead elements of both armies ended poorly for the Zhao: General Chieh was killed and his force of 5,000 destroyed. The Zhao army moved into a defensive position, while General Poh analyzed the strategic situation. Poh believed that an attritional strategy offered the best chance at victory. The Qin army operated over an extended distance that traversed difficult terrain comprised of mountains and rivers. If the Zhao army assumed a defensive position, it might exhaust the logistical and financial capacity of the Qin state, forcing them to withdraw or to attack fortified positions. General Poh deployed forces forward and constructed forts to the rear. Now the Zhao army waited for the attritional effects of time.

THE BATTLE

General Poh maintained a defensive position behind his forts and refused to engage in battle. The Zhao army easily repulsed attacks from the Qin forces. Unable to breach the Zhao fortification line, the Qin adopted a different strategy. Because General Poh refused to give battle and the Qin army could not dislodge, they decided to employ intrigue to remove General Poh from command. The Qin employed spies to spread rumors throughout the court of Zhao, resulting in the removal of Poh.

General Zhao Gua now assumed command of the army, with an additional 200,000 reinforcements. However, unlike his predecessor, Gua had never commanded soldiers in battle. In response, the Qin dispatched Bai Chi, their most capable commander. The two generals could not have been more different; Gua, an arrogant dilettante, opposed Bai, experienced and cunning.

After fortifying his position, Bai challenged Gua to battle, and he accepted. Bai had baited the Zhao army, and now he sprung the trap. The outlines are not unlike those of Cannae. The Qin center fell back slowly under the steady pressure of the Zhao army. The Zhao sensed the shifting momentum and pressed the Bai center all the harder. The Chi'in army was forced all the way back to their encampment, where supporting missile troops pushed the pursing Zhao army back.

As the Zhao pulled back to regroup, Bai sprung the trap. The Qin forces hidden among the heights emerged all along the Zhao flanks. Meanwhile, the Qin forces that had circled deep behind the Zhao army in order to cut its lines of retreat appeared from behind. Like a vise, enemy forces closed simultaneously from all sides. Chaos ensued and panic spread within the Zhao army. Cut off and surrounded, the Zhao army awaited relief efforts. A final breakout attempt led personally by Zhao Gua ended in failure and the death of the general.

The Zhao army, including the garrison, was forced to surrender. General Bai offered generous terms to the more than 200,000 Zhao prisoners, and a feast of wine and meat followed. But that night, Bai's soldiers entered the Zhao camps and slaughtered the slumbering prisoners almost to a man.

CONCLUSION

The Zhao kingdom ceased to be a significant player in the pursuit for hegemony over greater China after the battle. In fact, the kingdom no longer posed a serious threat to the power and expansion of the Qin kingdom. Many of the most experienced and best-equipped Zhao soldiers perished in the Battle of Chang-Ping. With the last major obstacle to Qin expansion destroyed, it was only a matter of time before the remnants of Zhao and the remaining kingdoms fell.

Further Reading

Tang, Long. *The Book of War: From the Series Tales of the Dragon.* New York: Algora Publishing, 2017.

7. Cannae

Date: August 2, 216 BCE
Location: Cannae, Italy

OPPONENTS

1. Carthage

   Commander: Hannibal

2. Rome

   Commanders: Gaius Terentius Varro and Lucius Aemilius Paullus

BACKGROUND

The Battle of Cannae was one of the most significant battles of the seventeen-year-long Second Punic War. Rome and Carthage would eventually fight three wars over hegemony in the Mediterranean. The Second Punic War began in 219 BCE, when Hannibal sacked Saguntum, a city allied with Rome, on the Iberian Peninsula. Hannibal then proceeded over the Pyrenees and Alps to progress down the Italian peninsula toward Rome. Along the way, Hannibal defeated two Roman armies: first at the Battle of Trebia, and the second along the shores of Lake Trasimene.

The Roman senate appointed Quintus Fabius Maximus Verrucosus to halt the Carthaginians before they reached Rome. Fabius fought a series of delaying actions, hoping to defeat Hannibal through attrition. Never seeking a pitched battle with Hannibal, Fabius was able to slow the Carthaginians, but his tactics did not sit well in Rome. The Roman senate wanted to defeat Hannibal decisively and end the Carthaginian threat to Rome before her allies began defecting to Carthage. In 216 BCE, the senate raised a new army, and Gaius Terentius Varro and Lucius Aemilius Paullus were elected as consuls and put in command. However, based on Roman law, the consuls would alternate command from day to day. This new army was the largest fielded by Rome up to that time, and it was comprised of roughly 40,000 Roman infantry, with an equal number of allied infantry supported by over 6,000 Roman and allied cavalry.

Hannibal forced the hand of Varro and Paullus when he seized a major supply point at Canusium, near Cannae. The two consuls led their armies southward to confront the Carthaginians. Along the way, Hannibal's light infantry and cavalry fought a small skirmish with the Romans, from which the Romans emerged victorious. Bolstered by their victory, the Romans continued their march and found the

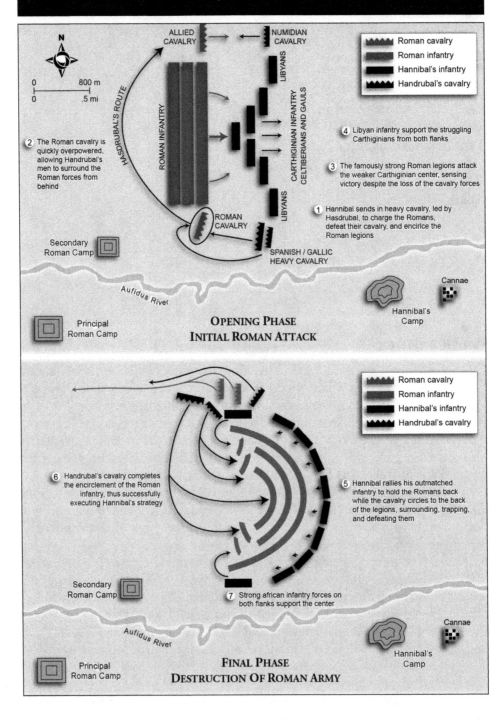

BATTLE OF CANNAE, AUGUST 2, 216 BCE

OPENING PHASE
INITIAL ROMAN ATTACK

FINAL PHASE
DESTRUCTION OF ROMAN ARMY

50,000-man Carthaginian army camped along the left bank of the Arfidus River. Hannibal's force consisted of roughly 32,000 heavy infantry, 8,000 light infantry, and around 10,000 cavalry, giving him a significant advantage in cavalry. For two days, both sides stayed in their camps. Paullus, considered the more prudent of the Roman commanders, was not sure of accepting battle on an open plain, given Hannibal's superiority in cavalry. However, in the current situation, he did not believe that it would be wise to withdraw either. Regardless, it would be Varro's turn to command on the day of battle.

THE BATTLE

Hannibal's army was a mix of contingents from his various allies. Along with his core of Libyans, he had with him Iberian, Gallic infantry, as well as Hispanic and Celtic cavalry. His soldiers were armed with a variety of weapons that generally represented cultural preferences. For example, the contingent from Balearic went into battle with short-, medium-, and long-range slings. Anchoring his line on the Arfidus River, Hannibal arrayed his force in a typical manner for that time. He placed his infantry in the center and his cavalry on the wings. What was different was the alignment. He arranged his infantry in a convex formation with his Iberians and Gauls in the center and in front of the main formation. Hannibal positioned himself with this force. Confident his cavalry could defeat the Romans, he intended for them to encircle the Roman infantry as his infantry pressed in from the flanks. The Roman deployment played into Hannibal's hands.

The Roman army equipped with spears, javelins, along with shields and body armor, was arrayed to mirror the Carthaginians. The Roman cavalry was on the flanks of the infantry, but the infantry showed a narrower front. Varro was hoping to capitalize on his superior numbers in infantry to force a hole in Hannibal's lines by focusing on one point in the Carthaginian front. Unfortunately, this tight formation only made it easier for Hannibal to outflank his opponent. Additionally, the Roman position faced east, meaning they would be blinded by the morning sun and would be marching into a southeasterly wind that would blow sand into their faces.

As the armies marched toward each other, the cavalry made first contact. On Hannibal's left flank, Hasdrubal, one of Hannibal's subordinates, led his Hispanic and Celtic cavalry in a desperate battle against the Romans. After a fierce fight, Hasdrubal's men broke the Roman cavalry, who fled the battlefield. At this point, Hasdrubal showed the presence of mind not to pursue the Romans; instead, he led his cavalry around the Roman infantry to support the Carthaginian cavalry on the other flank. The Roman cavalry, facing attacks from front and rear, fled the battlefield with Hannibal's Numidian cavalry in pursuit.

Meanwhile, the main attack was going on between the infantry. The Roman infantry pushed the center of the Carthaginian line. Hannibal, leading from the center, slowly began to withdraw in the face of the Roman attack. The Carthaginian infantry on the flanks held in place and Hannibal's concave formation became more convex as the center fell back. The further Hannibal's center retreated, the deeper the advancing Roman infantry was funneled into his trap. The Roman infantry to the rear continued to push forward, crushing those at the front to the point that it was difficult for them to use their weapons. After driving off the Roman cavalry, Hasdrubal led his force in an attack on the rear of the Roman infantry. Seeing the arrival of Hasdrubal's cavalry, Hannibal ordered his infantry on the flank, which up to this point had been harassing the flanks of the Romans to attack them. The Romans soon found themselves completely encircled with no way to escape. The Carthaginian army set upon the Romans with a vengeance, and the Romans were cut down. Hannibal's mixed infantry kept pressing in tighter, killing more and more of the Roman infantry.

When darkness ended the slaughter, roughly 60,000 Romans were killed or captured, and the rest escaped to Canusium. Varro escaped, but Paullus was among the Roman dead, along with 28 tribunes and 80 others of senatorial or higher rank. Historians number Hannibal's losses at 8,000 to 10,000 (though, as with any ancient battle, the numbers are only estimates at best).

CONCLUSION

With Hannibal's victory, some of Rome's allies began to doubt the empire's power. Philip V of Macedon allied with Carthage and initiated a war with Rome. Rome itself was gripped by panic when word arrived of the disaster that had befallen the Roman army. Legend has it that the Roman senate called for a day of mourning. Hannibal was urged to march on Rome, but he declined, hoping his victory would be enough to convince the Romans to negotiate. It did not. The Roman senate refused to meet with Hannibal's emissaries and instead vowed to redouble their efforts to defeat Carthage. These efforts paid off, and Hannibal eventually was forced to return to Carthage. In 202 BCE, the Second Punic War came to an end when a Roman army led by Publius Cornelius Scipio Africanus defeated Hannibal at Zama.

Further Reading

Daly, Gregory. *Cannae: The Experience of Battle in the Second Punic War.* London: Routledge, 2002.

Goldsworthy, Adrian K. *Cannae.* London: Cassell Military, 2001.

Hunt, Patrick. *Hannibal.* New York: Simon and Schuster, 2017.

O'Connell, Robert L. *The Ghosts of Cannae: Hannibal and the Darkest Hour of the Roman Republic.* New York: Random House, 2010.

8. Zama

Date: 202 BCE
Location: Zama, in modern-day Tunisia

OPPONENTS

1. Carthage
    Commander: Hannibal

2. Rome and Numidia

Commanders: Publius Cornelius Scipio Africanus (Scipio) and Masinissa of Numidia

BACKGROUND

The Battle of Zama was the decisive battle that brought about an end to the Second Punic War. After defeating the Romans at the Battle of Cannae, Hannibal remained in Italy hoping to bring the Romans to terms. However, the intransigent Roman senate refused to negotiate.

Meanwhile, the defiant Romans continued to rebuild their forces and eventually went on the offensive, and they scored a major victory over the Carthaginians by Scipio in 206 BCE at the Battle of Ilipa. During the battle, Scipio demonstrated his tactical skills by employing a clever stratagem. For several days before the battle, Scipio would deploy his forces as if to give battle, but then withdraw. Each time, he placed his Roman infantry in the center with his Iberian infantry on the flanks. However, on the day of battle, Scipio reversed his deployment, putting his Roman infantry on the flanks. With this switch, Scipio's Roman infantry easily defeated the weaker infantry on the Carthaginian flanks. Scipio's victory at Ilipa secured the Iberian Peninsula for Rome.

Scipio returned to Rome and, after being elected consul, argued that the time was ripe to end the war with a direct invasion of Carthage. The senate rejected his plan for being too dangerous. However, he was eventually permitted to form an army with volunteers and the remnants of the 5th and 6th Legions. Banished to Sicily for their performance during the Battle of Cannae, the veterans were eager to avenge their humiliation. With this force, Scipio set sail for the coast of North Africa in 204 BCE.

After landing, Scipio met up with Masinissa, the son of Gaia, the recently deceased chieftain of the Massylii. The Massylii was a Numidian tribal group, and when Masinissa met Scipio, he was in a fight with his brother over succession. Masinissa allied himself with Scipio, hoping to gain an advantage over his brother. With his new ally, Scipio led his army into the interior of Carthage. Hearing of Scipio's landing, the Carthaginian senate sent an army to intercept him. Scipio handily defeated this force at the Battle of the Great Plains.

After the defeat, the Carthaginian senate sued for peace. The Roman senate approved the terms, but not all of the Carthaginians were satisfied, and Hannibal was recalled from Italy. Buoyed by the return of Hannibal, it was not long before the Carthaginians breached the terms of the treaty. Events came to a head when a group of Carthaginians attacked some Roman ships that had washed ashore during a storm and the Second Punic War resumed.

THE BATTLE

After his return, the Carthaginian senate gave Hannibal command of three armies. The core of his army was the nearly 14,000-veteran infantry that had been with him throughout his campaigns in Italy and Spain. The second army was comprised of approximately 14,000 local civilians, with little or no training (as opposed to his previous army, a group of between 10,000 and 12,000 Celtic, Ligurian, and Balearic mercenaries). He would also have 4,000 cavalry and eighty elephants. On the day of the battle, Hannibal arrayed his forces in the typical fashion of the day—infantry in the middle and cavalry on the flanks. His first rank would be his mercenaries, followed by his civilian infantry. He held his hardened veterans in the third rank a little farther back, hoping to use them to reinforce success.

The Roman army numbered nearly 30,000 infantry and 6,000 cavalry, including Masinissa's 4,000 mounted Numidians. For the first time in facing the Carthaginians, the Roman army would have a cavalry advantage, in terms of both numbers and quality. Scipio intended to exploit this advantage. He also anticipated that Hannibal would lead with his elephants. To counter this threat, Scipio proved himself an innovative tactician. Rather that array his infantry in the typical checkerboard pattern as per Roman doctrine, he arrayed them in lines. He hoped to channel the elephants through his lines in the space between the formations. He placed skirmishers in the gaps to mask them until the elephants charged.

The battle opened on the plains of Zama Regia, as Scipio anticipated when Hannibal's elephants charged the Roman lines. As they elephants lumbered toward his infantry, Scipio ordered the cavalry on the flanks to blow their horns to frighten the charging animals. This ploy partially worked; some of the elephants turned and charged the Carthaginian left wing, while the rest pressed on. Then Roman skirmishers threw javelins to attract the elephants toward them. Next, the skirmishers moved away, revealing the gaps in the Roman infantry. The elephants charged down the lanes to the rear of the Roman formation, running into the soldiers that Scipio had placed there to deal with them. With the elephant threat neutralized, Scipio turned his attention to the main fight.

Masinissa, on the Roman left wing, saw the confusion caused by the elephant charge as his opportunity and charged the Carthaginian cavalry on the right wing. After a brief skirmish, the Carthaginian cavalry retreated and led Masinissa's Numidians away from the battle. There is some conjecture that this was a deliberate ploy by Hannibal to neutralize the Roman superiority in cavalry. Regardless of the reason, the effect was that Masinissa's horsemen were not present for the early stages of the battle. However, they would return.

Scipio sent his first line forward to engage Hannibal's mercenaries. After some intense fighting, the more heavily armed and armored Romans got the better of the mercenaries, who tried to pull back into the second line of Carthaginians. Hannibal, afraid of disrupting his formation, ordered the second line not to let them in. The surviving mercenaries moved off to the flank. Next, Hannibal charged with his second line of Carthiginian civilians. The fighting was intense, and Scipio was forced to commit his second line. Scipio's professionals eventually broke the Carthaginians, and they withdrew to the flanks. Both commanders now committed their third lines, and the battle entered its final stage.

Hoping to buy time for his cavalry to return, Scipio did not commit his reserve directly into the fight. Instead, he moved them to the flanks to extend the Roman

Hannibal (247–183 BCE)

Hannibal was the son of the great Carthaginian general Hamilcar Barca. As a young boy, Hannibal was brought to Spain by his father and eventually became an officer in the Carthaginian army after the death of Hamilcar in 229 BCE, eventually assuming command of the army. Over the next two years, Hannibal consolidated Carthaginian rule in Spain, and in 221 BCE, he attacked Saguntum on the east coast of Spain. Rome considered this an act of war, and it marked the beginning of the Second Punic War.

In 218 BCE, Hannibal crossed the Alps into Italy. For fifteen years, despite several successful battles against the Romans, including the Battle of Cannae, Hannibal ultimately could never defeat them. He returned to Carthage in 204 BCE after the Roman general Scipio landed in North Africa. Scipio was the equal of Hannibal in generalship and defeated the Carthaginian at the Battle of Zama in 202 BCE.

Following the war, Hannibal was made a civil magistrate, but his reforms made him unpopular among many of the aristocrats, and he fled to Tyre, and later to Antiochus, to resume his fight with Rome. After Rome defeated Antiochus, they demanded the surrender of Hannibal as part of the peace terms. Instead, Hannibal fled to Bithynia and served King Prusias in his war against Rome's ally, Pergamum. Once more, the Romans demanded Hannibal's surrender; and he could not escape this time. Around 183 BCE, rather than face the ignominy of Roman captivity, Hannibal committed suicide.

lines. Hannibal's battle-hardened veterans crashed into the thinner but wider Roman lines and were slowly gaining the advantage in the ferocious struggle. Scipio was afraid that the battle was slipping away from him when he saw a cloud of dust approaching from the direction where his cavalry had pursued the Carthaginians. Scipio rallied his men, and they held on long enough for the Roman cavalry to charge into the rear of the Carthaginians. Sensing their pending victory, the Romans began to slaughter the encircled Carthaginian soldiers. Hannibal managed to escape the melee, and the battle ended in a decisive Roman victory. Estimates claim that 20,000 of Hannibal's men were killed and perhaps another 15,000–20,000 taken prisoner, while Roman losses are estimated at between 1,500 and 2,500.

CONCLUSION

The Roman victory at Zama brought the Second Punic War to an end. Rome offered peace terms that it hoped would eliminate the Carthigian threat. One of the terms of the treaty required Carthage to ask Rome's permission before going to war. Rome hoped this would curb Carthage's military adventures. Even though Carthage was no longer a military threat, it eventually recovered enough to challenge Rome economically. When Carthage tried to defend itself against the Numidians without permission, the Roman senate had the pretext it needed to start the Third Punic War and crush Carthage once and for all.

Further Reading
Delbrück, Hans. *Warfare in Antiquity*, Volume I. Translated by Walter J. Renfroe, Jr. Lincoln: University of Nebraska Press, 1990.

Goldsworthy, Adrian. *The Punic Wars.* London: Cassell, 2001.

Hunt, Patrick. *Hannibal.* New York: Simon and Schuster, 2017.

Miles, Richard. *Carthage Must Be Destroyed: The Rise and Fall of an Ancient Civilization.* New York: Viking Penguin, 2011.

9. Pharsalus

Date: August 9, 48 BCE
Location: Thessaly, Greece

OPPONENTS

1. Julii Faction

    Commander: Julius Caesar

    Numbers: 22,000–30,000 infantry, 1,000 cavalry

2. Aristocratic Faction

    Commander: Gnaeus Pompey

    Numbers: 41,000 infantry, 6,700 cavalry

BACKGROUND

The Pharsalus engagement occurred near the end of the Roman Civil War during Julius Caesar's Greek campaign, which followed his successful campaign to secure Spain from the Aristocratic Faction, led by Gnaeus Pompey. The cause of the civil war had been Caesar's defiance of a senatorial decree to return to Rome without his armies to face charges of corruption. The forces against Caesar were led by Rome's other most famous general, Pompey. Caesar famously crossed the Rubicon with his Gallic legions, saying "Let the die be cast." This event then led to the first phase of the Roman Civil War, which lasted from 49–45 BCE. Initially, the odds were against Caesar, but through patient and skillful generalship, he managed to gain the upper hand after his Spanish campaign (49–48 BCE).

Although Caesar now had the advantage on land, Pompey and his allies still controlled the seas. Caesar formed up field forces in Brundisium (modern Brindisi) for a crossing of the Adriatic, and despite his weakness at sea, he managed to get eleven legions and his cavalry across the Adriatic in a daring gamble. First, he crossed with seven legions and while Pompey hesitated, his second-in-command, Marc Antony, sailed with four legions and the remainder of the cavalry. Caesar then proceeded to besiege Pompey's force at Dyrrhachium (modern Dures), but he was eventually defeated in a combined sortie and amphibious attack by the garrison and withdrew. Elated by their victory, Pompey's aristocratic advisors convinced the cautious general to pursue Caesar and his army into Greece. This accorded well with Caesar's wishes because his army was not that badly beaten and consisted of his most veteran legions. Also, the pursuit by Pompey took him away from the sea, where Pompey's fleets kept him well supplied and gave him more freedom of action.

After a series of maneuvers involving a detached force of two legions under Caesar's subordinate, Domitius, Caesar accepted battle at Pharsalus in Thessaly. Although outnumbered, Caesar felt confident that his generalship and his veterans would prevail. Pompey might have retreated, which would have wrecked Caesar's strategy, but with his army unbeaten and his advisors clamoring for battle, and probably against his better judgment, he took up the challenge.

THE OPPOSING PLANS

Pompey's plan was very straightforward. He anchored his right flank on the Enipeus River in relatively open ground. This open ground was probably another factor that convinced Caesar to risk a battle because of the tactical flexibility it offered him. Pompey formed up his eleven legions in three successive lines. He probably did this because of the newness of these legions compared to Caesar's, so they could support each other. On his left flank, he stationed most (or all, according to some accounts) of his much more numerous cavalry under the turncoat general Titus Labienus, who had served under Caesar in Gaul. His plan was to keep the bulk of his infantry on the defensive and to rely on his much larger and well-led cavalry to disperse Caesar's cavalry, and then attack his infantry in the flank and rear. He intended a single envelopment and probably kept his infantry on the defense to avoid pushing the quarry out of the sack created by his cavalry. Pompey stationed himself behind the left-flank infantry, commanded by Lucius Domitius Ahenobarbus.

Caesar made his dispositions once the great dust clouds of Pompey's cavalry deployment indicated Pompey's intent. His legions were not deployed as such, but rather as cohorts, and they, too, were arrayed in three lines, but with only four or five men to a rank. Caesar was already inferior in infantry, but such was his confidence in himself, his commanders, and his men that he withdrew one cohort from each of his nine legions and created a fourth line, which he deployed in a refused position hidden behind his cavalry and joined at an angle to his right flank. He also stationed his best legion, the Tenth, at the fulcrum on the right, and took his station there. He anticipated that Pompey's cavalry would overwhelm his own cavalry, but he intended to counterattack them as his cavalry withdrew. It is not certain if Caesar intentionally had his cavalry feign a withdrawal, but more than likely he did not.

THE BATTLE

Caesar's deployment of his fourth line went unnoticed by Pompey and Labienus. He opened the battle by advancing his first line of infantry within *pila* (a short Roman spear)–throwing range of Pompey, but then they stopped when Pompey's infantry refused to meet them in a rush of battle. Caesar's centurions and tribunes carefully redressed their battle lines within sight of Pompey's troops, as if on parade, and this probably increased the morale of Caesar's troops. Pompey then launched Labienus's mass of cavalry against Caesar's right flank and, as expected, the much inferior Caesarian cavalry was defeated and withdrew. However, Labienus was given no time and had no experience in reforming up his mass of disordered cavalry. Caesar committed his fourth line just as his own cavalry withdrew, and in the dust raised by the cavalry battle, their approach was not seen by Pompey's cavalrymen until the cohorts of the fourth line attacked them in the flank. Instead of hurling their *pila,* they used them as pikes, taking many of the cavalry mounts in the side and causing them to panic, which created even more disorder and confusion. It was one of the few times in history when maneuvering infantry defeated cavalry in battle. Only veteran infantry with superb small unit leaders could have done it in the noise, dust, and heat of battle on the plains of Thessaly.

Meanwhile, the main bodies of infantry on both sides joined battle. Caesar's infantry hurled their *pila* and ran at the stationary Pompeians. At first, Pompey's infantry remained steady, even after Caesar committed his second and third lines to what can only be imagined as a sort of giant rugby scrum-pushing match. However, the battle on the far flank proved decisive. As Pompey's cavalry fled in retreat and disorder, Caesar's fourth-line cohorts coolly wheeled around Pompey's left flank at it was held immobile by the Tenth Legion. Caesar's third line and flank pressure by the fourth line occurred nearly simultaneously, which caused Pompey's rookie legions to finally break and flee.

CONCLUSION

As with most ancient battles, casualties are a source of dispute, but the numbers from Pharsalus are more reliable than most because Caesar controlled the battlefield and was sure to get an accurate counting of both dead and prisoners because he intended to parole most of his enemies to highlight his magnanimity, as well as to get a good count of the prisoners who would now be joining his own ranks. He claimed some 15,000 enemies killed and 24,000 captured, more than 80 percent of Pompey's army. His own casualties are a testament to the leadership of his army at

The Marian Reforms

Gaius Marius (157–86 BCE) emerged on the stage of history in the second century BCE. He was what the Romans called a *novus homo* (i.e., a "new man"). He had money, but not the family lineage of the patrician class, and he was a self-made man. He used his talents, money, and influence to gain a military command during the turbulent period of the Barbarian Invasions of Rome, taking advantage of the emergency to advance himself until he eventually became one of two consuls who ruled the Roman Republic in concert with the senate. Prior to Marius, the Roman military had consisted of propertied citizens who purchased their own arms and through military service advanced in rank from Velites (light infantry) all the way to Triari (heavy spearman) and Equites (cavalry). However, this system did not produce the numbers to address the Barbarian threat or Rome's expanding military requirements in both Africa and Asia (modern-day Turkey). Accordingly, Marius recruited from among the lowest class, the unpropertied "head count," and used state funds to equip them. His second reform was to organize these men into legions of around 4,500 troops. They served Rome well but tended to transfer their loyalty from Rome to their generals (like Marius). Eventually, they served as the engine of the fall of the republic in the first century BCE during the turbulent period of Rome's internecine civil wars.

all levels—he lost about 250 soldiers, but of these, over 30 were officers, which highlights how important tactical leadership "from the front" was in Caesar's army.

It is reputed that Pompey fled before the battle was even over. The catastrophe was irredeemable. Pompey fled to Egypt, where he was murdered by King Ptolemy to curry favor with Caesar. The aristocratic faction, including Brutus and Cassius (pardoned by Caesar), were never able to mount effective resistance, and it was only after Caesar's murder (44 BCE) that the Civil War reignited and ground on until Augustus and Marcus Agrippa defeated Marc Antony at Actium in 31 BCE, which inaugurated the age of the emperors.

Further Reading

Delbrück, Hans. *Warfare in Antiquity*, Volume I. Translated by Walter J. Renfroe, Jr. Lincoln: University of Nebraska Press, 1990.

Goldsworthy, Adrian. *In the Name of Rome: The Men Who Won the Roman Empire*. London: Phoenix Books, 2002.

Plutarch. *The Fall of the Roman Republic*. Translated by Rex Warner, with introductions and notes by Robin Seager. London: Penguin Books, 1972.

10. Teutoburg Forest

Date: September 9 CE
Location: Germany

BELLIGERENTS

1. Germanic Tribe

   Commander: Chieftain Arminius

2. Roman Empire

   Commander: Publius Qinctilius Varus

BACKGROUND

Julius Caesar continued to expand the borders of the Roman Empire, and in early 59 BCE, he started making preparations to bring the rich and fertile land of Gaul under Roman control. Caesar completed the conquest of Gaul, now France, by 51 BCE. The military campaign lasted a little over eight years and brought vast new territory under Roman rule. The Rhine now served as the eastern edge of the Roman Empire.

Germanic tribes east of the Rhine made frequent raids across the river, plundering villages and trade caravans. In 55 BCE, and again two years later, Caesar crossed the Rhine and made a show of force, scorching small Germanic settlements and crushing tribal forces that gave battle. These punitive expeditions, often launched as retaliatory measures for Germanic raids, continued over the next fifty years, leaving a lasting impression on the memory of the Germanic tribes that lived there. Arminius would later capitalize on these hostile feelings.

Arminius hailed from the Cherusic tribe. His family, being one of means and reputation, provided him access to the upper echelons of Roman society in Gaul. He soon took command of an auxiliary unit in the service of Rome. In this capacity, he learned much about Roman culture and customs. He picked up Latin, which allowed him to become the close confidant of the Roman general Publius Qinctilius Varus. Perhaps most valuable, he gained knowledge of Roman military operations and became familiar with the strengths and weaknesses of Roman legions. The precise motivations that led Arminius to betray his Roman ally are largely speculative. However, Roman encroachments on native lands, combined with taxation, were widely unpopular. However, his motives may have been more complex, if personal, with designs on becoming a Germanic king.

PLAN

In the intervening years between Caesar and Varus, the Germanic tribes learned much about Roman methods of war. Germanic soldiers often filled axillary positions in the legions and, upon completion of their terms of service, returned to their respective tribes east of the Rhine. Thus, men with military knowledge and experience began to fill the ranks of Germanic tribes.

Arminius apprehended Roman strengths. Legionnaires were well paid, drilled, and usually competently led. When the legions were able to choose the field of battle and deploy in order, tribal forces stood little chance of securing victory. Thus, Arminius knew that any victory rested on securing an asymmetric advantage that exploited Roman tactical weaknesses.

Arminius devised a plan to lure the Roman legions into a position of vulnerability. He told Varus of a Germanic tribe farther to the north that was in open rebellion. Varus had experience putting down revolts in Syria. As such, destroying a nascent rebellion before it expands dictates that one respond quickly and in force. Varus directed the legions to march on the tribe.

The plan required that the Roman legions be lured into topography that limited their ability to organize into tactical formations. If the legions could be ambushed while in march formation, on terrain that severally limited their mobility and visibility, then the Germanic tribes stood a good chance of victory.

Arminius decided on a spot near the base of Kalkriese Hill. A narrow stretch of land, probably no more than twenty feet wide in places, ran between the hill on the south and a large bog to the north. Furthermore, numerous streams crisscrossed the area, further complicating movement. Germanic soldiers reinforced the ambush site by building a wall at the base of the hill. In this narrow, wet, and forested area, the conditions were stacked in Arminius's favor.

THE BATTLE

As Varus marched his legions deeper into the trap, the 20,000-man army, baggage train and camp followers now stretched out three to twelve miles along the route. Germanic scouts, probably in the service of Arminius, provided reconnaissance and led the legions blindly along. Ancient Roman sources record that the legions endured torrential downpours and poor visibility throughout this period. Roman shields became waterlogged and heavy. The soldiers were likely tired and in a mental stupor, as long marches are wont to do, each staring at the feet of the legionnaire in front of him. In this fatigued and exhausted state, the lead legion rounded the northern point of Kalkriese Hill.

Germanic soldiers attacked suddenly from atop the wall with a hail of spears. The Roman legionnaires struggled to orient themselves to the unexpected attack. They stumbled in the stream and struggled to bring their shields to bear as they faced the attack from their southern flank. Discipline waned under the surprise attack. The legionnaires strained to hear orders above the cries of the wounded, the battle cries of the attackers, and the clanking of metal. Then, without warning, legionnaires were impaled from behind as the Germanic tribesmen attacked from the northern flank. With the men halted to the front and assaulted from both flanks, Roman discipline now broke. Panic moved with an accordion effect from front to rear. Varus moved toward the front with his lieutenants to get commanders' eyes on the situation. Upon seeing the scale and ferocity of the ambush, he despaired and committed suicide, lest he be taken prisoner and tortured to death.

Over the next several days, the remaining men in Legions XVII, XVIII, and XIX were hunted down and killed. Of the survivors, the unlucky were captured and

Arminius's German tribes attack Varus's legions in the Teutoburg Forest, ca. 9 CE. Note the dress is probably patterned after a much later period. (Hulton Archive/Getty Images)

sacrificed to the Germanic gods, while a lucky few were enslaved and later ransomed back to Rome.

It was one of the greatest disasters to ever befall the Roman army.

CONCLUSION

In a matter of days, Rome had lost roughly 10 percent of its legions. And perhaps more damaging, the invincibility of Roman military might was now a question, not a forgone conclusion. Augustus Caesar, now in the latter years of life, never entirely recovered from the loss of the legions. Tiberius rushed to the Rhine to meet the coming Germanic invasion that never came. Arminius had successfully checked Rome. Augustus moved to fortify the Rhine, but outside of punitive raids across the Rhine, did not attempt eastward expansion.

The Battle of Teutoburger Forest is a cautionary tale. One might take note of the importance of leadership, the dangers of imperial overextension, or the tenuous nature of alliances. Varus certainly did not act prudently or heroically, ending his life before the capricious winds of war had finished. Fortunes in war have turned on less. In fact, Arminius had less—less men, arms, and armor than the Romans. In every measurable metric, the Germanic soldiers came up short of their Roman counterparts. But counting is a favorite pastime of military officers, and Varus undoubtedly ran the numbers and concluded that a force of three legions was more than adequate for anything the tribes might throw at him. That's the problem with arithmetic in war: More often than not; the scales don't tilt as they should. Those ethereal factors—those things one can't count—count for an awful lot.

Further Reading

Clunn, Tony. *In Quest of the Lost Legions: The Varusschlacht.* London: Minerva Press, 1999.

Wells, Peter S. *The Battle That Stopped Rome: Emperor Augustus, Arminius, and the Laughter of the Legions in the Teutoburg Forest.* New York: W. W. Norton & Company, 2003.

11. Adrianople

Date: August 9, 378 CE
Location: Adrianople, in the Balkans

OPPONENTS

1. Tervingi/Goths

    Commanders: Alavivus and Fritigern

2. Rome

    Commanders: Emperors Valens and Gratian

BACKGROUND

In 375, the Roman Empire was divided among Valens, who controlled the eastern provinces; Gratian, who ruled over the west; and Valentinian II (only four years old), who held Italy and North Africa. And for the moment, relations among the triumvirate remained stable and peaceful, but unrest encroached from the east. As the Huns pushed westward, the various Gothic tribes, like a giant bow wave, were pushed west, toward the eastern boundary of the Roman Empire. The Gothic tribes were caught between the advancing Huns to their rear and Roman legions at the front, guarding the Rhine and Danube rivers.

Rome still had massive resources at its disposal, but numerous fissures had begun to run through the once-firm foundation. Emperors were less secure, and perhaps less capable than their earlier predecessors, and their power was more fragmented now. The army remained formidable when competently led and able to deploy for battle. However, competence, like manpower for the legions, was in short supply.

The Gothic tribes pressing against the Danube numbered in the tens of thousands; some estimates have the number at closer to 60,000. The republic, and later the empire, occasionally resettled tribes within Roman borders. The tribes provided a new tax base and worked the agricultural lands. Furthermore, Germanic soldiers had filled the auxiliary components of legions for centuries. Young men born into these militant Germanic tribes made excellent soldiers. Valens needed a peaceful eastern front along the Danube while he took care of the Persian threat, and this certainly figured into his analysis. There were dangers when allowing migration of this magnitude, of course, but the benefits appeared to outweigh the risks. Nevertheless, Valens accepted the request made by Alavivus and Fritigern, both Goth chieftains, to resettle within the empire.

From the start, the mutually beneficial agreement began to unravel. First, the Romans were supposed to provide food for the Tervingi. And they did—just on a woefully inadequate scale. In fact, the food shortage became so acute that tribal children were sold for food. Second, the Roman officers responsible for the care and movement of the Tervingi abused their power for gain at every turn. Finally, Rome did not provide enough legionnaires to oversee the peaceful integration of the Germanic tribes. Valens was over 1,000 miles away and rightly assumed that he had neutralized a precarious situation, but in the lesser hands of inept officers, Valens's sound decision transformed into insurrection.

Yet, had the Roman officers left it at starvation and extortion, things may not have escalated to open warfare. But one evening, Lupicinus, the Roman officer in charge at Marcianopolis, held a banquet that the two chieftains, Fritigern and Alavivus, attended. During the banquet, a minor argument broke out between tribal forces, legionnaires, and peasants on the outskirts of the city. A small brawl ensued, and the Roman soldiers fled. Once news reached Lupicinus, he arrested the two chieftains. Word quickly spread to the Tervingian camp. Tribal warriors now gathered for battle. Fritigern convinced the Romans, that if released, he could convince the warriors to return to camp.

Lupicinus compounded the problem with one impulsive act after another and marched on the Tervingian camp. The Tervingian warriors attacked and destroyed much of the Roman force. The warriors now moved on Adrianople, but they lacked the necessary knowledge in siege craft and quickly abandoned the assault. Instead, the Goths moved on towns that lacked walls. As word spread, more Germanic warriors flocked to join Fritigern's force. They raided, burned, and pillaged; yet the Goths could not hope to prevail against Rome. Finally, in 377, Valens had restored order along the Persian border and headed back to deal with the Goths. The Goths had ravaged the provinces of Thracia and Macedonia for roughly two years before Valens marched on them for battle.

THE PLAN

The initial plan called for Gratian to move east and meet up with Valens, who was moving west. Then, the combined Roman armies would march against the Goths. However, like most military plans, this one fell short of the ideal. Gratian dithered, either intentionally or because he had to ward off raiding Germanic tribes of his own. Nevertheless, his absence left Valens with a choice: He could abstain from battle and wait for Gratian's army, which would provide him with a significant numerical advantage; or else he could commence the attack alone. He chose the latter. Valens confidently moved forward, secure in the knowledge he had. However, knowledge is imperfect, and all the more so in war, where the enemy attempts to mislead you at every turn. Valens's scouts reported an army of around 10,000. As it turns it out, that number was well below the actual figure.

THE BATTLE

As the armies approached each other on the battlefield, Fritigern sent several envoys to entreat with Valens. Fritigern's appeals for some kind of peaceful end to the hostilities were ignored. Perhaps Valens felt that Fritigern's overtures were insincere and he was only playing for time, or he may have sensed weakness in the appeal. Regardless, the requests were swept aside and the armies deployed for battle.

The Roman battle plan unraveled quickly, as cavalry on the right flank attacked before the Roman battle line had finished forming. The cavalry's attack triggered a general response down the Roman line. However, the premature attack put the deploying units on the left flank at a distinct disadvantage. The Roman cavalry were soon put to flight, leaving the flanks of the Roman army open.

The Roman infantry continued forward until a sudden attack by Gothic cavalry landed against the flanks and rear of the army. Meanwhile Gothic infantry pressed in from the front. The Roman left flank, given its inauspicious start, began to collapse under Gothic pressure. Organized command and control began to fail in the Roman army, although veteran units continued to resist. As evening approached, the Roman units were completely broken. Like most battles in antiquity, the losing side usually lost substantially more soldiers than the winners, as the pursuing cavalry slaughtered the routed army.

CONCLUSION

Roman losses were appalling, with its army losing nearly 10,000 soldiers. Valens's body was never found. The primary army of the eastern empire was lost by the afternoon. Its experienced officers were cut down and the army's equipment looted by the Goths, who now roamed unchecked. Valens, despite his experience fighting the Persians, demonstrated a casual overconfidence and poor leadership. Perhaps he didn't expect much of a fight from the Germanic warriors, but the catastrophic losses of three legions in the Battle of Teutoburger Forest should have given him at least some pause.

The Roman Empire spent a total of six years to bring the Goths to peaceful surrender. The fact that it took six years speaks to the declining power of Rome and the increasing effectiveness of Rome's enemies. In the end, the Goths got much of what they had been promised originally when they were given peaceful entrance to the empire. Theodosius, the new emperor of the eastern provinces, rebuilt the army, but it paled in comparison to what was lost.

Further Reading

Goldsworthy, Adrian. *How Rome Fell.* New Haven, CT: Yale University Press, 2009.

Grant, Michael. *The Roman Emperors.* New York: Sterling Publishing, 1985.

Ward-Perkins, Bryan. *The Fall of Rome and the End of Civilization.* New York: Oxford University Press, 2005.

12. Catalaunian Plains

Date: June 29, 451 CE
Location: Champagne-Ardenne region of northeastern France

OPPONENTS

1. Western Roman Empire
    Commander: Flavius Aetius
2. Visigoths
    Commander: King Theodoric I
3. Hunnic Empire
    Commander: Attila the Hun

BACKGROUND

The Battle of the Catalaunian Plains (also known as the Battle of Chalons), in 451 CE, was the high-water mark of the Hunnic Empire's incursions into western Europe. Forced out of Kazakhstan, the Huns migrated westward, leaving death and destruction in their wake. In the late fourth century, they reached the Danube River and crossed into the Eastern Roman Empire. Too weak to fight this new threat, the Romans opted to pay them off. This arrangement worked until 433 CE, when Attila took control after the death of his uncle. For a time, Attila honored the treaty, but in 441 CE, he led his Huns across the Danube, ransacking Roman towns as he marched farther westward.

In 305 CE, after decades of social unrest, civil war, and outside invasions, the Roman Empire had been divided into the Western and Eastern Roman Empires, with capitals in Ravenna and Byzantium, respectively. However, by the time of the split, the Roman army was not what it once was. Very few Romans served in the army, and it consisted mostly of foreigners. Also, both halves had to rely heavily on alliances with the various tribes and bands within their borders. Nonetheless, the western emperor, Valentinian III, knew that it was only a matter of time before Attila invaded the Western Roman Empire. By 447 CE, Attila had subdued most of the Eastern Roman Empire and was looking for an excuse to take the other half.

The sister of Valentinian, Justa Grata Honoria, may have provided Attila his pretext, though that is debatable. Honoria, hoping to get out of an arranged marriage, sent a letter asking for Attila's help. To prove her sincerity, she included her personal ring. Attila took the ring as her intent to marry him. He claimed not only Honoria's hand, but also half of the Western Empire as her dowry. Valentinian rejected Attila's demands, giving an insulted Attila the excuse he needed to invade Gaul.

In 451, Attila crossed the Rhine near Mainz at the head of a force of approximately 200,000 warriors, sacking the cities in their path. Attila and his main force moved through central Gaul attacking Trier, Metz, and Reims, while a secondary force looted and rampaged in the north along the coast. The two forces linked up near Paris before moving on to Orleans. The Alan king, Sangiban, promised Attila that he would hand over the city; however, the people of Orleans declined to surrender, forcing Attila to lay siege to the city. Weather and a determined defense thwarted Attila's plans for a quick victory. On June 14, as he prepared to launch his final assault, Attila received word of an approaching Roman army. More concerned with confronting this new threat than taking Orleans, Attila broke off the siege and withdrew.

When he heard of Attila's invasion, Valentinian appointed Flavius Aetius to command the army to repel the Huns. Aetius was a perfect choice. Not only was he capable and courageous, but he was also familiar with Hunnic culture and spoke the language. Other than some auxiliaries, Aetius had very few Roman soldiers. The rest of his force was comprised of a coalition of Franks, Burgundians, Alans, Saxons, Olibrones, and Armoricans. The largest contingent came from the Visigoths, led by their king, Theodoric I. Estimates of the size of the Aetius force ranges from 30,000 to 80,000.

After forming up near Arles, Aetius led his force toward Orleans to lift the siege. As they approached Orleans, Aetius's army was met by a rearguard of Gepids that Attila left behind to cover the withdrawal of his main force. After the Roman coalition dispatched Attila's rearguard, they continued to pursue the Huns, eventually catching them on a plain near the Marne River.

THE BATTLE

By most accounts, the focus of the battle became a ridge between the two forces. On the Hunnic side, Attila deployed his forces with his Ostrogoth allies on his left wing and the remnants of his Gepid allies on the right. Attila positioned himself with his Huns in the middle. Attila preferred to engage in mobile warfare and tried to avoid set-piece battles whenever possible. The Catalaunian plain would give Attila that advantage, so long as the Roman coalition did not close the range too quickly.

Aetius deployed his force with the Visigoths, under Theodoric, on the right wing opposite Attila's Ostrogoths. In the middle, he assembled his remaining allies, some of questionable loyalty, near his loyal ally, the Alans. Aetius hoped that the example of the Alans would steady the others. Aetius positioned himself with his Roman auxiliaries opposite the weakened Gepids, which he had bested in their rearguard battle.

The battle opened with the Huns attempting to take the ridge. However, the Visigoths, led by Thorismund, Theodoric's son, forced them off the ridge. Aetius and the Romans had taken possession of the ridge when Attila launched his main assault at 2:30 p.m. Some accounts claim that Attila chose this time in order to give his force the ability to slip away under cover of darkness should the outcome of the battle go against him.

Aetius engaged the Gepids on the Roman left and was able to separate them from the rest of Attilas's force. Meanwhile, the Ostrogoths threw themselves on the Visigoths, only to be pushed back down the ridge. Despite the death of Theodoric in this opening fight, the Visigoths, under Thorsimund, pressed their advantage. Thorsimund exploited the gap between the Visigoths and Huns by attacking into Attila's left flank. Attila was losing his mobility advantage as the Visigoths closed in. Seeing that the battle was not going his way, Attila withdrew to his camp. The bloody battle continued as the Roman coalition chased the Huns back to their camp. Once inside the protection of the camp, though, the Hunnic archers drove the Romans back with withering volleys of arrows. Some accounts suggest that as darkness fell, most of the Romans staggered about as they tried to regroup.

The next morning, the sun came up on a scene of great carnage, and once the scale became apparent, neither side wanted to resume the fight. Aetius met with Thorismund to work out their next move. They both agreed that they could keep Attila surrounded and wait him out. However, Aetius was concerned that with the Huns now in check, his Visigoth ally might seize the opportunity to turn on the Western Roman Empire. Therefore, Aetius convinced Thorismund that he should return home to defend his new throne against his brothers. After the Visigoths departed, Aetius gathered his remaining force together and retired to Ravenna. Attila remained in his camp until his scouts confirmed that the Romans had left the battlefield. For unknown reasons, Attila neither pursued Aetius nor resumed his ravaging of Gaul; instead, he led his Huns back home.

CONCLUSION

Even though both sides ceded the field of battle, most accounts give the victory to Aetius for repelling the Hunnic invasion. Nonetheless, Attila would return the following year, but famine and disease cut his campaign short. By 454, both Aetius and Attila would be dead. Attila died in 453 from internal bleeding. Following his death, fighting among his sons over control eventually led to the collapse of the Hunnic Empire. Aetius was assassinated by Valentinian in 454, either to eliminate a threat or because of Aetius's failures on the battlefield. Regardless, the Battle of the Catalaunian Plains halted the Huns' incursions and led to the rise of the Franks and Burgundians.

Further Reading

Heather, Peter. *The Fall of the Roman Empire: A New History of Rome and the Barbarians.* New York: Oxford University Press, 2006.

Hughes, Ian. *Aetius: Attila's Nemesis.* South Yorkshire, UK: Pen & Sword Books, 2012.

Kim, Hyun Jin. *The Huns, Rome, and the Birth of Europe.* New York: Cambridge University Press, 2013.

Man, John. *Attila: The Barbarian King Who Challenged Rome.* New York: T. Dunne Books, 2006.

13. Yarmouk

Date: August 15–20, 636 CE
Location: Jordan, near the Yarmouk River

OPPONENTS

Rashidun Caliphate
    Commander: Khalid ibn al-Walid
Byzantine Empire
    Commander: Vahan

BACKGROUND

The Battle of Yarmouk was the first significant clash between Christians and Muslims. After the death of Muhammad in 632, his successor, Abu Bakr, faced an open revolt over his rule. After defeating the rebels, Abu Bakr consolidated the Arabs and moved north to seize Iraq from the Sassanid Empire. The Arabs easily took Iraq, and in 634, Abu Bakr set his sights on Syria. However, in Syria the Muslims came up against the Byzantine Empire, under the rule of Heraclius.

Heraclius had just defeated the Sassanids in a long-running war to reclaim Byzantine territory lost to the Persians. Nonetheless, the Byzantine victory had left the army and the people exhausted, and both were in the process of rebuilding when the Muslim invasion began. Initially, Heraclius, not relishing another war, ignored or disregarded the Muslim incursions. However, when the Muslims threatened Syria, Heraclius could no longer ignore this new threat. In 634, the Muslims defeated the Byzantines in their first two battles, and they occupied Damascus. An outraged Heraclius assembled an even larger army, approximately 80,000–150,000 men composed of Christian Arabs, Armenians, Slavs, Franks, and Georgians, to crush the Arabs. Due to ill health, Heraclius was unable to lead the army, and he named a capable Armenian, Vahan, to command the coalition instead.

The year 634 also saw the death of Abu Bakr; however, his successor, Umar, saw no need to change the path of expansion that Abu Bakr had set, so the Arabs continued their northward conquest. As they expanded across the Levant, the Arab army divided into four smaller forces. When Khalid ibn al-Walid, the overall Arab commander, heard of the force that Heraclius was assembling, he recommended to the new caliph that the scattered forces pull back and come together to meet the Byzantine army en masse. Khalid knew the Arabs would still be outnumbered, but if they chose the ground, they might be able to overcome the Byzantines' superior numbers through courage and strategy. Umar agreed, and the four Arab armies, approximately 25,000–40,000 strong, gathered on a plain near the Yarmouk River.

The Byzantine army caught up with the Arabs at Yarmouk in May. However, the size of the force, coupled with the length of their supply lines back to Damascus, put the Byzantines in a precarious position logistically. The logistical difficulty put a further strain on an already tense command situation. Unlike the small but cohesive Arab army, there was much infighting among the leaders of the various groups. These disagreements led to mistrust, which in turn hampered coordination between the commanders. These tensions and mistrust would contribute to the Byzantine defeat in the upcoming battle.

From May to August, the two armies faced each other across the Yarmouk plains. Postponing the battle worked to the advantage of the Arabs. The lull not only gave them time to assess their Byzantine opponents, but also gave Khalid time to bring in 6,000 more reinforcements. Despite a few attempts at negotiation, neither side would bend. All the while, the Byzantine army was growing weaker and increasingly restless. Vahan, believing he had no other choice, decided to attack on August 15; the battle would last six days.

THE BATTLE

From August 15–18, the fighting was at times intense but inconclusive. Over those four days, the Byzantines launched numerous attacks in an attempt to find a weakness in the Arab lines, only to be rebuffed repeatedly by Khalid's men. The fourth day is sometimes referred to in Arab accounts as the "Day of Lost Eyes" because of the number of eyes that were put out by the deadly fire of the Byzantine archers. Nonetheless, the Byzantines still could not penetrate the Arab lines. On the fifth day, Vahan asked for a truce to reopen negotiations. Khalid surmised that Vahan's offer indicated the Byzantines were weaker than he believed, so he declined. Instead, he planned to attack the next day, August 20.

In preparation for the upcoming attack, Khalid reorganized his army. He massed his cavalry in one large formation, intending to throw them at the left flank of the Byzantine army and roll them up from left to right. To the rear of the Byzantines were three steep gorges, or *wadis*. Khalid intended to cut off the Byzantine routes with his cavalry and sent a small detachment to seize a key bridge across one of the wadis, at Ayn al-Dhakar.

On August 20, Khalid's cavalry charged the Byzantine left flank, driving off part of Vahan's cavalry. At the same time, the Arab infantry attacked across the entire Byzantine front. Khalid's plan was unfolding as he envisioned. His cavalry disengaged from the left flank to attack the bulk of Vahan's cavalry. The Arab horsemen quickly dispersed the Byzantine cavalry, who fled north of the battle area, taking Vahan with them. At the same time, Khalid's infantry was steadily rolling up the Byzantine left flank. The Arab cavalry now fell on the rear of the Byzantine line. This added pressure was enough to break the last of Vahan's army, and they began retreating, signaling the final phase of the battle.

Khalid's cavalry blocked any escape to the north, forcing the Byzantines westward and into the wadis and the Arab cavalry detachment at al-Dhakar. Once the Arabs had the Byzantines surrounded, the slaughter began. The crush of the Arabs forced some off the cliffs, while others were run down and killed as they tried to escape. A few were able to escape their Arab pursuers, but Khalid's men took no prisoners and killed all the survivors. As the battle was winding down, Khalid took part of his cavalry to pursue the remnants of the Byzantine army. He caught up with them outside of Damascus and, after a short fight, defeated them, killing Vahan in the process.

CONCLUSION

The defeat at Yarmouk left Heraclius a broken man, and he blamed the loss on God's displeasure with his sinful ways. Realizing that he had neither the manpower nor resources to mount an offensive to retake the province, he left Syria and returned to Constantinople. For the Muslims, their decisive victory at Yarmouk was the opening for further conquests throughout the Middle East—conquests that continue to shape and influence East-West relations.

Further Reading

Akram, A. I. *Sword of Allah: Khalid Bin Al-Waleed, His Life and Campaigns*. Maktabah Publications, 2007.

Kaegi, Walter E. *Heraclius, Emperor of Byzantium*. New York: Cambridge University Press, 2003.

Kennedy, Hugh. *The Great Arab Conquests: How the Spread of Islam Changed the World We Live In*. Boston: Da Capo Press, 2007.

Luttwak, Edward N. *The Grand Strategy of the Byzantine Empire*. Cambridge, MA: Harvard University Press, 2009.

14. Baekgang

Date: October 14, 663 CE (though accounts vary)
Location: Present-day South Korea (near the modern-day city of Kunsan)

OPPONENTS

1. Japanese and Korean allies (Paekche)
    Commander: General Abe no Hirafu

3. Tang Chinese and Korean allies (Silla)
   Commander: General Liu Rengui

BACKGROUND

The Battle of Baekgang occurred in the seventh century and was among the more significant engagements in this period of Asian history. According to the *Chronicles of Japan,* a Japanese invasion of Korea occurred during the reign of the Yamato empress Jingo (or Jingu). This began a period of extensive Japanese meddling in Korea and established the historical pattern for such actions. To this point, the Japanese armies, especially those that had gone to subjugate Korea, had been primarily infantry. However, in the fifth century, the Koreans revolted, aided by another Korean kingdom not under the Yamato kingdom's tribute. The circumstances of this successful revolt help explain why the Japanese began to take the horse more seriously as a weapon of war. Around 400 CE, the mighty Yamato warriors were put to flight by mounted Koreans of the Kingdom of Koguryo. It was not long after this defeat that the Japanese began to use horse-mounted units in their military formations. The continental Asians had invented the stirrup around the time of the birth of Christ, and so the Japanese benefited from this military innovation as well. By the seventh century, the Japanese had invented their own pouchlike stirrup that served them all the way to 1853, just before the arrival of Commodore Matthew C. Perry, who forced Japan into the modern era in 1854. One of the great ironies of history is that it was the hated and despised Koreans who bequeathed to future samurai their essential equestrian so-called birthright.

The rich area of the Kanto plain, on the eastern side of the island of Honshu, became the setting for Japanese warriors to practice mounted warfare and tactics. Because of an iron shortage, Japanese warriors tended to favor archery, even though it took quite a bit of practice; arrows used less iron (for their arrowheads) than swords did. The Japanese quickly saw the advantage of combining expert archery and horsemanship, and so was born the penultimate template for the fearsome samurai—the mounted bowman—of later legend. Also, by this time the Japanese had abandoned most plate armor in favor of chain-mail armor, which allowed more flexibility for archery and equestrian skills, especially given the small size of Japanese horses. By 553, the Japanese were ready to return to Korea for continued interventions and war, this time on horseback. At the same time, the powerful Tang Empire in China, as well as their Korean clients, had long experience in both mounted and naval warfare.

The politics in Korea were complicated, but essentially the Tang backed the Kingdom of Koguryo and the Japanese backed the rival Kingdom of Paekche. The two kingdoms were interminably at war over dominance of the peninsula, and eventually Japan got involved in the fighting, first sending 1,000 troops and 100 horses using forty ships. This was evidently not enough, and eight months later, the emperor ordered 10,000 more troops to be dispatched to aid Paekche. There was no mention of horses, but if the ratio of 10 to 1 in the earlier request continued, then there may have been as many as 1,000 horses. How these troops fought, in what sort of units, and how they were controlled and commanded (beyond the assignment of generals) are not apparent from the chronicles. By 562, the superior Sino-Korean armies from farther north in Korea had evicted the Japanese.

However, Japan's rulers remained enamored of their adventures in Korea, and an even larger Japanese expedition proceeded forth in 602, with Prince Kume commanding as shogun (meaning "general") to invade the Kingdom of Silla (near modern-day Pusan). It included over 25,000 troops, as well as a number of Shinto priests. Prince Kume's expedition also gives evidence of the emergence of a cadre of nonnoble leaders, or "local servants of the Court." These local strongmen fought as horsemen and commanded various units of peasants in the Yamato armies. Of particular note, at least at the time of Prince Kume, these men did not have the authority to "tax the people" (Farris, 1996). These in fact may be the forerunners of both the *daimyo* (great lords) and their samurai retainers. However, there were also noble families that specialized in military affairs. They went by the name of *gunji shizoku* ("military aristocrats"). This group's duties included command of the emperor's archers, as well as holding some of the Shinto priest positions with the armies.

Japan continued to play a tricky game of balancing the three major Korean kingdoms—Koguryo, Silla, and Paekche—against each other to continue the expansion of its own interests in Korea. Of the three, Paekche was most important, and Silla was the most hostile to Japan. The Korean states played it safe, though, presenting tribute to both their powerful Chinese Tang neighbors to the north and west and to the Japanese emperor Kotoku when he assumed the Yamato throne.

However, a dispute between the Chinese and the Koguryo kingdom brought the Chinese to the very door of Japan. A disastrous campaign by the short-lived, but powerful, Sui dynasty against Koguryo caused the new Tang dynasty to regard this more northerly kingdom as an enemy. As the Tang armies began to invade and campaign against the Koreans, members of the Japanese court decided that a more aggressive foreign policy was needed to aid their Korean allies in Koguryo, but especially the more southerly Paekche kingdom. The coup plotters, as well as the reformers who wished to introduce Buddhism to Japan, took action because of the urgency of the situation in Korea—in other words, the coup was not just a court power struggle, but a struggle over the defense of Japan.

THE PLANS

Emperor Kotoku immediately took steps that bore out how urgent he and his confederates deemed the military situation in Korea. He appointed eight military governors from the ranks of the nonnoble leaders (hereafter military leaders). These military leaders went to the key eastern provinces around the Kanto plain to sequester for the Crown all the weapons they could find.

In the meantime, the Tang advance into Korea continued. The Kingdom of Silla had the foresight to become an ally of the Tang. While the northern Kingdom of Koguryo reeled under the assault of the large Tang armies (numbering often as many as 100,000), the invaders turned their attention to Japan's closest ally in Korea, the Kingdom of Paekche, to open a second front against Koguryo from the south. In 660, the Tang launched an amphibious invasion of Paekche across the Yellow Sea from Shandong. Initially, all went well for the Tang forces and the enemy capital of Churyu (near modern-day Gongju) was captured.

However, as the Tang focused their efforts on Koguryo in the north, the people of Paekche rose up in an effort to expel the Tang in the winter of 660–661. By 663, an uneasy stalemate had settled over Paekche, with the Tang focusing on capturing the principal base of the rebels at Churyu. To this end, Paekche had already sent envoys to the emperor of Japan requesting aid. Japan had sent 5,000 troops as a sort of vanguard in 661, and then in 662, a fleet of 170 ships to aid the Koreans in controlling the Kum River—essential to the Tang and rebels alike for communications and supply.

According to the *Chronicles of Japan,* some of these troops and ships aided Koguryo against the Tang. Finally, in response to the Tang siege of the rebel base at Churyu in 663, Japan sent a large force of 27,000 troops under General Abe no Hirafu, composed principally of infantry but also including very valuable mounted troops, which indicates the seriousness of Japan's effort almost as much as the numbers of ships and men they sent. The *Chronicles* states the decision as follows: "The . . . shoguns . . . were sent at the head of 27,000 men to attack Silla." In this case, Silla naturally included the large Tang forces.

The stage was set for a major battle. Abe had to get his troops up the river to relieve the rebel fortress, and the Tang commander, the experienced general Liu Rengui, brought his fleet down the mouth of the river to keep the Yamato fleet from ascending it. The actual battle occurred on the river, near the village of Baekgang, not far from modern-day Kunsan.

THE BATTLE

The Tang fleet had to be driven off, so the Japanese were forced into the tactical offensive. Based on the accounts of the battle, several features emerge. First, the Japanese and Paekche operated as a loose military coalition and probably had more vessels than the Tang fleet did, possibly as many as double the number. The Tang fleet had a superior position, and the Japanese account says that the first Japanese units to arrive attacked without proper support; this probably occurred the day before the main battle on October 14, 663 (though some sources list the battle as having occurred in late August). Second, while the Japanese and Koreans cooperated little in their attack, the Tang forces maintained strict discipline and formation, as observed with some admiration by the Japanese chroniclers. Finally, a second combined attack by the Japanese and their Korean allies became strung out, probably because of a desire of either the Japanese or Korean captains to be first to engage the enemy (and thus win the glory). This allowed the Chinese fleet to conduct a virtual double-envelopment of the Japanese-Korean fleet and annihilate it in the same manner of Hannibal against the Romans at Cannae.

According to some sources, the Japanese and their Korean allies lost as many as 400 ships, 10,000 men, and 1,000 horses (which must have been loaded aboard the ships to go ashore after the presumed naval victory). The sources list 170 Tang ships, which makes the victory all the more a result of Tang tactical excellence, even factoring in the fact that perhaps the Tang "cooked the books" to make the victory look like an even bigger achievement than it was. Nonetheless, it was a crushing and paradigm-changing military disaster for Japan.

Certainly, the Japanese had a lot to learn about how to conduct war, especially when it involved fighting on the water. The professionalism of the Tang leaders and units also probably had much to do with the outcome. The Yamato kingdom lost the bulk of its disposal military force for overseas warfare, and the way was clear for the Tang to attack Japan because of the loss of the latter's navy to defend against invasion. The loss of warhorses was particularly grievous. By 668, the Tang had destroyed or absorbed the last remaining allies of the Japanese in Korea, placing rulers friendly to themselves in charge of the peninsula.

CONCLUSION

Tensions were so high after the defeat that the Chinese feared that their envoys, sent in 671, would be attacked as the vanguard of an invasion fleet. The Japanese emperor Tenji came to an understanding with the Tang that led to a truce, but relations remained strained. The militarization of Japan continued, with the court nobility now wearing sidearms. The long-term impact of the disaster at Baekgang was the removal of Japanese armies and influence from the affairs of Korea for almost 1,000 years (see the "Battle of Pyongyang" entry).

Further Reading

Chronicles of Japan (Nihon Shoki), scrolls that address the reigns of the Emperors. Available at http://nihonshoki.wikidot.com (accessed April 23, 2019).

Farris, William Wayne. *Heavenly Warriors: The Evolution of Japan's Military.* Cambridge, MA: Harvard University Press, 1996.

Graff, David. *Medieval Chinese Warfare, 300–900.* New York: Routledge, 2002.

PART II

Medieval Military Disasters

15. Tours

Date: October 10, 732 CE
Location: Between Tours and Poitier, France

OPPONENTS

1. Franks
    Commander: Charles (Karl) Martel
2. Umayyad caliphate
    Commander: Abdul al-Rahman

BACKGROUND

The Battle of Tours (also called the Battle of Poitiers) was the high-water mark of the Muslim Umayyad caliphate's incursion into Europe. In 1711, the warriors of the caliphate crossed the Strait of Gibraltar and quickly occupied the Iberian Penninsula. Seeking further expansion and plunder, the Muslims crossed the Pyrenees into the duchy of Aquitaine, under the rule of Duke Odo. In 721, at the Battle of Toulouse, Odo temporarily halted the Muslim advance. However, in 732, a new emir, Abdul al-Rahman, resumed the invasion of Gaul, easily defeating Odo at the Battle of the River Garonne and laying siege to the town of Bordeaux. When he was informed of even greater riches waiting in the Basilica of Saint Martin in Tours, al-Rahman lifted the siege.

Fearing he could not stop this latest Muslim invasion, Odo reached out to Charles, the Carolingian ruler of the Franks. Charles and Odo were not natural allies; however, Charles realized that the Muslims would probably move on his empire next, so he conditionally agreed to help Odo. The condition was Carolingian sovereignty over Odo's kingdom. Odo, left with little choice, agreed.

Charles was a battle-hardened ruler who had spent most of his reign repelling external threats such as the Saxons. Based on his study of the great captains of Greece and Rome, Charles had built a disciplined army to defeat his opponents. The bulk of his army consisted of heavy infantry armed with a variety of weapons, including shields, swords, javelins, and axes. After hearing about Odo's defeat along the Garonne, Charles gathered a force of roughly 30,000 and headed out to meet al-Rahman at a place of his choosing. Moving by a circuitous route to mask his movements from the Muslims, Charles crossed the Loire River and linked up with Odo and the remnants of his army. Charles eventually selected a piece of wooded high ground astride the route to Tours to set up his defense and wait for al-Rahman.

Composed mostly of light horsemen armed with lances and swords, al-Rahman's force of approximately 80,000 left Bordeaux and moved toward Tours. While the exact location is unknown (though it is believed to be somewhere between Poitiers and Tours), al-Rahman was surprised to find Charles and the Franks blocking his path. The Muslims halted and set up camp to prepare for the inevitable battle. For several days, there was some minor skirmishing as each side waited for the other to make the first move. Finally, on October 10, al-Rahman and his soldiers had had enough and decided to act.

THE BATTLE

The ground that Charles chose to defend was ideal for his forces. By occupying the heavily wooded high ground, Charles forced al-Rahman's cavalry to attack not only uphill, but also through a tangle of trees and bushes. Then they would come face to face with Charles's disciplined heavy infantry. If the Franks could stand firm in the face of the Muslims, they had a good chance of coming out victorious.

Now, al-Rahman unleashed his cavalry against the Franks; however, as antici-pated, the ground chosen by Charles afforded them protection from the charging horsemen. Charles's battle-hardened veterans stood firm and, in a rarity for the time, repulsed the Muslim charge. The cavalry of al-Rahman retreated to reform before charging a second time. Charles's men suffered some losses, but his disciplined infantry closed ranks and held off the Muslims one more time. Then al-Rahman would send his cavalry against the Frankish infantry several more times. At one point, some the horsemen penetrated the square but were quickly surrounded and killed before they could reach Charles.

During what would be the final Muslim charge, some of Charles's scouts slipped away and reached the Umayyad baggage train full of the loot they had collected en route. Word quickly spread among the Umayyad cavalry that the Franks were threatening their plunder, and some began breaking off to protect the camp. The remainder saw the horsemen and took that to be the beginning of a withdrawal. Taking advantage of the confusion in the Muslim ranks, Charles ordered his troops to advance; al-Rahman tried to stop the retreat and reform his army, but the Franks surrounded and killed him.

Rather than continue the pursuit, Charles halted to prepare his army to resume the battle the next day. The next morning, the Franks formed and waited for the Umayyads to return, but they never did. Charles, fearing an ambush, cautiously approached the Umayyad camp, only to find it deserted. During the night, the Umayyads had packed up and begun their long retreat to Spain. Counting the cost, Charles lost roughly 1,500 men and al-Rahman, by most accounts, 10,000.

CONCLUSION

There was still much fighting to be done before the Muslims were driven south of the Pyrenees; however, Charles's victory at Tours marked the peak of the Muslim advance into Western Europe. After the battle, Charles assumed the title of Charles Martel ("the Hammer"). He was also proclaimed king of the Carolingian Empire, consolidating its hold on Gaul and Europe. Charles's son, Pepin the Short, would continue his father's work in establishing the Carolingian Empire. However, it would be his grandson, Charlemagne, who would have the biggest impact on European history when the Carolingian Empire became the Holy Roman Empire, and the pope named him the first emperor in 800 CE.

Further Reading

Bachrach, Bernard. *Early Carolingian Warfare: Prelude to Empire.* Philadelphia: University of Pennsylvania Press, 2001.

Fouracre, Paul. *The Age of Charles Martel.* New York: Routledge, 2000.

Hanson, Victor Davis. *Carnage and Culture: Landmark Battles in the Rise of Western Power.* New York: Doubleday, 2002.

Riche, Pierre. *The Carolingians: A Family Who Forged Europe.* Philadelphia: University of Pennsylvania Press, 1993.

16. Hastings

Date: October 14, 1066
Location: Hastings, England

OPPONENTS

1. Anglo-Saxons
    Commander: Harold Godwinson
2. Normans, French, and Bretons
    Commander: William, the duke of Normandy

BACKGROUND

The Battle of Hastings was the decisive battle that paved the way for the Norman conquest of England. Leaving no heir, the death of Edward the Confessor on January 5, 1066, precipitated a succession crisis. The primary claimants to the throne were Harold Godwinson, the earl of Wessex; King Harald Hardrada of Norway; and William, the duke of Normandy. On his deathbed, Edward, with the backing of the English nobility, named Harold of Wessex his successor. Upon hearing the news, Harald Hardrada and William of Normandy each laying claim to the English throne began preparing to invade England. Hardrada claimed the thrown because of his lineage to King Canute, the King of England from 1016–1032. William's claim was based on a promise from King Edward.

Harald Hardrada's Norwegian army of about 15,000 landed in northern England in September. Harold's brother, Tostig, who had been gathering troops in Scotland to challenge Harold, allied with Hardrada. After the forces linked up, Hardrada led the combined force toward York. An English army, under the command of

BATTLE OF HASTINGS, OCTOBER 14, 1066

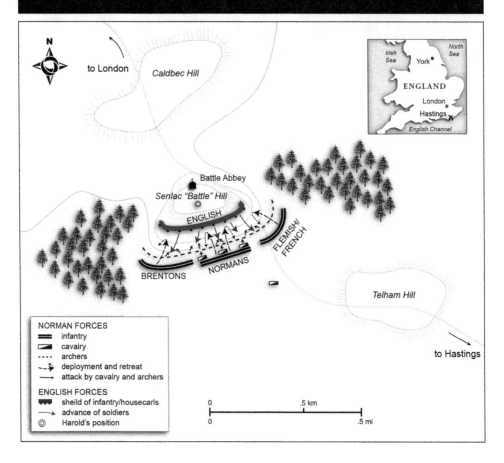

Edwin, the earl of Mercia, and Morcar, the earl of Northumbria, intercepted Hardrada and engaged him in battle. Hardrada defeated the English at the Battle of Fulford on September 20 and went on to occupy York.

Meanwhile, Harold had been waiting along the southern coast of England for William to land and challenge his claim. Growing weary of waiting, Harold had released his militia to help with the harvest when he received word of the Norwegian landing. Harold quickly headed north, gathering what forces he could along the way. On September 25, he met and defeated the combined armies of Hardrada and Tostig at the Battle of Stamford Bridge, which resulted in the deaths of Hardrada and Tostig and was an overwhelming victory for Harold. Harold secured his northern flank, but it had cost him most of his army. Unfortunately for Harold, William chose this moment to invade.

After months of preparation, William's army of approximately 10,000 infantry and 3,000 cavalry was prepared to sail in mid-August, but he postponed the invasion. Then, three days after the Battle of Stamford Bridge, the Normans landed at Pevensey in Sussex and began raiding the local area. Harold was returning to the southern coast to resume his wait for William when he received word of the

Norman landing. Harold spent a week in London reconstituting his forces before setting out to face William. On October 13, Harold assembled his army of approximately 7,000–8,000 men, almost all infantry, on a hill about ten miles northwest of Hastings. It was here that the battle would take place.

THE BATTLE

The English army was a combination of fyrd soldiers and housecarls. The fyrd soldiers were recruited from landowners and were roughly comparable to a militia. These soldiers usually provided their arms and provisions and were more lightly armed than the housecarls. The housecarls, soldiers in full-time service to the king, formed the core of Harold's army. They wore a conical helmet and chain mail and carried either battle-axes or swords. The site Harold chose was at the top of a slight slope, bounded by woods on both flanks. However, the frontage was too narrow for the size of his force, making it hard for the tightly packed soldiers to wield their weapons. Nonetheless, Harold chose to fight here, and the front rank of the infantry formed a shield wall and waited for the Norman attack.

William's army was a mix of infantry, cavalry, and archers. Like the English, they wore chain mail and carried shields. The infantry and cavalry weapon of choice was a long, two-edged sword, though some of the cavalry carried maces (a type of club). The archers used either curved bows or crossbows. In preparation for the battle, William arrayed his army with the Bretons on the left; Normans, with William, in the center; and French fighters on the right. Archers led this formation, followed by his infantry. Bringing up the rear were his three divisions of cavalry.

At 9 a.m. on October 14, William's army advanced toward the waiting English. Even at close range, William's archers opened fire to little effect. Because of the slope, many of their arrows went over the English formation, and the English shields deflected others. William sent his infantry forward next, but even with cavalry support, they could not breach the English shield wall. Unable to make any headway against the steadfast English infantry, William's cavalry and infantry retreated. At the sight of the retreating cavalry, a large portion of the English infantry began pursuing them. William personally intervened to stop the cavalry before the battle became a rout and led them in a counterattack, cutting off the impetuous English infantry. Not yet defeated, William regrouped his forces for the next phase of the battle.

After a brief lull in the fighting, William resumed his cavalry charges, supported by his archers. Each time the cavalry charged the English lines, they would break off the attack before they breached the shield wall, and they would then retreat. Some historians have suggested that this was a deliberate tactic by William, hoping to draw the English into another pursuit. Regardless, if deliberate or not, each charge began to wear on the English infantry. Nonetheless, Harold's shield wall held throughout the day until fate intervened.

Late in the battle, during one of the Norman cavalry charges, Harold was killed. Accounts of this incident vary; some suggest that he was killed by an arrow to the eye, while others suggest that he was felled by a sword blow or was trampled by a

The aftermath of the Battle of Hastings from *Military and Religious Life in the Middle Ages* by Paul Lacroix, ca. 1880. Note the armor is from the late Middle Ages. (Universal History Archive/Universal Images Group via Getty Images)

horse. While it cannot be definitively verified, the arrow to the eye is the legend that has come down through time.

Whatever the cause of his death, the loss of Harold, along with his two brothers, Gyrth and Leofwine, left the English leaderless. Many of the housecarls remained with Harold's body and fought to the end, defending his body. Many more of the infantry fled into the fading light, pursued by the Normans. In a final confusing engagement, a number of the housecarls may have fought a rearguard action at an unknown location that has come to be called "Malfosse." Many accounts question if the events at Malfosse ever took place at all. But whether or not the fight at Malfosse took place, by dusk, the English had ceded the field to William, and the battle was over. While exact casualty figures will never be known, some estimates put the English losses as high as 50 percent, and for the Normans, it was 25 percent. No matter what the exact figures were, the battle was a decisive victory for William.

CONCLUSION

Following the battle, William marched on London. He defeated one English force that attempted to intercept him at Southwark before reaching the capital. After a few more skirmishes outside London, William accepted the surrender of the English noblemen and entered the city. On December 25, William was crowned king of England in Westminster Abbey, beginning what would be nearly a century of Anglo-Norman rule of England.

Harold Godwinson (1022–1066)

Harold Godwinson was the son of Godwin, the earl of Wessex, one of the most power-ful men in England. Upon Godwin's death in 1053, Harold assumed the title of earl of Wes-sex. He quickly proved himself a capable and loyal supporter of the king of England, Edward the Confessor. His reputation was burnished by several military victories and for settling a revolt in Northumbria that was brought about by the actions of Harold's brother, Tostig. His loyalty was rewarded when Edward, on his deathbed, named Harold his successor. However, William, the duke of Normandy, laid claim to the crown setting off a war between the two.

Besides William of Normandy, Harold faced another claimant to the crown from Den-mark, Harald Hardrada. Harold defeated Hardrada and Tostig at the Battle of Stamford Bridge on September 23, 1066, before receiving word that William had landed in England. Harold gathered his army to face this new threat. Unfortunately, Harold's short reign and life both came to an end at the Battle of Hastings on October 14, 1066. Harold's passing also marked the end of 500 years of Anglo-Saxon rule in England.

Further Reading

Lawson, M. K. *The Battle of Hastings: 1066.* Stroud, UK: Tempus Publishing, 2002.

Marren, Peter. *1066: The Battles of York, Stamford Bridge, and Hastings.* Barnsley, UK: Leo Cooper, 2004.

Morillo, Stephen. *The Battle of Hastings: Sources and Interpretations.* Woodbridge, UK: Boydell Press, 1996.

Thomas, Hugh. *The Norman Conquest: England After William the Conqueror.* Lanham, MD: Rowan and Littlefield Publishers, 2008.

17. Hattin

Date: July 3–4, 1187
Location: Not far from the Horns of Hattin, near the western side of Lake Tiberius in Palestine

OPPONENTS

1. Crusader Army
   Commander: Guy de Lusignan, king of Jerusalem
2. Islamic Army
   Commander: Salah ad-Din (Saladin)

BACKGROUND

The Battle of Hattin came about as a result of an internal power struggle among the leaders of the Crusader states over the kingship of Jerusalem. There were two factions: the "old nobility" and the court party; they were dominated by Count

Raymond of Tripoli, who was also the ruler of Jerusalem's fiefdom of Galilee, and Guy de Lusignan, respectively. After Guy conducted a coup d'etat seizing power as king of Jerusalem, Raymond, who had intended to have his own candidate installed per a royal will by the deceased King Baldwin, retreated to his fortress at Tiberias. Guy had been supported in the coup by the patriarch of Jerusalem and the master of the Knights Templar, Gerard of Ridefort. Raymond requested aid from Salah ad-Din (Saladin), the Kurdish sultan of Egypt and Syria and a military leader of the Muslim world, who later founded his own Islamic dynasty (the Ayyubid). This occurred in 1186.

Saladin had signed a truce with the previous king for four years, but Raymond's request allowed him to break the truce prior to its expiration in 1189. Saladin further strengthened his strategic position by signing a peace treaty with the Byzantine Empire in 1186. Saladin remained in Galilee with substantial military forces. In 1187, a Christian-led attack on Muslim caravans by Reynald of Chatillion served as the official pretext for Saladin to declare a Jehad (or *jihad*, meaning "holy struggle") to protect the faithful and punish the Kingdom of Jerusalem for violating the truce.

Guy's best strategy would have been to stay put and let Saladin's army wither in the inhospitable country until it could no longer sustain itself with raids. This strategy had worked previously in 1183 and had been one factor in Saladin's subsequent signature of a truce. Saladin's strategy remained the same; if he could get the Crusaders to open battle, away from their system of fortifications in the north and east, he felt he could defeat them. Raymond's betrayal, and the use of his lands as safe ground through which to cross and raid, were key in this sense: They offered Saladin a logistical base much closer to his enemy. Recall, too, that the main opponent in the eyes of King Guy and his supporters was not Saladin—it was Count Raymond. However, early in 1187, Raymond allowed a large force from Saladin's army into his territory, and there they fought a smaller Christian force belonging to Guy at the Cresson oasis (May 1), not far from Nazareth. Raymond was shocked and embarrassed because he had guaranteed the safety of these emissaries, who were proceeding to Tiberias to negotiate. He realigned with his fellow Christians, but Saladin now had the advantage.

As for tactics, the Crusaders relied on a combined arms team known as the *infantry-knight symbiosis.* So long as the mounted arm worked closely with infantry and did not charge pell-mell without support, the Crusader army was tactically safe within a line of retreat to one of its fortresses or had access to water. This was because Saladin's tactical advantage lay in his mounted Turkish horse archers, a problem that very few states would be able to solve until gunpowder weapons became more ubiquitous. If his archers could get close enough to the Crusaders, with their compound bows to penetrate their armor, they would probably prevail. This might take time, though, so having a good supply of arrows was a necessity for these horse-archer armies. However, Saladin had to avoid massing within range of the heavy knights, who could win the entire battle with one or two well-delivered charges. The battle would thus hinge on a mistake by either party—a mistake that could prove catastrophic.

THE PLAN

With the return of Raymond to the fold, King Guy was able to assemble the largest Crusader army in the history of the Kingdom of Jerusalem—21,200 troops. It contained more than half the Christian knights in the Levant (perhaps as many as 75 percent). Guy had this army assemble at Saforie, just west of Nazareth. Count Raymond held the key fortress, at Tiberias. Hattin lay between these two places, in very inhospitable country not far from Mount Tabor, where Napoleon would defeat another Islamic army 600 years later. However, he had no real plan for its use, and during June and much of July, it sat inactive.

For this reason, Saladin had the initiative. His army was even larger than that of the Christians, possibly as many as 40,000 (including 12,000 cavalry). As the Crusaders dithered at Saforie and in councils at Acre, Saladin seized the high ground around the dominating terrain feature on the road to Tiberias, the so-called Horn of Hattin. Now on the high ground between Tiberias and Guy's army, Saladin besieged Tiberias, held by Raymond's wife, Eschiva. When the Crusader army did not respond, Saladin moved opposite their entrenchments at Saforie, hoping they might attack.

Count Raymond advised caution, and the Crusader army did not attack despite his wife's urgent situation. Saladin withdrew again to the high ground. It appeared that the Crusaders would wait him out. However, for reasons that are still unclear, King Guy reversed himself on the night of July 1–2 and ordered a general advance to the relief of Tiberias, which was about to fall. It appears that Guy had been advised by the master of the Templars to cement his authority as king by ordering the advance, in spite of general agreement with the course of action of waiting Saladin out. His barons meekly obeyed, against their better judgment.

On July 2, the largest Western Christian army in the Holy Land marched east toward Tiberias. It pressed on from the village of Mashan the next day into a valley formed between the Horns of Hattin (two extinct volcanoes), behind which Saladin's main army camped, and hills to the southwest toward Mount Tabor. The army advanced in three huge boxes, with the vanguard led by Raymond of Tripoli, the main body in the center led by Guy, and the rearguard under the command of Balian of Ebelin, with most of the Templars and Hospitallers. The most holy relic of Christendom, the "one true cross," accompanied the king in the center. The army was additionally weighed down with its baggage train, which was distributed throughout all three boxes.

In the meantime, Saladin moved in response. His light forces harassed the Crusaders as they marched. He had been caught somewhat by surprise, and by the time he arrived at Hattin overlooking the Crusader army, they had arrived at a strong position at Turan, which was well watered in those days. If Guy had stopped and entrenched, he would have put Saladin in an awkward position. Saladin may have been forced to attack Guy to prevent him from sending a relief column to Tiberias, which would have resulted in the kind of battle the Crusaders could win—a defensive one.

Fortunately for Saladin, the Crusaders did not intend this at all, but started to make the climb out of the basin and valley toward the plateau and the road to

Tiberias. Even so, they maintained their tactical integrity that had served them well in the past, with their heavy cavalry on the interior of the boxes, screened by infantry and light cavalry (Turcopoles). However, the near-constant harassing attacks and the separation of the army by the terrain, especially the rearguard, caused Guy to call a halt to ask Raymond, his most experienced military commander and most familiar with the terrain, for advice. Raymond advised that they turn farther north and seize the pass at Hattin itself, and then camp and entrench for the night. There was a spring nearby, and once Saladin realized what the Crusaders were doing, he sent the right flank of his army to seize the pass and block them. They succeeded, and now the battle proper began.

The rearguard, whose problems had caused the diversion to the north, now came under pressure from Saladin's left wing. Without access to water, at the end of a long day, Guy decided to simply halt the army and have it entrench for the night where it was. Saladin took this opportunity to bring up water to his larger army and more arrows (reputedly seventy camel loads). The Crusader army, without water for most of a day and a night and with another hot day in front of it, was assailed on the morning of July 4 by Saladin's rested, watered, superior forces. Saladin drew the fight out to try to take advantage of the stifling July heat. His forces were arrayed around the Crusader army in a large *U*, which had to be on the offensive to try to fight its way to water. Additionally, Saladin had fires set upwind of the Crusaders and used the smoke to further discomfit the Crusaders, now parched and desperate.

It was at this point that the infantry abandoned the cavalry and made for Hattin to escape the smoke and heat, heading toward Lake Tiberias, in the hope of breaking through to obtain water. Without the infantry to protect them, the cavalry, paradoxically, were now vulnerable to the horse archers of Saladin. Despite desperate and brave charges, the cavalry could not break through to their infantry and continued to fall. The tactical center of gravity of Guy's army was now melting away. In the final hours of the battle, just below the Horn of Hattin, the Crusader knights fought around the relic of the cross and a tent that the king has set up as a rally point.

The battle ended in the late afternoon with the Crusader army virtually annihilated. Most of the casualties were among the infantry and light cavalry, although almost all of the knights' splendid mounts died in the battle. The bulk of the knights and lords, as well as the king himself, surrendered. Raymond and Balian miraculously escaped with a few knights, riding over their own infantry to get away.

After the battle, Saladin had 200 of the Templar and Hospitaller knights, "the fiercest of all the Frankish warriors," executed. He personally executed one of the men most responsible for the disaster, Reynald of Chatillion, but he spared King Guy.

CONCLUSION

The political consequences of this military disaster were far reaching and profound. Hattin, rather than the capture of Jerusalem afterward, caused the initiation of the Third Crusade because of the destruction of the Crusader army and all its best warriors. Although Saladin did not go on to complete victory because of the Third Crusade, the battle destroyed the basis for Christian military power in the

The Knights Templar

The Knights Templar emerged during the period of the First and Second Crusades. After the capture of Jerusalem in 1099, several of the leaders of the First Crusade—including Hugh de Payens—realized that they needed an organization to protect pilgrims traveling to the Holy Land from both Christian and Muslim bandits. With seven other knights, they established the order in 1119 on the site of Solomon's Temple. Hugh de Payens is generally regarded as the order's first grand master, and it was he who argued successfully at the Council of Troyes for official papal recognition of the order.

Its early ordinances are still unknown, although it is accepted that the members swore the standard monkish vows of poverty, chastity, and obedience. However, under Bernhard of Clairvaux, "the Rule" was formalized and published. To become a Templar, one had to be a candidate before final initiation into full-fledged brotherhood. The organization was later changed to five classes: servants, squires, chaplains, knights, and bailiffs. Again, its primary purpose was as an armed holy order dedicated to protecting pilgrims traveling to the Holy Land. It was only later that its members became politicized, more worldly, and fabulously rich, which in the end probably sealed their final doom under King Philip II of France in 1307. This was because Philip probably wanted its financial holdings and resources and now had the papal backing to seize them to defray his debts incurred by war with the English.

Holy Land, and even this the Third Crusade could not resurrect. The Crusader states hung on for several more generations, the high point of their military power had been reached, and it declined after Hattin.

Further Reading

Baha al-Din Ibn Shaddad. *The Rare and Excellent History of Saladin.* Translated by D. D. Richards. Burlington, VT: Ashgate, 2002.

France, John. *Hattin.* From the Great Battles Series. Oxford: Oxford University Press, 2015.

Olsen, Eric. *The Battle of Hattin, 1187.* A master's degree thesis for the U.S. Army Command and General Staff College, Fort Leavenworth, KS, 1997.

Setton, Kenneth M., ed. *A History of the Crusades, Volume I: The First Hundred Years.* Madison: University of Wisconsin Press, 1969.

18. Kamikaze: The Second Mongol Invasion of Japan

Date: 1281

Location: Hakata Bay in Kyushu and coastal Nagato, in Japan

OPPONENTS

1. Yuan dynasty
   Commander: Kublai Khan
2. Japan
   Commanders: Hojo Tokimune (shogun) and Takeazki Suenaga

BACKGROUND

After 1225, stable government based on cooperation became the rule in medieval Japan. The military dictatorship (*Bakufu*), with the shogun effectively ruling from Kamakura, was comparatively mild and brought a period of peace to Japan. Such was the situation when the Mongols turned their gaze east to the rising sun and Japan.

The genesis for the Mongol invasion lay in their establishment of the Yuan dynasty in China. The founder of this dynasty was the new Mongol head chieftain Kublai Khan, grandson of Genghis Khan, whose power base was in north China. To eliminate the remnants of the Song dynasty in the south of China, Kublai Khan had to create a navy—something the Mongols had little experience with. Hence he turned to his Chinese and Korean vassals, and in 1270, they proceeded to build at a prodigious rate, with the goal of producing 5,000 ships. Japan had already attracted Khan's attention by its rejection of his overtures for submission and tribute in 1268. The Japanese component of Kublai Khan's grand strategy, then, was really that of a punitive expedition against some rude island so-called savages who needed to be taught a lesson in humility—but it occurred against the backdrop of a much bigger effort against southern China that eventually included seaborne attacks on Vietnam as well. In other words, the conquest of Japan was not Kublai Khan's only military goal.

The Mongol military machine never did anything by halves. After the latest round of Japanese rejections, it invaded and subdued the islands of Tsushima and Iki in late 1274 before moving on to the large southern island of Kyushu. The Mongols reputedly had 90,000 men aboard several thousand ships, mostly veterans from recent fighting against the Song Chinese the previous year.

Two things stand out in the Japanese response. First, some eighty horsemen met the initial wave, which must have included several thousand Mongol warriors. They seem not to have realized that the Mongols did not fight in the same way that they did, as individuals prior to a general engagement. The Mongol group tactics simply brushed this annoyance aside. Second, and more important, the *Bakufu* system used the centrally controlled land stewards and constables to perform two functions of national mobilization. First, they notified Kamakura of the threat, and second, they initiated the process of raising substantial numbers of troops from provincial headquarters as a sort of "emergency first response" force, while the administrators used the local records to call out more warriors from the various estates. The urgency of the situation was far greater than earlier civil wars, so the numbers of warriors generated in Kyushu probably exceeded what might normally have been seen in the first stages of a civil war, which was the only form of warfare Japan had known for almost 600 years.

Meanwhile, the Mongols invaded Kyushu at Hakata Bay. The Japanese tried the same tactic, opening the combat with a single warrior firing a single arrow, and "All at once the Mongols down to the last man started laughing." The Mongols then executed their advance-and-retreat tactics, controlled by a general on a hill with drums, and defeated the opposing Japanese force. Japanese chronicles highlight the bravery of their warriors in defending against the Mongolian steamroller, but they managed only to slow the enemy down as the *Bakufu*'s forces conducted a fighting retreat toward the interior of Kyushu at Mizuki.

What happened next supports the theory that this was a punitive expedition rather than a full-fledged invasion. The Mongols suddenly withdrew late in 1274 from in front of the fortifications of Mizuki. They then set ablaze the area around Hakata before reembarking on their ships to sail away, taking their garrisons in Tsushima and Iki with them. The ships were needed in 1279 for a series of sea and river battles near modern Hong Kong that once and for all destroyed the Song.

THE PLAN

The Japanese expected the Mongolians to return and prepared for the invasion that could come at any moment. The burden of conscription and warrior service for these campaigns fell naturally upon the warriors of Kyushu, which included those most experienced in sea-land warfare. The government also wisely sent Kyushu warriors home from distant guard duty in Kyoto and elsewhere so that they could defend their hearths. The Mongols dispatched another emissary in 1275, which also supports the view that the original invasion had been punitive. The shogun sent his head back to the Mongols in reply.

The Japanese also made the first tentative plans to conduct a counterinvasion of Korea as part of their ancient strategy of using that peninsula as a buffer between themselves and Asian threats. However, it was in the area of beach defenses and tactics that the samurai really innovated. The *Bakufu* recruited as many warrior mariners and helmsmen as possible. At the same time, they used the extra manpower they had gathered to construct a lengthy wall along the shore of Hakata Bay and the coastline in Nagato, where the best landing beaches acted as a countermeasure against a Mongolian descent at both locations. They built the walls with inclines on their reverse slopes so that roving bands of horse-archer cavalry could mount the walls and deliver their deadly volleys quickly, and then retreat down and reload as quickly as possible. They also gathered as many boats, and not a small number of ships, to contest the Mongolian fleet's approach at sea as well. They modified their vessels so that the masts could be lowered quickly to board the invaders' vessels, thus allowing the samurais' superior skills in personal combat to have the greatest effect.

The Mongols were busy with other more pressing matters, but in 1281, they returned to Japan, probably with the aim of conquest given that the Song no longer distracted them. The Mongolians organized two armies to subdue Japan, having no shortage of ships and men for this purpose. The larger of the two consisted of approximately 100,000 Chinese; the other comprised a coalition of Mongols, Koreans, and Chinese and was about half the size of the first army. These numbers may in fact have been much less, but still they were far superior to what the Japanese could muster and move. The strategy was for the smaller army to capture the strait islands and then to descend on Honshu in the province of Nagato, possibly as a feint. The key for the Mongols was to establish a substantial lodgment ashore, as they had in the earlier campaign, where they could unload their ponies to employ their mass mounted archery tactics.

THE CAMPAIGN

The invasion began in the spring of 1281 and again involved the capture of the strait islands of Iki and Tsushima as advance bases. It is likely that the Mongols hoped for a quick decision before the typhoon season became serious by late summer and early fall, as it does in that region at that time of the year. Iki was captured, but the Mongols were initially repulsed at Tsushima. The main army arrived at Hakata Bay on Kyushu in the summer, having been delayed in its departure by weather, finding crews, and loading supplies. They encountered the samurai-manned walls at both Hakata and Nagato that had been built to deny them an easy landing at the former or to contain their landing at the beach at the latter. At the islands of Shika and Noko off the coast of Kyushu, the smaller army waited in reserve. It came under attack by embarked samurai, such as the famous warrior Takeazki Suenaga, who afterward commissioned an illustrated narrative of the invasion.

The Japanese executed their forward defense at the walls and on the beaches as planned. The fighting along these beaches was fierce, but the samurai defenders held off the Mongols for six weeks, denying them any major landings and also being able to attack the forward bases mentioned previously. In the light of the previous campaign, this was nothing short of astonishing, and Suenaga discussed how he and his warriors fought from their horses on the beaches and then embarked in boats to attack the Mongols on the water. In one account, a single samurai warrior is said to have swum out to a Yuan vessel and killed everyone aboard with his weapons, all by himself.

It was at this point that the weather played its famous role. The admirals in charge of the invasion fleets intemperately took their ships into the enclosed Hakata Bay and the Imari Gulf for shelter, which enhanced the destructive power of the typhoon that followed. This may indicate that they had little confidence in their crews' ability to weather the storm on the open sea. The typhoon destroyed two-thirds of this fleet. A large number of the warriors drowned, and those who survived were massacred by the samurai, who sortied in their boats after the worst of the storm had passed.

The typhoon became known forever after as a *kamikaze* ("divine wind"), sent by the gods to disperse the barbarian invaders—recall that *shogun* translates as "general who defeats the barbarians." The Mongols withdrew and returned to the mainland, threatening a future invasion that kept the *Bakufu* mobilized for several more years.

CONCLUSION

After the disaster in 1281, the Yuan decided to try their luck exercising their naval power farther south against Vietnam, both that same year and again in 1287. But their ability to project naval power had been severely compromised by the great disaster off Japan. Their hegemony did not last, and they themselves were displaced in the following century by the powerful Chinese Ming dynasty.

Thus was established the myth of the divine deliverance of Japan by the gods. A more sober analysis should attribute equal credit to the organizational structure

Bushido

Bushido means "way of the warrior" in Japanese. Its origins can be traced to the rise of the samurai class to political preeminence in Japan during the twelfth century. From there, it evolved into a highly structured system for the next 600 years until taking its final form under the Tokugawa shoguns. Japan scholar Karl Friday has done much to undo the mythology surrounding bushido, finding that as a common term of understanding, it was not popularized in Japan until the nineteenth century. That said, its central tenets conformed to Confucianism, especially in its demands for loyalty to one's lord (*daimyo*). However, the medieval code of the warrior, as Friday has shown, was far more practical than often portrayed, and loyalties shifted as necessary due to political considerations.

The other common perception of bushido demanding ritual suicide (or *seppuku*) for a loss of honor or "face" must be tempered with the fact that most of the famous suicides in Japanese military history were symbolic and not widespread. Perhaps the best synthesis of the tenets of Japanese medieval bushido can be found in *The Book of Five Rings* by the great warrior and kendo swordsman Musashi Miyamoto, which was written around the early seventeenth century, at the time of the great disarming of the samurai under the Tokugawa shoguns. Finally, later pseudo versions of bushido were socially constructed by the Japanese military in the twentieth century and have little in common with the classic tenets of Confucianism and bushido represented by Musashi.

of the *Bakufu*, especially the tireless work of the Hojo regent Tokimune. Credit also goes to the strong performance of the warriors against an alien military threat and their innovative use of fortifications and tactics along the beaches. One might term this a thirteenth-century version of what today is known as an *antiaccess maritime defense.* Also, the Mongol dynasty was not interested in a lengthy campaign and probably thought the Japanese easy pickings given the results of their first invasion in 1274. Credit for the victory goes to the entire system rather than to any one general; however, it is hard to imagine the samurai prevailing against the Mongols had the enemy put significant forces ashore with room to maneuver.

There were several unintended consequences for Japan. Chief among these involved the idea of having a buffer zone against the barbarians in Korea. The *Bakufu* never fully implemented such a strategy, but the adoption of this scheme as a sort of final solution of the Asian barbarian problem lodged itself in the Japanese psyche. After 250 years, at the end of interminable civil war (*Sengoku*), the warlord Hideyoshi would again try to establish a Japanese-controlled buffer region in Korea against the foreign threat. Also, the narrative of the kamikaze became a seminal component in Japanese national identity as a nation protected by the gods.

Further Reading

Conlan, Thomas C. "Medieval Warfare," in Karl Friday, ed., *Japan Emerging Premodern History to 1850,* 244–253. Boulder, CO: Westview, 2012.

Lorge, Peter, "Water Forces and Naval Operations," in David A. Graff and Robin Higham, eds., *A Military History of China*, 81–96. Boulder, CO: Westview, 2002.

Turnbull, Stephen. *The Samurai: A Military History.* Trowbridge, UK: Japan Library, 1996.

19. Lake Boyang

Date: 1363
Location: The city of Nanchang, on Lake Boyang

OPPONENTS

1. Han
    Commander: Chen Youliang
2. Ming
    Commander: Zhu Yuanzhang

BACKGROUND

The decline of the Mongol Yuan dynasty in the fourteenth century led to its shrinkage to North China. To the south, along the great Yangzi River valley, South and Central China slipped into another period of warring states as revolts spread. Three kingdoms opposed each other in the region along the Yangzi: the Ming (in the middle), Han (in the west), and Wu (in the east). Of these kingdoms, the Han, led by Chen Youliang, were the strongest and most aggressive and the Ming the smallest in terms of both population and resources. However, the Ming, led by a former monk named Zhu Yuanzhang, held key cities along the Yangzi and its tributaries, including the larger fortress city of Nanchang at the southern end of Lake Boyang.

The warfare among these three states revolved around the seizure and retention of walled cities, most of them along lakes and rivers. Warfare in this period thus tended to involve what are today called *joint operations*—the use of navies and armies together.

The ships used on these rivers varied, but for city warfare, they involved large "tower" ships that both could transport large numbers of troops quickly along the river systems and be a means to attack cities. Many of these ships were built with iron-sided, towerlike sterns or forecastles (hence the name), and platforms could be let down on top of city walls so that the troops could assault the cities from the top down. This campaign also involved the first widespread use of gunpowder weapons and cannon, but the primary means of battle involved hand-to-hand combat in boarding other ships or "boarding" city walls from ships.

THE PLAN

In early 1363, the Wu attacked the Ming, who had defeated a Han fleet three years earlier which had tried to seize the key city of Nanchang that controlled access to the rich province of Jiangxi in the south. The Han had rebuilt their fleet and took advantage of Ming distraction to attack Nanchang. Chen Youliang gathered over

300,000 men and moved down the Yangzi, seizing smaller cities and strongpoints with his massive, waterborne host until he arrived at Nanchang in June 1363.

The city was defended by Zhu's nephew, Zhu Wengzheng. It differed from other cities in that its walls were not next to the shores of the lake, but rather were farther back, thus preventing the tower-ship method of attack and forcing Chen to employ traditional land-based siege methods. Zhu Wengzheng's spirited defense of Nanchang for his uncle caused Chen's forces to become bogged down until late August. One of the reasons for Chen's failure to take the city by storm was the Ming advantage in firearms, which they reputedly used to repel Chen's most serious assault on the city in June.

THE BATTLES

Zhu moved to address the threat to Nanchang. He attacked the Han fleet on August 28–29 with his own army and navy of 100,000 men, which were at a disadvantage on the lake. The battle involved the first widespread use of gunpowder in naval warfare between large fleets of ships. The "guns" used by the Ming were much smaller than later cannon and resembled short mortars, or swivel guns mounted on walls or bulkheads. They fired large stones or projectiles, as well as possibly smaller, canister-type projectiles and were mainly used as antipersonnel weapons up close. The Han also probably had this technology, but the Ming certainly did. And these were not the only gunpowder weapons. They used hand grenades, crude rockets, fire arrows, and all manner of other devices. The most interesting of these was something called the "No Alternative" weapon, which was basically a fused bag of gunpowder and objects that were slung over an enemy ship by poles and then dropped and ignited. Needless to say, these weapons could cause the bane of any sailor's existence, then and now—shipboard fire—and that they did in great numbers at Lake Boyang. What the Ming did in this battle was comparable to the new tactics and methods in Western military history that have come to be called a revolution in military affairs. The first day's battle was indecisive, but the most damaging result was the fires caused by the Ming tactics, although the enemy fleet remained undefeated but shaken.

The second day's battle was more successful. The Ming saw what the fires had done and created gunpowder-filled "fire ships," manned by volunteers who drove them into the heart of the Han fleet. At first, the wind was mild and the fires subdued, but the wind picked up and the fires increased until, according to the Ming records, several hundred Han ships were ablaze. This day's battle was enough to cause the Han fleet to move to the northern part of the lake, but the smaller, more maneuverable Ming vessels were able to block the straits leading out of the lake to the Yangzi River.

After September 2, both sides retired and waited, with the Ming fleet blocking the main exit from the lake up the river to the Han bases. This gave the Ming the advantage of having the current in their favor—even more so given their ships' better maneuverability and the additional loss of maneuverability of the Han ships if they tried to escape upriver against the current. There were some defections to the Ming fleet after the disasters of late August, but for almost a month, the two sides remained in a tense standoff. But time was on Zhu's side; the situation for the Han was worse, they had more mouths to feed and now risked losing the entire fleet and army if they did not break out. In a desperate gambit, they attempted to run through the Ming fleet and escape upriver to their bases, no doubt with the intent to try to return after they had revictualed, replaced their losses, and repaired (or modified) their damaged fleet. The reason? The Han had run out of food, so they had to leave or else starve on the lake.

The Han fleet approached the narrows leading from the lake into the Yangzi River on October 3, where the Ming fleet waited upriver in its blocking position. The current worked in the Ming's favor, as the Han fleet lost cohesion and the battle turned into a ship-on-ship fight as clumps of battling vessels drifted downstream. The Han might yet have survived and escaped by sheer force of numbers, but Chen was killed in one of these skirmishes, and his son and heir were captured. With that, the entire Han fleet surrendered to Zhu. It was a military catastrophe that literally changed the history of China.

CONCLUSION

With the disaster on Lake Boyang and the Yangzi, the Ming leader could now turn his attentions directly on the much-weakened Han while remaining on the defensive against the Wu (downstream of Nanchang). They never recovered from their losses in the Boyang campaign. Zhu's naval power was unmatched now, and he who controlled the rivers controlled this part of China. After the defeat of what remained of the Han, Zhu turned his attention to the east and the Wu, conducting the famous siege of Suzhou in 1366. His guns created a breach in the wall of that city, 300 years before the period of European siege warfare on a similar scale, and led to its capture. He overran the rest of Wu in 1367 and declared the founding of a new dynasty called the Ming (based on the names of dynastic instructions he issued). Zhu gave himself the dynastic name of the Hongwu (vastly martial) emperor. He then proceeded to the north and retook North China and the Chinese heartlands there from the Mongol Yuan. Under Hongwu, the Ming established the largest navy in the world, with immense shipyards at the capital of Nanjing. Had they not become insular in later years under Hongwu's successors, it may have been they, rather than the Europeans, who colonized the modern world.

Further Reading

Andrade, Tonio. *The Gunpowder Age: China, Military Innovation, and the Rise of the West in World History.* Princeton, NJ: Princeton University Press, 2016.

Dreyer, Edward L. "The Poyang Campaign, 1363: Inland Naval Warfare in the Founding of the Ming Dynasty," in John K. Fairbank and Frank A. Kierman, Jr., eds., *Chinese Ways in Warfare,* 202–242. Cambridge, MA: Harvard University Press, 1974.

Lorge, Peter. "Water Forces and Naval Operations," in David A. Graff and Robin Higham, eds., *A Military History of China,* 81–96. Cambridge, MA: Westview Press, 2002.

20. Grünwald

Date: 1410
Location: Northwestern Poland

OPPONENTS

1. Order of Teutonic Knights
    Commander: Grand Master Ulrich von Jungingen
2. Kingdom of Poland and Grand Duchy of Lithuania
    Commanders: King Wladislaw II Jagiello and Grand Duke Alexander Vytautas

BACKGROUND

The story of the military disaster of Grünwald (also known as Zalgiris, or the First Battle of Tannenberg) begins with the founding of the Order of Teutonic Knights, initially in the Holy Land as a brotherhood created to care for wounded Germanic knights during the Third Crusade. As the position of the Crusaders in Palestine began to collapse, the Order was invited by the king of Hungary to relocate and fight pagans in Transylvania in the thirteenth century. They soon wore out their welcome, as they attempted to establish an independent state and were expelled from Hungary. From there, they moved to Poland at the invitation of a Polish nobleman to help him defend his lands against some troublesome heathen Prussians (a Slavic, not Germanic people). With this, the Order became established in Poland and eventually succeeded in carving out a state along the Baltic, expelling their fellow Christian Poles from access to that body of water by the early fourteenth century. At the same time, the order forged an alliance with the Livonian Sword Brothers and conducted the Prussian Crusade, incorporating most of what became East Prussia and Pomerania into their domains and displacing (or converting) the Slavic Prussians with the help of Germanic colonists who came to be called *Prussians*. In the meantime, the Order had made the fortress at Marienburg (today the Polish town of Malbork) the capital of its Baltic empire.

After this, the Order turned its crusading/expansion efforts to the east, against the pagan Lithuanians. The Order expanded slowly, but it was a grinding, almost 100-year crusade until the Lithuanian grand duke Wladislaw Jagiello converted to Christianity in 1386. Jagiello found a willing ally to his southwest in the Poles, who were still resentful of the loss of their lands to the Order generations before. Jagiello's reward was the kingship of Poland and marriage to the only female heir to the throne, Queen Jadwiga.

Jagiello's alliance soon faced a crisis when a younger cousin attempted a coup to seize his crown. When this failed, the cousin, Alexander Vytautas (also known as Witold)—now a Christian convert as well—went to the Order to ask for help. The

Order agreed after getting promises from Vytautas for territorial aggrandizement, and they marched on the Lithuanian capital of Vilnius and besieged it in 1390. The siege was prosecuted off and on for two years without success until Vytautas switched sides and made peace with Jagiello. Eventually Vytautas became Grand Duke of Lithuania, while Jagiello remained King Wladislaw II of Poland, with suzerainty over the grand duchy.

It seemed the Order's fortunes were on the decline, especially because Poland-Lithuania had made peace with most of its surrounding neighbors, thus further isolating the Teutonic Knights from support. It was at this point that the Samogitians, whose territory lay between the Teutonic domains in Prussia and Livonia, rebelled against their overlords. The first rebellion was suppressed and a general peace signed, but in 1409, they rebelled again. In their efforts to put down the rebellion, the Order seized trading barges of Poland on the Neiman River at Ragnit (present-day Kaliningrad), violating a peace treaty that they had signed with Jagiello in 1404. With this, a general war broke out between Poland-Lithuania and the Order. The result was an ineffectual campaign that resulted in a six-month truce. During this time, the first several months of 1410, the Order managed a series of diplomatic coups that made the outcome of a renewed war appear to favor it, leading to an overconfidence on the part of Grand Master Ulrich von Jungingen that turned out to be misplaced.

THE PLANS

Initially, the Order had planned, under the cover of the truce, to invade Lithuania and conquer it, while trying to remain at peace with the Poles. Victory over Lithuania would result in a fait accompli for Poland, which would have to fight without the Lithuanian army and thus could probably be pressured in giving away territory for peace. The entire plan is reminiscent of the later partitions of Poland in the eighteenth century. Samogitia, which had allied itself to Poland, would be ceded permanently to the Order, along with Lithuania and parts of Poland. Moldavia, an ally of Poland, would be given to Hungary.

The only problem with this plan was that Vytautas discovered it and informed his cousin. When the truce expired in late June, all sides now actively mobilized again for war. The Poles wished to regain their access to the Baltic by recapturing Polish Pomerania, and the Lithuanians hoped to recapture Samogitia, which had been pacified and occupied by the Order and the Livonians. Thus they decided ahead of time to join forces to defeat the main Order army by invading it from the south, and then to destroy it by capturing the headquarters-capital at the fortress of Marienburg.

The key problem for the Order would be to prevent the juncture of the Polish and Lithuanian armies. Ulrich had at first relied on Vytautas's self-serving policies to prevent an effective alliance. When this failed, he had estimated that the king of Hungary, who had given him a substantial amount of money in support, would protect his investment by coming to his aid. Neither of these things panned out. Additionally, the Poles and Lithuanians, by mobilizing their forces in the north and south, convinced Ulrich that the real site of invasion would be from the east, north of the Narew River, and not from the south.

The other thing Ulrich had not counted on was the speed at which Jagiello and Vytautas moved their forces. The Poles, in particular, outmobilized the Order by incorporating large mercenary contingents, which moved quickly to join the Polish army. Jagiello and Vytautas combined their armies on July 2 after the Polish army crossed north of the Vistula, near Czerwinsk, which is about fifty kilometers northwest of Warsaw. Once united, they drove north, with Marienburg as their objective. Word soon reached Ulrich, though, and he marched east to block the enemy at the ford over the River Drweca at Kauernick. He succeeded in doing this. The combined Polish-Lithuanian host now turned northeast into Prussia to outflank the Order's forces by marching east to Soldau, through Gilgenburg, Grünwald, and then on Marienburg. Ulrich followed his adversaries, crossing the river to intercept the allied army on ground of his own choosing. It was these two marches that resulted in the final arraying of the two armies around the villages of Grünwald and Tannenberg.

THE BATTLE

The Order's forces arrived at Grünwald first on July 14, aligning themselves roughly north and south across the road to Marienburg and anchoring their position on the villages of Tannenberg and Ludwigsdorf, with Grünwald lying roughly behind the center of their line. While the Order's army raced to Grünwald, the allied army, some five miles to the south, stormed the fortress of Gilgenburg on July 13, capturing it and eliminating the threat of its garrison to its rear and its supply lines back to Poland. Ulrich was enraged after hearing of this defeat, and this further motivated him to give battle, especially after hearing of atrocities committed by the Tatars against the townspeople at Gilgenburg. Nonetheless, after he calmed down, he sent orders to Heinrich von Plauen at the fortress of Swiece (Schwetz) to take his 3,000 men to strengthen the garrison at Marienburg. It was a prudent course of action if he were forced back or if he offered a check to the allied army.

As already described, the Order's position was north-south between two villages. A small brook ran in front of the position, and northeast of the position lay a lake. The ground was generally open, with more wooded areas in the south, thus it was nearly ideal for the great cavalry armies of the day. At daybreak on July 15, the Teutonic army deployed and the king of Poland was informed of the event while at prayers. He sent orders for his army to deploy, the Lithuanians to the north and the larger Polish contingents to the south.

Evidently, the design for the battle was by the younger Vytautas, who was a renowned warrior and tactician. The older king remained in the rear, as his survival and escape should things not go well were considered imperative. Both armies consisted mostly of mounted knights and men-at-arms, although the Order's forces were said to include infantry. Ulrich also had some crude field artillery in the form of bombards. The allies numbered approximately 39,000 troops, and those of the Order around 27,000, perhaps less.

The actual battle was dramatically preceded the grand master sending two swords across the field between the armies "for assistance." The king had his emissaries formally reply that his army would do battle "in the name of Christ, before whom all stiff-necked pride must bow . . ." (Turnbull, 2003). The battle opened at about noon with a cavalry charge by the Lithuanians against the Order's forces on the left (north). The Polish charged shortly thereafter. Evidently, Vytautas's goal was simply to "bum rush" his outnumbered enemies. It was during these first charges that Ulrich used his artillery, but all observers agree it had no effect. The pressure on the Teutonic army's south by the Poles was successful, but in the north, the Lithuanian wing was repulsed with heavy losses and fell back. Some German knights pursued, and in so doing, they removed themselves from the key terrain of the battle between the two villages. In those days, if cavalry pursued too far, the horses would be blown and often could not be formed for a second charge if they were too far from the battlefield.

Ulrich now counterattacked the Polish center. During this charge, the main Polish standard disappeared and the Order's forces took heart, believing themselves about to win a divinely aided victory. However, the standard reappeared, as did the regrouped Lithuanian forces to their north. These events represented the turning point of the engagement.

The final phase of the battle involved a desperate counterattack led personally by Ulrich against what he believed was the faltering Polish right. The Poles observed this movement and met it resolutely, while at the same time the Lithuanians attacked the Order's last reserves from the rear. Jagiello then committed his reserves against the Teutonic army's left flank, thus achieving the equivalent of a single envelopment. Ulrich and his remaining knights were surrounded and slaughtered during this phase of the battle.

The final phase involved a pursuit to the Order's camp, which the survivors attempted to defend. Outnumbered, they too were overrun. Both Jagiello and Vytautas were sober men who were known for their abstinence from alcohol, and on their orders, the captured wine stocks of the Order were smashed to prevent their warriors from going on a drunken rampage, which might slow a follow-on pursuit to Marienburg.

The tactical victory was complete in every respect. Ulrich and over 200 of his brother knights were killed, along with 8,000 other troops. Over 600 knights and two allied princes were captured, which would provide a great bounty in ransom for the allied forces. Although the Poles listed their losses as insignificant, they had, in fact, suffered major casualties—over 12,000, including perhaps 4,500 killed. The fact that the defeat had been against another Christian army, despite the Order's propaganda about pagan Tatars and heretic Slavs, meant that few of the other Christian states of Europe felt very alarmed about the Order's defeat. Many agreed with Jagiello that it was divine punishment for the Order's stiff-necked pride, a comeuppance that was long due.

CONCLUSION

Because of the heavy losses, the allied army proceeded slowly north, which may have been a factor that allowed von Plauen, the defender of Marienburg, to ready his garrison for the coming siege. Gunpowder siege weapons were in their infancy, and those with the allied army were ineffectual in creating a breach—modern European siege methods would not come until more than 250 years in the future. After a siege of over 50 days, the Teutonic Prussians began to recover and rumors arrived that new Livonian forces were marshaling to enter the fray. Additionally, the Hungarians were finally stirring, threatening the Poles from the south. All these factors caused the allied army to fall back; Marienburg, its primary goal in the campaign, remained unconquered. Thus, the campaign concluded with less of a victory than the disaster at Grünwald seemed to have won.

As a reward, von Plauen was elected as the new grand master, and that December, the allies signed a new truce. The only significant result was the Order's loss of Samogitia to Poland-Lithuania, as well as a very large indemnity. No other territory of significance changed hands. All of this was confirmed by the Treaty of Thorn in 1411. However, war would continue to plague the region for much of the remainder of the century.

Further Reading

Christiansen, Eric. *The Northern Crusades.* New York: Penguin Books, 1997.

Rogers, Clifford J., ed. *The Oxford Encyclopedia of Medieval Warfare and military Technology,* Volume 2. Oxford: Oxford University Press, 2010.

Turnbull, Stephen. *Tannenberg 1410: Disaster for the Teutonic Knights.* Oxford, UK: Osprey Publishing, 2003.

21. Agincourt

Date: October 25, 1415
Location: Agincourt, France

OPPONENTS

1. England
    Commander: King Henry V
2. France
    Commander: Charles d'Albret, constable of France

BACKGROUND

The Battle of Agincourt occurred during the Hundred Years' War between France and England. In 1413, Henry V, the newly crowned king of England, claimed his hereditary title of king of France. Usually, the English king would renounce this claim, so long as the French abided by the terms of the Treaty of Bretigny, which gave England the rights to Aquitaine and other French holdings. However, Henry wanted to renegotiate the terms and demanded more French lands. Not surprisingly, the French rejected his terms and made a counteroffer, and from there, the negotiations broke down. Henry began assembling his army after the Great Council permitted him to go to war with France in April 1415.

BATTLE OF AGINCOURT (OCTOBER 25, 1415)

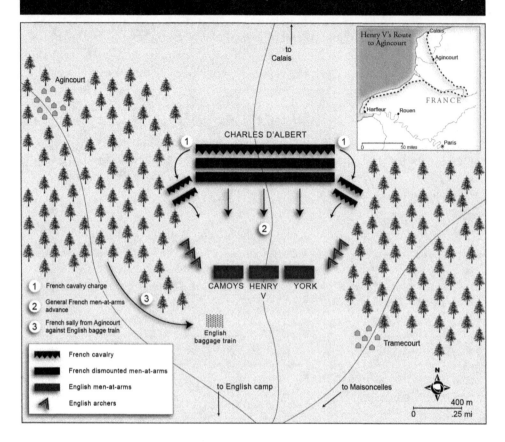

Henry landed in France with an army of about 12,000 in August 1415 and laid siege to the port of Harfleur. After several weeks of hard fighting, the town surrendered on September 22. However, the siege had taken longer than expected, and Henry lost many soldiers to disease. With the campaigning season coming to an end, Henry decided to retire back to England through the English port of Calais. On October 8, the English army headed for Calais; however, as a propaganda tool and to make his presence known to the locals, Henry elected to march his army through Normandy en route to Calais. Henry also hoped his action would provoke the dauphin, heir apparent to the French throne, to battle.

The French army, led by Charles d'Albret, the First Constable of France, moved to block the English army along the Somme River, forcing Henry to look for a ford farther from Calais. Charles kept his distance and shadowed the English army after it crossed the Somme, hoping to gather more nobles to aid him. Meanwhile, the English army was getting weaker as it marched through the French countryside. Henry realized that he would have to fight his way through the French. On October 24, Henry drew his army of 8,000–9,000 soldiers up at one end of a freshly plowed field near the village of Agincourt. Opposing him were roughly 12,000 Frenchmen under the command of Charles.

THE BATTLE

After a night spent in the open, Henry arrayed his force of approximately 1,500 men-at-arms and 7,000 archers in three lines across the 750-yard-wide field. The Duke of York led the first line, Henry the second line or main force in the center, and Lord Camoys commanded the left line. The archers, on the flanks, emplaced sharpened stakes to protect themselves from the French cavalry. The men-at-arms, in chain mail and plate armor, stood in ranks four deep. Satisfied with his deployment, Henry gave his men an inspiring speech to his men, reminding them of the justness of their cause. Then he waited, hoping the French would attack him.

Across the field, 1,000 yields away, Charles deployed his army in three divisions, with his cavalry on the flanks. Believing that victory was all but a foregone conclusion, the French men-at-arms were vying with each other to be in the first division. Charles planned to charge the English archers with his cavalry, followed by a dismounted attack by his men-at-arms to finish off the English. Unfortunately, heavy rains had turned the field into a muddy mess.

For most of the morning, both sides watched each other across the field. The French were not in a hurry to open the battle. With the English cut off from their escape route, time was on the French side. Charles was also awaiting the arrival of 9,000 more reinforcements that were en route. On the English side, Henry understood that time was not on his side. His soldiers were tired and hungry, and the months of campaigning had worn them down. Tactically, Henry knew his best choice was to let the French attack, but as the morning wore on, he also knew he had to do something to provoke the French. He decided to advance and establish his defensive line closer to the French.

Henry's move forced Charles to attack, but Charles hesitated, which gave the English time to reform their lines, including time enough for the archers to emplace their stakes. Once set, Henry's archers launched a volley of arrows at the French. The British arrows were enough provocation for Charles to launch a weak and uncoordinated cavalry charge toward the English longbowmen. The mounted Frenchman found themselves pinned in by the terrain and unable to overrun the archers because if the stakes. The archers now poured more arrows into the French cavalry at point-blank range, forcing the Frenchmen to pull back. Some accounts say the fleeing cavalry trampled the now-advancing men-at-arms, though most accounts agree that the main effect of the French charge and subsequent retreat was to churn up the already muddy field.

Following the failed cavalry charge, Charles sent the first line of French men-at-arms toward the English. As the French soldiers, burdened by their plate armor, struggled through the mud, they were under constant fire from the English archers. Still, they pressed on, and the survivors even pushed the English line back. However, the now-exhausted Frenchmen were set upon by the English archers, armed with mallets, daggers, and hatchets. To further complicate matters, the second French line had joined the attack and was pushing hard up against the struggling first line. The French men-at-arms, crushed from all sides, could not even raise their weapons to fight. Many Frenchmen fell or were knocked down during the difficult hand-to-hand combat and were unable to get up. Some suffocated in their armor, while many more of the helpless knights fell victim to the English archers' daggers.

As the fight wore on, more and more French prisoners were escorted to the rear, where an unfortunate decision by Henry left a stain on his reputation.

At some point during the battle, Henry ordered the slaughter of the French prisoners. The number killed has been estimated as high as several thousand. It is not clear what prompted Henry to make this decision. Some accounts attribute it to an attack by a small French force on the English baggage train. By this telling, Henry, fearing he might be facing an attack from the rear, ordered the killing to eliminate the prisoners as a threat. Other accounts assert that Henry observed the French regrouping and fearing another attack, he again did not want the prisoners to become a threat. Regardless of the reason, the fact remains that Henry ordered the killing of unarmed prisoners.

CONCLUSION

After about three hours, the battle was over. The French withdrew, ceding the field to the English. Henry's campaign in France was over, at least temporarily, and he returned with his army to a hero's welcome in London on November 23. The battle solidified Henry's title at home and added legitimacy to his claim to the French throne, making any future campaigns more palatable to the English parliament.

Counting up the cost of Agincourt is problematic because exact numbers are not available. Estimates for the French run from 1,500 to as many as 11,000 killed, including three dukes, eight counts, a viscount, and an archbishop. For the English, the figures are between 100–1,600, including the Duke of York. Despite the lack of precision in accounting, Agincourt is considered a decisive victory for the English.

Further Reading

Barker, Juliet R. V. *Agincourt: Henry V and the Battle That Made England.* New York: Little Brown, 2006.

Curry, Anne. *Agincourt: A New History.* Stroud, UK: Tempus Publishing Group, 2006.

Keegan, John. *The Face of Battle: A Study of Agincourt, Waterloo, and the Somme.* New York: Penguin Books, 1978.

Reid, Peter. *Medieval Warfare: Triumph and Domination in the Wars of the Middle Ages.* New York: Carroll & Graf Publishers, 2007.

22. Bosworth Field

Date: August 22, 1485
Location: Bosworth Field, central England

OPPONENTS

1. House of York

    Commander: Richard III, king of England

2. House of Lancaster

    Commanders: Henry Tudor and Lord Thomas and Sir William Stanley

BACKGROUND

The Battle of Bosworth Field has come to be regarded as the last act of a conflict known to history as the "War of the Roses." This conflict was a civil war inside England between two great families over succession to the throne. The York family crest included a white rose and the Lancaster crest included a red rose (hence the name of the war). The war began as the result of a combination of the insanity and bad government (while sane) of King Henry VI. Henry VI came from a branch of the royal family that had married members of the family Lancaster, and Henry VI was the most recent Lancastrian king. It was during one of his bouts of insanity that Richard, Duke of York—and heir to the throne should Henry die childless—became the protector of England and ruled.

When Henry regained his sanity, the battle lines were drawn between his supporters and those of Richard. The war began around 1455 and lasted off and on for the next thirty years. It seemed to have come to an end at Tewkesbury in 1471, when Richard's son, now King Edward IV, defeated a last Lancastrian challenge. After that, England remained at peace until Edward's death in 1483 at the relatively young age of forty-one, with both his sons, Edward and Richard, still too young to assume the throne. His younger brother, Richard, Duke of Gloucester, through a very confusing process usurped the throne after becoming Lord Protector, as specified in Edward's will. This caused a number of Yorkists, as well as previous supporters of the Lancastrian branch, to seek out the last Lancastrian heir to the throne, Henry Tudor, who was biding his time in Brittany, perhaps hoping for a chance to retake the throne.

Richard's ruthless actions, especially the disappearance and possible murder of the two young princes in the Tower of London, gave Henry Tudor his chance. At first, Tudor's bid for the throne seemed a long shot, but more and more of the great families either openly or secretly pledged him their support. Henry also had the support of the king of France, who provided the nucleus of an army: approximately 1,600 mercenary troops under French commanders, as well as 500 men-at-arms from various English exiles—slightly more than 2,100 troops in total.

THE PLANS

By the spring of 1485, the French agreed to transport this force with their navy and assume the costs of paying the mercenaries. Henry's plan was to land in Wales, where the Tudors had the base of their support, and then march east, gaining strength and followers as he went. The wild card in all of this was the forces of the powerful Stanley brothers, Lord Thomas Stanley and Sir William Stanley—Henry's stepfather and stepuncle, respectively. Lord Thomas Stanley was married to Henry's mother, through which his claim to the throne came. The Stanleys were notorious for sitting on the fence until it was clear who would win in any particular internecine conflict. Richard knew this, and when Lord Stanley requested permission to depart from the king's entourage to see to his own estates, he took Stanley's son, Lord Strange, as a hostage to guarantee his fidelity.

Richard's base of support came from the north, where he was well liked. His situation was not as dire as later historians (and certainly William Shakespeare) made it seem. He still had a very strong following and was an excellent soldier and leader, having been instrumental in many of his older brother's victories. Not everyone believed that he had murdered his nephews. However, one of the major lords in the north, the Earl of Northumberland, jealous of his popularity, also seemed less than committed to the royal cause.

Once Richard learned of Henry's landing, he gathered his forces at Leicester, including Northumberland's contingent. His plan was to accost Henry's army before it grew any stronger. The two armies came within range of each other on August 21, 1485, near the little village of Bosworth Market. Here, Richard seized the moment and the high ground, putting Henry Tudor at a disadvantage. He also made contact with the Stanleys, who had arrived, but remained unsure as to their loyalties. Henry, on the other hand, was banking on the Stanleys changing sides because his army had not grown to quite the size where he could be confident of victory without their support.

THE BATTLE

Both sides thus entered the battle uncertain about the outcome. King Richard had the advantage on the ground but was unsure of the support of the Stanleys and Northumberland. Meanwhile, Henry knew that he would have to attack and again, could not count on the Stanleys (who promised support but had not joined their forces with him).

Richard's army was parked atop the high ground, Ambion Hill, with a low area at its base. He had approximately 8,000–12,000 troops, if one includes those belonging to Northumberland. His vanguard, under the loyal Duke of Norfolk, reached the top of the hill first and established a defensive line along its crest. Henry's army had been slightly closer to the hill, but his march started late and approached the hill from a direction that did not allow him to get to the crest first. His army consisted of about 5,000–7,000 men-at-arms. As Henry's army filed into position at the base of the hill, Norfolk had an opportunity to attack his flank with archers, but for some reason, he held off—a clear mistake, probably due to a misplaced sense of fair play.

Now the Stanleys arrived on the flanks of both armies, Sir William to the north of the hill and Lord Thomas to the south. Between them, they had around 7,000 men, so whichever side they joined would probably win the battle. However, if they waited to see how the battle went, then Richard, with the better tactical position and superior numbers, would probably win. So the great question in everyone's mind that morning was, "What would the Stanleys do?"

Henry could not afford to either wait or retreat, and after receiving a cryptic reply to a message he sent to Sir William Stanley to join him, he began the battle. The engagement started with both archery and cannon fire. Both sides remained steady through this opening, and then, almost simultaneously, the armies attacked each other, Richard's downhill and Henry's uphill. They met about midway down the slope, and a savage hand-to-hand melee ensued. After an hour of fighting, the Stanleys finally began to move, but here the accounts begin to diverge as to what happened. It was not clear which side the Stanleys were moving to support. What is clear, though, is that Richard himself led a cavalry charge toward the north against Sir William Stanley. He might have been trying to intercept Henry, who was spurring toward his stepuncle to clarify his loyalty, or he might have simply decided that Stanley was clearly a threat and must be dealt with sooner rather than later. Also, Richard may have been going for a knockout blow by killing Henry Tudor while he moved with a relatively small force toward Stanley.

What is not in dispute is that in the melee that followed, Richard was unhorsed and killed. This knocked all of the wind out of the Yorkist sails—there was no longer any reason to fight because now only one legitimate heir to the throne remained on the battlefield. Also, it seems clear that the sizable contingent of Northumberland was not supporting the main battle or making any moves to block either of the Stanleys. The battle thus hinged on the treason—or loyalty—of the Stanleys, and possibly Northumberland.

The battle thus was short, but very bloody, with over 3,000 Yorkists, including the king, dying on the field of battle. The casualties of the Tudor forces were probably less, possibly even half as much. Legend has it that Richard's crown fell from his head and was retrieved by Lord Thomas Stanley and brought to Henry, where he was crowned king of England right there on the battlefield.

CONCLUSION

Bosworth Field was a disaster for the Yorkist cause. It had precious few adherents, and although there were other claimants to the throne, none had nearly as strong a claim as Henry, a direct descendent through his mother, of the Plantagenet line. Henry thus became Henry VII and established the Tudor dynasty. To cement the legitimacy of his claim, Henry married the daughter of Edward IV, Elizabeth of York, the "white princess," thus uniting the two houses. Their son would become Henry VIII.

Bosworth Field, interestingly enough, did not prove to be the final battle of the war. There was still enough jealousy and dissension among the nobles, and enough support for the Yorkist cause in the north, for a serious challenge to be mounted two years later, at the Battle of Stoke (1487), where a pretender was placed at the head of an army in Ireland, which then invaded England. Henry easily disposed of this mostly mercenary force, and the War of the Roses finally ended for good. Henry VII proved one of England's better kings; he left his nation prosperous and at peace when his son, Henry VIII, assumed the throne upon his death in 1509.

Further Reading

Haigh, Philip A. *The Military Campaigns of the Wars of the Roses.* Gloucester, UK: Sutton Publishing, 1995.

Rowse, A. L. *Bosworth Field and the Wars of the Roses.* London: MacMillan, 1966.

PART III

Military Disasters from the Early Modern Period

23. The Conquest of the Aztecs

Date: 1519–1521
Location: Aztec Empire (south-central Mexico)

OPPONENTS

1. Spanish Empire
    Commander: Hernán Cortés
2. Aztec Empire
    Commander: Montezuma II (sometimes spelled Moctezuma)

BACKGROUND

The Aztec Empire was an alliance of three city-states: Tenochtitlan, Texcoco, and Tlacopan. For this reason, it is sometimes referred to as the *Triple Alliance*. Over time, as the alliance expanded throughout central Mexico, the Tenochtitlan dominated it and eventually ruled the empire. In return for their protection, the Aztecs required the conquered cities to pay semiannual tributes and provide soldiers as needed. However, the Aztecs were not the most benevolent of rulers, so they eventually began to alienate most of the cities under their control. When they arrived, the Spaniards would exploit this animosity and turn the peoples of these cities into allies.

The first Spanish expedition to Mexico in 1517 ended in disaster, as the Mayans killed most of the Spaniards. Nevertheless, two Mayan prisoners let their captors know that there was plenty of gold to be found farther inland. The mere hint of the possibility of more gold was enough for the governor of Cuba, Diego Velasquez, to send a second expedition. This time the explorers returned with enough treasure to convince Velasquez to send an even larger expedition under the command of his brother-in-law, Hernán Cortés. At the last moment, Velasquez doubted the loyalty of his brother-in-law and decided to remove him from command. However, Cortés got word of the impending change and on November 18, set sail with his fleet of eleven ships and 600 soldiers and sailors.

THE CONQUEST

Cortes's first encounters with the local inhabitants were friendly, with the natives hoping to appease the Spaniards with gifts and women. In March, Cortés met his first resistance from the Mayans at Centla. After a short battle that was never in doubt due to the Spaniards' superior firepower and discipline defeated the Mayans offered tribute to the victors. Among the offering was a young woman named Malinalli (or Malintzin). In some accounts, she is called La Malinche. Malintzin spoke not only Mayan, but also Nahuatl, the Aztec language. Cortés named her "Marina" and appointed her his interpreter. Marina eventually married Cortés and became known as "Dona Marina."

Next, Cortés sailed farther north, landing near the town of Cempoala and established the settlement of Veracruz. He and his men were warmly welcomed the Totonacs when they marched into Cempoala. After arresting two of Montezuma's tax collectors, Cortés was able to convince the Totonac chief to join him and overthrow the rule of the Aztecs. With his new ally, Cortés prepared to move inland toward the Aztec capital at Tenochtitlan. However, before he could set off, he received word of a pending mutiny among his soldiers because they believed he was overstepping his mandate from Velasquez. Cortés quickly squelched the mutiny by hanging two of the conspirators and scuttling his ships. There would be no turning back.

Montezuma, upon hearing about the approach of Cortés and his men, decided he would negotiate with the Spaniards. Some sources attribute this to his belief that the appearance of the Spaniards fulfilled an ancient prophecy about the return of ancient gods. Other sources suggest that Montezuma's actions were rational, given the little he knew about these strangers. Regardless, Montezuma chose diplomacy, and as a peace gesture, he sent Cortés gold and silver gifts. These gifts, more than likely, only confirmed for Cortés that there were more riches to found in Tenochtitlan.

Moving inland, the Spaniards encountered the Tlaxcalan confederacy. The Tlaxcalans chose to fight the Spaniards. After winning a series of battles in early September 1519, Cortés was able to convince the Tlaxcalans that it would be better for them to ally with him. After decades of fighting the Aztecs, the Tlaxcalans were eager to ally with the Spaniards and help them overthrow the Aztecs. Cortés and his army spent the rest of September in the capital of Tlaxcala, resting and recuperating, before resuming the march to Tenochtitlan.

Along the way, Cortés and his force of 40 Spaniards and 4,000 Tlaxcalans reached the sacred city of Cholula. The Cholulans did not prevent Cortés and his men from entering the city, nor were they welcomed by the locals or greeted by the city leaders. After three days, Cortés received a rumor that the Cholulans planned to kill the Spaniards in their sleep. Cortés confronted the city elders, who did not deny the rumor but admitted that Montezuma had ordered the attack. The Spaniards quickly seized and executed several of these leaders before setting the city on fire. They went on to kill around 3,000 of the inhabitants. Word of the massacre spread quickly and served as a warning to the other Aztec cities. After hearing about the events in Cholula, Montezuma invited Cortés to visit him.

Montezuma led the welcoming committee that greeted Cortés as his men entered the Aztec capital. After a cordial exchange of gifts, he offered the Spaniards a royal palace for their quarters. During their discussions, Cortés offended Montezuma and his followers by suggesting that the Spaniards be allowed to raise a cross and an image of the Virgin Mary the on the main temple pyramid. This offense began to sour relations between Montezuma and Cortés. However, events came to a head with the murder of seven men whom Cortés had left on the coast. Holding Montezuma responsible for this act, he secretly took him hostage but allowed him to act as emperor. Montezuma went along with the charade to prevent further violence.

Meanwhile, Cortés's scouts reported that a large force of Spaniards, under the command of Panfilo de Narvaez, had landed to arrest or kill Cortés for his actions in Mexico. In response, he gathered his most loyal soldiers and headed out to confront Narvaez. In his absence, he left Pedro de Alvardo in charge. A surprise night attack by Cortés quickly defeated Narvaez's force. Left with little choice, Narvaez and his soldiers joined forces with Cortés. Returning to Tenochtitlan, he received reports that Alvarado and his men were under attack by the Aztecs.

After rescuing Alvarado's soldiers, Cortés inquired into the events that led to the Aztecs attacking Alvarado. He learned that Alvarado had provoked the fight by attacking the Aztecs during one of their religious festivals. In his defense, Alvardo told Cortés that he believed the Aztecs were going to attack him, so he struck first. Regardless of the cause, Cortés tried to calm the situation by having Montezuma address his people. Speaking from a balcony, Montezuma was struck and killed by a rock. Cortés realized that the situation was becoming desperate and elected to leave the city. Unfortunately for the Spaniards, Tenochtitlan was built on an island, and the Aztecs had removed all the bridges. Using a rainy night to mask their retreat, the Spaniards tried to leave by crossing a temporary bridge. The Aztecs immediately attacked when they realized the Spaniards were trying to slip away. The orderly retreat turned into a rout, with many of the Spaniards drowning under the weight of their loot. Some sources cite Cortés's losses as more than 800 Spaniards and nearly 1,000 Tlaxcalans. The events of this night so shocked the Spaniards that it became known as *La Noche Triste* ("The Night of Sorrows"). The Spaniards recovered enough to defeat the Aztecs at Otumba to secure their retreat to the safety of Tlaxcala.

Once he was safe, Cortés spent his time planning and preparing to retake the Aztec capital. He sent a messenger to the royal court in Spain to explain his situation and request reinforcements. He also began building small ships called *brigantines,* which he could use on the lake to besiege Tenochtitlan. More important, he gathered more allies, and on December 26, 1520, he led his new army out to reconquer the Aztecs. Unknown, to Cortés, a smallpox outbreak had swept through the Aztecs, reducing their numbers and making his task easier.

In the spring of 1521, Cortés surrounded Tenochtitlan and laid siege to the city. The inhabitants held out for three months, but the lack of food and water began to take its toll. Finally, on August 13, the Spaniards and their allies entered the capital. The invaders found Tenochtitlan in ruins, ransacking and destroying what little remained. The Spaniards eventually captured the last Aztec emperor as he tried to flee in a canoe. With that, the Aztec Empire came to an end.

CONCLUSION

The fall of the Aztec Empire paved the way for Spain to conquer the rest of Mexico. It also became apparent to the local allies of Spain that they had merely

Montezuma II (1466–1520)

At the age of thirty-six, Montezuma II (sometimes referred to as Moctezuma) succeeded his uncle to become the ninth Aztec emperor. Under his reign, the empire fought four more wars to expand its lands, eventually stretching from Mexico to modern-day Honduras and Nicaragua. However, Montezuma was not a particularly benevolent monarch, and his lavish lifestyle irritated his subjects. The tribute he required from neighboring tribes created resentment, and he was forced to put down several rebellions during his rule. The Spaniards would exploit these divisions.

When he first heard of the Spaniards' approach, Montezuma first attempted to buy them off with gold and other lavish gifts. Montezuma's offerings, more than likely, had the opposite effect and only encouraged the Spanish. Nonetheless, Montezuma warmly greeted the Spaniards when he let them enter the city. Initially, relations between the two were amicable until Hernán Cortés took Montezuma hostage. However, Cortés had to leave to secure his position in Veracruz. In his absence, a fight broke out between the two sides. Upon Cortés's return, he urged Montezuma to present himself and calm his people. Unfortunately, many of Montezuma's warriors were no longer willing to listen. Montezuma faced a hail of rocks when he stepped out onto a balcony. One of the rocks hit Montezuma in the head, and he died. During the ensuing turmoil, the Spaniards fled but returned nine months later, bringing an end to the Aztec Empire.

traded one oppressive regime for another. In a matter of years, the Spaniards subjugated all of the Mesoamerican tribes, and the site of the Aztec capital of Tenochtitlan would eventually become Mexico City.

Further Reading

Clendinnen, Inga. *Ambivalent Conquests: Maya and Spaniard in Yucatan, 1517–1570.* New York: Cambridge University Press, 1987.

Hassig, Ross. *Mexico and the Spanish Conquest.* Norman: University of Oklahoma Press, 2006.

Marrin, Albert. *Aztecs and Spaniards: Cortes and the Conquest of Mexico.* New York: Atheneum, 1986.

Thomas, Hugh. *Conquest: Montezuma, Cortes, and the Fall of Old Mexico.* New York: Simon and Schuster, 1993.

24. Lepanto

Date: October 7, 1571
Location: The Gulf of Corinth

OPPONENTS

1. Christians/the Holy League
    Commander: Don Juan of Austria
2. Muslims/Ottoman Turkish Empire
    Commander: Pasha

BACKGROUND

The sixteenth century was marked by constant warfare in the warm waters of the Mediterranean Sea. The Ottoman Empire, the superpower of the Islamic world and ruled by Suleiman the Magnificent (1520–1566), seemed on an inexorable march to control most of the littorals of the Mediterranean. Its maritime opponents were a varied host of Christian states and entities, from the Knights of St. John to the oligarchic republics in Genoa and Venice to the great Catholic empires of Spain and the Holy Roman Empire. The Turks had the great advantage of unity—or at least more unity than their Christian opponents, who time and again could not coordinate or cooperate enough to turn back the great threat from the east.

The voyage to Lepanto for the great Turkish fleet began with Suleiman's conquest and ejection of the Knights of St. John (sometimes called the *Hospitallers*) from their eastern bastion of Rhodes in late 1522 after a lengthy siege. This campaign had been initiated by Suleiman as a means of starting his reign in style, with a great military victory. It also opened the Mediterranean to its west to further conquest by the surging Ottoman superpower. The Knights of St. John were allowed to evacuate, and they took up residence in the fortress on Malta. For the next forty years, the Ottomans extended their influence and power west, by the sea. They subdued the remaining Christian outposts in North Africa (the Maghreb) and raided routinely along the coasts of Spain, France, and Italy—the most famous of these invaders was the red-bearded "king of evil," Hayrettin, and his fearsome Corsairs.

This expansion came to a head at the epic siege of Malta in 1565, where Suleiman's legions at last tasted defeat. Suleiman's army was ruined, and his greatest general, Mustapha Pasha, humiliated. The "king of kings" (as he was known to the Ottomans) marched north the next year into Hungary and besieged a small fortress, but he died, embittered by the failure at Malta.

However, the threat from the sea by the Ottomans had not been eliminated. Suleiman's successor as sultan, Selim II, sought revenge against Cyprus, the last Christian bastion in the eastern Mediterranean, held by the sometimes fickle Venetians. A measure of revenge was obtained with the reduction and capture of Cyprus's major fortresses of Nicosia and Famagusta. Lala Mustapha Pasha (a different Mustapha than the one at Malta) received the Venetians' surrender in August 1571, but then he slaughtered them afterward during the ceremony. Selim now turned his eyes westward once again, for the Christians had finally made common cause in a Holy League to come to the aid of Cyprus and Famagusta, raising an enormous fleet.

This fleet was led by nominally by "Christ's general," the popular and handsome Don Juan of Austria, illegitimate brother of the king of Spain. Also in command were Marcantonio Colonna of Rome, Andrea Dorea of Spain, and Sebastiano Venier of Venice. This coalition of nominal enemies, which included the triumphant remains of the Knights of St. John and various other western Christian states, also counted contingents from frightened Protestant realms newly separated from the Catholic universe. The stage was set for an epic clash of civilizations, this time at sea, not ashore in an island siege.

THE PLANS

Don Garcia of Toledo, the leader of the successful relief expedition to Malta in 1565, advised Don Juan on how to approach the coming challenge. Garcia, and many of Juan's other advisors, had learned from previous naval defeats versus Hayrettin and the Turks in the previous forty years. Garcia advised caution above all. Loss of the Holy League's fleet would be a disaster of the first order. He further advised that if it did come to battle, Juan should organize his fleet into three semi-independent squadrons (roughly Spanish, papal, and Venetian) for better command and control and less confusion. As for when to open fire, his words would have pleased Admiral Horatio Nelson 230 years later: that the Christians should get close enough "to the enemy that their blood spurts over you."

Don Juan absorbed this advice, but based on intelligence that the Turkish fleet was smaller than expected, he convened a council of war at Messina on September 10 and recommended that they attack while the weather was still good. The motion passed, and the fleet proceeded toward Corfu, which was still in Christian hands. If the Turks wanted a fight, they would oblige them.

Don Juan had one tactical surprise up his sleeve. His fleet included six Venetian galleasses, large, virtually round ships with oars used to turn and heavily armed with cannon. His plan was to couple these up during his approach in front of his fleet and use them like fixed batteries to batter and disrupt the enemy fleet. Because of their ability to turn, they could fire almost constantly at whatever came within range of them.

On the Turkish side, they had been using their fleet the entire season in support of land operations in the Balkans in the Adriatic Sea. After raiding Corfu, the overall commander Ali Pasha retired to his base in the Gulf of Corinth at Lepanto. The fleet, though large, had been very active, so it was in poorer material shape than the less used ships of Don Juan's fleet, with fouled bottoms. The crews, especially the galley slaves, were tired from an entire season of active sailing, and the embarked soldiers suffered from extended time at sea on a restricted diet; many had scurvy. Others had deserted to the shore forces at the first opportunity. However, Ali Pasha and his captains believed that the Christian coalition fleet would become a victim of disunity and dissent and disperse before it ever could pose a threat to their larger fleet. He also had incorrect intelligence as to the size of his opponent's fleet, believing it to be 60 ships smaller than it really was. If it came to a fight, he believed that his larger fleet of almost 300 ships, though much used and tired, would prevail. As noted, the Christians too believed the enemy fleet smaller than it actually was. On top of all this, Ali Pasha received stern orders from Selim and his grand vizier to aggressively confront the so-called infidel fleet.

THE ENGAGEMENT

The collision was not long in coming, although in the Christian fleet, tensions boiled over in the days before the battle between the Spanish and the Venetians that almost fractured the fragile unity that the Turks hoped would crumble. Fighting broke out between Venetian sailors and embarked Spanish and Italian troops, and order was restored only with difficulty. However, as the fleet sailed south in its

A contemporary rendering of the Battle of Lepanto (1571). Note the organization of the opposing formations. (Fine Art Images/Heritage Images/Getty Images)

formation of three squadrons, unity was restored when a Cretan frigate arrived with the news of the bloody and criminal martyrdom of the Venetian defenders of Famagusta by the hated common enemy. Although the nominal reason for the creation of the fleet in the first place—the relief of Famagusta—was gone, the Christians pressed on now in grim resolve, animated by a desire for vengeance.

As the Turkish hope faded that the Christians might disperse, they gathered and discussed what to do. Despite the advice of some of his subordinate commanders, Ali Pasha ordered the fleet to confront the Christians, rather than stay put inside the safety of the well-guarded harbor of Lepanto, where it could hold off the Christians easily. He made the famous comment, "If Allah wants it, no harm can come to us" (Crowley, 2008). The scouts for both sides confirmed the other's presence, and as the morning dawned clear and bright on October 7, the Turkish fleet sallied forth with an easterly wind at its back, making the rowing easier.

Don Juan approached from roughly the northwest and Ali Pasha from the southeast. The Christian fleet, as planned, formed a straight line abreast for all three squadrons, with Don Juan in the middle with sixty-two ships, Dorea on his right with fifty-three, and on the left, nearer to the Greek islands and shoreline, the Venetian contingent with fifty-seven ships. Don Juan kept another thirty veteran galleys in reserve just behind his center, under the command of the Spanish admiral Alvaro Bazan. Also behind his main line were his six galleasses in groups of two, being towed up but hidden from the view of Ali Pasha. The Turks approached in their favorite crescent formation, with Ali Pasha in the center, Ali Uluch opposite Dorea, and the Bey of Alexandria opposite the Venetians. The Turks also stationed cavalry ashore to hunt down the Christians should they beach their vessels and the crews attempt to escape. Tactically, the Christians were relying on their heavier firepower at close range, especially by the galleasses, to give them the edge. The Turks were relying on their better maneuverability and ram-and-board tactics, which had served them so well in every previous naval engagement.

As the two fleets approached each other, each side gave public prayers to give a fighting edge to its sailors and soldiers. Don Juan had his galley slaves unshackled and promised them freedom after the battle, while the Turks left theirs shackled and handcuffed to their benches, although Ali Pasha promised the Christian slaves their freedom should he win. The approach occurred almost until noon, and both sides worked mightily to maintain the cohesion of their formations. The lines were spread out opposite each other, over four miles. Then the wind died and then picked up again from the west, regarded by some as a sign of divine favor for the Christian cause. Just before noon, Ali Pasha's lookouts spotted four of the galleasses as they were towed in front of the infidel line, while the two on the far right of the Christian line (Dorea) lagged and had not been spotted yet. The battle opened when Ali Pasha spotted Don Juan's flagship, *Real,* and fired a blank round at it from four miles away. It was answered by a live shot from *Real*—and the greatest sea battle until World War I commenced.

The Turks surged forward in the center, led by Ali Pasha's flagship, *Sultana.* The galleasses here reportedly sank three Turkish galleys with their first volley, and Ali Pasha desperately maneuvered to avoid the lumbering, fire-spitting contraptions. On the Christian line, the order went out to fire at will. The heavier Christian ships had had their rams cut away and replaced with forward-firing heavy cannon and, in accordance with the plan, waited until the last possible moment to fire. Some sources estimate that a third of the Turkish line was obliterated in in this exchange of fire before the two lines even collided. Ali Pasha's apprehension about the galleasses was all too correct.

The Turks, however, were not done. On the left, the lighter Turkish galleys slipped around the Venetian squadron through the shallow water inshore and started to have considerable success. The flagship, commanded now by the second-in-command, Barbarigo, attempted to block the gap, but it was overwhelmed. An arrow killed Barbarigo with a shot through the eye. However, galleys from the reserve and the sheer murderous determination of the Venetians to avenge Famagusta balanced the danger. The Venetians fought the lighter and more nimble Turkish ships to a standstill. Bey Shuluch Mehmet saw his fears realized, as the hard fighting dispirited his already tired men and they began to desert and swim ashore. The Venetians massacred them, pursuing them in longboats and taking no prisoners.

In the center, 150 galleys collided with each other, but the Christians, rowing more easily and slowly, maintained their positions within supporting range of each other, while the Turkish line was ragged and disorganized, both from its exertions and the horrific fire of the galleasses and the opening volley. This battle turned into one gigantic melee, and firepower won out over the tactics that had given the Ottomans victory in a dozen other naval engagements. Confusion reigned, and most eyewitnesses who survived remembered only the deafening noise and chaos as ships crashed into each other and crews boarded and counterboarded each other. Here too, galleys from the reserve helped swing the tide of battle in Don Juan's favor. The battle raged around the two flagships, which engaged in personal combat like two knights at a tournament, but finally both Colonna and Vernier came to Don Juan's aid, and Ali Pasha was killed and beheaded and both his sons captured.

Meanwhile, on the right, Dorea and the Spaniards were outnumbered by Ali Uluch's more numerous and nimble galleys, which attacked in a double line on the seaward side of the battle. The wily Uluch managed to pull Dorea away from the center as he continually tried to outflank Dorea seaward, then as a gap appeared on Dorea's left, Uluch sailed into it and then against the right flank of Don Juan's main body. This maneuver nearly turned the tide of battle, but it was too late. Uluch mauled several Sicilian and Hospitaller ships, but when he saw Don Juan and Dorea closing in on him, he ran to the north with fourteen galleys and escaped. The butchery continued for the remainder of daylight, and the battle was effectively over, the Ottoman fleet dispersed and destroyed, and its commander killed.

CONCLUSION

The slaughter of this one battle, just over four hours in length, would not be equaled until the great land battles of the Somme and Loos in World War I, almost 350 years later. At least 40,000 men died and almost as many were wounded—25,000 were Muslim. Another 12,000 Christian galley slaves were liberated. Over 100 ships on both sides were destroyed, with the Holy League capturing another 137 Muslim ships.

The Ottoman ability to threaten the Christian realms west of Lepanto seriously by sea was effectively neutralized. The threat from the Ottoman world remained dangerous, but it now mostly came on land. Many observers see Malta as the more important battle, but if not for Lepanto, Selim and his admirals may have tried again to capture it.

Further Reading
Crowley, Roger. *Empires of the Sea: The Siege of Malta, the Battle of Lepanto, and the Contest for the Center of the World.* New York: Random House Publishing Group, 2008.

25. The Spanish Armada

Date: July–August 1588
Location: English Channel

OPPONENTS

1. England

   Commanders: Sir Francis Drake, Sir John Hawkins, and Sir Martin Frobisher

2. Spain

   Commander: Alonso Pérez de Guzmán y de Zúñiga-Sotomayor, Duke of Medina Sidonia

BACKGROUND

The source of conflict between Spain and England began when, under orders from Henry VIII, the Church of England broke away from papal authority. Henry's eldest daughter, Mary, succeeded him and married Philip II of Spain. Their marriage quelled the conflict for a time. However, their marriage produced no heirs, and upon Mary's death in 1588, her half-sister Elizabeth acceded to the throne. For a time, Philip accepted the new Protestant monarch, but he never gave up his aspirations of bringing England back to the Catholic fold by placing Elizabeth's cousin, Mary, Queen of Scots, on the throne. Fearing these machinations, and supposing

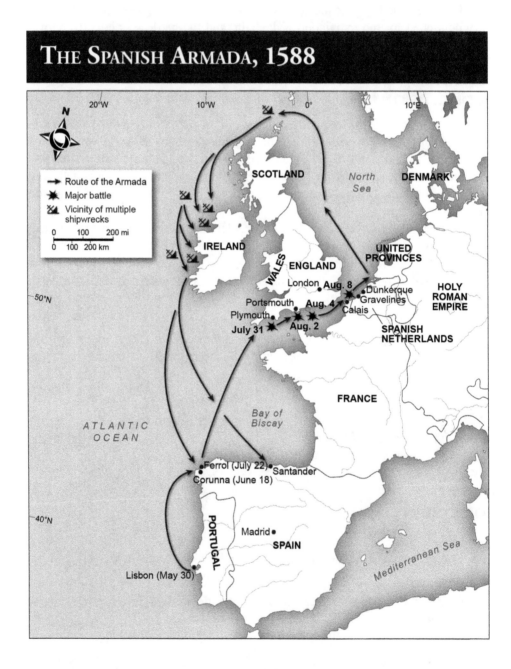

that Philp was behind them, Elizabeth had Mary imprisoned and eventually executed, furthering England and Spain's slide to war.

Two of Elizabeth's actions galled Philip the most. The first was England's open support for the Protestant Dutch rebels in their bid to overthrow Spanish rule in the Netherlands. Elizabeth began providing aid almost as soon as the revolt began in 1568, and eventually she sent soldiers to help the rebels. Second, Elizabeth issued Letters of Marque to several privateers, authorizing them to raid Spanish ships. These English captains gained much fame and notoriety for their exploits in plundering Spanish ships and holdings and became known as Elizabeth's "Sea Dogs." Three of the most famous of these was Sir Francis Drake, Sir John Hawkins, and Sir Martin Frobisher. Each of them would play a vital role in the battle with the Spanish Armada.

By 1586, Philip had enough; he decided to invade England and end Elizabeth's Protestant rule. Pope Sixtus V heartily approved and gave his blessing to this great Catholic undertaking. However, it would take time for Philip to assemble the force necessary for the invasion. It did not help that his preparations were disrupted in April 1587, when Drake raided the port of Cadiz. Drake's raid destroyed nearly thirty ships, as well as the large quantities of supplies that were destroyed or captured by the English. This raid set Philp's planned invasion back by a year. During that year, the original commander, of the operation, the Marquis de Santa Cruz, died, and Philip appointed the Duke of Medina Sidonia to take his place. Sidonia was a good soldier but not a sailor. Nevertheless, Philip waved off Sidonia's objections and pressed on with his plans.

His plan called for the Spanish Armada to sail from Lisbon through the English Channel to link up with the Spanish ground forces, under the command of the Duke of Parma, in the Netherlands. The Armada was then to protect the duke's 30,000 soldiers as they crossed the channel in barges to land near Kent. Still not clear as to how he was to contact Parma, or even the status of Parma's army, Medina Sidonia and his fleet of 130 ships set sail on May 30 for the English Channel. Waiting for them would be nearly 200 English ships. Only 34 of these belonged to the queen's Royal Fleet, but having a new and faster design, they were the best ships in the English fleet. This edge would be critical as the fleets maneuvered against each other during the battle. The rest were of different types, including 12 owned by Drake, Hawkins, and Lord Howard of Effingham, Elizabeth's "Sea Dogs."

THE BATTLE

After a storm-wracked trek that cost his fleet several ships, Medina Sidonia and the Armada passed the Lizard Peninsula in Cornwall on July 19. A series of beacons that had been established along the coast to alert the English fleet of the arrival of the Armada went into effect. Unfortunately, the tide was against the English fleet, as it rode at anchor in Plymouth Harbor and it could not sail. Medina Sidonia was faced with a crucial decision. He could attack the English fleet while it was still in Plymouth Harbor or continue up the English Channel to link up with Parma. Medina Sidonia cautiously chose to follow his orders and bypass the English fleet.

The next day, the English fleet set sail to confront the Spanish. With the Armada upwind, the English used their superior speed and maneuverability to sail around it and gain the "weather gage," meaning they would have the wind in their favor. The next morning, the English were in position and sailed toward the Armada. The Spanish adopted their standard naval formation: a densely packed crescent shape, with the heavier ships on the wings and the smaller ships and transports protected in the middle. Both sides closed and spent the day trading shots, to no effect. The Spanish preferred to get in close, grapple the other ship, and then board it, engaging in a melee between crews. The English, relying on their superior gunnery and guns, refused to get close enough for the Spanish to grapple with them.

On the other hand, because of the longer range, the English guns could not penetrate the Spanish hulls. Neither side lost any ships; however, the Spanish abandoned two ships after they collided with each other in the confusion of the battle. Seizing the opportunity, Drake turned back to plunder the ships. Unfortunately, he was also supposed to guide the English fleet that night as they shadowed the Armada. When Drake doused his signal lanterns, the English fleet became scattered, and it took most of the next day to regroup. Meanwhile, the Armada continued to sail through the English Channel.

Both sides continued their desultory engagements over the next few days, and both sides were running low on ammunition. Medina Sidonia wanted to resupply and find a safe harbor to await word on the status of Parma's force. He chose an area called the Solent, off the Isle of Wight. However, the English pressed on, and Medina Sidonia was forced to weigh anchor and set sail for the next safe port. On July 27, the Armada anchored off Gravelines, between Calais and Dunkirk. That same day, Medina Sidonia received word that Parma's force was only about half the size he expected, but more important, that it would take up to a week to get sufficient barges to transport even this smaller force. Medina Sidonia and his commanders were not comfortable being at anchor for that long, with the English right behind them.

Howard, nominally in command of the English fleet and low on ammunition, was not going to let this opportunity slip by him. He gave orders to convert eight small merchant ships into fire ships, fire being the biggest fear of most seamen during the age of sail. Making these *hellburners,* as they were sometimes called, involved packing the ship with extra gunpowder and other combustibles setting it alight and letting it drift into the enemy fleet. On the night of July 28, the English launched their eight hellburners toward the Spanish ships. Two quick-thinking Spanish captains each grabbed a burning ship and towed it away.

Nonetheless, the sight of the remaining six fiery ships bearing down on them caused a panic among the packed Spanish ships. The majority of the ships cut their anchor lines and made for the open sea. The next morning, the English fleet was in a position to take advantage of the scattered Spanish ships.

Still wary of getting too close to the Spanish ships, the English captains now pressed home their attacks to within 100 yards to penetrate the Spanish hulls. Then they would use their maneuverability to back away and come around again for another broadside. This tactic proved effective, and losses began to mount on the Spanish ships. The battle ground on for eight hours and only came to an end around 4 p.m., when the English ships began running low on ammunition and withdrew.

The Spanish Armada lost five warships, but Medina Sidonia realized that the plan to invade England was in shambles, and he should save the Armada and return to Spain. Facing another crucial decision, he could force his way back through the

English fleet and return by the English Channel, or he could continue through the North Sea going around Scotland and Ireland to return to Spain. He chose the latter. The Spanish Armada reformed and headed north with the English fleet in pursuit. The "Sea Dogs" chased the Spanish as far as Scotland before they had to return to resupply.

Unfortunately, the ordeal was not over for the Spanish sailors. As the ships rounded Scotland and Ireland, unusually strong storms greeted them with westerly winds, forcing many ships aground. Those Spaniards that survived this ordeal then faced further depredations by the local inhabitants. The lucky ones whose ships made it through the storms had to endure starvation and sickness as the Armada limped back to Spain. Between the fighting and the storms, of the 200 ships that set sail in May, only 67 returned to Spain. In contrast, the only English losses were the 8 ships sacrificed as fire ships.

CONCLUSION

On paper, the Spanish Armada should have been the clear winner, but as so often is the case in war, the intangible factors came into play. The weather worked against the Spanish from beginning to end, and then the technical and tactical differences came into play. The English ships were faster and more maneuverable, and this allowed the English to negate Spanish tactics and emphasize their own. Rather than close in and fight on Spanish terms, the English engaged and withdrew, using their superior gunnery to devastate the Spanish ships. However, the most significant outcome was that the defeat of the Spanish Armada marked the beginning of a long slow decline for Spain as a world power, while England's victory over the Spanish marked its first steps onto the world stage and established the nation as a leading naval power.

Further Reading

Hanson, Neil. *The Confident Hope of a Miracle: The True History of the Spanish Armada.* New York: Alfred A. Knopf, 2005.

Mattingly, Garrett. *The Armada.* Boston: Houghton Mifflin, 1958.

Parker, Geoffrey. "Why the Spanish Armada Failed." *History Today*, May 1988, 26–33.

26. Pyongyang

Date: February 8–10, 1593
Location: Pyongyang, in present-day North Korea

OPPONENTS

1. Ming Dynasty Northern Army
   Commander: General Li Rusong
2. Samurai Armies of Japan
   Commanders: So Yoshitosi, Kato Kiyomasa, and Konishi Yukinaga

BACKGROUND

In the spring of 1592, the warlord of all Japan, Hideyoshi Toyotomi, decided to invade Korea as a prelude to a direct attack on the vast Empire of the Ming Chinese. Hideyoshi saw himself as the reincarnation of Genghis Khan, and his confidence in his samurai armies, hardened by over a century of civil war, was unbounded. In the invasion, 150,000 samurai-led troops, well armed with modern firearms, landed at Pusan and captured the city rapidly against the outnumbered and outgunned Korea defenders, who used archery, swords, and spears. By June, the Japanese armies had shattered the Korean army and captured Seoul, causing the Korean king to flee to the north and beg for aid from his powerful Ming protectors in China. The Ming regarded Korea as a tributary kingdom and pledged to defend it.

Meanwhile the Japanese pushed north of the Imjin River and captured Pyongyang. The Ming, alarmed at having the Japanese only 80 miles from their border, put together a force of 3,000 troops to try to recapture Pyongyang quickly, but they fell into a Japanese trap by the samurai generals Kato Kiyomasa and Konishi Yukinaga, who easily defeated them.

However, the Japanese offensive had outrun its supply lines. As the Japanese languished in their garrisons that fall and their fleets suffered at sea from attack by combined Korean-Ming fleets, the Ming conducted intensive preparations to retake Pyongyang. They decided to build up supplies of food, gather and build over 200 cannon, and then wait for the dead of winter to enable them to bring 75,000 men and the cannon on wagons over the frozen ground against the exposed Japanese outpost in northern Korea. The Japanese, on the other hand, had only very light cannon, more like large matchlock arquebuses, to oppose the Ming heavy artillery.

In command of the Ming army was Li Rusong, one of its most celebrated generals. A contemporary account describes him as follows: "Wearing a nine-dragon helmet and pure gold armour adorned with images of the sun and moon . . . of nine-foot stature . . . on his Red Rabbit horse and [holding] a Blue Dragon sword." It was this hero who now advanced swiftly over the frozen landscape on Pyongyang. Li had just put down a mutiny in northern China, and many of his troops were veterans of that campaign. He arrived in early January with sweeping powers and instructions to use everything from diplomacy and peace talks prior to a winter counteroffensive. His army probably numbered no more than 50,000, of which 20,000 were Korean allies. The advance began the day after he arrived (January 11, 1593).

THE PLANS

Li's army was about half cavalry and half infantry, but his ace in the hole were his heavy cannon, which far exceeded in weight and number the light hand cannon that the Japanese used. Often the Japanese used a type of canister shot in these weapons, which made them even more limited in range (although lethal up close). The key advantage was the same one that the Japanese had over the Koreans—weapons range. The Chinese could pound the Japanese from afar with their heavier cannon, should they manage to get them to stand and fight or trap them in a city. Li knew his advantage and boasted, "Japanese weapons have a range of a few hundred paces while my great cannon have a range of five to six *li* [nearly two miles]. How can we not be victorious?" (Swope, 2003). Using diplomacy to lull the Japanese into complacency while moving with his cannon secured to wagons, Li rapidly approached Pyongyang. He attempted to surprise the Japanese further by asking for a meeting with envoys to work out the details of a peace treaty between the Ming and the Japanese. Li's goal was to capture the envoys, and then, while Yukinaga awaited their return with the good news, the Ming army would debouch on Pyongyang and surround it on all sides with around 200 cannon. Ultimately, he wanted to achieve the complete annihilation of the two Japanese "armies" (but really divisions) garrisoning the city. The Japanese plan, once they realized they were under attack, was to rely on the superior skill and discipline of their superb infantry.

THE BATTLE

As it turned out, Li's ambush did not succeed, and the Japanese that escaped sounded the alarm, but he still stole many marches on his foes. His vanguard, under his younger brother Li Rubo, managed to cut Yukinaga and a contingent of troops off from the walled city in their camp on a nearby hill. Yukinaga was rescued, however, by General So Yoshitosi, and he and his remaining troops were brought into the city. Li Rusong arrived the following day and surrounded the city, putting his Korean forces on the eastern side and disguising some of his men as Korean soldiers at the southwest corner. He then launched fire arrows and noxious smoke grenades into the city.

Yukinaga decided to attack the Ming and, if not defeat them, at least take his army away, avoiding being trapped inside the city. At dawn on February 8, his drums sounded a general attack. The fighting lasted almost three days, but in the end, the longer range of Li's cannon, plus much hard fighting against the determined Japanese, decided the issue against the Japanese and their muskets, pikes, and disciplined infantry. The high point of the battle came when Yukinaga decided to break out against the pseudo "Korean" troops at the southwest corner of the city, and when these were revealed as Ming veterans, the Japanese troops lost their composure. Yukinaga was able to retreat via a different route, however, and according to some accounts, this was because Li offered him this choice to prevent further Chinese losses, having already suffered high casualties.

Those Japanese that escaped retreated in relatively good order, administering a sharp rebuff to a pursuing force as they moved south toward Yongson. This very modern battle saw high casualties on all sides, and even the Koreans fought well. Overall, casualties for the Japanese totaled nearly a third of their force, probably around 7,000, with many of those killed. On the Chinese side, the Ming admitted to 795 killed in action, and certainly the Korean numbers were as high or higher.

CONCLUSION

The results of the disaster were far reaching. The Japanese, who until now had maintained an aura of invincibility, at least on land, had been defeated by another land-based force. They would never meet the main Ming armies in a set piece battle again; instead, they resorted to raids, ambushes, or protracted sieges (and often they were the besieged). Their momentum was halted, and some observers compare this reversal of initiative to that which overtook the Japanese navy at the Battle of Midway in 1942. However, they were not utterly defeated, and during his pursuit with about 3,000 cavalry, Li received a sharp check in an ambush about 90 miles north of Seoul, although the Japanese continued their retreat to that place after the engagement. Once in Seoul, they assessed their situation and then continued south after the Chinese and Koreans had destroyed a critical grain storage depot nearby.

This emphasizes the impact of Korean guerilla warfare and Korean naval victories on the fragile Japanese logistics situation. As the Korean king moved back to Pyongyang, and then Seoul, negotiations between the Ming and the Japanese began in earnest. By the spring of 1593, the Chinese had agreed to a truce with the Japanese that left the latter in a small pocket around Pusan. They did this without consulting their Korean allies.

Further Reading

Kuehn, John T. *A Military History of Japan: From the Age of the Samurai to the 21st Century.* Santa Barbara, CA: Praeger, 2014 (see esp. Chapter 5).

Swope, Kenneth. "Turning the Tide: The Strategic and Psychological Significance of the Liberation of Pyongyang in 1593." *War and Society*, 21(2) (October 2003): 1–26.

Turnbull, Stephen. *The Samurai: A Military History.* Trowbridge, UK: Japan Library, 1996.

27. Sekigahara

Date: October 21, 1600
Location: Central Honshu, between Edo and Kyoto

OPPONENTS

1. Tokugawa Eastern Army (Japanese)
     Commander: Tokugawa Ieyasu
2. Mitsunari Western Army (Japanese)
     Commanders: Mitsunari Ishida, Kobayakawa Hideaki, and Konishi Yukinaga

BACKGROUND

After the death of the great warlord Hideyoshi Toyotomi in 1598, the cycle of power struggles resumed, and civil war returned to Japan. Tokugawa Ieyasu, now in his fifties, was one of five regents appointed over Hideyoshi's five-year-old heir, Hideyori—included among these regents were the heads of the powerful Mori and Uesugi clans. Tokugawa had a better claim to the title of shogun than Hideyori. His position was now very strong, with domains stretching from the Tokugawa capital in Edo (Tokyo) through the province of Mikawa to Kyoto, the cultural and spiritual capital of Japan.

Tokugawa had not sent his veteran troops to Korea and now occupied the central position in Japan, much as the shogun Oda Nobunaga had. One of the returning samurai generals from Korea was Ishida Mitsunari, who immediately began to forge a coalition to seize power to protect the rights of the young Hideyori. This caused an open split among the regents in 1600, with many of Hideyoshi's rough-and-tumble generals like Honda Tadakatsu and Kato Kiyomasa supporting Tokugawa. Mitsunari gathered up many of the *daimyo* who had been late to submit to Hideyoshi, including the Mori, Uesugi, and Shimazu. His forces also included a number of veteran Korean War generals such as Konishi Yukinaga, Ukita Hideie, and most important, Kobayakawa Hideaki (who had opposed signing the truce with the Ming dynasty in China in 1593).

Tokugawa established himself in Osaka Castle, gathered intelligence on his enemies, and stockpiled arms, including muskets, cannon, and gunpowder. It became clear that Mistunari's intention was to draw Tokugawa away from Osaka and Kyoto by using the Uesugi from their domains north of Edo to threaten his capital. Tokugawa's intent was to manipulate the coalition against him into a set piece battle because he desired to spare Japan and himself the sort of long and protracted wars of siege and position that might undo the stability that Nobunaga and Hideyoshi had worked so hard to establish. Tokugawa decided to feign a reaction to the threat from the northeast and moved his army east, abandoning Osaka. In a complicated series of maneuvers, Tokugawa used a subordinate's defense of a castle outside Kyoto astride a key line of communication to delay the advance of Mitsunari's army through central Japan upon Tokugawa's supposedly undefended rear. The ploy succeeded, and he pulled Mitsunari into the mountainous area east of Lake Biwa, to which he rapidly countermarched.

THE PLAN

Mitsunari and the western army had decided to conduct a forced night march in horrible weather to intercept the road and attack Tokugawa's rearguard at a crossroads near the little village of Sekigahara, along the Fuji River. Like the Duke of Wellington at Waterloo, Tokugawa had picked the ground for the battle ahead of time. Also like Wellington, he was facing a wet and tired enemy, even though his 74,000 troops were outnumbered by the western army's 80,000 troops. Unlike in the Battle of Waterloo, his position was ideal for both offense and defense. Tokugawa aligned his forces along some foothills astride the road and the river. Mitsunari was trapped; with no nearby forces coming to his relief, he had to fight. According to contemporary accounts, the battlefield was covered in a dense fog on the morning of October 21, 1600. In his final instructions to his generals, the sanguine Tokugawa reportedly told them to either come back with bloody heads or with their own heads detached from their bodies. Another account has his generals telling him this, with Tokugawa grunting his approval.

The wily Tokugawa could well be confident. He had already arranged with the commanding general of Mitsunari's right flank, Koboyakawa Hideaki, to betray the western army. Koboyakawa nursed a grudge from the Korean campaign against Mitsunari.

THE BATTLE

Tokugawa's generals launched a preemptive attack that morning against Mitsunari's soaked minions, first skirmishing, then unleashing a volley of musket fire, and finally charging with pikes into hand-to-hand combat. Parts of the battle became pushing matches between sword and pike-wielding infantry. Mitsunari used a fire to signal Kobayakawa to attack, as well as the Shimazu division, which was in reserve. Tokugawa decided to push Kobayakawa off the fence so he had his musketeers fire some shots at the enemy's right flank, where that general was stationed. This action spurred Kobayakawa to turn and roll up the flank of his nominal ally. As disaster engulfed the western army and Mitsunari, Yoshihiro realized his peril, and his men cut their way through the Tokugawa forces and retreated to Kyushu. There they found the ruthless samurai general Kiyomasa ravaging their domains and those of Konishi Yukinaga. Konishi and Mitsunari were both captured after the battle and put to death—Konishi, in obedience to his Christian faith, refused to commit suicide when offered the option.

Mitsunari's decision to put men of doubtful loyalty in the key positions on his flank and in reserve probably did the most to contribute to the disaster. Nonetheless, Tokugawa had more forces in reserve marching to the battle, and it is unlikely his army would have been rolled up in the manner of Mitsunari's had the treachery not occurred. Instead, everything went nearly according to plan, and his instincts proved correct about trying for a decision in a provoked battle.

The overall casualties estimated for the battle vary and are uncertain, but it seems clear that Tokugawa's losses were minimal, while those of the western army, apart from the defections, numbered in the thousands. Many of the cutting wounds at the battle can be attributed to the pikes rather than the swords. Of the missile weapons, most of the casualties came from gunfire, although 20 percent also came from bows. Due to their lack of mobility (especially on a muddy field like Sekigahara), cannon did not play a significant role in this battle, although they would in Tokugawa's final battles, 14 years later.

CONCLUSION

Sekigahara did not end the fighting, but it did lead the emperor to appoint Tokugawa Ieyasu as *seii taishogun* (shogun) in 1603 because the Tokugawa family could trace its lineage back to the Minamoto. With that, the third (and last) *Bakufu* (military government) was established in Edo. Tokugawa continued policies initiated by his predecessors that froze the social order, disarmed the farmers, and limited both the samurai and the *daimyo*. Hideyoshi's heir, Hideyori, continued to be the rallying point for rebellions against Tokugawa. By 1614, Hideyori was a young man, and he gathered around himself many of the disenfranchised and dissatisfied warriors who were alienated by the shogun's ruthless policies of

The Shogunate

The origins of the institution of the shogunate can be found very early in Japanese military history. The idea of a military man assigned for special missions was firmly established by the time earliest chronicles of Japan were written on ancient scrolls. By 797 CE, with the elevation of the warrior Tamuramaro as "The Great General Who Quells the Barbarians [seii tai-shogun]," one sees the first of the type of shogun that we often think of in Japanese military history. However, the post was only temporary, not the permanent position it later became. The first permanent shogun was established by Yoritomo of the Minamoto clan during a series of civil wars known as the Genpei Wars (1180–1185). Yoritomo established the first warrior-based dictatorship at Kamakura on the Kanto Plain (today the Greater Tokyo area). It was also nicknamed after a general's tent in the field—Bakufu.

The establishment of the Kamakura Bakufu (also known as the shogunate) changed the political dynamic in Japan for the next 600 years, becoming the paradigm to which the nation's new ruling class, the samurai, always returned. Even after the fall of the Kamakura Shogunate, it too was replaced by the Muromachi Bakufu, located nearer Japan's cultural center in Kyoto. Finally, after an almost 150-year civil war following the collapse of the Muromachi Shogunate, Japan's final shogunate was established by the cunning politician-warlord Tokugawa Ieyasu, which lasted nearly 250 years until the arrival of the Americans in Tokyo Bay in the 1850s.

disarmament. Tokugawa had allowed Hideyori and his family to continue living in Osaka, and it became a haven for disaffected samurai and ronin who threatened the Tokugawa peace. Finally, in an epic siege in 1615 at Osaka, Tokugawa established his complete domination over his remaining enemies and annihilated them, posting the heads of the defeated ronin and samurai rebel warriors along the road from Osaka to Fushimi.

Further Reading

Friday, Karl, ed. *Japan Emerging.* Boulder, CO: Westview, 2012.

Sadler, A. I. *The Maker of Modern Japan: The Life of Shogun Tokugawa Ieyasu.* 5th ed. Rutland, VT: Charles E. Tuttle, 1982.

Turnbull, Stephen. *The Samurai: A Military History.* Trowbridge, UK: Japan Library, 1996.

28. The Sack of Magdeburg

Date: May 17–21, 1631
Location: Northern Germany

OPPONENTS

1. Protestant Germans
    Commander: Dietrich von Falkenberg
2. Catholic League and Imperialists
    Commander: Johann Tserclaes, Count of Tilly

BACKGROUND

The sack of Magdeburg in 1631, one of the most notorious events of the Thirty Years' War, stemmed from a variety of causes. Ostensibly, the first had to do with the arrival of Gustavus Adolphus, the king of Sweden, to champion the Protestant cause against the Holy Roman Emperor, who had issued the Edict of Restitution (1629), aimed at restoration of Catholic control in Protestant parts of Germany. With Sweden's entry into the war, bankrolled by Catholic France, the situation for the imperial armies, surviving on the land in Germany, became critical.

Another cause came from the animosity between the two principal generals fighting nominally on the behalf of Emperor Ferdinand III of Austria—the Count of Tilly, commander of the Catholic League army; and Count Albrecht von Wallenstein, commander of what was in effect a private army of mercenaries. Tilly was nominally Wallenstein's superior. However, Wallenstein's ambitions caused him to feel jealous of Tilly. Circumstances found him reduced to de facto control of Tilly's army, and he undermined its logistical situation by failing to pay or feed it. By the time Tilly resumed his command, his army had become a famished mob. Meanwhile, Tilley's subordinate, General Gottfried Heinrich Graf von Pappenheim, a dashing cavalry commander, besieged the city of Magdeburg, which was allied with the Protestants.

The defense of Magdeburg had been placed in the hands of Dietrich von Falkenberg, a Hessian general. Falkenberg found the citizens of Magdeburg unwilling to support his garrison, and some of his men mutinied, causing Falkenberg further difficulties. Tilly's hungry mercenaries turned south to join von Pappenheim in reducing Magdeburg. Gustavus's plan to try to pull the Imperialists away by attacking the city of Frankfort-on-the-Oder in the east failed. By May 1631, the leading citizens of Magdeburg had had enough of the siege and demanded that Falkenberg surrender. The king of Sweden's army lay about 150 miles from Magdeburg, and he exhorted its defenders to await his relief. However, the two neutral electors of Saxony and Brandenburg, through whose territory he must pass and whom he wanted as allies, now refused him passage at the key moment. Gustavus frightened the elector of Brandenburg, Georg Wilhelm, by seizing the fortress of Spandau to secure his cooperation.

THE ASSAULT AND SACK

While Gustavus was doing this, events at Magdeburg came to a head. The rumor that the Swedish army was closer than it actually was, and marching hard to Magdeburg's aid, infused the Imperialists with desperate resolve. Beginning on May 17, it assaulted the city. The assault lasted for two days and was bloodily repulsed. Fearing the worst, however, the burghers of Magdeburg begged Falkenberg to surrender. The Hessian general refused. While Tilly vacillated under the weight of his belief that the king of Sweden was approaching, Pappenheim took matters into his own hands and resumed the assault on May 20, leading the troops personally in the storm. He attacked at two points and caught the defenders unprepared. His courage and that of his desperate soldiers were rewarded when Magdeburg fell.

But the disaster was only just unfolding. Falkenberg was killed, and the bloody-minded Imperialist troops lost their discipline and went on a drunken, murderous rampage. Pappenheim was forced to personally protect the wounded administrator of the city from his own troops, while Tilly tried to rally and bring the men under control. He personally rescued an infant from the dying arms of its (probably raped) mother and was seen thereafter despondently cradling the baby as he made his rounds. Tilly managed to save about 600 women and children in the old Gothic cathedral and defend it from his rampaging men. However, by this time, the city had caught fire in many different places.

Now Pappenheim and Tilly tried to organize their drunken men into fire brigades, if for no other reason than to save their inebriated comrades trapped in various quarters of the city by the fire. For over a day, the city burned, and by May 21, it lay a smoking, blackened ruin—with the Gothic cathedral and its terrified inhabitants as one of the few buildings still standing. Both civilians and many of their drunken tormentors perished. It took 14 days for wagons to empty the city of all its corpses; Tilly had them thrown into the river to prevent disease. Even after that, his troops returned to search for more booty or alcohol, and they found enough in the cellars for many of them to remain drunk for two more days. Tilly retreated with his wounded and disorganized army, sure that Magdeburg could no longer feed his army, or any other for that matter.

AFTERMATH

It is estimated that over 20,000 of Magdeburg's 30,000 presiege inhabitants perished, in addition to the thousands of soldiers on both sides killed in the various assaults or the fire. Those left behind were mostly women, who were kidnapped by Tilly's soldiers and removed from the city for their amusement. Soon after, it was rumored that before he died, Falkenberg had ordered the city burned, much as Moscow would be 200 years later by the Russians, but no proof could ever be found in the charred remains of the grand old city on the Elbe.

However, the extent of the disaster resonated as the "Rape of Magdeburg"; it became a Protestant rallying cry and the news spread through Europe, almost as quickly as the flames had through the city. Before long, the king of Sweden saw thousands of willing recruits joining his army to fight the "legions from hell" that had so pitilessly destroyed a Protestant city. Politically, the catastrophe finally forced the electors of Saxony and Brandenburg to make common cause with Gustavus Adolphus, the Dutch estates also agreed to finance the Swedes. All these actions led to the so-called Swedish phase of the Thirty Years' War, as Swedish arms threatened the very existence of the Hapsburg monarchy itself.

Further Reading
Wedgewood, C. V. *The Thirty Years War.* New York: Doubleday, 1938.
Wilson, Peter. *The Thirty Years War: Europe's Tragedy.* Cambridge, MA: Belknap Press, 2007.

29. Breitenfeld

Date: September 17, 1631
Location: Breitenfeld, northwest of Leipzig, Germany

OPPONENTS

1. Sweden
    Commander: King Gustavus Adolphus
2. Catholic League
    Commander: Johann Tserclaes, Count of Tilly

BACKGROUND

The Battle of Breitenfeld was a major Protestant victory during the Thirty Years' War. This war began as a religious conflict between Catholics and Protestants within the Holy Roman Empire, but over time, it grew into a war over hegemony in Europe. In fact, by the time of Breitenfeld, the Protestant king Gustavus Adolphus was receiving substantial financial support for Catholic France.

The Thirty Years' War began in 1618 following the election of Ferdinand II as Holy Roman Emperor. Ferdinand created fear and anger among Protestants when he attempted to force Roman Catholicism on the people. The first act of the war was the defenestration of two Catholic regents by Protestant representatives, an event that became known as the Second Defenestration of Prague. The warring factions became known as the Protestant Union and the Catholic League. For the next twelve years, there were widespread revolts, and battles with atrocities committed by both sides were commonplace. In 1630, King Gustavus Adolphus of Sweden decided to come to the aid of the German Lutherans to check the expansion of the Hapsburgs and to gain a foothold on the continent.

After entering the continent of Europe in Pomerania, Gustavus fought a few successful skirmishes but was not having much luck gathering allies among the Protestant princes. But his luck changed when a Catholic League force under the Count of Tilly sacked Magdeburg in May 1631. Imperial troops killed over 20,000 of the 25,000 inhabitants as they rampaged through the town. Word of the horrors inflicted upon the residents spread through the Protestant countryside. While some blamed Gustavus for not lifting the siege of Magdeburg, others began to join with Gustavus. John George I provided Gustavus with 16,000 soldiers from the electorate of Saxony. Buoyed by his new reinforcements, a confident Gustavus marched his 42,000-man force south to seek out Tilly. At the same time, Tilly turned north with a force of around 35,000 to check the now-growing Swedish threat. The two sides met on September 17 on a plain near the village of Breitenfeld, about five miles northwest of Leipzig.

THE PLAN

Tilly and Gustavus faced each other across a plain about a mile apart. Both commanders arrayed their forces in the typical fashion for the day, with infantry in the middle, cavalry on the flanks, and artillery in the front. However, the details of their respective force structures would help decide the day. Tilly's infantry still fought in large pike squares, referred to as *Spanish tercios,* with musketeers placed on the corners. The Imperial cavalry, armed with pistols, fired them into the massed infantry before retreating to reload and repeat the process, in a tactic called the *caracole.* Tilly's artillery was heavier and less mobile than that of his Swedish opponents.

Gustavus had instituted changes in the Swedish army based on observing the Dutch army's reforms. Rather than fighting in tightly packed squares, he thinned the ranks, increased the number of muskets, and organized them into brigades that covered a broader front, were more flexible, and could reorient faster than the Imperial *tercios.* His cavalry had given up the pistol and returned to sabers; they relied on the shock effect of the mounted charge to rout the infantry. Gustavus would also surprise Tilly's cavalry by placing musketeers among the Swedish cavalry. His artillery was equipped with smaller-caliber guns, which not only made them more mobile but also increased their rate of fire.

Perhaps the most significant innovations he brought to the Swedish army were in the area of recruitment and training. Most of Gustavus's army was made up of Swedes because he believed that his people would be more loyal and steadfast in combat. The remainder of his army was composed of Scots and Germans. However, it was his emphasis on training that made his army so effective. Gustavus had full confidence in his army, but he was less confident about his Saxon ally. The Saxon army of John George I was a quickly gathered band of conscripts and militia and did not meet the high standard of training of Gustavus's main force. He placed the Saxons on his left flank, where one of his trusted subordinates, Gustav Horn, could keep an eye on them.

THE BATTLE

Around noon, the battle opened with a two-hour artillery duel. The Swedes got the better of this opening exchange because they could maintain a higher rate of fire. Watching the action from the Imperial left flank, Gottfried Heinrich Graf von Pappenheim, the commander of the Black Cuirassiers, decided that he could wait no longer and charged the Swedish right flank. Pappenheim's 7,000 horsemen were bearing down on the Swedes when they halted short of the enemy line to execute the *caracole.* As they began to fire into the Swedish lines, Pappenheim's cavalry received a nasty surprise. The Swedish musketeers positioned among the cavalry opened fire on the Imperial riders. A counatercharge by the Swedish cavalry drove off Pappenheim's cavalry. However, a determined Pappenheim attacked six more times, with the same result, before he finally withdrew from the battlefield.

Tilly did not authorize Pappenheim's attack, but he decided to support him, so he sent his right-flank cavalry to attack the Saxons on Gustavus's left flank. The Imperial charge chased the Saxon cavalry away, followed soon after by the Saxon infantry. Tilly now saw an opportunity to attack Gustavus's left flank and roll up the Swedes from east to west, so he ordered his infantry *tercios* into the gap left by the Saxons.

It was at this point that Gustavus's training regimen paid off. Horn, watching the Saxons flee the battlefield and observing the movement of Tilly's infantry, knew what he had to do. As the Imperial *tercios* lumbered forward, Horn took the initiative to reposition his more flexible Swedish brigades to refuse the left flank. His troops now faced the approaching enemy head on. The massed Imperial squares moved like an inexorable force; however, as they closed in on the Swedes, much like the Imperial cavalry, they would receive a terrible shock. Rather than firing individually, the Swedish musketeers fired in mass volleys. The Imperial infantry had never faced anything like this, but they pressed on nevertheless. They were held at bay by the Swedish pikemen as the musketeers reloaded before receiving another salvo from the Swedish musketeers. All the while, the regimental guns were adding to the carnage wreaked upon the Imperial infantry. At this moment, Gustavus noticed that Tilly's line begin to waver and decided to counterattack.

Gustavus led his cavalry on a charge toward the middle of the Imperial line. The Swedish cavalry seized Tilly's cannon and turned them on the Imperial right flank. Caught in the crossfire from Horn's cannon and the recently captured guns, Tilly's men began to break and flee the battlefield, with the Swedish cavalry in pursuit. Roughly 7,600 soldiers of the Catholic League were left dead on the battlefield, and another 3,000 were taken prisoner. The Swedish casualties came to around 2,000; however, Gustavus had won the first significant victory by the Protestants over the Catholics during the Thirty Years' War.

CONCLUSION

Gustavus's overwhelming victory crippled the Catholic League until it could rebuild its army. More important, for the Protestant cause, more German princes began allying with Gustavus. The fighting in northern Germany would continue

Johann Tserclaes, Count of Tilly (1559–1632)

Johann Tserclaes was born into a devoutly Catholic family in Walloon Brabant, Spanish Netherlands, which is now Belgium. Following his Jesuit education, Tserclaes, the Count of Tilly, joined the Spanish army at the age of fifteen. He saw action during the Eighty Years' War and fought as a mercenary in the army of the Holy Roman Empire against the Turks, rising to the rank of field marshal. When the Thirty Years' War broke out in 1610, Tilly was selected to command the Catholic League. Despite many successful campaigns during the war, he is best known for two events: the Sack of Magdeburg and the Battle of Breitenfeld. After a two-month siege, Tilly's men entered Magdeburg and went on an uncontrolled rampage, killing 20,000 of the 25,000 inhabitants before order was restored.

In 1630, the king of Sweden, Gustavus Adolphus, landed in Europe to gain a foothold in the Baltic and assist the Protestant cause. Though Tilly did not rate the Swedes as much of a threat, he could not ignore them. Both sides met at the Battle of Breitenfeld on September 17, 1631. At Breitenfeld, new Swedish tactics bested the Catholic League veterans, forcing Tilly and his army to flee the battlefield. Tilly next faced the Swedes as they tried to cross into Bavaria near Rain am Lech. During the battle, he was struck by a cannonball and died fifteen days later of tetanus on April 30, 1632. Tilly is buried in Altötting, Germany.

for another four years, culminating with the Peace of Prague. However, the terms of this treaty did not appease France, who still feared a resurgence of Hapsburg influence in Europe, so the Thirty Years' War entered the French Intervention phase.

In the history of warfare, the Swedish victory at Breitenfeld was significant because it ushered in a new era. After Breitenfeld, all armies would drop the old style of warfare, with massed pike formations, and adopt the Swedish innovations. Gustavus's form of combined-arms warfare continued to evolve until another dynamic leader, Napoleon Bonaparte, would introduce a new paradigm to the evolution of warfare.

Further Reading

Parker, Geoffrey. *The Thirty Years War.* New York: Taylor and Francis, 1997.

Stephenson, Donald S. "Breitenfeld: A Battle Piece." Fort Leavenworth, KS: US Army Command and General Staff College, July 2000.

Wedgewood, C. V. *The Thirty Years War.* New York: Doubleday, 1938.

Wilson, Peter H. *The Thirty Years War: Europe's Tragedy.* Cambridge, MA: Belknap Press of Harvard University, 2009.

30. Nördlingen

Date: September 5–6, 1634
Location: Bavaria, Germany

OPPONENTS

1. Imperial Forces

    Commanders: Ferdinand, Cardinal Infant of Spain, and Archduke Ferdinand, king of Hungary (Austria)

2. Swedes and Protestant Allies

    Commanders: Bernhard of Saxe Weimar and Marshal Gustavus Horn (Sweden)

BACKGROUND

The Battle of Nördlingen was a result of the overextension of the Swedish-German Protestant alliance along the Danube after the death of the Swedish king Gustavus Adolphus in late 1632, during the Protestant victory outside Lützen in central Germany. The defeated general in that battle, Count Albrecht von Wallenstein, also died, murdered by his men when he attempted to switch sides and take his army to the Protestants in February 1634. The armies supporting both sides now came under the command of various leaders.

On the Protestant side, the German allies of the Swedes were led by the ambitious Bernhard of Saxe Weimar, and the main Swedish contingent fell into the capable hands of Marshal Gustavus Horn. The extreme threat posed by these forces caused Emperor Ferdinand II to bring the excellent Spanish infantry into the fight under the Cardinal Infant of Spain (also named Ferdinand). These forces arrived from Italy in 1633 and were used to secure the upper Rhine as a means to perhaps unite the Spanish and German forces in the next year. However, Saxe Weimar swept down the Danube and captured Regensburg in November 1633, which had been the proximate cause of Wallenstein's attempted defection and then murder.

On the Imperialist side, what remained of the mercenary army of Wallenstein was placed into the hands of the emperor's son, the young Archduke Ferdinand of Austria, king of Hungary. Because of the close friendship of the two Catholic prince-cousins, the unity of the Catholic forces would never be greater, at least on the field. Conversely, on the Protestant side, disunity would be the order of the day, despite the fearsome military reputations of both Saxe-Weimar and Horn. Additionally, the French, always very involved in the politics of Germany, attempted to curry influence with the Protestant princes in opposing Hapsburg power via the machinations of the brilliant prime minister of France's King Louis XIII, Cardinal Richelieu. However, because of Swedish military power and French reluctance to commit military forces to a direct fight with the Imperialists, French activities were limited to continued financial support and diplomatic maneuvering. French meddling ironically created even more disunity on the Protestant side that it was nominally supporting. Nördlingen would change all of these relationships and dynamics.

The campaign in 1634 hinged on the recapture of the key Imperial city of Regensburg on the Danube. This outcome in turn depended on the unification of the armies led by the Cardinal Infant of Spain and the king of Hungary—the two Ferdinands.

THE PLANS

The plans for the campaign of 1634 highlight how unity of effort occasionally trumps leadership. The Catholic plan was to have the king of Hungary recapture Regensburg and then unite with the Spanish army and jointly defeat whatever force the Protestants sent against them. For Saxe-Weimar and Horn, the goal was obvious—to interpose their united armies between the two Catholic forces and defeat each one. There was a wrinkle in this overall plan—at the same time, their Saxon allies invaded Bohemia to threaten Prague. Horn and Saxe-Weimar decided that if they marched to assist the Saxons, the Imperial army would be drawn away from Regensburg and a subsequent union with the Spanish. They united and then defeated a secondary force of Bavarians and Imperialists at Landshut and marched north. However, Ferdinand adhered obstinately to the plan and recaptured Regensburg in their absence.

The operation against Prague was abandoned, and they rushed back to try to do battle with Ferdinand at Regensburg. He managed to slip away from their pursuit and marched to Nördlingen in western Bavaria, not far from Ulm. Ferdinand halted here because the Swedes held the town with a strong garrison and he did not want to leave this threat to his flank untended. He besieged the place. The Protestants—who outnumbered Ferdinand only by 3,000 or 4,000 troops—might yet have attacked him, but they had mere days to do so, and their troops, who had been marching and countermarching all summer, were exhausted. On September 2, the Cardinal Infant and his Spanish army arrived in Donauworth, which his cousin had secured, and a union of the two armies was affected in the presence of the combined Protestant armies. The Catholics now outnumbered the Protestants almost two-to-one.

The Catholic armies took up a strong position anchored on hills south of Nördlingen, covering any approaches that the Swedes and their allies might take to relieve the town. The country was broken and wooded, although an area of open country lay just southeast of the town. The far left flank of their position was in the air (that is, not secure). The two cousins intended to defend this line; there was no need for them to attack because time was on their side—the garrison was starving and near surrender. Horn decided to attack the insecure flank with a night march and then a sudden rush with his Swedish component of the combined army. Saxe-Weimar would fix the Spanish infantry on the plain to ensure that they could not come to the aid of the Imperialists. Once on the high ground and in contact with the beleaguered garrison, the Protestants hoped to defend their position from Catholic attacks and cause the enemy to give up the siege and withdraw. This plan took advantage of the moral superiority that the Swedes had maintained in battle over the Imperialists since arriving in Germany four years before. It was the Protestants' best hope for success.

THE BATTLE

The actual battle was a two-day affair; it started on September 5 with a Protestant success, when Saxe-Weimar, who arrived first, drove off musketeers guarding the road access to the Catholics' exposed left flank. However this skirmish decided little—only that the larger battle would occur the following day with the Swedes a little closer than they might have been before. When informed by a captured officer that the Spanish had brought almost 20,000 troops to reinforce the Imperialists, Saxe-Weimar refused to believe it. Had he realized the man was correct, he might have tried to get Horn to agree to a withdrawal.

That night, Horn got his columns moving. Everything then began to go wrong for the Protestants. Instead of bringing lighter cannon with the infantry in the advance guard for a quick coup de main to seize the hill, heavy cannon were moved up instead and became bogged down. The noise as the Swedes tried to dislodge these guns, mired in the difficult terrain at night, gave away the surprise that Horn was supposed to achieve at daylight, alerting the Imperialists of his presence and causing them to entrench. Nonetheless, when the sun came up, Horn attacked. His tactical plan was to overawe the Imperialist defenders with his superb infantry and then use his cavalry to either finish them off or as a reserve to defend against the Spanish component of the army down on the plain. Instead, the cavalry attacked first due to a mistake by one of Horn's subordinates. They hit a lightly defended portion of the line and caused the defenders to flee, but then they took themselves out of the battle in pursuit of an unimportant component of the enemy army.

It was now the infantry's turn, and despite all the missteps, they advanced up the hill and put the Imperial infantry to flight. However, a wagonload of gunpowder exploded in the midst of their victorious infantry, and another two brigades mistook each other for the enemy and became disorganized and intermixed as a result. The Swedes had taken the hill but were too tired, confused, and stunned by the sudden explosion to establish a secure defense.

The explosion alerted the two Hapsburg cousins, positioned on a small hill behind the Spanish army near its hinge with the Imperialists, to the danger on their left. The Cardinal Infant dispatched a mixed force of Spanish infantry and cavalry to retake the hill, which they promptly did. The battle then became an effort by the Protestants to do what they had initially wanted the Catholics to do: attack and take the key ground from a determined defense. Saxe-Weimar opened fire in the valley with his artillery to keep the Spanish busy, and the rest of the battle became a grueling, close-range firefight, especially at the hill. In the meantime, the Imperial infantry was rallied and reinforced the lines. However, the superiority and discipline of the Spanish infantry proved the decisive factors.

The Swedes exhausted themselves trying to retake the hill. At midday, Horn decided that he had had enough and advised Bernhard of Saxe Weimar to cover him as he retired. As the beaten Swedes began to retire, the two cousins chose that moment to attack Bernhard's outnumbered and wavering troops, with their relatively fresh men, and rallied the Imperialists, especially their cavalry. The Protestant army disintegrated. Saxe-Weimar tried to rally his men but eventually fled the field of battle. Horn was not so lucky and was captured.

The mythical invincibility of the Swedes was shattered. Casualties on the Protestant side were catastrophic—nearly 16,000 killed or wounded and 4,000 prisoners, most of whom went into the Imperial service, as was the custom of the time. The Catholic forces suffered about 3,500 casualties, most of them to the Imperial army. However, because of the addition of the mercenaries from their beaten foes, their army was actually stronger after the battle than before it.

CONCLUSION

The Battle of Nördlingen was a disaster for the Protestant cause, but it did not end the war. Although Sweden was effectively knocked out of the ranks of the major belligerents, it was now replaced by France, who had subsidized the Swedes to begin with. French armies now entered the lists and the war became a more direct contest between the French Bourbons and the Spanish and Austrian Hapsburgs, with Germany, the Low Countries, and northern Italy the main theaters of the conflict. Germany would have to wait another fourteen years before the ruinous war ended.

Further Reading
Wedgewood, C. V. *The Thirty Years War.* New York: Doubleday, 1938.

Wilson, Peter. *The Thirty Years War: Europe's Tragedy.* Cambridge, MA: Harvard University Press, 2009.

31. Naseby

Date: June 14, 1645
Location: Northamptonshire, Great Britain

OPPONENTS

1. Royalists
   Commanders: Charles I and Rupert, Prince Palatine
2. Parliamentarians
   Commanders: Sir Thomas Fairfax and Oliver Cromwell

BACKGROUND

The Battle of Naseby occurred during the English Civil War (1642–1649). The occasion of this conflict was the incompetent rule of King Charles I and fears by Puritan groups and others of his reintroduction of Catholicism as the state religion of England. The proximate cause consisted of a conflict between the authority of the king and that of Parliament, especially as it concerned the king's often arrogant behavior and profligate spending and debt. The king had attempted to force ecclesiastical mandates on the Scottish Presbyterians and they resisted them. The king then called Parliament for the first time in eleven years to ask for money to discipline the Scots with military force. Parliament instead presented its demands for reform. After Parliamentarian leaders refused to disband when ordered by the king (who had earlier arrested certain of their members), the king fled London and raised his standard at Nottingham on August 22, 1642, to forcibly disband Parliament and quell the "rebellion." The king's forces became known as the Cavaliers, and those of Parliament, derogatorily, as Roundheads. The war occurred against the backdrop of the disastrous Thirty Years' War in Europe, and its generals and leaders copied many of the same tactics used by the Protestant and Catholic armies battling in Germany.

The war did not go well for the Parliamentarian forces at first. Their ill-trained levies were initially defeated at Edgehill (October 23, 1642), but in a trend that continued for most of the first two years of the war for both sides, the Royalists did not effectively follow up their battlefield victory. Roundhead armies remained in the field under the earls of Essex and Manchester, and the behavior of the king's troops, many of them mercenaries led by his German nephew, Rupert, the dispossessed third son of the elector of Palatine, alienated various factions in towns and the countryside that might have supported the king. Additionally, the king's tolerance of Catholicism, abhorrence of Puritanism, and inability to control his nobles, especially in the south and west of England, alienated other constituencies.

In 1644, the Parliamentarians managed to unite with Protestant Scottish allies and defeat a large Royalist army commanded by Prince Rupert at the Battle of Marston Moor (July 2), not far from York. It was after Marston Moor that Rupert, a fine soldier and commander, nicknamed Cromwell "Ironsides," and this name

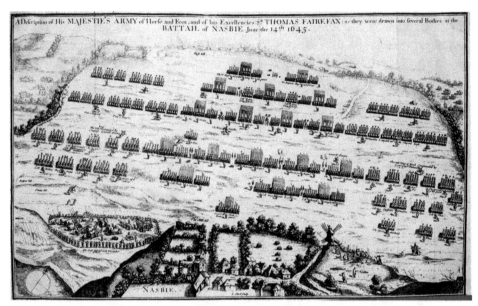

Based on how the Old English words are spelled, this is a nearly contemporaneous depiction of the Battle of Naseby (1645). Note the tactical formations, which are representative of the Thirty Years' War. (Hulton Archive/Getty Images)

attached itself to the regiments of cavalry that Cromwell raised, trained, and led. However, the Parliamentarian leadership under Essex and Manchester wasted the fine victory by failing to pursue the king's beaten forces, and then the earls frittered away their advantage by trying to recapture the south of England. Instead, they lost several small battles late in the year.

THE PLANS

At the beginning of 1645, the situation seemed promising for the Royalists and dismal for the Parliamentarians. Their Scottish allies were tied down dealing with the rebel Marquess of Montrose (one of the great unheralded commanders in history), and the king had raised a new army and intended to attempt to reassert control over the midlands prior to a reconquest of the north, which he had lost after Marston Moor. The plan revolved around first seizing the town of Taunton in the south and then marching north to secure the midlands. However, there was much dissension over this plan—Prince Rupert did not like it—as well as in the ranks of the king's other lieutenants, especially the surly and often drunken Baron Goring, who was supposed to lead his forces north to join the king for the final extinguishing of the rebellion. The king's optimism about the upcoming campaign was almost certainly misplaced.

On the Parliamentarian side, which in 1644 had suffered from disunity and disaffection, a new spirit reigned. Parliament raised a new army and placed Sir Thomas Fairfax, an ally of Cromwell and one of the most popular generals, in command. Fairfax and Cromwell, fast friends, together integrated the new levies with their veterans and then trained all of them assiduously over the winter. The army was known as the "new model" army because of the bill passed in Parliament that funded it. Fairfax's intention was to deny the midlands to the king and to threaten his lines of communication and support from the south.

Accordingly, the campaign began with an attempt to seize Taunton from the Parliamentarians, but its successful defense and a rumor of relief caused the king's army to march north to attack Leicester in the midlands instead, as Rupert had originally recommended. This had two results: It probably prevented Charles from receiving reinforcements that he might have gotten had he stayed farther south, and it led to the storm and sack of Leicester by the Royalists. This outrage added moral power to the approach of the New Model army under Fairfax, which was determined to fight the king if his army gave battle.

The Royalists, meanwhile, dithered. Hoping for reinforcements, they abandoned any further drive to the north and marched toward Harborough, where they expected to meet with reinforcements. Fairfax, who had been marching to the relief of Taunton, now moved to intercept the king's army, while his own outnumbered it. Cromwell had joined the army as second-in-command and overall commander of the cavalry, and thus the Parliamentarians were reinforced by well-trained troops, while the Royalists were not. Southwest of Harborough, the king's pickets came under attack near the little village of Naseby by Fairfax's cavalry. The king called a council of war, which advised giving battle. Rupert, on the other hand, recommended avoiding battle and retreating to the south, given the reported size of the Roundhead host and his personal experience fighting troops led by Fairfax and Cromwell at Marston Moor. His advice was rejected because it was thought it would lower the morale of the entire army. Additionally, the troops in the Royalist army were loaded down with their booty from the sack of Leicester and reluctant to abandon their ill-gotten gains to the Roundheads.

THE BATTLE

Rupert prepared the battle plan for the Royalists by picking a low ridge with the northerly winds at its back, facing southwest toward the village of Naseby and the broad moor to its northwest that ended in some swampy terrain. Thus, any smoke created by cannon and musket fire would blow into the eyes of the Roundheads. Fairfax took a corresponding position on a low rise of ground above the swamps. Both armies positioned their cavalry on their wings. Rupert commanded the Cavalier cavalry on that army's right wing, while Cromwell commanded the cavalry on the Parliamentarian right (i.e., opposite the Royalist left wing). Fairfax also positioned dismounted dragoons in the rough terrain, flanking any approach Rupert might make against the Roundhead left with musketry. The Royalists had the advantage in trained infantry but were still outnumbered nearly two-to-one in that arm.

Fairfax kept most of his newly conscripted infantry behind the low hill as the king's battalions and squadrons deployed for battle. He did this to avoid them witnessing that army's disciplined maneuvering, which might shake their confidence.

The first move was made by Prince Rupert, who charged down on the Roundhead left with his cavalry. He was met by Cromwell's son-in-law, Henry Ireton, and the cavalry on that wing. Despite the flanking fire from the Roundhead dragoons, Rupert kept his men in good order and burst through the left wing, wounding Ireton as he went. As some of the Parliamentarian regiments fled the field, Rupert's men followed and then rode up to the baggage train behind Fairfax's army, ready to plunder it. However, the baggage train was well defended, and when Rupert realized this, he rallied his troopers and led them back to the field of battle.

While Rupert was gone, the battle went poorly for Charles. Initially, his infantry was successful in pushing the Roundhead infantry back, but Cromwell charged against the enemy left and carried all before him. Rallying his troopers much closer to field of battle, he attacked the Royalist infantry in the rear. He was joined by dragoons from the left, who had not been dispersed by Rupert and rode northeast to join Cromwell in his second attack. The Royalist army now disintegrated about the king, who tried to lead his Lifeguards in a personal charge against Cromwell and Fairfax as they surged into the reserve on the hill. However, another officer ordered the Lifeguards to withdraw, and the king was carried away with them as they retreated. This mischance probably saved Charles from either death or capture at that point. Rupert returned to the field to find the battle lost, and he did what he could to rally the fugitives and take them away to safety. However, many of them, loaded down with coin after the so-called rape of Leicester, could not escape, or they stopped to try to pick up coins as they fell from their pockets while they ran and were scooped up by the Ironsides cavalry in that manner.

The final result was the complete destruction of this Royalist army. It lost nearly 5,000 troops, either wounded or captured or left dead on the field of battle. Meanwhile, the Roundhead losses probably totaled less than 500 due to all causes. There were no more veteran cadres around which the king could form any armies for the foreseeable future.

CONCLUSION

Naseby marked a turning point in the English Civil War. After the battle, Cromwell and Fairfax captured all of the king's baggage and his correspondence to the queen, wherein his schemes to introduce French and Irish Catholic armies into England were laid bare. This caused even more Englishmen to abandon the Royalist cause, if not actively take up the Parliamentarian cause. It also brought Cromwell and Fairfax to the fore as the generals of most merit, who would go on to prosecute the war much more aggressively, leading finally to the capture and beheading of the king in 1649 and the establishment of a Commonwealth that lasted until Cromwell's death in 1659.

Further Reading

Hibbert, Christopher. *Cavaliers and Roundheads: The English Civil War, 1642–1649.* New York: Charles Scribner's Sons, 1993.

Roberts, Keith. *Cromwell's War Machine: The New Model Army, 1645–1649.* Yardley, UK: Pen and Sword Publishers, 2005.

32. Rocroi

Date: May 19, 1643
Location: Rocroi, France

OPPONENTS

1. Hapsburg Spain
     Commander: General Francisco de Melo
2. Bourbon France
     Commander: Louis II de Bourbon, Duke of Enghien

BACKGROUND

The Battle of Rocroi is considered one of the major battles of the Thirty Years' War. Beginning in 1618, the Thirty Years' War initially pitted Hapsburg Spain under Philp IV against the Protestant powers of Europe. France, a staunchly Catholic nation, remained neutral until 1635, when it appeared that Spain might gain hegemony in Europe. In that year, France declared its support for the Protestant cause. A French invasion of the Spanish Netherlands the following year ended in defeat for France. For the next several years, French forces were content to remain behind their borders. The situation changed with the death of Cardinal Richelieu in December 1642. Richelieu, one of the primary advisors to Louis XIII, had kept a tight grip on the French army and limited French operations. General Francisco de Melo, the Marquis of Tordelaguna, commanding the Spanish forces in the Netherlands, saw Richelieu's death as an opportunity to support the other theaters by invading France.

In April 1643, Melo led a force of approximately 20,000 infantry, roughly 7,000 cavalry, and eighteen cannon through the Ardennes forest, reaching the fortress of Rocroi on May 12. Rocroi sat along Melo's lines of communication, and he wanted to eliminate it before advancing deeper into France. Believing the fortress was lightly held and in disrepair, Melo assumed that it would not take long to seize Rocroi, and then he could continue his invasion of France. Unfortunately for Melo, the fortress was not lightly held, nor was it in disrepair.

The twenty-one-year-old Duke of Enghien commanded the French forces assembling to repel the invasion. Two experienced generals, Marshal Francois de l'Hopital and Jean de Gassion, who had fought with King Gustavus Adolphus of Sweden, were there to assist him. With approximately 17,000 infantry, 6,000 cavalry, and twelve cannon, Enghien set out to intercept the Spanish forces and relieve Rocroi. Upon hearing the news of the approaching French forces, Melo shifted his forces from Rocroi to meet the new threat.

THE BATTLE

By nightfall, both armies deployed on the plateau southwest of Rocroi between the Meuse and Oise rivers. The main Spanish line comprised of ten *tercios*: eight

Spanish *tercios* and a Burgundian *tercio* on the left and an Italian *tercio* on the right. Despite some innovations by the Dutch and the Swedes, the Spanish *tercio*, a densely packed formation of pikemen augmented with arquebusiers, was still the paradigm fighting formation for European armies and would be Melo's strength. This infantry was backed up by ten Walloon and German battalions. Melo placed his cavalry on either flank, with his eighteen cannon in front of the infantry.

The French forces deployed similarly, only they used the thinner and more linear Dutch-style formation. Enghien deployed his infantry in two main lines of fifteen infantry battalions. He arranged them so that the front line did not obscure the view of the second line. Behind this line were three infantry battalions and four smaller cavalry formations. On either flank was Enghien's strength—his cavalry. Even Melos knew that his cavalry would be no match for the French. In the front, the duke placed his twelve cannon.

At 4 a.m., Enghien ordered his artillery to open fire, and the Spanish immediately replied, and the battle was waged. Enghien planned to attack both flanks of the Spanish line simultaneously with his cavalry. He hoped that his superior cavalry would drive off the Spanish cavalry and he could roll up the less mobile *tercios*. Unfortunatel, for Enghien, his cavalry conducted a weak and uncoordinated charge toward the German cavalry anchoring Melo's right flank. Sensing an opportunity, the commander of the German cavalry, Count Ernst von Isenberg, ordered a charge into the disorganized French horsemen, forcing them to seek safety in the nearby woods. However, the Germans did not follow up on their success. Some of them continued west, hoping to raid the French supply trains. The rest milled about, unsure of what to do next.

Once Isenberg got his cavalry sorted out, he directed them to attack the left flank of the French infantry. At the same time, the Spanish *tercios* on the right of the line moved forward to attack the French. Assuming that this was the opening of a general Spanish assault, the commander of the French cavalry reserve, Baron Claude Sirot, led his horsemen into the flank of the German cavalry. This move stalled the German attack and saved the French left flank. However, it was the actions on the French right flank that would decide the battle.

At the same time, the French cavalry on the left flank was advancing, Gassion led his horsemen forward to attack the Walloon cavalry on the Spanish left flank. The Walloons put up a better fight than Gassion anticipated, repelling his first attack. The battle on the right flank became confused after a countercharge by the Wallonians. Enghien, watching the battle and encouraging his men, sensed that the moment was right to send in the second echelon of French cavalry. This cavalry charge was enough to shift the momentum of the battle to the French.

Enghien found Gassion, and the two worked out a plan to finish off the Spanish. Gassion would take a portion of the French cavalry and ride around behind the Spanish and prevent any reinforcements from arriving. Meanwhile, Enghien would lead the majority of the cavalry to attack the weaker second echelon Spanish *tercios*. Catching the *tercios* by surprise, Enghien's horsemen began rolling up Melo's second echelon and eventually found themselves at the northern end of the Spanish formation, effectively surrounding Melo's forces. At the sight of Enghien's cavalry, the German cavalry fled the field. The battle now entered its final and conclusive phase.

The French cavalry owned the battlefield, and the Spanish *tercios* found themselves under attack from all sides. The French musketeers and artillery were steadily firing into the mass of the Spanish *tercios*. As their numbers dwindled, the commander of the Spanish infantry, the incapacitated Count of Fontaine, assessed the situation, weighing his chances. He concluded that a withdrawal would only lead to more casualties and decided to hold fast and wait for reinforcements. Fontaine formed his remaining five *tercios* into one massive square to repel the French cavalry. Due to their superior training and discipline, the Spanish infantry held firm and repelled three French attacks, but in the process, Fontaine was killed. To the north, Spanish reinforcements were approaching Rocroi. However, after running into the retreating German and Walloon cavalry, assuming the battle was lost, the commander elected to collect the survivors and reorganize for the next day.

Enghien prepared for one last attack on the Spanish square. The French attacked from all sides, supported by the artillery firing grapeshot into the thinning Spanish ranks. Still, the Spanish held firm, and after three more French attacks, the Spanish were offered the chance to surrender, but they refused. Frustrated, Enghien continued to pound the square with artillery. Eventually, a Spanish colonel who had taken command following Fontaine's death accepted the inevitable, but not until his infantrymen were low on ammunition did he signal that he wanted to negotiate a surrender. Unfortunately, not all of the Spaniards got the word, and as Enghien and his staff approached, some soldiers shot at them. The incensed French soldiers resumed the attack, quickly overwhelming the Spanish ranks and killing any Spaniard they could find. This massacre went on for nearly thirty more minutes before the French commanders established order, ending the battle.

CONCLUSION

Of the 27,000 soldiers and cavalrymen that Melo led into France, nearly 16,000 were killed or captured. After linking up with his reinforcements the next day, Melo, who had slipped away during the battle, led the rest of them out of France. Other than laying siege to the fortress at Thionville, Enghien, who had lost only 2,000 men, failed to exploit his success. Even after the fall of Thionville, the French did not invade the Spanish Netherlands, and both sides were content to accept a stalemate. However, the battle was considered a significant defeat by Hapsburg Spain, and it led to the rise of Bourbon France as the preeminent power on the continent.

Further Reading

Guthrie, William P. *The Later Thirty Years War: From the Battle of Wittstock to the Treaty of Westphalia.* Westport, CT: Greenwood Press, 2003.

Parker, Geoffrey. *The Thirty Years War.* New York: Routledge, 1984.

Wilson, Peter H. *The Thirty Years War: Europe's Tragedy.* Cambridge, MA: Belknap Press of Harvard University Press, 2009.

33. Ramillies

Date: May 23, 1706
Location: Austrian Netherlands (modern Belgium)

OPPONENTS

1. French

   Commander: Marshal Francois de Neufville, Duc d'Villeroi and Elector of Bavaria

2. British coalition

   Commander: John Churchill, Duke of Marlborough

BACKGROUND

The greatest disaster to befall the French during the War of the Spanish Succession occurred in 1706, a year after the famous, but strategically indecisive defeat of the French and Bavarians at Blenheim in southern Germany by Sir John Churchill and Prince Eugene of Savoy. During the previous battle, the two commanders had altered the strategic equation of the irresistible power of Louis XIV (the "Sun King") and his seemingly invincible French armies. Blenheim resulted in the salvation of the tottering position of the Hapsburgs, not the imminent defeat of the Bourbons. The French were not out of the war, and its cause, the succession to the Spanish throne of Louis's grandson Philippe, was still in play because the British and Austrian political goal was to get Louis to renounce the Spanish throne. It would take a lot more than a Blenheim to do that. A major secondary goal was to threaten, or even reverse, Louis's conquests in the low countries, especially the Austrian Netherlands (modern Belgium), against which the French perhaps could extract concessions, or even a peace, from the Hapsburgs. Accordingly, the major seat of effort in 1706 moved to the area of the Meuse and Sambre rivers in northern France and southern Belgium. This was an area of fortified towns and rivers, and it promised the sort of early eighteenth-century *pavane* (slow dance) of military tactics so common to the era—sieges, reliefs, exhaustion, and indecision.

THE PLANS

Marlborough's opponent in this campaign was Marshal Francois de Neufville, Duc d'Villeroi. Villeroi owed his advancement more to his skill at court and his family bloodline than to military talent. Marlborough employed a simple deception to begin the campaign, feinting with his forces toward the fortress of Namur at the juncture of the Meuse and Sambre rivers. Villeroi reacted as expected, leaving an opening for Marlborough to maneuver into his rear through the line of fortresses known as the Lines of Brabant, which supposedly protected it.

Marlborough's army was a coalition force composed of his English troops, Dutch, and various German allies. His successful maneuver was intended to set the conditions for him to fight a defensive battle in the vicinity of ground that later became known as the Battle of Waterloo. However, his Dutch allies failed to agree to an engagement (unlike Marshal Gebhardt von Blücher years later), and so he was forced to improvise further. In the meantime, spurred on by Louis, Villeroi crossed the Dyle River to give battle against the coalition army with an army of 60,000 men. The two armies confronted each other near the small village of Ramillies, north of Namur.

Villeroi evidently intended to fight a defensive battle. He deployed his army between and behind two rivers, trying to take advantage of several small villages at both ends of his line as strongpoints. His left, in particular, was well protected behind the Little Geet River. Marlborough's plan again involved deception. He would feint against Villeroi's left and then engage him on his right flank with his cavalry. As Villeroi rushed reserves about, Marlborough banked on the Frenchman weakening his center. The battle had an almost Napoleonic design: flank attacks followed by a massive blow delivered in the center to crack the enemy army.

THE BATTLE

Marlborough opened the engagement on the morning of May 23, slightly outnumbering Villeroi with 62,000 troops against the 60,000 French. Marlborough's artillery outnumbered those of his opponents by almost two to one, and he concentrated a large battery of twenty-four-pound cannon in his center. They opened the battle at 11 a.m., pounding the center around the strongpoint of Ramillies.

The battle went as according to plan as any battle in history. Villeroi reacted as expected to Marlborough's feint on his left wing, sending his reserves toward that threatened sector. At that point, Marlborough launched his cavalry, outnumbered, against Villeroi's cavalry on the French right flank. This was one of the greatest cavalry actions of the age, not to be repeated in scale until Eylau in 1807, and even then not matched as a cavalry-versus-cavalry action. Marlborough actually participated in second and third charges and was dehorsed, and one of his aides was killed. The British regiments of cavalry performed gloriously, especially the Household regiments (Life Guard and Horse Guards) and the Royal North British Dragoons (the "Scots Greys"), who were allowed to replace their miter headgear with bearskins in honor of their achievement.

Villeroi again reacted predictably to this coup, moving reserves to shore up his right. The battle was not won, but it had reached the key decision point. Marlborough now unleased his infantry against Villeroi's weakened center, using his steady, well-trained Dutch troops. Reinforced by infantry who had moved stealthily from Marlborough's right, they carried all before them, and the center cracked. Marlborough then rolled up Villeroi's line from south to north with his victorious and unbroken cavalry. The French army fled the field, abandoning all its artillery, with a loss of over 13,000 troops. Marlborough had suffered fewer than 4,700 casualties.

CONCLUSION

The aftermath of Ramillies was devastating because the victory occurred early in the campaigning season. Marlborough's army reconquered the Spanish Netherlands, seizing Antwerp and Brussels and recapturing the fortresses that had belonged to the Spanish that had long threatened the Dutch. The tragedy of Ramillies was that it emboldened the British to continue the war as one of conquest. Louis was ready to negotiate a compromise peace that was favorable to the British and their allies. The Dutch also wanted peace, but the scale of the victories in 1706 caused the British and the Hapsburgs to overreach and continue their war, dragging the Dutch and other German states along with them. Ironically, the war effort bogged down in the next couple of years in Spain, where the Spanish people rejected the efforts of allies to "liberate" them from their new Bourbon king, whom they revered, and install a Hapsburg one. The war lasted another seven years, until a series of treaties signed at Utrecht (1713–1715). Ramillies was a disaster for Louis XIV, but the French military had more than one army. Its very success proved a larger disaster for the rest of Europe as well, in that it extended a war that could have ended in 1706.

Further Reading

Lynn, John A. *The Wars of Louis the XIV, 1667–1714.* New York: Routledge, 1999.

Weigley, Russell F. *The Age of Battles: The Quest for Decisive Warfare from Breitenfeld to Waterloo.* Bloomington: Indiana University Press, 2004.

34. Poltava

Date: June 28, 1709
Location: Central Ukraine

OPPONENTS

1. Swedish
   Commanders: King Charles XII and Field Marshal Carl Gustav Rehnskjold
2. Russians
   Commander: Tsar Peter the Great

BACKGROUND

The occasion for the Battle of Poltava was the outbreak of the Great Northern War in 1699 engineered against the Swedish Baltic Empire by Russia, Denmark, and Poland-Saxony. It occurred shortly after the accession to the Swedish throne of the young Charles XII, of the line of the great Gustavus Adolphus. Trained from infancy as a soldier, Charles XII turned out to combine the ferocious habits of a warrior with the efficacies inferred by the new modern military professionalism in Europe. It was not long before he had stunned all of Europe, and not just his

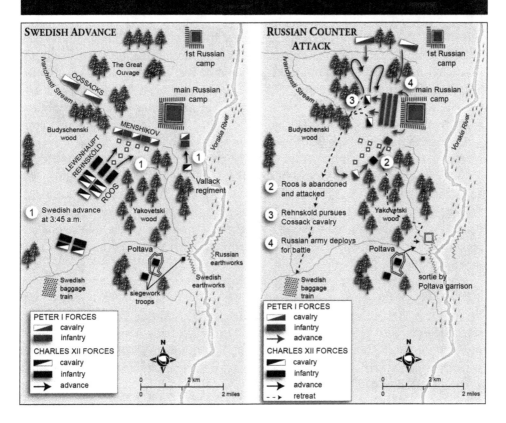

enemies, with his skill at warfare and warmaking, reclaiming the legacy of invincibility for the Swedish army from the days of Gustavus Adolphus.

From 1799 to 1704, Charles defeated, in order, the Danes, Russians, and Poles, turning the Poles into his allies. Russia now remained his only enemy. Tsar Peter (later the Great) offered a conciliatory peace, but he underestimated the young king's desire to see his enemies not only defeated, but personally ruined and destroyed. Charles aimed at nothing less than removing Peter from the throne of Russia. On New Year's Day 1708, Charles invaded Russia. Peter employed his Tatar and Cossack cavalry in a scorched-earth campaign, trading space for time. Charles seized Grodno in a lightning thrust, almost capturing Peter. The tsar continued a Fabian strategy of avoiding battle directly with Charles, depopulating towns and driving the refugees before his armies as he pulled back into Russia's vast interior. His goal was to deny Charles any support from sympathizers and appeasers inside Russia who opposed his modernizing reforms.

In July, Charles followed and crossed the Berezina River at the same point that Napoleon later crossed over a century later during his infamous retreat in 1812. However, despite Swedish victories, Peter's strategy was causing the Swedish army extreme difficulties in terms of supplies. Charles halted his advance eastward toward Moscow and turned south to feed his army after an offer of alliance by Mezepa, the Hetman of the Cossacks in Ukraine, who had switched sides. Because almost half of Charles's army consisted of cavalry, the rich fields and grains of the Ukraine offered a solution to his operational difficulties. As he proceeded south across the Dnieper River, he defeated Peter's army, which was blocking the way, at Dobry, but not as easily as in the past. Peter's modernization efforts with the Russian army were starting to have results on the battlefield. Charles briefly pondered waiting for a relief column with supplies to join his army, and then returning to Livonia to stay the winter, but he decided turning south was the better course, given Mezepa's offer.

Little did Charles realize that Mezepa himself was under threat of defeat as Peter turned on the turncoat to his south. When Charles turned away from his relief column, Peter doubled back and defeated the 11,000-man Swedish column, who abandoned their cannon, with only 6,000 supply-less, hungry soldiers eventually making it to join Charles. This was Charles's first major military setback of his career. Worse, most of the Cossacks abandoned their allegiance to Mazepa and renewed their loyalty and service to the tsar. Peter then won the race to the supply depot at Baturin.

Charles's situation was desperate. On top of everything else, as would occur 100 years later, the frosts came early, and the winter of 1708–1709 developed into one of the coldest in recorded Ukrainian history. The subsequent Ukrainian winter campaign, with Peter harassing Charles's army and attacking his bases of supply, saw the Swedish army reduced from 40,000 troops to 20,000 by the time the warmer weather arrived in the spring. Many of these men had frozen to death or starved instead of dying in battle.

THE PLANS

Charles's obsession with Peter turned into a kind of insanity. Instead of retreating into friendly Poland, he continued to campaign, placing the fortress of Poltava under siege in late spring. His army was too weak to invest the fortress properly in the eighteenth-century style. His hope was to get some support from the Zaparogian Cossacks and defeat any army of relief that Peter might send. He also believed that his position in Peter's southern realms, close to the Ottoman enemies of Russia, might bring the Turks to his aid. In addition, he called on the Poles to send him reinforcements. The Turks remained neutral, content to see the Russians and Swedes kill each other.

Peter, on the other hand, methodically dealt with all these eventualities in a professional, rational manner. First, he took on the Zaparogian Cossacks, suppressing them enough to then march on Poltava in relief, although he was careful in his approach. He also prevented any Polish reinforcement by dispatching forces to keep them busy while he dealt with Charles's dwindling army. Peter's army numbered 80,000 troops, and unlike the Swedes, they were healthy and well fed. Charles was wounded in the foot during a skirmish as the two armies maneuvered and subsequently fell into a coma after surgery (probably due to loss of blood).

Peter learned of this and decided to risk provoking a battle with the temporarily leaderless Swedes. He did this by moving his field army (41,000 troops) in a threatening position northeast of Poltava on Charles's flank. He then fortified the main camp, as well as constructing several defensive redoubts. The rest of his forces were used to watch Poltava and his own lines of communication. He also built redoubts in a defile that existed on the approach march to his fortified camp in case Charles tried a surprise attack. Peter outnumbered Charles in artillery, most of the Russian guns being in his fortified main camp, but he also put sixteen cannon in the various redoubts. Charles's artillery had little powder and shot in any case, and only four guns accompanied the army so that it could move quickly.

The tsar's hopes were partially realized. Charles, still recovering but conscious, decided to do what he always did—attack. He took 17,000 of his best troops (of 23,000 total available) to attack the Russian fortified camp on June 28, 1709. The Swedes were so short of powder that it was understood that the bayonet would be the main weapon for the infantry. Charles was unable to ride a horse, which curtailed his ability to command at this engagement. Normally, the king rapidly moved about on horseback from crisis point to crisis point, inspiring his troops and making quick, effective tactical decisions. He would be able to do little of either. The battlefield, too, was very spread out, with the Russians having created broadly separated strongpoints as well as protecting their flanks with their position astride the wooded Vorskla River, which forced Charles's army to approach exclusively from Poltava, to the southwest.

Charles relied on shock action by his infantry and cavalry to decide the battle by sealing Peter into his fortified camp, with no means of escape. He nominally deferred the actual command to his military tutor and most trusted subordinate, Field Marshal Carl Gustav Renhskjold, the commander of the cavalry. Charles's infantry forces were under General Count Adam Carl Lewenhaupt, who did not get along with Renhskjold. Worse, Renhskjold did not share Charles's plan of battle with Lewenhaupt, although the king did accompany one of Lewenhaupt's four infantry columns in his litter.

THE BATTLE

The Swedes began their approach march shortly after dark the night before, at 11 p.m. It was just after midnight when they discovered that that the Russians, under Prince A. D. Menshikov, were building additional redoubts at right angles to the first line to split the Swedish columns into two groups, with the goal of firing into their flanks as well as their front as they passed. A hasty council of war was held in the dark, and the infantry was reorganized into five columns; four would press on into the plain in front of Peter's camp, and the fifth would screen the redoubts until the others had passed. But no one informed Lewenhaupt, commanding two of the columns on the right, of this decision. Just before 4 a.m., it was light enough for the Russians to see the stationary Swedes waiting for their new orders, and they opened the battle by opening fire with their cannon from the forward redoubts. The Swedish army reacted violently and lurched into the attack. The first two redoubts fell quickly to the Swedish infantry, with their cold steel. However, at the third and fourth, things began to go awry. Instead of falling easily, the redoubts absorbed more and more Swedish combat power as forces were detached to try to reduce them, rather than simply marching past them as envisioned in the original plan. This was a direct result of Rehnskjold not sharing the plan with his infantry commanders. Meanwhile, the king lay helpless on his litter, unaware that his well-conceived plan was slowly falling apart.

Nearly one-third of the Swedish infantry swirled around the bravely defended redoubts when Menshikov attacked with his dragoons. The Swedes responded with their own superb cavalry. This melee continued without result for an hour, and Menshikov, who felt he was winning, sent back to Peter the recommendation that the whole army sally forth and fight at his location. Peter cautiously refused to come forth and instead ordered Menshikov to break off the action with his cavalry. This he did, under the protective fire from Peter's cannon in the main camp. Meanwhile, the redoubts had achieved their purpose, splitting Lewenhaupt's column of infantry out of supporting range on the far right of the Swedish line. Once in position opposite the camp, Lewenhaupt simply did what the Swedes always did—he prepared to attack the huge Russian camp with his solitary six battalions of infantry (2,400 Swedes versus the 25,000 Russians behind defensive works with plenty of cannon).

On the far left, only the third component of the Swedish infantry under Rehnskjold actually executed the plan correctly. It was at this point he saw Lewenhaupt storming the southern works of the camp unaided, and he ordered him to break off the attack and rejoin the main body under him. Unbelievably, Lewenhaupt had been having some success in this sector and was furious that he was being recalled at his moment of triumph. He had unintentionally discovered the weakest area of Peter's defenses, and the battle may have hung in the balance, although the likelihood that the Russians would panic was very low. In any case, Lewenhaupt withdrew, in part because he knew the king was with Rehnskjold.

However, all was not well. The other third of the infantry, under Major General Carl Roos, was now entirely separated from the Swedish army and any support in its own continuing battle around the redoubts; he lost almost 40 percent of his men in the fruitless assaults and finally received a recall order. Then Peter saw him withdraw to reform and try to find the main Swedish army. With Lewenhaupt no longer blocking the approach to Roos, Peter launched an overwhelming attack on this isolated force, led by Menshikov with infantry and dragoons. The attack was devastating, and the shock of discovering that these were Russians and not Swedish comrades caused a panic. Roos fled with 400 men but was surrounded and captured just outside Poltava.

Meanwhile, the battle continued to the north. Rehnskjold dispatched a small force to go find Roos, and as they waited, the Russian artillery began shelling that stationary Swedish army and almost hit the king. It was now roughly 8 a.m. Rehnskjold now regretted leaving most of his artillery behind and sent for one battalion in the camp before Poltava to bring what artillery it could to the main army. This message never arrived. Rehnskjold had three choices: He could try to take the ford to the north of the camp and cut Peter off, but this would divide his weakened army even more. He could attack Peter and his seventy-three guns and 25,000 infantry in the entrenched camp. Or he could retreat and try to save the army to fight another day. He ordered the retreat.

As the Swedes formed to go, the Russian army issued forth in tight professional columns and then spread out, inviting an attack by the Swedes on the open ground. Peter was positioned with the troops on the left side of the army, elite soldiers who had been uniformed in plain gray to hide their identity. Rehnskjold realized that if he continued the retreat and the Russians attacked, the army would certainly disintegrate, so he formed them again to face the Russians, who continued to bombard him with about half their artillery, which was still on the ramparts in the camp and was firing over the heads of the nearly 21,000 troops assembled on the plain below.

Charles was consulted, and he recommended attacking the Russian cavalry on the wings first. Rehnskjold disagreed and recommended a main attack in the center on the infantry. Charles meekly deferred. The remaining 5,000 tired Swedish infantry now advanced against nearly 21,000 Russian infantry, with another 7,000 cavalry in support on its flanks. The Swedes had won against similar odds early in the war, but these Russians were well trained, steady, and confident, led by their tsar in person. Amazingly, the attack seemed to succeed against Peter's side of the line.

However, on the left side, the Swedes were in dire straits, being chewed up by the bulk of the Russian cannon fire, which had shifted because firing at the Swedish right would kill Russians and Swedes alike. Also, there was no cavalry in support of the temporary success on the left. As the Swedes under Lewenhaupt advanced farther on the left, they became dangerously separated from the stalled right wing. Peter, in the second line behind the left, now personally led his elite troops forward into the gap between the two separated Swedish wings. They carried all before them, rolling up the northern Swedish line from the south and the southern one from the north. Peter reinforced this success with the bulk of his infantry, achieving an envelopment of both infantry wings.

The Swedish cavalry, which might have saved the day, was slow to deploy for the main attack and then became distracted by the Russian cavalry on its flank and the broken ground that it had been assigned on the left. Only one squadron made it into the maelstrom in the center, and it was annihilated. When it finally did engage, the infantry was already broken and the cannon continued their deadly work.

Rehnskjold was captured as the Swedish army now fell completely apart, for the first time since the Battle of Nordlingen over 74 years earlier. Lewenhaupt managed to save the king and retreat to the camp outside Poltava in the south, utilizing the troops there as well as the Cossacks to prevent a further disaster. Peter, meanwhile, celebrated his victory on the field and then ate dinner. The Swedish army had been crippled, with almost 10,000 men killed, wounded, or captured. The Russians had suffered fewer than 4,500 casualties.

CONCLUSION

After the battle, Charles fled toward the south, but the remainder of his army of 40,000 was now down to less than 11,000 Swedes plus 6,000 Cossacks. The retreat was poorly conducted, again a reflection of Charles's poor health from his wound. Charles left the army at Perevoluchna, at the confluence of the Dnieper and Vorskla rivers, with about 2,900 Cossacks and soldiers and crossed the Dnieper in small boats. Only he and 600 others eventually found sanctuary in the Turkish dominions to the west of the Bug River. What was left of his army, however, did not fare so well. It tried to countermarch north and cross the Vorskla to flee south to the Crimea and seek safety with the Tatar Khan. Instead Menshikov caught up to it at Perevoluchna before it could get away and surrounded it. Charles's army surrendered on July 1, 1709. His disastrous campaign, like Napoleon's 100 years later, broke the military power of Sweden and heralded the arrival of a new major power in the north—tsarist Russia. Sweden would never again be a major military power.

Further Reading

Englund, Peter. *The Battle of Poltava: The Birth of the Russian Empire.* London: Victor Gollanz, 1992.

Weigley, Russell G. *The Age of Battles: The Quest for Decisive Warfare from Breitenfeld to Waterloo.* Bloomington: Indiana University Press, 1991.

35. Rossbach

Date: November 5, 1757
Location: Saxony, in eastern Germany

OPPONENTS

1. France and the Holy Roman Empire

   Commanders: Marshal Charles de Rohan, Prince de Soubise, and Duke Josef of Saxe-Hildburghausen

2. Prussia

   Commander: King Frederick II (the Great)

BACKGROUND

The Battle of Rossbach occurred within the context of the Seven Years' War, which began in 1756 in Europe, although it was really the outgrowth of an earlier colonial war that had broken out in North America between France and Great Britain. On one side were Great Britain and the Kingdom of Prussia, plus some of their minor allies, and on the other side were the greatest powers of Europe: France, the Holy Roman Empire (Austria), and the Russian Empire.

Frederick II, the king of Prussia, fought the war in order to retain his Silesian province, which he had seized in an earlier war from Austria. It was he who broke the fleeting peace via a preemptive invasion of Saxony, an ally of Austria, seizing that electorate and incorporating its army into his own. However, it soon became clear that he faced a two-front war against the major powers. After a failed invasion of Bohemia to capture Prague in the spring and summer of 1857, he seemed doomed as a French army invaded from the west, an Imperial army approached from the south, and another large Austrian army advanced from the southeast. Frederick conducted a forced march from Bohemia against the foe he considered easiest to beat, the Imperial army, composed of an array of German forces allied with Austria. This force, though, retreated into fortresses, denying Frederick his quarry. While considering his next step, he learned that the Austrian cavalry had raided his capital in Berlin. He further weakened his own small army by dispatching forces to see to this threat in his rear. Defeat seemed almost certain.

THE PLANS

Frederick saw a chance when components of the Imperial army united with the French, forming a field force of 42,000 troops. He had little more than 21,000 men to spare, even after most of his cavalry returned from Berlin. The combined French-Imperial army was led by two military "non-entities," the Prince Soubise, Charles de Rohan (French), and Duke Josef of Saxe-Hildburghausen (Imperial Army). Soubise owed his position to the favor of the French king's mistress, Madame Pompadour, rather than to any particular military skill or achievement. The duke owed his position to the archaic system of seniority by which the Holy Roman Empire selected its field marshals.

The combined army was located just west of the city of Merseburg in Saxony. It was on the high ground overlooking the area of Frederick's camp between the villages Bedra and Rossbach. The allies decided their two-to-one advantage meant that they should attack. Their plan seems to have been simply to overwhelm Frederick as he defended his camp and baggage trains. Frederick had no plan beyond waiting to see what the enemy might do and then taking advantage of any mistakes the Allied commanders might make. It is certain that had they not attacked, Fredrick probably would have.

THE BATTLE

The first thing to go wrong for the Allies was their disunified command. Instead of breaking camp and attacking at dawn, they dawdled all morning, only getting the entire force of 42,000 troops on the march by 11 a.m. This probably reflected a reluctance by Soubise to attack Frederick. Frederick initially misunderstood the approach by the enemy army; he thought it was retreating, but then he realized it was marching to take up positions to attack him. He was relying on his own generalship and the disciplined valor of his troops to overcome the long odds. Accordingly, he instantly decided to attack before the Allies could get into position.

The Allied march formation consisted of two large infantry columns on the left (nearest to Frederick), their artillery, and another column of infantry in reserve, all heading southeast. At the head of the column was half their cavalry, and at the rear was the other half. Their intent was to align in front of Frederick and then turn 90 degrees in place, which would have put their cavalry on the wings, protecting the flanks of the army. Frederick's infantry broke camp quickly and repositioned itself facing southwest, behind Rossbach. As for his cavalry, commanded by Baron Frederich Seydlitz, who had just returned from liberating Berlin, he brought all of it around to his far-left flank. He screened the cavalry movement from the enemy by having it redeploy behind Janus Hill to his left, with his infantry on the right. Once in position, he put his entire army in motion, using his famous oblique order, but with the cavalry now closest as the Allied army wheeled to face northward against Frederick's new position. The Allied army was simply too clumsy to deal with Frederick's nimble, smaller army.

Seydlitz made first contact, hitting the Allied cavalry in the van before it had sorted itself out from its march columns, right after Frederick's artillery opened the battle. Seydlitz's charge is justly famous; his troopers were mounted on the best horses in Europe. They trotted forward in two lines, 1,500 troopers in the first line and 1,800 in the second. The Allied cavalry tried to turn to face them, and its formations became unsteady and intermixed as they attempted to receive the charge. The Prussians, at the last moment, spurred into a headlong gallop and hit the muddled allied squadrons and some of their infantry in the front and flank, which caused a huge melee. The discipline of the men and horses of the Prussians prevailed, as French and Imperial squadrons melted away during the melee.

Now the Allied right flank was uncovered at just the moment when Frederick's lead elements of his infantry made contact in their own advance. They halted and began to pour steady musket fire into the Allied infantry in a stupendous firefight, as their cavalry melted away on their flank. Seydlitz, in the meantime, had rallied and reformed his cavalry—a feat that no other army could have equaled because most cavalry forces could charge only once and then were out of the battle. The Allied force never overcame the confusion that it had been thrown into by Frederick's not giving it time to form a line of battle. Some French formations used columns instead of lines to try to counter Frederick's infantry attack, but the shock of the cavalry rout and the intermixing of the Allied army were too much for this new tactic to do much good.

The firefight went poorly for the Allies, as the Prussians continued to pour accurate artillery and musket fire into the confused ranks of their enemies. Just as the Allied line began to crack from the intense weight of this musket fire, Seydlitz hit the line again in the flank and turned the beginnings of a withdrawal into a rout. For a loss of only 550 killed, wounded, or missing, Frederick inflicted over 7,700 casualties on the Allies, who stumbled back in headlong retreat to the west. The battle lasted only 90 minutes—it was one of the quickest (and cheapest) tactical victories in the history of warfare.

CONCLUSION

Rossbach proved to be more than just a humiliating tactical disaster for the French and Imperialists. It also prevented this army from uniting with another Austrian army in Silesia that was besieging Breslau. Frederick now raced to Silesia to relieve

Breslau, but it fell before he arrived. This army, under Charles of Lorraine, was forced to fight Frederick at the village of Leuthen in early December, not far from Breslau. The Prussians and Frederick again defeated an army twice as large using maneuvers and the tactical excellence of Frederick's infantry deployed in the oblique order once again on the enemy flank.

It was a much bloodier battle, but it saved Frederick's kingdom and his army to fight another day after active campaigning ceased for the winter. Additionally, using the criteria established in the introduction for the choices of these disaster, at the political level, Frederick's victories led to further loans from Great Britain that actually strengthened the coalition and put Frederick on a sounder financial footing. None of this would have been possible without the disaster at Rossbach.

Further Reading
DiMarco, Louis A. *War Horse: A History of the Military Horse and Rider.* Yardley, PA: Westholme Publishing, 2008.

Duffy, Christopher. *The Army of Frederick the Great,* 2nd ed. Chicago: The Emperor's Press, 1996.

Weigley, Russell F. *The Age of Battles: The Quest for Decisive Warfare from Breitenfeld to Waterloo.* Bloomington: Indiana University Press, 2004.

36. Quebec

Date: 1759
Location: Quebec, French Canada

OPPONENTS

1. French
    Commander: Marquis de Montcalm
2. British
    Commander: General James Wolfe

BACKGROUND

The first years of what was known in Europe as the Seven Years' War (and the French and Indian War, to Americans) did not go well for the British Empire. The conflict began in 1754 just outside modern-day Pittsburgh, in what is now the state of Pennsylvania in the United States, with the massacre of French envoys by the Indian allies of a British colonial mission sent to ascertain French intentions. Only later did it spread to Europe, and then to the rest of the globe, the first modern world war. In 1755, the British attempted to correct their early ham-handed conduct of the war by sending several British and colonial regiments through the Allegheny Mountains under General Sir Edward Braddock. Braddock marched into an ambush on the Monongahela River, and his forces routed into headlong retreat back over the mountains by the French and their Indian allies. The seat of war in North America then moved to a different front, along the line of the Hudson River Valley, and then through the natural invasion route to Canada up Lakes Champlain and George. Here, the British overreached again, building a European-style fortress at Fort William Henry.

In a surprise maneuver of great daring, the overall French commander, Louis Joseph Marquis de Montcalm, placed Fort William Henry and its garrison under siege in 1757. The garrison surrendered when it became clear that no relief would be forthcoming under fair terms offered by the French that same year. They were massacred after they marched out with their arms and colors, along with many civilians, women, and children, by Montcalm's disappointed Indian allies. Montcalm lost control of his Indian allies altogether, and the war entered a grim, bitter phase characterized by frontier ambushes and no-quarter engagements.

These disasters brought into power a new leadership in Great Britain, composed of William Pitt in the commons, who was determined to provide everything needed to prevail in the conflict. Included in the shakeup were new commanders in the various theaters of the war in North America. Chief among these were James Wolfe and Jeffrey Amherst. These two generals arrived in 1758, and their first order of business involved the capture of the great French island fortress off the coast of Newfoundland at Louisburg. At the same time, other British commanders methodically built roads across the Alleghenies that had led to the withdrawal of the French from the Ohio Valley and the loss of many of their Indian allies. Amherst succeeded at Louisbourg, which fell to standard eighteenth-century siege tactics. However, as payback for Fort William Henry, the British did not allow the French honors of war and took them prisoner. They also deported the civilian population back to France.

At the other end of the St. Lawrence River, another British commander, Colonel James Bradstreet, secured Britain's western flank north of Fort Pitt by capturing France's Fort Frontenac in a daring coup. With the flanks secure, the British could implement a plan to conquer Canada that involved securing the St. Lawrence Valley, invading from the south along the traditional invasion route up Lake Champlain, and going up the St. Lawrence River to capture Quebec. Additionally, they might go down the river from their new base at Fort Frontenac. The first phase of this operation involved General Wolfe's expedition to take Quebec in 1759.

THE PLAN

The long-delayed conquest of Canada could only be achieved by controlling the St. Lawrence River. The British controlled the entrance and outlet, but not the majority of the course of the river between Lake Ontario and the Gulf of St. Lawrence. Quebec was the natural target for the first phase of this conquest. Wolfe did not intend to waste time, given the short period for campaigning in those northern climes, conducting a methodical campaign as Amherst had at Louisbourg. He did not have the time, as the campaign began in late June. However, the geography of

Quebec conspired against him and favored Montcalm. His overall force numbered 9,000 British regulars and about 500 American colonials, plus his naval support. About half of these troops ended up being used to garrison and guard his line of communication. His efforts to land his troops farther upriver to invest Quebec in some manner were constantly frustrated by Montcalm. It seemed Quebec was impregnable, much as Vicksburg would seem over a century later.

As the weather started to turn, Wolfe's naval commanders, Rear Admirals Saunders and Holmes, advised him that they would have to withdraw to avoid their ships becoming iced in for the winter, which would enable the French to attack them at their leisure or starve them out. Wolfe had to act right away.

ENGAGEMENT

Wolfe convened a council of war in mid-September with his three brigadier generals to discuss his courses of action. All of them were from a higher social class than Wolfe and to some degree felt him unfit to command them. They advised him to ascend the river and cut the French line of supply. Wolfe rejected their advice and consulted Captain Robert Stobo, a relatively junior officer who had been held captive by the French. He had escaped from Quebec earlier in the year. Stobo probably informed Wolfe about a little-known footpath up the cliffs on the river southeast of the city, which gave access to the Plains of Abraham, from which operations might commence to besiege Quebec. Wolfe seized on this opportunity, his plan being to ascend this path on the night of September 12–13 and then *hope* (there is no other word for it) that Montcalm would come out and do battle.

Luck was on Wolfe's side—the path proved navigable enough, even at night, for him to move the bulk of his army of 4,800 troops up to the Plains of Abraham and form a line of battle on the morning of September 13. Montcalm, serene in his confidence, was caught completely off guard. As Wolfe's red-coated columns fell into line, Montcalm considered his options. Unknown to Wolfe, Montcalm had gone through most of his supplies and had less than a week's rations left, with little possibility of resupply while the British controlled the river. There was another French column of around 2,000 men about eight miles away, under Colonel Louis Antoine de Bougainville, guarding the landward line of communications with Montreal. However, it would take hours for them to arrive, and Montcalm thought that he could see the British building entrenchments with each passing minute. The troops were actually lying down to avoid French cannon fire, but the French general did not know this. After waiting for two hours with no news about the arrival of Bougainville, Montcalm assembled his 4,500 troops and marched out on the plain to face the British.

By this point in the campaign, Wolfe was horribly ill (possibly from consumption), and the climb up the cliffs had exhausted him. Nonetheless, in the best style of the age, he led his troops personally forward, established his line, and waited for Montcalm to respond. Because of the ad hoc nature of the battle, with Wolfe *hoping* that Montcalm might come out (but not knowing of his supply difficulties), the two commanders simply adopted the standard eighteenth-century approach of lining up opposite each other and conducting a traditional close-range firefight. This gave the advantage to the steadier, healthier, better-trained British regulars—a confirmation of the idea that he who can take the most punishment wins, an approach that historian John Lynn (2005) calls the "battle culture of forbearance."

Montcalm then made the key error that sealed his doom. Instead of awaiting a British attack, or waiting inside Quebec until Bougainville arrived in the British rear, he decided to attack first. The order to advance caused his ill-trained militia to abandon the field and left the bulk of the attack to his now-outnumbered regular regiments. Despite Wolfe's own mistakes, the Frenchman delivered his army into the hands of Wolfe's regulars, who then proceeded to methodically destroy it with disciplined, sustained musket volleys. The French attack ran out of steam and stalled, and then fell apart altogether.

The British then counterattacked, with Wolfe personally leading the attack on the right. It was a bloody affair. Wolfe was mortally wounded in the pursuit and soon bled to death. Montcalm was mortally wounded during the retreat but lasted until 4 a.m. the following day, although he had turned over his command to whoever was left to take it. The campaign was actually won by the actions of Brigadier General Townshend after the battle, who halted the pursuit to regain control of his men in case Bougainville showed up. The command of the remaining French fell upon the Marquis de Vaudreuil, who made the key decision to abandon Quebec and to join Bougainville and retreat toward Montreal, with the intention of fighting another day. The British could have Quebec, empty of supplies and provisions—the French would simply return and retake it in the spring.

Quebec put up a token resistance, but the events of September 13 guaranteed that it would not be able to resist long, and a junior officer surrendered the city to the British and the remainder of the French garrison was transported back to France by the Royal Navy and repatriated. This was a wise move because it meant the British would not have to feed them over the winter.

CONCLUSION

The British left Quebec garrisoned under the junior brigadier Sir James Murray, who had no guarantee that it would hold out against the certain French attempt to retake it in the spring. The remainder of the expedition departed ahead of the winter ice. The battle was a tactical victory, but it was catastrophic for the French in the political realm because it represented a complete shock and, combined with all the other defeats, including the destruction of a French fleet that November, caused the French to begin seeking peace in earnest. Fortunately for the British, they were able to return and prevent its recapture the following year. Quebec spelled symbolic doom for the French enterprise in Canada—the last gasp of French efforts to retain a colony that simply could not be held in the long term against the more populous and enterprising British to the south.

Further Reading
Anderson, Fred. *The Crucible of War: The Seven Years' War and the Fate of Empire in British North America, 1754–1766*. New York: Vintage Books, 2000.

Lynn, John, A. "Forging the Western Army in Seventeenth-Century France," in William-son Murray and MacGregor Knox, eds., *The Dynamics of Military Revolution, 1300–2050*. Cambridge: Cambridge University Press, 2001.

Lynn, John A. "States in Conflict," in Geoffrey Parker, ed., *The Cambridge History of War-fare*. Cambridge: Cambridge University Press, 2005.

37. Kunersdorf

Date: August 12, 1759
Location: Near Frankfurt on Oder in Silesia (today, part of Poland)

OPPONENTS

1. Kingdom of Prussia
   Commander: King Frederick II
2. Empires of Austria and Russia
   Commanders: Marshal Peter Saltykov (Russia) and *Feldmarshalleutnant* Ernst Laudon (Austria)

BACKGROUND

By 1759, the Seven Years' War in Europe had turned into an attritional slugging match. The superb troops that Frederick the Great had led earlier in the war were almost all gone, replaced with conscript levies, unwilling prisoners of war, and whomever the Prussian press gangs could kidnap or hoodwink into serving. For the most part, only the officers were Prussian. The campaign of 1758 had only delayed a reckoning with Frederick's enemies, who had spent the winter leisurely encamped and half-heartedly besieging the Saxon city of Dresden.

The goal of Frederick's strategy had been to prevent the unification of the Russian and Austrian armies facing him by using his central position on interior lines. However, because of the siege of Dresden, when the summer campaigning weather arrived, his enemies finally achieved their goal after a Russian army defeated a Prussian Corps near Kay, in eastern West Prussia, in July. The Russians, whom he had met at Zorndorf the previous year and failed to cow, were led by the redoubtable Marshal Peter Saltykov, and the Austrians by the steady, if unimaginative, Marshal Ernst Laudon. After Saltykov captured Frankfurt on Oder, the Austrians slipped by Frederick and the combined Russo-Austrian army entrenched near that city at Kunersdorf in early August.

THE PLAN

Frederick believed that his only hope perhaps was to retrieve his fortunes with another lightning march and battle to stun his opponents and thus get the initiative back long enough to make it to another winter. However, his adversaries held all the cards, having captured a major city and now being in a good defensive position to defend their gains. Nevertheless, Frederick was counting on his tactics and his own genius to retrieve territory despite the weakness of his army. Also, the Russians and Austrians were not on the best of terms, and the two top commanders distrusted each other. Saltykov was already miffed that Laudon had brought a corps of only 22,000 troops, not a much larger force. Frederick may have been right in believing that, as at Rossbach, his allies' disunity in high command would lead to a great outcome for his army.

However, the Austrians and Russians had picked their position well—a series of low hills with their flanks protected by marshy forests in which armies could easily become lost or misdirected. They had no intention of attacking or moving; rather, per standard Russian practice since Poltava, they dug into field fortifications, with the strongest components in the center, able to defend their redoubts in any direction as a counter to any flanking movements Frederick might make. Also, with the approach of Frederick's army from the west, they abandoned Frankfurt and pillaged the city of any food or sustenance.

None of this deterred Frederick, whose reconnaissance revealed to him only the general outlines of his enemies' positions. Frederick returned to his standard game plan of using some terrain feature to screen a march of a flanking force to gain a tactical advantage. In the case of Kunersdorf, he chose the Reppen Forest to screen the march of his army to attack the northwest-facing enemy from the southeast, much as he had at Zorndorf the previous year. It is fascinating that he went with this plan against an enemy that had not panicked and that had inflicted nearly crippling casualties on him in the previous battle—which he could barely claim as a tactical victory. Frederick's confidence in his understanding of the terrain and enemy was misplaced.

THE ENGAGEMENT

Murphy's law went into effect almost immediately for Frederick, whose army was roughly divided into two unequal columns, one with him on the "screened" march, and the other a diversionary force under General Finck approaching the Russo-Austrian position from the west. On August 11, the day before the battle, Saltykov realized that Frederick was going to outflank him through the forests and refused both his flanks on his central position. Thus, Frederick ended up attacking both flanks, but they were ready to meet him.

Additionally, Frederick's attack became desynchronized because both columns, especially his, got lost in the woods during their approaches. Finck's column, with most of the artillery, did manage to deploy and perform its mission of demonstrating against what was thought to be the main Russian position, facing northwest. However, the Russians and Austrians remained unperturbed, especially because they had superiority in artillery. Frederick, in the meantime, realized his errors and tried to redeploy his troops around what he thought was the new enemy position, facing southeast on his front. The difficult terrain and several ponds and small lakes made this maneuver challenging, and it was under the Russian guns, which punished the Prussians with heavy fire as they milled about. Frederick lost all the element of surprise and further exhausted his soldiers, who had been up and marching for almost nine hours.

Instead of calling it a day, Frederick grimly pressed the attack. His onslaught against the entrenched Russians finally captured part of their southern position at Muehlburge, but the Russian central position remained strong and the light of the long August day wore on. Frederick might have stopped then. One of his columns had pressed on and recaptured Frankfurt, thus cutting the Russians' line of retreat if they decided to do so. However, Frederick continued to press his attacks on the Allied position, with no success. In days past, as at Rossbach, the Prussian cavalry might have retrieved territory for Frederick, but the Russians had felled trees along all the various roads and tracks around their positions, and the Prussian cavalry met sustained and confident fire wherever they met the enemy. A cavalry coup would not win this fight, and to add to Frederick's woes, his best cavalry general, Frederick Wilhelm von Seydlitz, was wounded in the fighting.

It was at this point that Saltykov and Laudon committed fresh Austrian infantry reserves and cavalry to the attack against the exhausted Prussians to their southeast. The Prussian army broke and streamed off to the south and west. Frederick and a detachment of his Life Cuirassiers were surrounded by Cossacks on a small hill. Fortunately, one of his subordinates led a hussar detachment to his rescue, and they cut their way through the Cossacks to safety.

CONCLUSION

This was Frederick's most significant defeat—a military disaster that was almost unrecoverable. His army lost almost half its strength in killed, wounded, and captured, as well as all of its artillery. The enemy, because of Frederick's earlier seizure of the Muehlburge and use of captured Russian guns, had suffered heavily too, with 15,000 casualties killed or wounded. It was as bloody a day as one finds in military history, comparable to the Battle of Antietam in the American Civil War. However, unlike Antietam, one of the armies was shattered.

The entire war was nearly lost on this day. Frederick fled, and Dresden fell shortly after, which resulted in the liberation of Saxony from the Prussians. He contemplated suicide, and only a partial victory by a Prussian-English army at Minden over the French partially restored the balance. Fortunately, the Allies now split up to pursue their own objectives. The French sought peace after their numerous defeats in Europe, North America, and elsewhere in this eighteenth-century world war. The Austrians proceeded to turn south to subdue the rest of Silesia, their main object in these wars since Frederick had conquered that province in 1740.

The Russians also decided to await another year to finally remove Frederick once and for all from the scene as chief troublemaker in Europe. In this, they failed. Frederick abandoned his disastrous policy of fighting battles, for a time, and waited the allies out, keeping his small army together until the "Miracle of the House of Brandenburg" occurred: the death of one of his most implacable foes, the Tsarina

Elizabeth of Russia in 1761. Her son, a slavish devotee of Frederick, became tsar and immediately withdrew from the war. Abandoned by their French and Russian allies, the Austrians finally submitted to the will of history and agreed to a peace that left Frederick with Silesia. Frederick had survived the disaster of Kunersdorf, but just barely.

Further Reading

Duffy, Christopher. *The Military Life of Frederick the Great.* New York: Atheneum (Simon and Schuster), 1986.

Duffy, Christopher. *Russia's Military Way to the West.* London: Routledge & Kegan Paul, 1981.

Weigley, Russell F. *The Age of Battles: The Quest for Decisive Warfare from Breitenfeld to Waterloo.* Bloomington: Indiana University Press, 2004.

38. Quiberon Bay

Date: November 20–21, 1759
Location: Quiberon Bay, on the southwest Atlantic Coast of France

OPPONENTS

1. French Royal Navy

     Commander: Admiral Herbert de Brienne, Comte de Conflans

2. British Royal Navy

     Commander: Admiral Sir Edward Hawke

BACKGROUND

The single greatest maritime disaster during the Seven Years' War in Europe occurred against the French in the third year of general war. French strategy around Great Britain had revolved around her army defeating British forces and allies on land in Europe. After being humiliated by Frederick the Great at Rossbach (1757), and then afterward being unable to threaten the British dominion of Hanover, the French resolved to invade Scotland or Ireland, as the best way to bring their hated enemies to the table. At the same time, victories in North America in 1756–1758 emboldened the new French maritime strategy.

The problem remained, as it had been in previous wars and would be again in later wars, how to wrest command of the English Channel away from the British long enough to invade the British Isles. This task was assigned to Admiral Herbert de Brienne, the Comte de Conflans, and late in 1759, events conspired to make the threat a dangerous reality. Although the ideal sailing season for invasion had passed, Conflans managed to combine his rather weak squadron with that of a squadron returning from the West Indies at Brest, allowing him to create a powerful squadron of twenty-one fully manned ships of the line (battleships) to oppose the blockading British fleet.[1]

These events occurred in the late autumn, during a period of storms and gales that made operating for both the British and French fleets hazardous. The French had the extra problem of moving and protecting their invasion fleet with its embarked French troops, and so their problem was more difficult. Conflans managed to collect his squadron and head south toward the invasion fleet at Quiberon Bay, which is south of French Brittany, during one of these storms because he had learned that the blockading British squadron under Sir Edward Hawke had been scattered by the same storms and gales that allowed him to concentrate at Brest.

Hawke, one of the most daring and enterprising officers in the British fleet, managed to collect his ships into a force of twenty-three battleships and also set sail in the bad weather for Quiberon Bay. On November 20, both fleets arrived nearly simultaneously off the bay.

THE PLAN

Conflans's plan was simple: He intended to take shelter in the relatively shallower waters of Quiberon Bay and hope that perhaps the storms would allow him to sally forth with the invasion flotilla. Hawke, on the other hand, made the extremely bold decision to pursue the French ships into the narrow waters of the bay and seek a decisive battle to eliminate the French threat once and for all. He intended to do this by completely ignoring the infamous Fighting Instructions of the Royal Navy, which dictated that he form a line and do battle with the opposing enemy, also in line. Such a plan could not be executed due to the weather and geography of Quiberon Bay. Hawke instead intended to execute what are now called *melee tactics,* also allowed in the Fighting Instructions, but only sanctioned in pursuit of a beaten foe, not one that had not yet been engaged or defeated. British admirals had been executed for less, most recently Admiral John Byng at Minorca, of whom Voltaire had quipped that "it was a good thing from time to time for the British to execute one of their admirals, as an example to the others."

THE BATTLE

One of Hawke's frigates located the French fleet that morning around 8 a.m. Hawke gave the signal to form a line abreast—meaning side by side, and not line stem to stern—so as to be ready to engage the French wherever he found them. He had earlier detached the battleship *Magnamine*, commanded by the equally daring Captain Lord Richard Howe, to make the land, and as luck would have it, Howe spotted Conflans's main body and signaled Hawke. As Hawke's after-action report attests, Conflans was slowed in his retreat by his attempts to escape while still keeping the body of his fleet concentrated. Hawke realized this, and at 2 p.m., he gave the order to his captains for a general chase, essentially giving them the authority to engage the enemy in their individual ships as they saw fit. Howe, being closest, instantly obeyed in his ninety-gun battleship.

Conflans was thrown into confusion, trying to form a line ahead and only making things worse as his captains realized that the British were not playing by the rule book. Confusion ensued. Howe managed to sink the French battleship *Thesee* and cause another, the *Formidable*, to strike its colors (i.e., surrender). Not long after that, another French battleship, the *Superbe*, sank and yet another, *Heros*, surrendered. However, in the fading light of that November day, Hawke realized that he must break off the action or risk losing his own ships in the treacherous shallow waters farther up the bay and into the estuary of the Vilaine River estuary. The French continued their retreat, tossing tackle and guns over their ships to escape and to get over the bar at the mouth of the river. This did almost as much to cripple their fleet as those ships lost to combat because these ships would never be able to get back out to sea over the bar. Capping it all off was Conflans's decision to anchor his ship *Soleil Royale* in the bay in the hope of escaping in the morning. When morning came, he found himself anchored among the ships of Hawke's fleet. He ran aground in his attempt to escape, and he had to abandon his flagship and burn it to prevent it falling into the hands of the pursuing British.

Hawke ended up losing two ships, both which had ran aground and could not be recovered. He had them burned, although he was able to recover the crew from only one, the other crew having abandoned ship already and then gotten lost in the storm in its rafts and boats, most probably drowning. Further, Hawke suffered fewer than 40 killed and 200 wounded. The French, on the other hand, had effectively lost their entire fleet, six in outright battle, as an organized unit, with only a couple ships escaping to other ports. The French had lost as many as 2,500 sailors killed, wounded, and taken prisoner.

CONCLUSION

The destruction of Conflans's fleet had an immediate effect, which was only strengthened by the news of the victory at Quebec that arrived not long afterward. It removed the option for France of invading Great Britain for the remainder of the war and gave the British almost complete command of the sea, which they intended to use to divest France of as many overseas colonies as they could. It also led to the beginning of negotiations with France to end the war; two more years of fighting would be required, but Quiberon Bay was certainly the agency that convinced France's leaders that they must negotiate or face the complete loss of their empire.

NOTE

1. A ship of the line roughly corresponded to a large warship, with fifty or more cannon. From here on, the number of cannon carried by these ships will follow in parentheses like this: HMS *Victory* (100).

Further Reading

Anderson, Fred. *The Crucible of War: The Seven Years' War and the Fate of Empire in British North America, 1754–1766*. New York: Vintage Books, 2000.

Hore, Captain Peter. *The Habit of Victory: The Story of the Royal Navy, 1545 to 1946*. London: National Maritime Museum, 2005.

39. The Siege of Pondicherry

Date: 1760–1761
Location: Southeast India

OPPONENTS

1. British and Indian allies

   Commanders: Major General Sir Robert Clive (later Earl Powis), Admiral George Pocock, and Lieutenant Colonel Eyre Coote
2. French and Indian Mahratta allies

   Commanders: Thomas-Arthur, Comte de Lally, Antoine Comte D'Ache, and Marquis de Bussy-Castelnau

BACKGROUND

The Seven Years' War (1756–1763) constituted a global conflict, with fighting on four continents and across the world's oceans. In India, British interests were represented by the United East Indian Company, and this brought about conflict with French commercial and trade interests on the subcontinent. The Company had its own troops, and these were augmented by a few British regular troops. The commander of these forces was Robert Clive, an Englishman who had first arrived in India as a young man. In 1751, he came into prominence by defeating the French and their ally, Chanda Sahib at Arcot, in Madras.

After the outbreak of the war in 1756, Clive resumed active operations, this time in the area of Bengal (today, part of India and Bangladesh). After the atrocity known to history as the "Black Hole of Calcutta," which saw the murder of over 100 British prisoners. Clive marched from Madras on Calcutta with an army of 900 Europeans and 1,500 natives. Here, he faced the forces of the Nawab (Viceroy) of Bengal (assisted by some French troops) that had perpetrated the Calcutta massacre and defeated them decisively at the Battle of Plassey (June 23, 1757).

These operations alarmed the French governor, Thomas Arthur, the Comte de Lally, at Pondicherry in southern India, where British and French commercial interests competed more directly and openly with each other. Now Clive had no distractions to keep him from turning on Pondicherry.

THE PLANS

The key to Pondicherry, a strongly fortified outpost of France, was controlling the sea. Initially, the British Royal Navy had had difficulties in securing command of the sea in the Indian Ocean as the war began, due to its far-flung operations and Indian waters being essentially a secondary theater to the Atlantic, Channel, and Mediterranean theaters. The Comte de Lally was an active commander, and while Clive was in the north, he threatened the base of British power in Madras. At one point, he besieged Fort George. Only the timely arrival of naval stores ships prevented de Lally from successfully concluding his siege of Fort George in Clive's absence. Accompanying these ships was a Royal Navy squadron under the command of Admiral George Pocock. As a result, de Lally abandoned the siege and moved back to his base at Pondicherry.

Clive returned to Madras and began active operations against the French to the south. Clive's plan was simple: Besiege de Lally in Pondicherry and remove the threat, while expanding British influence. The Comte de Lally relied on the strength of his defenses and the French navy to keep him supplied.

THE SIEGE AND THE NAVAL ACTIONS

Shortly after de Lally abandoned the siege of Fort George, the eleven French ships under Admiral Antoine Comte D'Ache fought a desultory but bloody battle with Pocock's inferior squadron (nine ships) on September 10, 1759. This action constituted the naval Battle of Pondicherry. Although neither side lost any ships. D'Ache felt compelled to return his damaged ships to his base on Mauritius to the south. He never returned, "leaving India to its fate." according to naval historian A. T. Mahan, continuing, "From that time the result was certain,"

Clive sent an army under his subordinate, Lieutenant Colonel Eyre Coote, to besiege Pondicherry by land while the Royal Navy blockaded it by sea. Coote's force, centered on the British 84th Regiment, arrived north of Pondicherry at Wandiwash in January 1769 and numbered just over 5,000 troops, 2,000 of them European. The Comte de Lally outnumbered him and sent Marquis de Bussy-Castelnau with over 7,000 troops, including more than 2,400 Europeans, against Coote. However, Coote's force was the more professional, and he had more artillery. He defeated the Franco-Mahratta force sent against him on January 22. This force retreated into Pondicherry, and active siege operations by Coote began in August.

The Comte de Lally was desperate to feed his demoralized and almost mutinous men and took the extreme action of expelling civilians from Pondicherry. Many of them died as they made their way between the lines, with the two armies firing at each other. This further demoralized the garrison. The comte's hope for the French fleet to arrive and resupply his men was in vain. On January 16, 1761, he surrendered Pondicherry and his nearly starving army to Coote.

CONCLUSION

This campaign spelled the doom of French influence in India. Although Pondicherry would be given back to the French at the peace table, the ability of the French to expand their influence in the face of Clive's more successful administration and political skill in isolating them from local Indian rulers would never be overcome. Pondicherry was besieged again in 1778, during the American Revolution, and fell again. Britain's dominance of India was sealed near the end of the French Revolutionary Wars in the early 1800s with triumphs by the young, almost unknown, "sepoy," General Sir Arthur Wellesley (later the Duke of Wellington).

Further Reading

Anderson, Fred. *Crucible of War: The Seven Years' War and the Fate of Empire in British North America.* New York: Vintage Books, 2001.

Mahan, A. T. *The Influence of Sea Power Upon History, 1660–1783.* Boston: Little Brown, 1890.

40. Yorktown Campaign

Date: August–October, 1781
Location: Yorktown Peninsula and surrounding waters, Virginia

OPPONENTS

1. Americans and French

    Commanders: General George Washington and Jean-Baptiste Donatien de Vimeur, Comte de Rochambeau

2. British

    Commander: Lord Charles Cornwallis

BACKGROUND

The genesis of the 1781 Yorktown campaign resulted from a British strategic decision to move the seat of war in the American colonies to the south. This decision was made after the colonial insurgency in Britain's North American colonies broadened into a global war as France, Spain, and the Netherlands joined in support of the Americans, mostly to regain the influence and colonies they had lost to the British from the Seven Years' War (1756–1763).

On the ground in the southern colonies, the British achieved victory after victory under the aggressive, but often brutal, leadership of Lord Charles Cornwallis. Cornwallis assumed command of the forces in the south after the capture of Charleston, South Carolina, and the surrender of an American army in the summer of 1780, which was the greatest military disaster of the war to that point for the Americans. General Horatio Gates then took command of the American forces remaining in the south but was utterly defeated by Cornwallis at the Battle of Camden on August 16, 1780.

Cornwallis then proceeded to subdue most of South Carolina and drive into North Carolina. Here, he overreached, and his detached forces were defeated at King's Mountain in October 1780, and again at Cowpens by part of Nathaniel Greene's small army on January 17, 1781. Greene was probably General George Washington's most talented general. Cornwallis, stung by the defeat at Cowpens, relentlessly pursued the smaller American force. Greene finally offered battle far to the north, not far from Virginia, in the bloody Battle of Guilford Courthouse; though this was a tactical victory for Cornwallis, Cornwallis was forced to abandon most of North Carolina and retreated to Wilmington to reestablish his supply lines and give his hard-pressed army some rest.

YORKTOWN CAMPAIGN, AUG–OCT 1781

MASSACHUSETTS   42°N

NEW
YORK
                    Hudson River
CONNECTICUT   R.I.

HEATH

0   40   80 mi
0   40   80 km

WASHINGTON   CLINTON
ROCHAMBEAU

PENNSYLVANIA   New York City

Princeton   Sandy
                  Hook
Delaware River   40°N

Philadelphia
Chester

Elkton   NEW JERSEY

MARYLAND

Baltimore
                                          ATLANTIC
Annapolis
                                          OCEAN
Mount
Vernon
                    Potomac   Delaware Bay
                                                    38°N

VIRGINIA
              LAFAYETTE   GRAVES
James River   19

                    Chesapeake Bay   BARRAS
Williamsburg   ROCHAMBEAU
                                      (8)
          Yorktown
CORNWALLIS   Second Battle of
Portsmouth   the Chesapeake,
                                Sep 5, 1781

                    ■ American/French troops

                    □ British troops   36°N

                    → American/French troop
                      or ship movement

NORTH CAROLINA   HOOD   ⇢ British ship movement
                    (14)

                         French ships
                         (number indicated)

DE GRASSE   British ships
(28)   (number indicated)

78°W   76°W   74°W   72°W

In the meantime, British forces began raiding in Virginia, including a mixed Tory and British force under the turncoat Benedict Arnold. Virginia had been relatively untouched by the war, and Cornwallis decided that if he ravaged that colony, he might draw the American forces north, where he could defeat them once and for all. He could also easily sustain his army in the region so long as the Royal Navy maintained command of the sea, which to that point in the war had not been a challenge.

Washington and the commander of the French forces contained by the British in Newport, Lieutenant General Jean-Baptiste Donatien de Vimeur, Comte de Rochambeau, agreed to send parts of their forces south to deal with Arnold. The British overall commander in New York, Sir Henry Clinton, sent 2,600 troops south under Major General William Phillips. After Phillips landed at Portsmouth, Virginia, on March 26, he superseded Arnold in overall command and was directed to subordinate his operations with Cornwallis once that officer arrived in Virginia. The Marquis de Lafayette made it to Virginia with a force of 1,200 light infantry, but the French never joined him, their navy under the French admiral René Destouches having been defeated by a British squadron under Mariot Arbuthnot. Destouches returned to Newport and rejoined Rochambeau there. Lafayette, meanwhile, was exposed, with only Virginia militia and a continental regiment under the command of the redoubtable Baron von Steuben available locally to reinforce him. Arnold attempted to preempt this juncture; he attacked some of the Virginia militia near Petersburg and defeated them.

It was at this point that Cornwallis arrived with his much-reduced force, only 1,500 men. But to this, he added another 1,500 sent by Clinton, those of Arnold, and those of Phillips. His force now outnumbered Lafayette's, consisting of over 7,200 men and well supplied through Portsmouth and other Tidewater area ports.

THE PLAN

The British position suffered from too many moving parts. Essentially, Clinton wanted Cornwallis to return to New York, while Cornwallis wanted to keep his independent command in Virginia. The decision was made to base out of Yorktown, from whence Cornwallis could easily be supplied by the Royal Navy. This strategy was flawed from the outset because it abandoned the south to Greene but didn't leave Cornwallis enough forces to control Virginia. It must be remembered, too, that the British had more than North America on their minds—there was great concern because a large French fleet, with more embarked troops, had crossed the Atlantic and joined forces with the Spanish in the Caribbean. The British expected the main Franco-Spanish effort in this theater, not in the north.

The man who might be given most credit for the Allied plan was the French fleet commander in the Caribbean, François Joseph Paul, the Comte de Grasse, who obtained the permission of the Spanish to proceed north, with a promise to return in October 1781 to cooperate with the Spanish in attacking British possessions. Washington's own plan was his long-deferred attempt to retake New York from Clinton. However, he and de Grasse now conceived a new plan, by which they might eliminate Cornwallis altogether by feinting toward New York and combining all the French forces, sea and land, into one force and supporting the movement of the bulk of Washington's army south to join Lafayette. Lafayette was somewhat better off when on June 10, General Anthony Wayne joined his force with 800 Pennsylvania troops.

Clinton had subsequently learned of the expected arrival of a new French fleet and army from the Indies, but his fear was that they would join with Washington to attack New York. Based on this intelligence, he subtracted another 3,000 men from Cornwallis's force to bring north to defend against this anticipated attack. However, de Grasse, Rochambeau, and Washington had other plans. Rochambeau informed Washington of de Grasse's intention to come north, not to Newport but rather to the Chesapeake Bay, and to effect a juncture with the Americans there. Washington agreed to leave half his army on the Hudson Heights as a deception force to mask his departure with the other half of his army. By mid-August, he was on the march. Rochambeau, too, departed with almost 5,000 troops marching overland and Admiral Jacques Barras (who had relieved Destouches) left Newport with a siege train to join de Grasse at the bay.

THE CAMPAIGN

In Virginia, Lafayette, with around 4,000 troops, continued operations that attempted to contain the British and prevent further raids in Virginia. Cornwallis pulled back down the peninsula to cross the James River and send 3,000 reinforcements to Clinton in late June. Lafayette followed and attacked him with his advance guard under Wayne on July 5, 1781, at Greenspring Farm. This attack nearly resulted in disaster when Cornwallis turned and almost trapped Wayne's force. However, Wayne recognized his danger and managed to withdraw without catastrophic losses. Cornwallis crossed the river and arrived at Portsmouth, where he sent the 3,000 troops north. His doom had already left the Caribbean in the form of the Comte de Grasse's fleet.

On August 30, de Grasse arrived at Hampton Roads and made contact with Lafayette. Cornwallis had remained serene in his confidence. By the time the British fleets, under Admirals Graves and Hood, arrived on September 5, 3,000 French troops had joined Lafayette, raising his army to nearly 7,000 men. The British arrived too late to keep de Grasse out of the Chesapeake Bay, and neither had they intercepted Barras's expedition with Rochambeau's siege train coming from Newport. They had little time to react. Immediately, de Grasse sortied and the fleets pounded each other in the so-called Battle of the Virginia Capes. The outcome was little in doubt, given the French fleet's clear superiority and firm leadership. While the battle ensued, with both fleets sailing generally to the south-southeast, Barras's squadron slipped into the Chesapeake. The Comte de Grasse did not realize this until he returned to his anchorages inside the bay five days later.

By this time, Washington and Rochambeau's armies had arrived at the Head of Elk embarkation point on the northern portion of the bay, and the French now ferried his forces down to the area of operations on the narrow peninsula between the York and James rivers. All the French and American forces were concentrated by late September at Williamsburg, with Cornwallis now occupying a strongly defended position at Yorktown with a small detachment across the York River at Gloucester. The Americans numbered almost 9,000 troops, the French 7,800, with Washington in overall command and Rochambeau his second-in-command. Cornwallis could only oppose them with approximately 8,000 men. His hope for the Royal Navy being able to rescue him was forlorn, and yet he was determined to force a siege that might buy him enough time for a miracle to occur.

The miracle never occurred. The French and Americans proceeded to methodically invest Cornwallis's forces on both sides of the river, but with the bulk around Yorktown on the south. The combined Franco-American army included the extremely professional artillery and siege troops of the French Royal Army, perhaps the most professional siege engineers and artillerists in Europe. Included among the French ranks was a young engineering officer named Alexandre Berthier, who later served at Napoleon Bonaparte's penultimate chief of staff.

By early October, the siege was ready to commence, and the digging of trenches, or *saps,* began in order to slowly advance the heavy artillery to within range to start battering down the British defenses, especially their line of redoubts. The siege of Yorktown was primarily an exercise in extended digging to slowly zigzag closer to the British defenses. By October 9, the French batteries opened fire. American artillery batteries joined in the battering on October 10. Slowly but surely, the siege lines tightened according to the inexorable calculus of eighteenth-century siege warfare. On the night of October 14, the infantry joined the fight, and two outlying redoubts on the left and right were taken by the French and Americans, respectively. Cornwallis refused to give up; he attempted to move parts of his small army across the York River to Gloucester to perhaps drive off the besiegers on that front and escape with part of his army. When he tried to do this with several regiments on the night of October 16–17, a storm arose that prevented his boats from returning and dispersed them downriver.

The next morning, the British were greeted with a general bombardment all along the line. Cornwallis bowed to the inevitable and sent a drummer to "beat a parley" (i.e., ask for a conference to discuss surrender), and once his presence was noted, the guns ceased. Notes were exchanged, and on October 18, 1781, the American and French armies came up to accept the surrender of the British. Cornwallis dishonored himself by remaining supposedly sick in his tent and sent his second-in-command to tender his sword to Washington, who graciously had him take it to General Benjamin Lincoln, whom Cornwallis had humbled at Charleston the previous year. Over 8,000 British soldiers and sailors were surrendered, along with hundreds of cannon and thousands of small arms.

CONCLUSION

Cornwallis nearly escaped the disaster. Once Clinton realized the danger, he collected 7,000 troops and headed south to relieve his subordinate. However, he set sail only the day after the surrender and arrived a week later, so the outcome was perhaps a bit closer run than some histories portray it. As military disasters go, Yorktown is among the more significant. It subtracted one of the most populous and extensive geographical collection of colonies from the British Empire, creating, as it were, a new competing power on the North American continent, and one that was none too friendly to British interests for several generations. The war did not end immediately due to the involvement of France, the Netherlands, and Spain, and it could have been even more disastrous had Britain's sea power not retrieved the nation's fortunes and prevented an even greater, global defeat for it. Nonetheless, the myth of British invincibility had been shattered, not just on land but also at sea, although the British learned lessons that would serve them well in a much bigger war that came with another revolution closer to home—the French Revolution.

Further Reading

Greene, Jerome A. *The Guns of Independence: The Siege of Yorktown, 1781.* New York: Savas Beatie, 2005.

Ward, Christopher. *The War of the Revolution*, Volume II. New York: Macmillan, 1952.

41. Rivoli

Date: January 14–15, 1797
Location: Northern Italy

OPPONENTS

1. Austrian army

    Commander: Marshal Baron Joseph D'Alvintzy

2. L'Armée D'Italie (French Army of Italy)

    Commander: General Napoleon Bonaparte

BACKGROUND

After a hard-fought three-day battle in and around the Adige River near Arcola (November 15–17, 1796), General Napoleon Bonaparte gave his army what might be termed an operational pause. His opponent, Marshal Baron Joseph D'Alvinzty, had been placed in command of the third Austrian army that Napoleon faced that year, charged with relieving a large body of Austrian troops under Field Marshal Dagobert Sigismun Count von Würmser that were trapped in the fortress of Mantua in northern Italy. Through hard fighting and some luck, Napoleon had survived the key crisis of the campaign, although D'Alvintzy's army was still "in being." Nonetheless, Würmser remained under siege at Mantua, his large garrison rapidly dwindling due to disease and starvation. Napoleon now turned and pursued a second Austrian column that had been moving down the valley of the Adige from the north toward Verona and was approaching Rivoli in his rear. When Napoleon turned on this column, it retreated north and rejoined the rest of D'Alvintzy's army.

THE PLANS

The Austrians were chastised but not defeated. Despite this latest setback, the Austrian Imperial War council (*Hofkriegsrat*) demanded another push to relieve Mantua, and D'Alvintzy gathered more than 28,000 troops to descend the valley of the upper Adige through Rivoli to do just that. He also pushed out another column by the eastward route under the Marquis di Provera, with another smaller column in support, to attack the along the southern Adige and perhaps break through to Würmser while he fought Napoleon in the north. D'Alvintzy hoped to lure Napoleon into thinking that the main effort would thus be southeast of Verona, as it had been the previous time, and thus catch the French unprepared for a thrust from the north. D'Alvintzy and his chief of staff, Colonel Franz Weyrother, believed that the bulk of Napoleon's army was south of the Po River below Mantua, when in fact the reverse was true.

Napoleon, however, had finally received more reinforcements and created another separate division under General Barthelemy Joubert, which he stationed at Rivoli. He kept his best-commanded division, under General André Masséna, in a central position at Verona and covered the southern approach with the division of General Pierre Augereau. In addition to these forces, he left another division to cover the siege of Mantua, along with his improvised fleet of gunboats that patrolled the swamp around the fortress. Napoleon had the advantage of the central position and, as usual, would rely on his instincts and the speed of his troops to deal with any Austrian threat.

They key to the Battle of Rivoli (officially the second battle of Rivoli) was the terrain of the Alpine mountains to its north that blocked the Austrian advance between the narrow valley of the Adige and Lake Garda to the west. These mountains went by the name of *Mount Baldo* (the most prominent one among them). The Austrians would have to advance in six narrow columns and could not bring all their troops along the road south at one time. Additionally, they could advance across this terrain in only two ways: over the mountains (and with only infantry), or along the river road and then up a narrow approach a plateau that took the road through Rivoli, and then south to Verona and Mantua. D'Alvintzy decided to try to bring more troops against Rivoli in just this way to avoid being bottled up along the road. Two columns would cross the mountains—one to his far right, which would conduct a wide flanking march with the intent of erupting in the French flank and rear *behind* Rivoli; and then the main column, again almost entirely infantry, would come down over Mount Baldo and approach Rivoli from the front, hopefully to distract the French from a third force, which included most of the Austrian cavalry and artillery, coming up from the valley. Finally, D'Alvintzy had artillery advance along the east bank of the Adige that would set up and fire across the river to cover the leftmost (eastern) column as it climbed the road to the valley and to fire into the French flank. It was an overly complicated plan, and for the first day and much of the morning of the second day, none of these forces would be able to support each other.

On the French side, Joubert had a fairly secure defensive position that controlled these approaches with good roads behind him to move reserves. He would also be secure in the knowledge that Massena's division would be marching hard in his support once he notified Napoleon of the presence of the enemy.

THE BATTLE

The disjointed Austrian columns of the main effort were detected by the French cavalry and light forces on January 12, and the next day, Joubert notified Napoleon of very strong forces to his front as he withdrew his skirmishers into his main defensive positions at Rivoli. Napoleon had first detected Provera's columns and brought his troops north of the Po in that vicinity, but he intuited the Austrian plan and rushed to Rivoli. Napoleon also ordered Massena's division and some of his reserves to Rivoli, leaving the trusty General Pierre Augereau to watch Provera.

Meanwhile, the Austrian plan began to come apart on the field of battle. Although outnumbered, Joubert repulsed D'Alvintzy's lead columns on January 14. The battle resumed on the next day as both sides fed troops into the battle. Massena's division was split, with the smaller part peeled off to deal with the threat on the French left, while the other part took up a position on Joubert's left and repulsed another Austrian assault from the mountains. A timely cavalry action and fierce defense at the road defile further disconcerted the Austrian attack, and then two ammunition wagons blew up in one of the Austrian columns. D'Alvintzy's troops began to falter.

Meanwhile, more French divisions arrived, and Napoleon's fresh troops turned a final attack by D'Alvintzy into a bloody repulse and headlong catastrophe for the Austrians. The flanking column arrived to find itself trapped between Napoleon's arriving reserves and the now-victorious French that it was supposed to attack in the flank. This column was thrown into headlong retreat and lost hundreds of men who surrendered rather than be cut down as they fell back.

Augereau, meanwhile, let Provera get by him, but the French division besieging Mantua kept Provera and Würmser apart as Napoleon marched hard from Rivoli with two divisions to try to bag Provera. Provera was caught between these defenders, Napoleon, and Augereau on January 16 and surrendered with 5,000 troops; 2,000 had been lost from his original 7,000 in earlier battles crossing the Adige and around Mantua.

CONCLUSION

In two days of battle, the French inflicted 15,000 casualties upon D'Alvintzy's army, 22,000 if one adds Provera's column, ruining it for further offensive operations. Rivoli and its aftermath amounted to the most decisive French battle of the campaign. Napoleon had been very ably served by his subordinates, Masséna and Joubert in particular. Mantua's doom was sealed, and Würmser finally surrendered on February 2, 1797, to spare his men any further suffering and death. With the surrender of Mantua, Napoleon had destroyed the equivalent of another Austrian army. The Austrians now scrambled to defend their empire in the south, recalling Archduke Charles, their best general, from Germany to try to establish a defense against a French offensive.

Napoleon and his victorious army gave them no rest, and by spring, they were within several days' march of Vienna at Leoben, having pushed through or flanked every defensive position that Charles had attempted to establish with the makeshift forces he was given to command. An armistice was signed at Leoben (April 18), which eventually led to the peace of Campo Formio (October 17, 1797) between Austria and France, marking the first time in five years that the French were at peace with all their continental opponents. Rivoli, thus, contributed directly to the end of the War of the First Coalition (1792–1797).

Further Reading

Chandler, David. *The Campaigns of Napoleon.* New York: MacMillan, 1966.

Fremont-Barnes, Gregory, ed. *The Encyclopedia of the French Revolutionary and Napoleonic Wars*, Volume III. Santa Barbara, CA: ABC-CLIO, 2006.

42. The Nile

Date: August 1–2, 1798
Location: Aboukir Bay, near Alexandria Egypt

OPPONENTS

1. Great Britain
    Commander: Admiral Horatio Nelson
2. Republican France
    Commanders: Admiral Francois-Paul Brueys

BACKGROUND

The Battle of the Nile occurred off the coast of Egypt on the night of August 1–2, 1798. The Nile numbers among the most decisive naval engagements in modern history and remains a monument to the superior training, tactics, organization, and—especially—leadership of Britain's Royal Navy of the period. But it was also a military disaster for France, and particularly for General Napoleon Bonaparte.

France and Great Britain had already been at war for five years, and the war between France and most of the rest of Europe had gone back and forth. The stalemate had been broken in 1797 by the electrifying victories of a young French general in Italy named Napoleon Bonaparte. For much of 1797, Britain faced the French alone, including an invasion threat. The French had hoped to invade England using a combination of three fleets: the Spanish, Dutch, and French. However, British admirals had smashed the Spanish fleet at the Battle of Cape St. Vincent (February 1797) and the Dutch at Camperdown (October 1797). Fortuitously, a late-season hurricane destroyed many of the French bateaux that were being built up for the invasion of England in late 1797.

Napoleon proposed to the French government that he instead attack Great Britain by the indirect route, by seizing Malta and Egypt to threaten Britain's long and vulnerable lines of communication with her most important colonies in India via the Levant. The Directory, wanting to get rid of the political threat posed by Napoleon, agreed and dispatched him with over 44,000 troops and the entire French Mediterranean fleet to accomplish this task. Napoleon captured Malta and then

BATTLE OF THE NILE, AUGUST 1, 1798

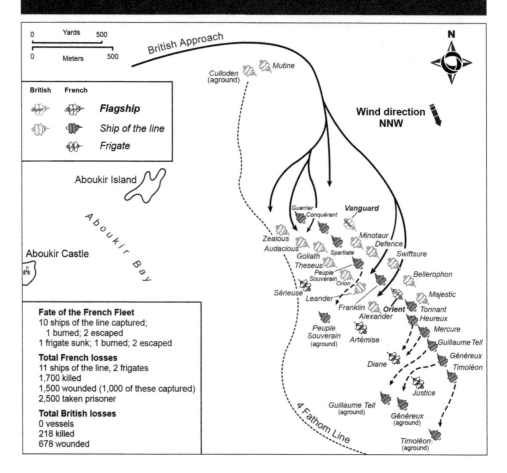

proceeded leisurely to Egypt, where he landed unmolested and defeated the local Mameluks at the famous Battle of the Pyramids (July 1798).

The French were opposed by the Royal Navy's Mediterranean fleet under Lord John Jervis, the victor at Cape St. Vincent. Admiral Horatio Nelson's heroic actions at Cape St. Vincent ensured his assignment to the critical theater of the war in 1798 under Jervis. Nelson sailed on *Vanguard* (74) in late March and set sail for the Gulf of Cadiz. Jervis's confidence in Nelson was unbounded. As soon as Nelson arrived to join the fleet on blockade duty of Cadiz, Jervis detached him on an independent command to keep an eye on the French fleet in Toulon. Jervis forwarded another eleven battleships to Nelson in May 1798, an unprecedented command for such a junior admiral which caused much grumbling in the many admirals senior to him without sea command. Jervis instructed Nelson to interdict Napoleon's invasion force, suspected to be bound for Egypt. Nelson's plan was simple: Intercept the invasion fleet and destroy Napoleon's army at sea.

Nelson's impatience almost did him in, but he was tenacious in pursuit of his quarry. Nelson had been off Toulon prior to his reinforcement but had sailed off, and then his small squadron was scattered by a storm. On May 19, Napoleon, escorted by the French fleet under Admiral Francois-Paul Brueys, had departed. Nelson was desperately short of frigates (he had only three) to provide him intelligence, and he decided Napoleon's destination was Naples. Napoleon instead went to Malta and conquered it, as previously noted.

Nelson realized his mistake and decided that Napoleon's next objective was Alexandria, Egypt. He rushed off, arriving off Alexandria on June 29, but he found nothing. Brueys and Napoleon had taken a different route via Crete and sailed far slower than Nelson imagined. Nelson missed a great chance by not waiting off Alexandria, second-guessing himself and sailing north to Turkey. While Nelson sailed north, the French arrived and began to debark their troops. It seemed that Nelson had lost the game of cat and mouse and missed a golden opportunity to destroy both a French army and a French fleet.

THE PLAN

Nelson did not give up. Off Sicily, he learned of his mistake and doubled back to Alexandria. Late on August 1, he arrived and found the transports empty, but Brueys's thirteen battleships and many smaller warships lay anchored close to shore, in the shallow and treacherous waters of Aboukir Bay. Brueys had unwisely sent half of his gun crews ashore to assist Napoleon with the land campaign. He also thought himself unassailable so close to shore. The final nail in his coffin was the late hour of the day. Surely Nelson would not attack in such dangerous waters in the dark? Nelson, demonstrating his intuitive grasp of the weakness of the French, instantly decided to attack.

Nelson had already planned for this moment and thus could decide almost instantaneously to attack the vulnerable French ships. Nelson had the complete confidence of his captains, and he returned the favor. He also had the advantage of probably having some of the best captains, ships, and crews in the entire Royal Navy under his command at this battle. The ten battleships that Jervis sent him under Sir Thomas Troubridge—who had served as a midshipman with Nelson—were later referred to by Nelson himself as "the finest Squadron that ever sailed the Ocean." Nelson instituted the policy of bringing his captains individually aboard his flagship to meet with him and to share their ideas.

Returning to the battle, Nelson had fourteen battleships to thirteen of the French, but the French had the heavier weight of gunnery (bigger ships and bigger guns). Upon sighting the enemy fleet, Nelson issued signals 53 and 54 from the Royal Navy's official signal books. The first simply alerted all the crews of his fleet to "prepare for battle." The second directed them to be ready to anchor at a moment's notice by the stern of the ship, an evolution requiring the rigging of a very large anchor and cable at the rear of each ship because anchoring by the stern was not something the ships were normally rigged for. In addition, it meant that each captain and his crew would have to do this under enemy fire. Its purpose was to stop the British ships so they could fire a full broadside into the French ships without waiting for the ships to come around and anchor by the bow. Further, each ship accepted the mission and executed without signaling back to Nelson for any further guidance. Neslon intended for this to take place in a single line of battle between the French ships and the open sea.

THE BATTLE

Nelson effectively gave his captains the initiative when he sent the signal to his ships at that evening "to form line as most convenient," leaving it to their discretion how to approach the French fleet because he was in the rear aboard the *Vanguard*. The execution was not without some hiccups, Captain Troubridge on *Culloden* ran aground just north of the French on the approach, but this also served to let the ships behind know where *not* to go. Several ships performed the anchoring maneuver badly and paid with heavy casualties as a result of being out of position. But Nelson's other captains served him well. The aggressive captain of the lead ship *Goliath* was Captain Sir Thomas Foley, who instantly made the decision to go behind the first French ships and inside the French line. About half the other captains followed his initiative, while Nelson signaled the remainder to follow the *Majestic* (seventy-four guns) on the northern side. This resulted in a double envelopment of the French ships in the first part of the line. Their mates farther down the line were anchored solid and could not help them.

To make matters worse, some of the French ships had not strung cable between their neighbors to counter the known British tactic of "breaking the line" and then shooting longitudinally into the aft and bows of the anchored French ships. Again, taking the local tactical initiative, several British ships of the line performed this maneuver, especially the *Leander* (fifty guns) and *Alexander* (seventy-four guns), dealing out further bloody devastation against the hapless French ships that were their targets. The night sky of Alexandria was lit up with the din and spectacle of burning French ships as Nelson pounded the French fleet to pieces as his ships proceeded down the line. Brueys's huge flagship *L'Orient* (120 guns), surrounded on two sides in this manner, blew up after absorbing incredible punishment, lighting up the night sky. Only Admiral Pierre Villeneuve in the rear escaped with two battleships and two frigates. The rest of the French fleet—including eleven battleships—was destroyed or taken.

Nelson, in the thick of the fighting as usual, received a nasty head wound. The battle continued through the night, although it was clearly won before midnight. The last two French ships surrendered around daybreak. Nelson had not lost a single ship and had fewer than 900 casualties, most of these in ships that had mishandled the anchoring maneuver. Meanwhile, the French losses numbered in the thousands.

CONCLUSION

Nelson had effectively checkmated Napoleon's strategy by stranding his army in Egypt. When Napoleon attempted to fight his way through Ottoman Turkish territory to gain passage to Europe, or even India, he failed at Acre and returned to Alexandria. In 1799, Napoleon abandoned his army and returned to France to take over the government in a *coup d'etat*. Many historians consider the Battle of the Nile Nelson's most important victory, strategically and tactically. However, for the French and Napoleon, it was a naval military disaster that nearly destroyed Napoleon's career.

Further Reading

Herman, Arthur. *To Rule the Waves: How the British Navy Shaped the Modern World*. New York: HarperCollins, 2004.

Hore, Captain Peter. *The Habit of Victory*. London: National Maritime Museum, 2005.

Knight, Roger. *The Pursuit of Victory: The Life and Achievement of Horatio Nelson*. New York: Basic Books, 2005.

43. Second Battle of Zürich

Date: September 25–26, 1799
Location: Zürich, Switzerland

OPPONENTS

1. Republic of France
    Commander: General de Division André Masséna
2. Empires of Russia and Austria
    Commander: General Alexander Rimsky-Korsakov

BACKGROUND

While Napoleon Bonaparte was away in Egypt, trying to attack Great Britain's line of communications to India and the east, a second coalition formed at the instigation of the British to challenge France in Europe. It came to include France's old enemy, the Austrians, along with, for the first time since the Russian Revolution broke out, the armies of Tsar Paul I of Russia.

The Austro-Russian armies took the offensive and rapidly reconquered many of the French gains made in Italy and Germany solidified by 1797. In Italy the legendary Marshal A. V. Suvorov led a combined Austro-Russian army that recaptured much of northern Italy after two bloody battles at the Trebbia River and then at Novi. In Switzerland, the combined forces were led by Archduke Charles of Austria, with a Russian corps of considerable size under General Alexander Rimsky-Korsakov approaching in support. In June 1799, Charles attacked the French at Zürich under the command of General de Division André Masséna, in the first battle for that city, and managed to force him to withdraw from the key high ground that dominated that city, the Zürichberg. However, Masséna escaped with his army intact.

It was at this point that the Austrians decided to pull Charles out of the theater with the bulk of his Austrian forces and send them to the middle Rhine to achieve

Austria's objectives on that front. Correspondingly, Suvorov's meddling in northern Italian politics resulted in orders being sent to transfer his Russian army to Switzerland to replace the forces taken north by Charles. By late June, Masséna had stabilized his position east of Zürich along the Aare and Limmat rivers and the Albis Mountains. He sensed that he had a window of opportunity for a counterstroke based on his opponent's lethargy. In the southern portion of his theater, an independent division of 12,000 troops under General Jacques Lecourbe operated east of Lucerne. Masséna made successful probing attacks to the east at Alstettin, and Lecourbe probed toward the critical St. Gotthard Pass, by which Suvorov would have to come north with his Russian troops once he left Italy after the Battle of Novi.

By August, Masséna was ready for more than tentative measures; he had Lecourbe move directly against the St. Gotthard Pass, guarded by one Austrian brigade. Lecourbe, as much an expert in mountain warfare as Masséna, seized the critical pass on August 18. Masséna had his forces, principally the divisions of Generals Nicholas Soult and Jean Lorge, demonstrate on the Limmat to distract Charles. Charles, who was preparing to leave the theater, assumed that offensives before Zürich and in the south must mean that the French left was weak; he attempted to throw a bridge across the Aare River on August 17, but this attempt was handily defeated by light artillery and Swiss riflemen from Masséna's reserves. Finally, other French forces further secured Masséna's right flank against the Austrians by capturing the town of Glarus to his southeast on August 29.

As August came to an end, Masséna found at his front approximately 48,000 Russians and Austrians, with Rimsky-Korsakov covering the front from the Rhine to Zürich and about 24,000 Austrians under General Frederick Hotze covering the northern shore of Lake Zürich and the Linth River. It was against this extended front that Masséna now massed. To the south, Lecourbe was directed to continue his own offensive toward the Grisons against the strung-out forces of Hotze, leaving only light forces covering the St. Gotthard Pass. Suvorov approached this pass with more than 21,000 of his Russians and an Austrian brigade under Auffenberg assigned to join his command once he forced the St. Gotthard Pass.

THE PLANS

Masséna had all the advantages of interior operational lines during this delicate period, but he had to act before Suvorov erupted from the St. Gotthard Pass on his flank and into Lecourbe's rear. He had also been reinforced considerably by General Jean Bernadotte, the new war minister for the Directory. Bernadotte also informed Masséna of an opportunity to attack after Masséna reported Charles's departure, leaving Rimsky-Korsakov with just his Russian troops to defend Zürich. By September 20, Masséna had resolved to attack in three different places: with his main army against Rimsky-Korsakov at Zürich, with Soult's division against Hotze on the Linth, and with Lecourbe, as already mentioned, toward the Grisons. His main effort at Zürich involved an operational deception against the widely deployed Russians on their right flank near the Rhine in order to get their attention, while he sent a column of 14,000 troops over the Limmat toward Zürich. At Zürich, he employed tactical deception by stealthily moving cannon and bridging elements directly opposite the city. The Russians and Austrians realized their vulnerability but stayed on the defensive to await the arrival of Suvorov.

THE BATTLE

The second Battle of Zürich began on September 25 with Masséna's cannon waking up Rimsky-Korsakov and his troops in the city, achieving both operational and tactical surprise. The crossing of the Limmat occurred without opposition, as Rimsky-Korsakov focused on the forces immediately to his front. The key to the battle was the seizure of the Zürichberg high ground, and Massena's main column did this at great cost, while at the same time, it seized the western suburbs. Rimsky-Korsakov desperately tried to retake the high ground but then moved his forces in front of the city, where it was savaged by the French artillery. By the end of the day, Rimsky-Korsakov had pulled back inside the city. Masséna offered the Russians the opportunity to evacuate the town without further bloodshed. Meanwhile, to the south, Soult had also achieved tactical surprise in crossing the Linth and eliminating any possibility of Hotze's Austrians coming to Rimsky-Korsakov's aid. The brave Hotze was killed at the beginning of this engagement.

Rimsky-Korsakov, learning of Hotze's death and Soult's success, oddly refused Masséna's offer to evacuate and resolved that night to retake both the suburbs and the Zürichberg, while he broke out with the rest of his army to the north (probably to save his many cannon). These attacks were initially successful but ultimately resulted in many more losses, as the French counterattacked and slaughtered the packed Russians as they retreated through the narrow streets of the city. Rimsky-Korsakov lost over one-third of his army (9,000 troops, including over 5,000 taken prisoner) and most of his cannon. The losses of the Austrians to the south were also heavy.

CONCLUSION

The results of the disaster of Zürich, as well as the other engagements north and south of the city, changed the entire dynamic of the War of the Second Coalition, not just the military situation in Switzerland. Masséna pressed his advantage after the battle and gave his enemies no rest. In the south, he had Soult link up with Lecourbe, and jointly they inflicted another 5,000 casualties on the leaderless Austrians, causing them to retreat. In the first week of October, Rimsky-Korsakov lost another 3,700 men in an ill-advised attempt to regain some of the initiative when he attacked the far left of the French line along the Rhine. After that, his force was no longer capable of offensive operations.

At the other end of the wavering Allied line in the north, held by the émigré corps of the Louis Joseph, Prince of Condé, at Lake Constance, Masséna continued his operations, taking Constance on October 8. Suvorov arrived after forcing the St. Gotthard Pass, only to find himself outnumbered and potentially cut off. He valiantly led his army of 21,000 men over the Alps in an epic retreat, but it took heavy casualties, especially from stragglers in the high mountain passes, and this force was ruined for use in further operations, just avoiding annihilation by three converging French columns. These defeats, along with the failure of a British-Russian expedition in Holland, led Tsar Paul to angrily pull out of the coalition. Now Britain and Austria fought on alone against the French. The overall plan to invade France faded into an impossibility, as Napoleon, just returned from Egypt, seized power in a coup. The Second Coalition lasted another two years, but its high point for victory had been immolated by the Russian catastrophe at Zürich.

Further Reading

Duffy, Christopher. *Eagles over the Alps: Suvorov in Italy and Switzerland, 1799.* Chicago: The Emperor's Press, 1999.

Ross, Steven T. *Quest for Victory: French Military Strategy, 1792–1799.* New York: A. S. Barnes and Company, 1973.

Shadwell, Lawrence, translator of the Swiss Narrative compiled from the writing of Archduke Charles, Baron Jomini et al. *Mountain Warfare: Illustrated by the Campaign of 1799 in Switzerland.* London: King & Company, 1875.

PART IV

Nineteenth-Century Military Disasters

44. Trafalgar

Date: October 21, 1805
Location: Cape Trafalgar, southwest of Cadiz, Spain

OPPONENTS

1. British
    Commander: Admiral Lord Horatio Nelson, Baron of the Nile
2. Franco-Spanish Combined Fleet
    Commanders: Admirals Pierre Villeneuve and Frederico Gravina

BACKGROUND

The Battle of Trafalgar was the culmination of a maritime campaign begun by Napoleon with the resumption of war with Great Britain in 1803. His strategic plan was to draw the British fleet away from the English Channel and then invade England and dictate terms to the British at the head of his *Grande Armee*, which numbered nearly 170,000 veteran troops. This would involve drawing Britain's greatest naval hero and the Mediterranean fleet away from the Channel long enough for the Spanish and French fleets to combine and escort Napoleon's army across the channel. The plan took real form in early 1805, when Admiral Pierre Villeneuve eluded Nelson's fleet blockading his fleet in Toulon and slipped out of the Mediterranean, with 6,400 troops, joining a portion of the Spanish fleet under Admiral Frederico Gravina. They crossed the Atlantic to threaten British colonies in the West Indies and managed to draw Nelson after them. However, poised on the edge of success, Napoleon's plan now came apart.

First, Nelson, upon arriving in the West Indies and finding Villeneuve had gone, dispatched a fast frigate to alert the British admiralty to the danger. The admiralty dispatched the squadron of Admiral Robert Calder to intercept the Franco-Spanish fleet. In a confused naval engagement off Cape Finisterre in northwest Spain (July 22), Villeneuve's nerve broke, and he retreated into port instead of proceeding into the channel to cover the crossing of Napoleon's army. Worse, the other French admirals, especially Admiral Joseph Ganteaume at Brest, failed to break out to join him, thus ensuring that even if he had proceeded north, the British squadrons under other commanders, such as Lord William Cornwallis and Calder, would probably still have defeated him.

Villeneuve then withdrew to Cadiz, where Nelson, now returned from the West Indies, blockaded him. Napoleon, disgusted by these events and now threatened by Britain's formation of a third coalition against him with Austria and Russia, marched east to face the new threat almost two months before the Battle of Trafalgar occurred. Nelson left his fleet there and returned to England for a short period to help defend Calder from an unjust court-martial, who had been surprised to find his victory over Villeneuve turned into a "defeat" by the press.

THE PLANS

When Nelson rejoined his fleet blockading the Franco-Spanish force off Cadiz in late September 1805, he convened a meeting with his subordinate commanding officers aboard his flagship HMS *Victory*. He had already sent a letter to all of them explaining his intention to attempt to trick Villeneuve into a battle. Once battle was imminent, he would attack with two columns of ships, with the intent to break the traditional battle line of the enemy into three groups: the van, the main body, and the rear. Of these groups, those in the van would be effectively unavailable for the initial phases of the fight because they would have to sail back into the wind (i.e., tack) to reach the battle, by which time Nelson intended to have defeated the other two groups of ships. In this way, Nelson would rectify any numerical superiority that the enemy might have, as well as deny him the ability to refuse battle with the entire fleet. Nelson explained all of this in further detail in person aboard his flagship to his captains.

Nelson reiterated his intent in a famous memorandum written after his conferences and dinners aboard the *Victory* on October 9. He outlined for his captains that he did not intend to form new lines of battle once they sighted Villeneuve's fleet. To take advantage of superior British seamanship and trap Villeneuve, he intended to waste no time forming up for battle, but rather his ships' positions—what was called their order of sail—would also be their order of battle. This would give him speed. Second, he wrote that "no captain can do very wrong if he places his Ship alongside that of an Enemy."

Villeneuve had no plan for the battle other than avoiding it. He was under strict orders by Napoleon to sail back into the Mediterranean with the entire combined fleet and then await further instructions once he arrived at Toulon. In fact, Napoleon intended to relieve him of command and had already sent his replacement, Vice Admiral Francois Rosily, to join the fleet in Cadiz. Villeneuve knew this, and that may have been the reason that he chose to sortie with the entire combined fleet of thirty-three battleships (ships with over fifty guns). On October 18, the wind blew favorably, and Villeneuve ordered his fleet to unmoor. On October 19, the first ships began to leave the harbor, although the wind occasionally died, which caused Villeneuve to have several of his battleships towed out of port. Nelson's frigates signaled the good news that Villeneuve was finally leaving port, bound for the Mediterranean.

THE BATTLE

Nelson continued to stalk Villeneuve the next day as the Frenchman proceeded east-southeasterly toward Gibraltar with the combined fleet; however, the pace of

BATTLE OF TRAFALGAR

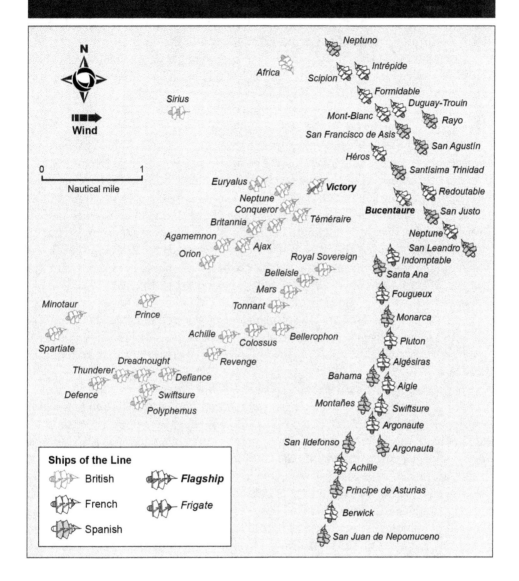

the French and Spanish advance was so slow that Nelson outran Villeneuve and had to bring his entire battle line around 360 degrees to fall back into a correct position vis-à-vis the combined fleet. Villeneuve by now had learned he was being stalked. Despite his numerical superiority at 7:30 a.m. on the morning of October 21, Villeneuve ordered his fleet to wear back toward Cadiz and began a gradual turn of the entire fleet back to port; this movement also gave him the correct disposition for battle based on the winds. He was literally running away from battle. This did not affect Nelson's plan appreciably—the only difference would be that Nelson's column would strike near the main body of the combined fleet's line, while that of Admiral Cuthbert Collingwood would now strike the rear. Nelson also employed tactical deception by having his own column feint toward the enemy van of ships to confuse them as to his real intention, and then he turned at the last possible moment toward Villeneuve's flagship (*Bucentaure*) in the main body. The result of this action was that the van was forced to maintain its line ahead and to delay its turning back to come to the aid of the rest of the fleet.

Nelson then added a final edge to his fleet's fighting mettle when he sent, sequentially, two significant signals. The first signal elicited a spontaneous outbreak of cheering throughout the fleet: "England expects every man will do his duty." He followed this with a signal for his captains: "Engage the enemy more closely." Cheering broke out again aboard the British ships.

The last minutes of the approach were harrowing, as the lead ships of each column traveled under the concentrated fire of the combined fleet. Nelson was on *Victory*, at the head of the northwestern column, and Collingwood was on *Royal Sovereign*, with the southeastern one (the French were heading north, back to port). Collingwood won the race, and *Royal Sovereign* crashed into the rear portion of the French-Spanish fleet just past noon. He had minimized his casualties by having his sailors lie down during the final minutes of the approach so he would have every man possible to work the guns and deliver the first devastating broadsides, simultaneously, into the ships on his left and right as he pierced Villeneuve's line. This tactic, combined with the excellent British gunnery, accounts for the extremely high casualties aboard the French and Spanish ships as the British cannonballs traveled the entire longitudinal expanse of their opponents' ships. The French and Spanish could only reply with the relatively few guns mounted on the bow and stern of their vessels.

The battle now became a melee, as Nelson's *Victory* plowed between Villeneuve's flagship *Bucentaure* and the battleship behind her, *Redoubtable*. The French gunners had had much better success against *Victory*, which lost many of her sails and had her helm shot away, and yet her momentum carried her ahead as planned. *Victory's* point-blank broadsides into the two French ships caused horrendous casualties. Not long after, a sharpshooter aboard *Redoubtable* sighted the bemedaled Nelson, who had refused to take cover below deck, and fired. The ball hit Nelson in the left shoulder and then ricocheted through his lung, finally lodging in his spine. This combination of wounds led to Nelson's slow, painful death. The *Redoubtable* crew now prepared to board the ailing *Victory*, but her boarding party was wiped out by a devastating broadside from the *Téméraire*, following in line behind *Victory*.

Much of the remainder of the battle followed this same pattern of devastating close combat, but in all cases, the British had the better of it, both up and down the line. Meanwhile, Villeneuve was frantically signaling his van, under the French admiral Pierre Dumanoir, to come about to assist in the battle. However, Dumanoir did not see the initial signals due to the smoke of battle and continued sailing toward Cadiz. It was only at 3 p.m. that he came about, and by this time, about fifteen ships of the combined fleet had struck their colors (surrendered), including Villeneuve aboard *Bucentaure*. Virtually all of them were blazing charnel houses full of dead and dying men. What remained of the French van, unable to affect the outcome of the battle, fled to Cadiz.

Naval Warfare in the Age of Sail

Warfare in the age of sail, after Lepanto, evolved rapidly due to four factors: finance, naval artillery developments, navigation, and ship design. Finance undergirds the other three, as well as providing the routine pay for the crews as the emerging nation-states of Europe built standing navies to go alongside their standing armies, especially the maritime nations of Spain, France, England, and the Netherlands. As for gunnery, it is well attested that as metallurgy and the Scientific Revolution developed every more reliable cannon and gunpowder, only those nations with wealth could develop them. Modern ship designs enabled larger and larger hulls that thus could carry more guns. Finally, the development of precise navigation via the sextant and accurate clocks allowed warships to undertake global navigation in support of the expansion of maritime trade by the European powers.

These developments led to a transformation in naval warfare from melees near land to engagements farther out to sea. By the mid-eighteenth century, the accepted method of warfare was for opposing fleets to form a line and sail by each other, blasting away. It also involved complicated sailing maneuvers to seize a downwind position that enabled a fleet to either accept battle or refuse it. However, even by the mid- to late eighteenth century, admirals such as Sir Edward Hawke and Baron Rodney of the Royal Navy of Great Britain were beginning to turn once again toward melee tactics that finally became standard by the time of the Battle of Trafalgar in 1805.

Not a single British vessel had been lost. Nelson died at around 4:30 p.m., but he did so with the knowledge that his men had won the most complete victory at sea ever obtained by a modern sailing fleet.

CONCLUSION

In total, the British captured ten French and ten Spanish ships in the battle; however, a subsequent storm damaged or sank many of them, and the British were able to salvage only four battleships and add them to the Royal Navy's order of battle. British casualties at Trafalgar numbered 449 killed (including Nelson) and 1,241 wounded. French and Spanish casualties, including prisoners, were almost ten times that of the British, including more than 4,000 killed. Several days later, four of the French ships that had escaped sortied from Cadiz and were intercepted, attacked, and captured by the British admiral Sir Richard Strachan. Thus, the Royal Navy gained eight battleships from the enemy as a result of Nelson's and Strachan's battles. French and Spanish sea power was effectively neutralized—for the remainder of the war, as it turned out. This caused Napoleon to adopt his ruinous economic blockade of Britain known as the *continental system,* which led to Napoleon's strategic errors in Spain, Portugal, and Russia and his eventual downfall.

Further Reading

Hore, Captain Peter. *The Habit of Victory.* London: The National Maritime Museum, 2005.

Knight, Roger. *The Pursuit of Victory: The Life and Achievement of Horatio Nelson.* New York: Basic Books, 2005.

Kuehn, John T. *Napoleonic Warfare: The Operational Art of the Great Campaigns.* Santa Barbara, CA: Praeger, 2015.

45. Jena–Auerstedt

Date: October 14, 1806
Location: Jena and Auerstedt, Germany

OPPONENTS

1. Prussia and Saxony

   Commanders: Charles William Ferdinand, Duke of Brunswick, Friedrich Ludwig, Prince of Hohenlohe, and General Ernst von Ruchel

2. France

   Commanders: The Emperor Napoleon and Marshal Louis Davout

BACKGROUND

Napoleon's decisive victory over the armies of Russia and Austria at Austerlitz in December 1805 led to the dissolution of the Third Coalition (Holy Roman Empire, Britain, and Russia). Rather than the period of peace he had anticipated following his decisive victory, Napoleon soon faced a Fourth Coalition (Prussia, Saxony, Great Britain, Russia, and Sweden). In August 1806, the Prussian king, Frederick William III, decided to go to war against Napoleon, though Prussia did not formally join the coalition until October of that year. Nevertheless, Saxony would be Prussia's only coalition partner in the upcoming battle.

The Prussian army had a reputation for being the paradigm army of Europe, and in a limited war, it was. Frederick the Great was the acknowledged master of limited war, but his successors were not equal to him, and the Prussian army had fallen into disrepair. Many of the generals were in their sixties and seventies and well past their prime, but they were of noble lineage and maintained their positions by birthright. On the other hand, the French Revolution brought about a new kind of army—an army of patriotic citizens, not oppressed subjects. Napoleon used that army to unleash a new kind of war on Europe: total war. The French army under Napoleon was more agile and mobile than the other armies of Europe and handily defeated them, even when outnumbered. Nonetheless, the Prussian army took the field in 1806 confident that the army of Frederick the Great would easily defeat the upstart Napoleon.

THE BATTLE

Rather than waiting for the Russian army to augment his force, the Prussian king decided to go on the offensive to oust the French from his territory. He divided the Prussian army into three forces. The main force, of nearly 61,000, was under the command of the seventy-one-year-old Duke of Brunswick. Frederick Wilhelm III colocated his headquarters with this force near Auerstedt. Outside Jena, Friedrich Ludwig, the Prince of Hohenlohe, commanded 38,000, backed up by another 15,000 under the command of Ruchel, located in Weimar. This arrangement put the Prussian army in position to protect Berlin or to strike at the French army, located near Bamberg. Satisfied with this disposition, the Kaiser held several councils of war to formulate a plan, but no definitive plan came out of them.

Napoleon, anxious to bring Prussia to heel, was not willing to stand on the defense and wait for the Prussians—he intended to destroy them before the Russians could intervene. To do this, he would advance the Grand Armee along three routes to position it between the Prussian army and Berlin, forcing the Prussians to attack. Following a couple of minor clashes with the Prussian army, which caused some panic among the Prussians, Napoleon decided to confront his enemy along the Salle River, near the town of Jena. The main body of the Grand Armee, 96,000 men, would attack there, while Napoleon's two remaining corps continued northeast to locate the rest of the Prussian army.

On the morning of October 14, Napoleon's main force attacked the flanks of Hohenlohe's smaller force at Jena. Hohenlohe believed the main French army was continuing toward Berlin and that he was only facing a flank guard, so he placed 8,000 men between the villages of Clausewitz and Cospeda. Napoleon's V Corps, under Marshal Jean Lannes, attacked the Prussian flank at Clausewitz while, simultaneously, the VII Corps, led by Marshal Pierre Augereau, attacked the opposite flank, anchored on Cospeda. After hard fighting, both villages were captured. To keep up the momentum, Napoleon committed a third corps, the IV, commanded by Marshal Jean de Dieu Soult, and the combined weight of the three corps pushed the Prussians back to a second line. The Prussians halted the French advance along this second line.

By now, Hohenlohe realized he was facing more than a security force; he called for Ruchel's force to come forward from Weimar to augment his forces. Unfortunately for Hohenlohe, Marshal Michel Ney and his VI Corps arrived and Napoleon launched another assault before Ruchel's force could arrive. Desperate, Hohenlohe was forced to commit the last of his reserves. Sensing his enemy's weakness, Napoleon characteristically seized the moment and launched Marshal Joachim Murat's Cavalry Reserve. The Prussian lines broke, and the soldiers fled the field. Amid this chaos, Ruchel arrived with his 15,000 men and immediately attacked the French, but his force was handily defeated. By 4 p.m., the entire Prussian force at Jena was in full retreat, and the Battle of Jena was over. More important, Napoleon believed that he had defeated the main Prussian army and the war might be over. However, one of his corps was already waging a desperate fight against the main Prussian force.

The night before, October 13, Napoleon directed Marshal Louis Davout to take the 28,000 men of his III Corps through the town of Auerstedt before turning south to attack what he believed to be the main force, near Jena, from the rear. Napoleon suggested that Davout might be able to march his corps along with Marshal Jean Bernadotte's I Corps. However, Bernadotte elected not to support Davout. Bernadotte's decision would become a point of contention after the battle. The next morning, Davout's III Corps crossed the Saale and headed toward Auerstedt. On the way, they were attacked by the 52,000 men under the command of the Duke of Brunswick. Davout kept his head and centered his defense around the village of Hassenhausen.

Throughout the morning, Davout's three divisions defeated the numerous but uncoordinated Prussian cavalry charges and infantry assaults. By midday, Davout, sensing that the Prussians were finished, ordered his corps to advance, and the Prussians retreated. The Battle of Auerstedt was over. Fortunately for the Prussians, Davout did not possess any cavalry to exploit his success, and they slipped away. Napoleon did not believe the first reports that Davout had single-handedly defeated the Prussians at Auerstedt. However, as he assessed the situation and realized it was true, he began to heap praise on Davout, making him the Duke of Auerstedt and giving his corps the honor of being the first into Berlin. On the other hand, Bernadotte was nearly court-martialed for failing to support either Napoleon or Davout.

CONCLUSION

After the battle, the Prussian army disintegrated as Napoleon consolidated his gains. On October 24, the Grande Armee, led by Davout's III Corps, marched through Berlin. There were still more battles to come before the Fourth Coalition was defeated, but Napoleon had eliminated a major member of the coalition and shattered the aura of invincibility around the Prussian army.

In a matter of hours, a more modern and battle-experienced French army crushed the paradigm army of Europe. For the Prussians, the defeat signaled a long-overdue need to reform the army. Many of the reformers, such as Gerhard von Scharnhorst and Carl von Clausewitz, were present at the battle. With the support of Frederick Wilhelm III, the reformers rebuilt the Prussian army on some radical notions for the time. Among these reforms was the notion of promotion on merit, universal military service, and the establishment of military academies to train and educate staff officers. The result was that, seven years later, the Prussian army would participate in the final defeat of Napoleon and be on its way to becoming the paradigm army of Europe once again.

Further Reading

Chandler, David. *Napoleon's Marshals.* New York: Macmillan, 1987.

Clark, Christopher. *Iron Kingdom: The Rise and Downfall of Prussia, 1600–1947.* New York: Penguin, 2007.

Hurtoulle, Francois Guy, and Andre Jouineau. *Jena, Auerstaedt: The Triumph of the Eagle.* Paris: Histoire and Collections, 1998.

Petre, F. Lorraine. *Napoleon's Conquest of Prussia 1806.* London: Kessinger Publishing, 2010.

46. Tippecanoe

Date: November 7, 1811
Location: Near the confluence of the Wabash and Tippecanoe rivers

OPPONENTS

1. United States
    Commander: William Henry Harrison
2. Tecumseh's Confederation
    Commander: Tenskwatawa ("The Prophet")

BACKGROUND

The 1795 Treaty of Greenville between the Native Americans and the United States was supposed to have settled the ongoing dispute over land in the Old Northwest territory. However, as so often happened in U.S. history, the settlers' desire for land was greater than the desire for peace with the Native Americans. The newly appointed governor of the Indiana Territory, William Henry Harrison, negotiated many land deals with the local tribes to help keep the peace, and his efforts culminated in the Treaty of Fort Wayne in 1809. But not all the tribal leaders were pleased with the treaty, which ceded approximately three million acres to the United States. The most vocal among them was Tecumseh, a Shawnee chieftain.

Tecumseh and his brother Tenskwatawa, who was known as "The Prophet," were the primary leaders behind a movement encouraging the Native American tribes to return to their ancestral ways. The brothers established a settlement at the confluence of the Wabash and Tippecanoe rivers that came to be known as "Prophetstown." Tecumseh traveled among the tribes, encouraging them to join his resistance movement at Prophetstown. Few took him up on his offer, especially among those who had signed the Treaty of Fort Wayne. Tecumseh next took his grievances directly to the territorial governor.

Meeting with Harrison in 1810, Tecumseh demanded that Harrison nullify the new treaty. Harrison refused. Tecumseh left the meeting warning Harrison that the settlers should not attempt to enter any of the lands covered by the treaty. Behind the scenes, but directly affecting the negotiations, was a growing trade dispute

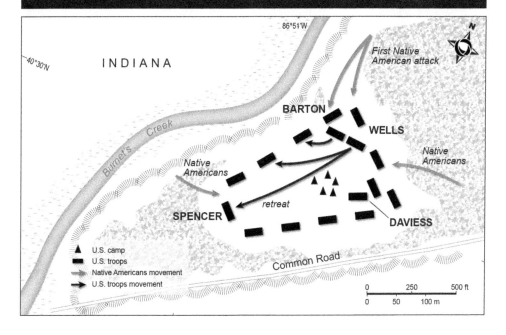

between the United States and Great Britain. Hoping to secure Native American support in case of a war with the United States, the British were encouraging Tecumseh and his war faction. Tecumseh tried to use this as leverage against Harrison, threatening to ally with the British. Harrison, who would not be cowed, still refused Tecumseh's demands.

In August of the following year, Tecumseh met once more with Harrison, but neither side would budge, and the meeting ended without settling the dispute. Following the meeting, Tecumseh resumed his recruiting drive, while Harrison left to see to territorial business in Kentucky. John Gibson, the acting territorial governor, got word of an impending attack by the Shawnee and immediately recalled Harrison and called out the local militias. Harrison returned in time to take command of the expedition. Along with authorization from Washington, D.C., to use whatever force was necessary to bring the Shawnee confederation into line, he arrived with a force of U.S. army regulars. After procuring supplies, Harrison led his force of 600 Indiana militia, 100 Kentucky volunteers, and 250 regulars toward Prophetstown. Along the way, they stopped to build a fort, Fort Harrison, near Terre Haute and waited for more supplies before continuing their march on October 29.

As they approached Prophetstown on November 6, a representative of Tenskwatawa met Harrison and his force, requesting a truce so that the two sides could meet the next day. Harrison agreed but was wary of intentions. He camped his forces on the high ground between the Wabash and Tippecanoe rivers. Burnett Creek was on one side of the campsite and a steep embankment on the other. Harrison arranged his command in a box formation on the hill, with his regulars inside the box as a reserve. Even though he suspected that the Shawnee might attack that night, Harrison believed that the terrain afforded his men sufficient protection, so he did not order any improvements to the defenses. However, he posted sentries around the perimeter.

It was a wise decision. Encouraged by Tenskwatawa and his assurances of casting spells to protect them from the U.S. soldiers' guns, the warriors headed out in the early-morning darkness of November 7 to attack the camp.

THE BATTLE

Around 4 a.m., the first Shawnee warriors struck the north end of the camp. Return fire from the sentries alerted the rest of the camp. As the half-awake defenders scrambled to their fighting positions, the Shawnee suddenly attacked from all sides. The determined and motivated warriors had some initial success at the southern end against an Indiana militia named the Yellow Jackets, killing the militia commander. However, a bayonet charge by a detachment of the regulars pushed the Shawnee back and restored the line. At about the same time, a second charge by the Shawnee hit the northern end of the perimeter. The results were similar. The aggressive attack by the Shawnee pushed the militia back, only to face a determined counterattack by the regulars held in reserve in the middle of the perimeter.

For two hours, the Shawnee repeatedly charged the soldiers and militia, only to be repulsed by counterattacks. As the sun began to come up, they were running low on ammunition and began to disengage. Harrison directed a final charge by his dragoons to keep the pressure on the withdrawing Shawnee. Eventually, the dragoons broke off their attack and pulled back to the camp. Meanwhile, the warriors returned to Prophetstown to confront Tenskwatawa. Feeling betrayed, the agitated warriors blamed Tenskwatawa for the disaster, but he assured them that he could cast more powerful spells that would make them successful in another attack on the camp. The warriors (perhaps wisely) refused to listen and elected to leave Prophetstown before the soldiers could arrive.

For his part, Harrison was not sure if or when Tecumseh might arrive with reinforcements, so he decided to remain in place, preferring to improve his defenses than getting caught out by Tecumseh. The rest of the day was uneventful, and the next morning, Harrison sent out a small group to reconnoiter the Shawnee village. All they found was one elderly woman who was too feeble to leave with the rest of the tribe. Harrison ordered his men to raze Prophetstown to deny its future use by the Shawnee. The soldiers took time to bury their dead and evacuated their wounded back to Fort Harrison. On November 9, the campaign was effectively over when the majority of the militia troops were released from duty.

CONCLUSION

During the battle, Harrison's command suffered thirty-seven killed and another twenty-five wounded. The Shawnee casualties are not certain but are estimated at fifty killed and another seventy-five wounded. Nonetheless, initial reports were not clear if the battle was a victory, and it took some time for information about it to make the newspapers. Regardless, the battle weakend Tecumseh's confederation, and the disgraced Tenskwatawa lost influence among the Shawnee. However, the defeat at Tippecanoe did not stop attacks on the settlers in the Indiana Territory. As word of the battle spread back east, many placed blame on the British for inciting the Native Americans and began calling for a war with Great Britain. This sentiment would contribute to the start of the War of 1812. For his efforts, Harrison came out the big winner, and during his successful bid for president in 1840, his campaign slogan was "Tippecanoe and Tyler Too" (referring to John Tyler, Harrison's vice president) to remind voters of his role in the battle.

Further Reading

Jortner, Adam. *The Gods of Prophetstown: The Battle of Tippecanoe and the Holy War for the American Frontier.* New York: Oxford University Press, 20111.

Langguth, A.J. *Union 1812: The Americans Who Fought the Second War of Independence.* New York: Simon and Schuster, 2006.

Owens, Robert M. *Mr. Jefferson's Hammer: William Henry Harrison and the Origins of American Indian Policy.* Norman: University of Oklahoma Press, 2007.

47. Leipzig

Date: October 15–18, 1813
Location: Leipzig, Saxony (central Germany)

OPPONENTS

1. French Empire

> Commander: Emperor Napoleon I

2. Allied powers (Prussia, Russia, Sweden, and Austria)

> Commanders: Tsar Alexander I, King Frederick William III, Emperor Francis I, Crown Prince Carl Johan Bernadotte, and Prince Karl Schwarzenberg

BACKGROUND

After the destruction of the bulk of French military power in Russia in 1812, Napoleon dashed back to Paris to create a new army, composed of raw conscripts, sailors, levees from the armies in Spain, and levees from his remaining allies in Germany, Italy, and Poland. By the spring of 1813, he was able to meet the advancing allied armies in the southern part of Saxony, south of Leipzig, near the village of Grossgorschen (Lutzen). Here, his young conscripts, under his personal command, delivered a sharp check on the combined Russian-Prussian army, driving it back toward Lusatia and Silesia. In May 1813, he defeated that army again at Bautzen but could not capitalize on his victory; he agreed to an armistice over the summer that would allow him to further rest, train, and equip his army, especially his cavalry. During the armistice, Napoleon rejected allied terms for peace, which caused the Austrians and Swedes to join in the Sixth Coalition with Russia, Prussia, and Great Britain against him. The allies adopted a Fabian strategy known as the Trachenberg Protocol (from a meeting held at Trachenberg, in Prussian territory). The agreement was to avoid battle with forces commanded by Napoleon and instead battle his flank forces, commanded by Marshals Nicolas Oudinot, Michel Ney, and Etienne MacDonald. They were positioned in three major armies surrounding Napoleon's central position in Saxony, based in the cities of Dresden and Leipzig.

When the main Austrian-Russian-Prussian force of over 250,000 fought with Napoleon at Dresden (August 26–27)—in contravention of the agreement—it was badly beaten, but this setback was counterbalanced by defeats of Napoleon's generals at Grossbeeren (Oudinot), the Katzbach (MacDonald), Kulm (General Dominique Vandamme), and Dennewitz (Ney). From that point on, Napoleon marched back and forth as the coalition slowly tightened the noose, finally marching on Napoleon's rear from two directions. By October 14, they had managed to cut off part of Napoleon's army in Dresden and cornered the rest of it in the general vicinity of Leipzig. Napoleon could either retreat or fight—he chose to fight.

THE PLAN

Napoleon had decided to try to fight the main Allied Armies to his south and east, under Prince Karl Schwarzenberg and Barclay de Tolly (almost 280,000 troops) before the armies of Gebhard von Blücher, Crown Prince Carl Johan Bernadotte, and Count Levin Bennigsen (leading Russian troops) could arrive, thus hopelessly outnumbering him. Napoleon had left Marshal Auguste Marmont's corps in the north, perhaps to be joined by the corps of General Jean Reynier, as an insurance policy to hold Blücher's 85,000 troops at bay. He estimated that the main fighting would be over before Bernadotte and Bennigsen arrived with another 155,000 fresh troops. Tactically, he was counting on the separation of the main allied armies by various rivers to allow him to do what he had done at Dresden—remain on the defensive in certain areas while conducting an offensive drive against one formation at a time. This would allow him to destroy that component and then confront the others in turn.

The allies' plan developed slowly and conformed to the precombat desire to eventually concentrate all the armies in one place and time and fight Napoleon, possibly with his army cut off, in more like a siege. To this end, they hoped to get troops along Napoleon's line of retreat and managed to get one Austrian corps across the Elster and to his rear prior to the beginning of his main offensive against them. Three of their five armies were not under the control of the main command under Schwarzenberg, and so they marched and moved according to their various commanders' preferences. Blücher advanced far more aggressively than they expected, while Bernadotte did so more cautiously. As for Bennigsen, he adhered to the timetable provided to him and only appeared on the last two days of the battle.

THE BATTLE

The allies had 1,500 cannon—over twice Napoleon's number. The battle was, in many ways, a microcosm of the entire fall campaign. Napoleon had success in some areas, but in others, his lieutenants were bested, or the enemy behaved in ways that unhinged the careful timing needed for Napoleon's admittedly risky plan to work. The battle actually began on October 15 with a gigantic cavalry action on Napoleon's southern flank. This allowed Napoleon time to concentrate the bulk of his army and decide that the key to the battle would be in the south against Schwarzenberg's unwieldy mass (200,000 men) on the left and Barclay's army (75,000) on the right. On the next day, Napoleon furiously attacked both these forces in turn but was forced to halt his success against them by diverting troops to deal with the Austrian corps in his rear that were attacking him on the western side of the Elster River. This surprise forced him to divert reserves that might have allowed him to take advantage of his victory in the southeast.

The second element that unhinged Napoleon's tactical plan was Blücher's aggressive offensive into the northern suburbs around Mockern on October 16. Marmont's troops fought furiously, but they were driven back, and again Napoleon had to divert troops meant to help him cap his success in the south and in destroying the Austrian corps in his rear. By the end of October 16, the fighting had died down.

Napoleon had reopened his avenue of retreat but was surrounded on three sides. He further exacerbated his situation by sending envoys to the allies to propose an armistice, which strengthened their somewhat-shaken resolve to press the battle.

October 17, the third day of the battle, saw the Coalition armies finally establish communications with each other and seal off Leipzig from three sides as mentioned. Napoleon's position looked like a *U* on its side with the mouth facing west, across the Elster River to safety. Most of the day was spent with the French conducting skillful retreats and the allies following as they brought up the armies of Bernadotte and Bennigsen. With the arrival of these forces, Napoleon realized he was only buying time to secure his retreat. He probably made his decision to retreat soon after the allies rejected his armistice proposal and his scouts reported the fresh troops arriving from the east (Bernadotte's in particular). He was also running low on ammunition, especially for his artillery. Napoleon's plan now was to escape with the bulk of his combat forces—which were still in relatively good condition—and attempt to establish a defensive line on the other side of the Thuringian Mountains, and perhaps even along the Rhine.

What happened on October 18, which began in a promising way for Napoleon with an effective defense all along the front, sealed this battle as a military disaster. In some of the earlier fighting, some of Napoleon's German cavalry units had defected to the allies. Napoleon had gotten more than half his army across the key bridge over the Elster leading down the narrow causeway when a confluence of factors caused chaos. Napoleon crossed the bridge and directed that it not be blown up until the other corps still defending got across. However, the officer assigned to this duty became distracted by the sounds of German defectors from Baden and Saxony firing at their retreating French comrades. While this officer was absent, a shaken French corporal blew up the bridge—the only means of escape—while

---

The Trachenberg Plan

With Napoleon's victories in the spring of 1813 at the battles of Gross-Goerschen Lützen) and Bautzen, the leaders of Prussia, Russia, and Austria realized that they needed an overall strategy to defeat him. They met at the castle of Trachenberg in the domain of Prussia in the summer of 1813 during an armistice with Napoleon to discuss this plan. On July 12, their representatives signed the Convention of Trachenberg, which agreed that none of the main armies would fight Napoleon singly, and instead retreat if he confronted them, while the others attacked his flanks. Authorship of this basic plan has been claimed variously by Marshal Bernadotte (Sweden), Gerhard Scharnhorst (Prussia), and Joseph Radetzky (Austria). What is likely is that the original convention was taken to Radetzky and modified in discussions with the Prussian chief of staff General August von Gneisenau.

In this plan, the basic formulation of avoiding battle with Napoleon directly was maintained, but it modified the size of the various field armies, especially the Prussian field army commanded by Marshal Gebhardt von Blücher and Gneisenau. The plan also specified that the flank armies were to engage those armies not commanded by Napoleon, with the hope that eventually all the armies would make the "enemy camp the point of rendezvous."[1] This is generally what happened in Napoleon's defeat that fall at Leipzig.

1. John T. Kuehn, *Napoleonic Warfare* (Santa Barbara, CA: Praeger, 2015), 215–216.

French troops were still on it. The French army east of the river fell apart. Marshal MacDonald managed to save himself by swimming across, but the Polish marshal, Prince Poniatowski, drowned in his attempt, while two other corps commanders, Reynier and Jacques Lauriston, were captured.

CONCLUSION

The French lost over 38,000 casualties in the actual fighting and another 30,000 were captured along with 300 cannon—the worst disaster for Napoleon since the Russian retreat. The allies did not come off lightly themselves, losing 52,000 casualties. Napoleon's loss of 30,000 veterans on the last day of the battle proved a bitter blow that would haunt him in 1814, when he tried to fight off the huge allied armies with teenage conscripts and what was left of his Imperial Guard. This decisive victory by the allies caused them to decide against any peace with Napoleon, which eventually led to the emperor's abdication and exile to the island of Elba later that year.

Further Reading

Chandler, David G. *The Campaigns of Napoleon*. New York: MacMillan, 1966.

Kuehn, John T. *Napoleonic Warfare: The Operational Art of the Great Campaigns*. Santa Barbara, CA: Praeger, 2015.

Leggiere, Michael V. *Napoleon and the Struggle for Germany: The Franco-Prussian War of 1813*. Cambridge: Cambridge University Press, 2015.

48. The Alamo

Date: February 23–March 6, 1836
Location: San Antonio, Texas

OPPONENTS

1. Texas rebels

    Commanders: Colonels William Barret Travis, James Bowie, and Davy Crockett

2. Republic of Mexico

    Commander: General Antonio López de Santa Anna

BACKGROUND

The Battle of the Alamo was one of the decisive battles during the Texas Revolution. The Texians (residents of Mexican Texas) were in a rebellion over the increasingly centralist policies of Antonio López de Santa Anna after he seized power in Mexico in 1832. By 1835, the federalist Constitution of 1824 was repealed, to be replaced by a unitary republic. One of Santa Anna's major concerns was the influx of illegal immigrants from the United States, so he outlawed immigration, along with abolishing slavery; however, this did nothing to stop immigrants from crossing the border. Despite concessions made by Santa Anna in what he hoped would calm the situation, the Texians put out a call for volunteers to come to their aid.

Santa Anna was not ready to face a civil war, nor could he afford to lose the territory of Tejas. In September 1835, he sent his brother-in-law, General Martin Perfecto de Cos, with 500 soldiers to Tejas to restore order. Throughout Tejas, the call went out for the settlers to form militias to defend themselves.

By late October, after a series of unsuccessful skirmishes with the Texians, Cos and his forces found themselves isolated in San Antonio de Bexar. Rather than surrender, Cos elected to defend the town, leaving the Texians with little choice other than to lay siege to Bexar. Eventually, the Texians grew tired of the siege. As winter closed in and rations dwindled, many of the volunteers returned home. On December 4, the Texian commander himself considered lifting the siege and returning in the spring. Rejecting this plan, a group of soldiers instead entered the city, and after four days of house-to-house fighting, the Mexicans retreated to the Alamo mission outside Bexar. Believing they were surrounded, Cos and his soldiers surrendered, promising never to fight the Texians again. Most Texians believe the war was over, and the militias began to stand down.

Santa Anna, displeased by this turn of events in Tejas, assembled an army of 6,000, mostly recruits, to put down the rebellion once and for all. Before departing, Santa Anna requested that the Mexican Congress declare any foreigner fighting for the rebellion to be pirates. By early nineteenth-century custom, captured pirates could face summary execution. With that, Santa Anna led his soldiers into Tejas. He led the main force directly to Bexar, while one of his subordinates, General Jose de Urrea, led a smaller force along the Gulf Coast. Poorly provisioned, Santa Anna's march to Bexar was beset by record low temperatures and attacks by Commanches before reaching Bexar in February.

After the Texians seized Bexar in December, approximately 100 soldiers were left to defend the city. At the news of Santa Anna's incursion, the commander of the Alamo, Colonel James C. Neill, requested more troops. However, there was not much that the fledgling Texas government could provide. Instead, the newly appointed commander of the Texian army, General Sam Houston, sent Colonel Jim Bowie with thirty men to recover the artillery pieces at the makeshift fort and then destroy it. After meeting with Neill, Bowie agreed that the Alamo could serve as a deterrent to Santa Anna and give the Texian army more time to prepare. In early February, Colonel William Travis arrived with thirty soldiers, followed a few days later by a small band of volunteers led by former congressman and frontier legend Davy Crockett. Neill left on February 11 to appeal to the Texian government for more men and supplies. After Neill's departure, Bowie and Travis divided command of the Alamo.

In the meantime, Santa Anna's men were closing in on Bexar, and on February 23, a Texian sentinel reported Mexican soldiers approaching the city. The locals fled the area as the defenders gathered what supplies they could and retreated behind the walls of the Alamo. By late afternoon, nearly 2,000 Mexican soldiers occupied Bexar. Santa Anna had a blood-red flag, representing no quarter, raised for the defenders to see. Travis replied to Santa Anna's threat by firing his largest cannon in the direction of Bexar, and the battle for the Alamo officially commenced.

One of the most dramatic battles of the Texas Revolution occurred at the Alamo in 1836. (National Archives)

THE BATTLE

The Mexicans' first order of business was to deploy their artillery. Santa Anna's gunners positioned their pieces about 1,000 feet opposite of the east, south, and southeast walls of the fort. Over the next several days, the sides engaged in an artillery duel until Travis, not knowing how long the siege might last, ordered his gunners to conserve their powder.

During the first week, along with the artillery duel, several smaller skirmishes took place between the Mexican and the Alamo defenders. These primarily were over some wooden huts near the Alamo walls that Travis wanted destroyed to prevent the Mexicans from using them for cover during an assault. After the temperature dropped some more, there was a brief fight over firewood. Nonetheless, the Texians usually got the better of these engagements, bolstering their morale.

After Bowie became incapacitated on February 24, the exact cause is unclear, Travis assumed overall command of the Alamo. From the beginning of the siege, he sent out couriers requesting men and supplies. One of his letters, sometimes referred to as the "Victory or Death" letter, not only captured the imagination of the Texians throughout Tejas, but also garnered support for their cause in the United States. Despite the calls for reinforcements, few were forthcoming. On February 27, the last significant number of reinforcements arrived when thirty-two men from Gonzales made it through the Mexican lines to join the defenders.

Unknown to Travis, the defenders of another mission at Goliad did attempt to relieve the Alamo. Colonel James Fannin, the commander of the Goliad garrison, began marching his command to Bexar to help Travis. On February 26, Fannin led over 300 soldiers, along with four cannon and some supply wagons, toward Bexar. After traveling no more than a mile, Fannin halted and decided to return to Goliad. Fannin and his men would face a fate similar to the Alamo defenders when they surrendered to General Urrea's forces on March 20. Seven days later, Fannin and his men were marched out of Goliad and executed.

In the meantime, Santa Anna was steadily receiving reinforcements. On February 24, 600 Mexican soldiers under the command of General Joaquin Ramirez y Sesma arrived at Bexar. About a week later, 1,000 more Mexican soldiers entered the city. By the time of the final assault, Santa Anna would have over 3,000 men under his command, compared to the approximately 185 soldiers and volunteers behind the walls of the Alamo.

With the arrival of the last set of reinforcements, Santa Anna wanted to launch an immediate attack on the fort. His subordinates talked him out of it, suggesting they await the arrival of their heavy cannon in a few days. That same day, a woman came to Santa Anna to negotiate a surrender. Some sources suggest this woman may have been Juana Navarro Alsbury, Bowie's cousin-in-law. Regardless, Santa Anna was in no mood to accept the surrender of the rebels, and her efforts proved fruitless. On March 5, Santa Anna informed his subordinates that the final assault would begin the next day.

It was that same day that one the greatest Alamo legends may or may not have taken place. Legend has it that Travis, expecting the final battle for the Alamo to take place any day, gathered his men together and drew a line in the sand with his saber. He then asked those willing to fight and possibly die for the Texian cause to cross the line. The authenticity of the story is in doubt, but one of the survivors, Susannah Dickinson, later recalled that Travis offered any man who wanted to the chance to leave.

Throughout the night of March 5–6, the Mexican soldiers prepared for the early-morning assault. Santa Anna was going to send four columns against the fort—one each to the northwest corner, the north wall, the east wall, and the wooden wall near the chapel. The front ranks were equipped with ladders and other tools to breach the walls. A total of 500 cavalry troops would stand off around the Alamo to catch any defenders who tried to escape. Hoping to catch the Texians asleep, Santa Anna refused to begin the attack with any preparatory fires from his artillery. He also kept 400 soldiers in reserve under his control in Bexar.

Moving quietly in tightly packed columns, the Mexicans began their advance at 5:30 a.m. The Mexicans quickly killed the sleeping sentries and continued toward the waiting walls. The first intimation that the Mexicans were attacking is when the sleeping Texians awoke to the shouts of "Viva Santa Anna!" Now fully alert, the defenders quickly moved to their positions and began engaging the approaching columns. The muskets of the Texians easily outranged the Brown Bess muskets of the Mexicans, and the Mexicans began taking casualties as they approached the walls. However, the press from the soldiers behind them kept the front ranks moving forward.

As the Mexicans tried to breach or climb the walls, the Texians easily picked them off. After a few shots from the cannon loaded with rocks and small pieces of metal, the Mexicans withdrew a short distance to regroup. Unfortunately, Travis was one of the first casualties in the first assault. Despite the loss of Travis, the defenders remained unshaken and repelled the second Mexican attempt. A short time later, the Mexican soldiers, urged on by their commanders, made a third attempt. This time, Texian fire unintentionally channeled three of the columns toward the north wall. The Mexican soldiers found the going easier here and began climbing the wall. After overpowering the defenders, the first soldiers over the wall opened a gate, and more rushed inside. The Texians on the south wall turned their cannon on the Mexicans breaching the north wall. However, this left the south wall unprotected, and the Mexicans breached that. At this point, the Texians retreated into the barracks and chapel. Outside, the Mexican cavalry ran down and killed a few Texians who were trying to get away.

Meanwhile, inside the compound, the Mexicans, giving no quarter, were killing the last of the Texians in the open areas. In front of the chapel, Davy Crockett and his Tennessee Volunteers engaged the Mexicans in hand-to-hand combat before succumbing to superior numbers. The fate of Crockett is in dispute. Legend has it that he went down swinging his musket like a club; other sources say he surrendered and Santa Anna had him executed. Regardless, Crockett and his men were among the last to fall before the fighting shifted to the barracks. The Mexicans methodically cleared the low and long barracks room by room, aided by the Texian cannon they captured. It was in one of these rooms that Jim Bowie was either bayoneted or shot as he lay in his sickbed. The interior of the chapel was the last area left for the Mexicans to clear. The Mexicans turned one of the captured cannon on the doors and blew them open. The Mexican soldiers rushed in, and after a brief skirmish, the last of the Texian defenders fell.

CONCLUSION

After the battle, Santa Anna had the bodies of the Texians stacked up and burned. The Tejano women who survived were allowed to return to their homes. Susanna Dickenson, the wife of Captain Almaron Dickenson, and her daughter, Angelina, were allowed safe passage out of Bexar to spread the word of Santa Anna's victory. Santa Anna allowed Travis's slave, Joe, to escort them.

Santa Anna's victory cost him between 400 and 600 total casualties, while the Texians lost over 185 soldiers, along with eighteen cannon. Santa Anna may have won the battle, but his actions following his victory hardened the resolve of the Texians as word of the massacre spread. On April 21, General Sam Houston located Santa Anna and a portion of his army near the confluence of the San Jacinto River and Buffalo Bayou. Houston and his men caught the Mexicans by surprise and charged them, shouting, "Remember the Alamo!" In eighteen minutes, the objective of Santa Anna's campaign (preventing the loss of Tejas) was forfeited, and Santa Anna lost the war strategically.

Further Reading

Donovan, James. *The Blood of Heroes: The 13 Day Struggle for the Alamo, and the Sacrifice that Forged a Nation.* New York: Little, Brown and Company, 2012.

Groneman, Bill. *Eyewitness to the Alamo.* Plano: Republic of Texas Press, 1996.

Hardin, Stephen L. *Texas Iliad: A Military History of the Texas Revolution.* Austin: University of Texas Press, 1994.

Roberts, Randy, and James S. Olson. *A Line in the Sand: The Alamo in Blood and Memory.* New York: Touchstone, 2002.

49. San Jacinto

Date: April 21, 1836
Location: Along the San Jacinto River, near present-day Houston, Texas

OPPONENTS

1. Texian rebels

    Commander: Major General Sam Houston

2. Mexico

    Commander: General Antonio Lopez de Santa Anna

BACKGROUND

General Antonio Lopez de Santa Anna was elected president of Mexico in April 1833 after helping oust President Anastasio Bustamante the previous year. Among his first acts was abrogating the Constitution of 1834 and abolishing local authority on the states of Coahuila and Texas. Santa Anna's actions set in motion the Texas Revolution.

In October 1835, Texian rebels laid siege to San Antonio de Bexar, the headquarters of the military governor of Texas, General Martin Perfecto de Cos. After a two-month siege, Cos surrendered his forces in December 1835. Santa Anna formed an army of 6,000 soldiers in February 1836 to march on Bexar. He also issued a decree declaring any foreigners who entered Texas to support the rebels would be labeled "pirates" and put to death if captured.

After a grueling march, a force of 1,800 Mexicans laid siege to the 180 Texians holed up in the Alamo Mission outside of Bexar on February 23. For thirteen days, the Texians held the Mexicans at bay, but at 5:30 a.m. on the morning of March 6, the Mexican infantry silently crept up on the fort, killing the sleeping sentries and then advancing to the walls. Now alerted, the Texians beat back two assaults; however, a third push by the Mexicans succeeded in getting inside the fort. Once inside, the fighting became confused, but the Texians were steadily pushed back into little pockets and killed. By 6:30 a.m., the fighting was over.

Meanwhile, on March 1, forty-five delegates gathered at Washington-on-the-Brazos to propose a Declaration of Independence, which passed the following day. After news of the fall of the Alamo reached the delegates, they set about writing a constitution for their new republic. Mainly lifted from the U.S. Constitution, it was ratified on March 17. The Republic of Texas now had a government.

With the bulk of his forces besieging the Alamo, Santa Anna sent General Jose de Urrea along the coast to seize the Texian forces at Goliad. Urrea's men fought several skirmishes on the way there. At the same time, Colonel James Fannin, the commander of the garrison in the Presidio La Bahia at Goliad, renamed Fort Defiance, was preparing to evacuate the fort. After delaying for several days, Fannin's force began a slow retreat from Goliad on March 19. Urrea caught the Texians out on the plains and surrounded them. After a two-day battle, Fannin and his 300 men surrendered to Urrea and marched back to the Presidio. On March 27, the Texians were led out of the fort and executed. Word of the Goliad massacre spread quickly, and along with "Remember the Alamo!" "Remember Goliad!" became rallying cries for the Texas rebels.

Santa Anna appeared to be gaining the upper hand, and General Sam Houston, with the bulk of the Texian army, began a series of retreats eastward to the Gulf Coast. Refusing to engage the Mexicans, Houston was losing the support of the Texian government and, more important, his men were losing confidence in him. Nonetheless, Houston knew that his army was not ready for a fight with the Mexicans, and he continued to avoid the Mexican army. On April 18, Houston's scouts captured a Mexican courier who happened to be carrying Santa Anna's plans for his campaign to end the rebellion. The plans indicated that Santa Anna and a small force were near Lynchburg. Houston realized that he had to move quickly if he was going to capitalize on this intelligence, and he immediately began moving his 900-strong force toward Lynchburg. Houston beat Santa Anna to the area and occupied the better terrain. On April 20, Santa Anna and a force of 700 arrived and set up camp on a plain 500 yards from the Texians. Santa Anna's subordinates pointed out that he had not chosen very defensible terrain, but Santa Anna arrogantly dismissed their advice.

Throughout the rest of the day, both sides' cavalry skirmished to no effect. Meanwhile, Houston's men were upset that he did not engage the Mexicans right then and there. Santa Anna, realizing his inferior position and fearing a full-scale assault by the Texians, had his men spend the night improving their positions.

THE BATTLE

When the Texians did not attack the morning of April 21, the Mexicans began relaxing a little. At 9 a.m., General Cos arrived with 500 more men, boosting the morale of the Mexican soldiers. However, Cos reported to Santa Anna that his men were tired and hungry and asked if he could rest them for a few hours. Santa Anna relented and agreed to let the rest of his command eat and rest. Santa Anna himself went off to his tent to nap.

At 4 p.m., following a council of war, Houston ordered his men to attack. Pulling their only two cannon with them, the Texians began quietly advancing toward the Mexican lines. Meanwhile, Houston's cavalry rode around the flanks to encircle the Mexicans. The Texians crept to within 200 yards before the Mexican sentries sounded the alarm. After firing one volley, the Texians rushed the defenses. Houston tried to regain control, but after days of retreating, the Texians just wanted to get at the Mexicans. With cries of "Remember the Alamo!" and "Remember Goliad!" they quickly overcame the defenders and were in no mood to show any mercy. The Mexicans broke and began fleeing to a nearby lake. Santa Anna lost control of the defense and ran from the battlefield. After eighteen minutes, the fight was over, but the massacre of Mexican soldiers continued longer.

Santa Anna, hiding in a nearby swamp, was captured the next day and brought before Houston. Despite demands for his immediate execution, Houston began negotiating with the vanquished dictator. Santa Anna agreed to order the remainder of his army to march south, though he admitted that, as he was a prisoner of war, his generals might feel no obligation to follow his orders. However, by this time, the Mexican army was in dire straits logistically and fell back across the Rio Grande. Texas had won its independence.

CONCLUSION

In October 1836, the newly formed Republic of Texas held elections, and the voters ratified the new constitution and chose Sam Houston as its first elected president. Also, the voters approved a resolution to seek annexation by the United States. The United States officially recognized the Republic of Texas in March 1837; however, annexation had to wait eight years. In March 1845, Texas was

Antonio Lopez de Santa Anna (1794–1876)

Santa Anna was born in Jalapa Vera Cruz into a *criollo* (middle-class) family. In 1810, the sixteen-year-old Santa Anna joined the Fijo de Vera Cruz infantry regiment as a cadet. As a *criollo*, he remained loyal to the Spanish crown during the Mexican War for independence; however, in 1821, he switched to the rebel side. After several years of internal fighting, Santa Anna emerged as the duly elected president of Mexico. However, in 1834, Santa Anna declared that Mexico was not ready for democracy, and he repealed the Constitution of 1824. This action led to widespread unrest. Santa Anna successfully put down all of these uprisings except in Texas. During the Texas Revolution, Santa Anna was taken prisoner and eventually retired to Mexico, but not for long. He lost a leg fighting the French during the Pastry War. Following the war, he took control of Mexico once more.

During the Mexican-American War, Santa Anna once again oversaw the defeat of his army and was sent into exile, only to be recalled as president in 1853. However, within two years, he was overthrown and exiled for eleven years. In 1867, he attempted to return but was arrested and sent back into exile. In 1874, Santa Anna finally gave up his designs on political power and was allowed to return to Mexico. He spent the last two years of his life in Mexico City, where he died on June 21, 1876. Santa Anna was buried in Tepeyac Cemetery near Guadalupe Hidalgo.

annexed as the twenty-eighth state, and this action contributed to the start of the Mexican-American War.

Further Reading

Brands, H. W. *Lone Star Nation: How a Ragged Army of Volunteers Won the Battle for Texas Independence—and Changed America.* New York: Doubleday, 2004.

Hardin, Stephen L. *Texas Iliad: A Military History of the Texas Revolution.* Austin: University of Texas Press, 1994.

Moore, Stephen. *Eighteen Minutes: The Battle of San Jacinto and the Texas Independence Campaign.* Dallas: Republic of Texas Press, 2004.

50. Siege of Nanjing

Date: 1855–1864
Location: Nanjing, central China

OPPONENTS

1. The Taiping

Commander: Hong Houxiu (later Hong Xuiquan) and Li Xuicheng

2. Qing dynasty

Commanders: Various Qing generals, primarily Zeng Guofan

BACKGROUND

The Taiping (Great Peace) Rebellion was perhaps the most cataclysmic event in nineteenth-century China, which is saying a lot because so many catastrophes and rebellions befell Imperial China during that turbulent century. China was in the midst of collapse, and with the Taiping Rebellion, it nearly became the failed state that it would be in the first part of the twentieth century.

The genesis for the rebellion began with a lowly Chinese scholar named Hong Houxiu, who had been stymied in his attempts to climb the Mandarin ladder of scholarship and influence due to failure to pass the required exams. After one of these failures, he had a nervous breakdown accompanied by torrid dreams and hallucinations, which he later interpreted as divine revelation that he was Jesus Christ's younger brother—God's Chinese son. He interpreted this in a way somewhat akin to Joan of Arc—that he had been chosen by God to liberate China from the "barbarian" Manchu (Qing) dynasty, which was not ethnically Han Chinese. With his revelation in hand, he was ready to establish an era of "Great Peace" that would bring Heaven and Earth into harmony with each other. Hong came from a poor area of south China populated by a Han minority known as the Hakka, who were hardy mountain people. It was among these people that Hong's message resonated. Hong changed his name to Xuiquan to reflect his new divine status— "completeness" (xiun) versus "fire" (Hou).

THE REBELLION

The rebellion started as a local phenomenon, as did most similar events in Chinese history. By 1849, Hong had over 10,000 followers, including armed women's units, because the Taiping preached equality for men and women. One of Hong's followers, a coal miner named Yang Xiuqing, proved to be a brilliant tactician and demolitions expert (because of his mining background). These attributes informed Hong's revolutionary ideology with real military talent.

In 1850, a Qing army attempted to oust the Taiping from their mountain sanctuary at Thistle Mountain in Guangxi, but it was badly defeated. The Taiping then began a slow advance toward the north, capturing the important southern city of Yongan by 1851, and their army swelled to 60,000. The rebellion gathered momentum and continued north. They used human wave attacks and, once victorious, they slaughtered thousands of Manchus and their supporters: men, women, and children. Their message of Qing decadence and the punishment of China by God through the Qing as well as European foreigners resonated. Despite some setbacks, by March 1853 they had captured China's ancient southern capital of Nanjing and began to rule like an established dynasty.

It was at this point that the Taiping movement began to have real problems. As with all great revolutionary movements, the founder began to have problems controlling his subordinates. Hong was forced to share power, especially with his most successful general, Yang, who declared that he too was channeling a divine element of the Christian Trinity (namely, the Holy Spirit). This state of affairs went on for eleven years (1853–1864), with the Taiping ruling significant parts of southern and central China from Nanjing but never entirely displacing the Qing, who eventually allied with various European-led forces, like that of General Charles Gordon and his "Ever Victorious Army" at the front near Shanghai.

THE SIEGE OF NANJING

The siege of Nanjing began not long after the Taiping seized it. The Qing had devised a strategy of trying to squeeze the Taiping Rebellion by creating two fronts to attack the Taiping from both north and south. After an abortive northern expedition (1853–1855) failed to capture Beijing, Nanjing was almost always under siege or threat of siege from the north. In the south, the Taiping managed to defeat all comers. However, the divided leadership of the Taiping ultimately led to their downfall. Hong had Yang, who had grown too powerful, assassinated in 1856, and then his other best general, Shi Dakai, became estranged and established his own "kingdom" to the west in Sichuan, where he was overthrown and conquered by the Qing in 1863. They also failed to coordinate their rebellion with key rebellions by the Nian in the north and the "Red Turbans" in the south.

The final events that led the Qing to overcome the Taiping were military in nature. In reaction to the Taiping excesses in the south, a Hunanese official named Zeng Guofan raised local troops to defend himself against them. Zeng had participated in the earlier failed southern-front offensives, but when the emperor officially sanctioned Chinese militia armies, Zeng managed to rebuild and to learn from his earlier experiences. Eventually, his army, composed of local Chinese recruits and not as easily defeated as the mercenary Manchu "banner" armies, became one of the most effective threats to the Taiping. They opposed the Taiping not as foreigners, but as Chinese who rejected Hong's anti-Confucian doctrine and totalitarian overlordship. Zeng's army eventually became known as the Xiang army.

Hong was fortunate in bringing to the fore another talented young general, Li Xuicheng. To relieve the pressure on Nanjing from the northern front, Li launched the first of several so-called Eastern Expeditions in 1860. With only 6,000 elite troops, Li struck southeast and captured Hangzhou using a mix of deception and the trademark demolition tactics unique to the Taiping. While the Qing reinforced Zhejiang, Li doubled back to Nanjing and attacked their weakened forces there, relieving the pressure on Nanjing. The eastern strategy at first seemed to work, and the Taiping reached all the way to Shanghai. However, the Europeans, now committed to support the Qing regime after signing the Tianjin treaties that summer, aided the Qing in defending Shanghai from the Taiping. Meanwhile, Nanjing came under siege again.

This pattern continued, with Li advancing again in 1861 to the east. But now Zeng approached the southern flank and recaptured the territory that was lost after the southern front's earlier defeats. The key city of Anjing, only recently recaptured by the Taiping, fell to Zeng's army in September 1861. Hong became more and more insular, retreating into his palace at Nanjing with his concubines (despite enforcing a doctrine of celibacy for his rank and file). Ultimately, his core Hakka followers were themselves regarded as "foreign" invaders with an "anti-Chinese" religion and rejected by the populations that the Taiping ruled.

Zeng, now appointed as overall commander, began the final campaign to exterminate the Taiping by driving on Nanjing from the south beginning in February 1862. By 1864, the Taiping were defeated on all fronts, retaining ownership of nothing but Nanjing and other small, isolated enclaves. Zeng now settled down for the most hated military operation in the Chinese playbook: a lengthy siege of a large, walled city. He was aided that June by the death (probably by suicide) of Hong, which left his weak, sixteen-year-old son as heir to the Kingdom of Heavenly Peace.

With that, much of the energy in the movement seemed to drain. Zeng marshalled his modern artillery and breached the walls of Nanjing after fifty days of bombardment on July 19, 1864. His forces penetrated the city, killing the Taiping leadership that remained in scenes of massacre and mayhem. Zeng reported to the Qing emperor: "Not one of the 100,000 rebels in Nanjing surrendered themselves when the city was taken but in many cases gathered together and burned themselves and passed away without repentance. Such a formidable band of rebels has been rarely known from ancient times to present."

The siege of Nanjing, nearly nine years long, was over. The final remaining enclaves of "unrepentant" Taiping were only exterminated finally and completely over the next two years by the Qing armies.

CONCLUSION

Zeng was more right than he knew as to the exceptionalism of this rebellion. By the time it ended in 1866, over twenty-five million Chinese (a low estimate) had lost their lives to this terrible, violent, and bloody insurgency. As a disaster, it is unequaled by anything else that took place in the nineteenth century, anywhere else on the face of the planet. It may be the most destructive rebellion in human history.

Further Reading

Franz, Michael, with Chung-li Chang. *The Taiping Rebellion, Volume I: History.* Seattle: University of Washington Press, 1966.

Graff, David A., and Robin Higham, eds. *A Military History of China.* Boulder, CO: Westview, 2002.

Spence, Jonathan D. *God's Chinese Son: The Taiping Heavenly Kingdom of Hong Xiuquan.* New York: W. W. Norton, 1996.

51. The Capture of New Orleans

Date: April 1862
Location: Lower Mississippi River, south of New Orleans

OPPONENTS

1. U.S. navy and army

   Commanders: Flag Officer David G. Farragut and Major General Benjamin Butler

2. Confederate army and navy

   Commander: Major General Mansfield Lovell

BACKGROUND

One of the major elements of the Union strategy in the first year of the American Civil War was the opening of the Mississippi River, which transected the Confederacy, cutting the trans-Mississippi region and its resources off from the rest of the Confederacy. Its political and economic value was even higher because doing this allowed the produce of the Midwest to be transported down the river and out to other markets via water, as well as helping President Abraham Lincoln and the Republicans solidify their political support in the Midwest and old Northwest, Union areas negatively affected by the Confederacy's closure of the Mississippi.

Key to securing the Mississippi was the seizure of New Orleans near its mouth, which would effectively close the river to Confederate access to the sea and simplify the blockade. Also, New Orleans was the most populated city in the South and its second-largest manufacturing center, and it had extensive shipyards, which in fact were building two large ironclads, *Louisiana* and *Mississippi,* to help defend it. Also being built there was a mysterious "submarine boat" by H. L. Hunley—a terror weapon intended to help break the Union blockade. The Confederacy losing New Orleans would be equivalent to the Union losing New York or Boston.

THE PLANS

The plans for seizing New Orleans were already well underway in 1861, and the important decision to appoint David G. Farragut to carry them out was made that November by Lincoln and his two key naval advisors, Navy Secretary Gideon Welles and Assistant Secretary of the Navy Gustavus Fox. Fox was a former commander in the U.S. navy, and his appointment as Welles's assistant had effectively made him equivalent to today's position of chief of naval operations. He was an astute judge of men, and in Farragut, he made an extremely wise choice—although there was some initial concern because Farragut hailed from Tennessee and had married a Southerner. But Farragut had spent most of his life at sea and had been adopted into the very Yankee Porter family, so he was legally the brother of David Dixon Porter, who would serve in Farragut's fleet, commanding a flotilla of schooner's armed with thirteen-inch mortars.

The plan had two components that were based on the defenses that the Confederates had constructed below New Orleans in an impassable area of swamps based on two forts—Jackson and St. Philip—opposite each other on the eastern and western sides of the great Mississippi. A chain connected to the two forts and these cannon covered this obstacle with 100 well-mounted guns. Additionally, the Confederates hoped to have their new ironclads support the defense of the city. On the Union side, Porter had successfully convinced Fox that he could reduce both forts with large mortars mounted on schooners. Once the forts were reduced, Farragut would take his seagoing squadron, race up the Mississippi, and put New Orleans under his guns, both literally and figuratively, because the river would be high at the time the assault was expected to occur, in the spring of 1862.

The Confederates underestimated the ability of the Union to move so quickly. At the same time, their defenses were stretched thin in the west, as joint Army-Navy expeditions penetrated down to Memphis and into the Tennessee and Cumberland river valleys. On top of this, when the Confederate leadership learned that Major General Benjamin Butler, a Democrat, was commanding the Union ground forces, they dismissed the idea that Lincoln would let a prize like New Orleans fall to a political rival. This opinion was shared by General Mansfield Lovell, who commanded the defense of New Orleans. Unfortunately for the Confederates, it was not the Yankee generals they needed to fear, but the Yankee admirals.

THE ENGAGEMENTS

Farragut and Porter arrived with the fleet and mortar squadron at Ship Island, off Mississippi, in late February, joining Butler and his transports with their troops. The Union intelligence estimated that the deepest of the passes at the mouth of the Mississippi was the one to the southwest, and Farragut immediately proceeded there and began passing his fleet over the bar at its mouth in early March. He had gotten his flagship *Hartford* across when he ran into problems with some of the heavier ships. For the next two weeks, he towed the rest of the warships across the bar so that by early April, he had seventeen warships (but he had to leave his most powerful one, the *Colorado,* behind) and Porter's twenty-one mortar schooners across. Farragut had lost the element of surprise and now steamed up the river to attempt the penetration of the barriers posed by the two forts and their 100 cannon.

Porter began pounding the forts with over 5,000 shells from April 18–23. This part of the plan failed. Some Confederate guns were disabled, but the forts were still in action and dangerous. During the bombardment, Farragut had had two of his gunboats go up the river and cut the chain. On the night of April 24, Farragut executed the second part of the plan, running his main fleet by the forts. He ran into a stiff fight with the tiny Confederate fleet but ended up sinking all but two of the ships, including the armored ram *Manassas*. At one point in the battle, the rebels had set the *Harford* ablaze with fire rafts, but the Union sailors quickly doused the fires and continued the fight.

Farragut promptly steamed up the river and demanded the surrender of the city. It fell without a shot, but Farragut could occupy only a small part of it with his 250 marines. The Confederates were able to remove much valuable rolling stock and war materials (such as the material for the "submarine boat"), as well as their 3,000 troops before Butler arrived with his troops on May 1. Butler had been delayed by the two forts, both of which he had been able to cause to surrender by a landing behind Fort St. Philip suggested by Porter.

CONCLUSION

The fall of New Orleans sent shock waves through the Confederacy and the rest of the globe. It showed the power that could be exerted by a dominant navy led by an audacious commander. It also shored up support for Lincoln in the critical Northern states that relied on the Mississippi for commerce. New Orleans remained in Union hands for the rest of the war, although it would take over a year for the Union forces, led by Major General Ulysses S. Grant and Rear Admiral David Porter, to secure the rest of the Mississippi with the fall of Vicksburg in July 1863.

Further Reading

Catton, Bruce. *This Hallowed Ground: The Story of the Union Side of the Civil War.* New York: Doubleday, 1956.

Chaffin, Tom. *The* H. L. Hunley: *The Secret Hope of the Confederacy.* New York: Hill and Wang, 2008.

Hoogenboom, Ari. *Gustavus Vasa Fox of the Union Navy: A Biography.* Baltimore: Johns Hopkins University Press, 2009.

52. The Vicksburg Campaign

Date: March 29–July 4, 1863
Location: Vicksburg, Mississippi

OPPONENTS

1. United States
   Commander: Major General Ulysses S. Grant
2. Confederate States of America
   Commander: Lieutenant General John C. Pemberton

BACKGROUND

The fall of Vicksburg was a significant turning point in the American Civil War. With that, control of the Mississippi was completely in Union hands and the Confederate States of America was divided.

By the spring of 1862, the Union controlled most of the Mississippi other than a stretch from Vicksburg to Port Hudson. To prevent Vicksburg from falling, the Confederacy decided to turn it into the "Gibraltar of the West," an allusion to the fortified British island of Gibraltar at the entrance of the Mediterranian Sea. The Union challenge would be to crack it.

The man selected to carry out this task was Major General Ulysses S. Grant, commander of the Army of the Tennessee. Grant's subordinates included Major General's William Tecumseh Sherman, James B. McPherson, and John A. McClernand. The latter was a politically appointed general and was permitted to raise an independent army. He was in the process of recruiting for his command when Grant began his opening drive to Vicksburg. When Grant took command of McClernand's recruits, it only compounded the animosity between the two strong-willed men. Rear Admiral David Dixon Porter commanded the naval vessels on this portion of the Mississippi. The success of the naval operations in support of the battle would be due in no small part to the personal relationship that formed between Porter and Grant.

In October 1862, the Confederate lieutenant general John C. Pemberton assumed command of the Department of the Mississippi, which included the city of Vicksburg. Pemberton, a native of Pennsylvania but married to a woman from Virginia, interpreted his orders to mean that his focus should be on defending Vicksburg. However, the command arrangements hampered Pemberton's efforts. First, Pemberton commanded only the forces on the east side of the river, preventing him from coordinating his efforts with forces on the west side. Next, his department was part of the larger Department of the West, under the command of General Joseph E. Johnston. Nonetheless, Pemberton's orders were to report directly to the War Department, bypassing Johnston. This confusion would contribute to the fall of Vicksburg.

Grant tried an overland approach to Vicksburg as his first attempt to seize the city. In November 1862, he led a force from Tennesse toward Jackson, hoping to outflank Vicksburg and force its evacuation. However, Pemberton would not stand and fight. A frustrated Grant, sensing that Pemberton was not strong enough to fight two threats, sent Sherman down the Mississippi to attack Vicksburg directly while he continued toward Jackson. However, before Grant could resume his march, Confederate cavalry captured his logistics base in Holly Springs and a raid by Nathan Bedford Forrest's cavalry tore up the rail line behind Grant, forcing him to withdraw.

Meanwhile, Sherman quickly loaded his force into barges and headed down the Mississippi. In late December, Sherman landed his force near Chickasaw Bayou. Unfortunately, after landing, the Union troops took several days to sort themselves out before Sherman could launch an attack. On December 29, Sherman attacked, but the Union delay gave Pemberton time to prepare, and Sherman ran into a force of 15,000 Confederate soldiers. A second attack set for December 31 was called off due to fog. Sherman admitted defeat and withdrew.

Grant regrouped and reassessed the situation. The problem was how to bypass the heavy defenses and get his army out of the wet lowlands and onto the dry bluffs on either side of Vicksburg. Between January and March, he made five attempts to get at Vicksburg, in what has become known as the *Bayou Expeditions.* The first of these was to dig a canal in front of Vicksburg. The engineers were making good progress when the river broke through a dam at the upper end, and the operation was called off.

Simultaneously, McPherson's corps was making the second attempt, by breaching a levee near Lake Providence in the hope of flooding the area and making it navigable. This operation was also aborted, though, when it became too difficult to cut through the cypress swamps.

The third attempt looked promising after soldiers from McLernand's corps cut a levee near Yazoo Pass. This cut created a navigable route for the Union ironclads and barges. However, they ran into the newly built Fort Pemberton. For three weeks, the stalled Union forces tried to capture the position before giving up and withdrawing.

Admiral Porter led the fourth expedition, in an attempt to find a route through the swamps to a point above Snyders Bluff. All was going well until the Confederates began dropping trees in front of and behind Porter's boats, and he backed out.

For the last expedition, Grant dug a three-mile canal near Duckport, Louisiana, hoping to bypass the guns at Vicksburg. All seemed to be going well until the Mississippi began receding, and this operation, like the others, was called off. Nevertheless, Grant would not admit defeat and was already formulating a more daring plan.

THE MAIN CAMPAIGN

Grant gathered his three corps on the west bank of the Mississippi, south of Vicksburg. However, Porter's boats were north of Vicksburg. To get Grant's troops across, Porter agreed to "run the guns" of Vicksburg. On the night of April 16–17, Porter, on his flagship, led a force of seven ironclads, three transports, a tug, and a ram ship down the Mississippi. Tied to the sides of these ships were eighteen barges. These would eventually ferry Grant's men across, but on this night, they also were loaded with coal for the ships and supplies for the army. Around 9:30 p.m., moving in trail, the ships came under musket fire from the sentries on the shore. Alerted by this fire, the Confederate gunners quickly manned their cannon and began firing on the Union ships, while others onshore lit bonfires to illuminate the river. For two hours, the Confederate shore batteries exchanged fire with the Union ironclads as they forced their way along the two-mile stretch in front of Vicksburg. By 2 a.m., the last of the Union ships were out of harm's way. Miraculously, Porter lost only one barge and one transport, and only twelve men were wounded. Five days later, he made a second attempt; however, without support from ironclads, the Union side did much worse, losing one transport and six barges. Miraculously, Porter's force suffered only thirteen wounded, and no fatalities. Nonetheless, Grant had his navy with him and could go on the next phase of his campaign.

Grant first tried to land on the east bank with elements of McClernand's corps at Grand Gulf. Early on April 29, Porter's seven ironclads began engaging the

Confederate shore batteries, planning to put McClernand's troops ashore after silencing the Confederate guns. However, after five hours, the Confederate guns were still firing, and Grant called off the landing. He tried again the next day, this time twelve miles downriver from Grand Gulf. The landing at Bruinburg was unopposed, and McClernand's men raced across a mile of the floodplain to secure the bluffs. By the end of the day, McClernand was driving inland, and elements of McPherson's corps began disembarking at Bruinsburg.

During the night of April 30–May 1, McClernand's corps ran into a Confederate brigade near Port Gibson and halted. All the next day, his corps, reinforced with elements of McPherson's corps, fought several Confederate brigades under the command of Brigadier General John S. Bowen. Bowen's badly outnumbered troops held up Grant's advance for most of the day, finally retiring before his force could be overwhelmed.

With Grand Gulf secured, Grant had three options for his next move. He could send part of his forces to assist in seizing Port Hudson and then turn his attention on Vicksburg. Grant rejected this plan. His second option was to drive straight for Vicksburg, but this would mean attacking two divisions that Pemberton had placed along this route. His final option was to keep going east toward Jackson and cut off Pemberton's rail lines.

Grant chose the third option. After taking a few days to gather provisions, he sent his three corps toward Jackson on May 10, with McClernand on the left, Sherman in the middle, and McPherson on the right. Sherman and McClernand successfully crossed Fourteen Mile Creek; however, on May 12, as McPherson's corps approached Fourteen Mile Creek near Raymond, he ran into a Confederate brigade. This brigade held up McPherson's corps for most of that day before pulling back to the Confederates.

The next day, Grant sent Sherman behind McPherson's corps to attack Jackson from the south as the corps marched north to attack the city from the east. Grant then placed McClernand's corps between Jackson and Vicksburg to protect his forces from any attack from the west. By May 13, approximately 6,000 Confederate troops were in Jackson, with more on the way. President Jefferson Davis sent General Johnston to Jackson to take direct command of the battle. Johnston arrived on May 13, and after assessing the situation, he determined that he was too late and ordered an evacuation of the city. The next day, Sherman and McPherson each sent a division into the city. A Confederate rearguard kept the Union soldiers engaged until the last of Johnston's main body could get out. Without much effort, Grant then seized Jackson.

Believing that Pemberton was going to leave Vicksburg to link up with Johnson, Grant immediately turned west, hoping to catch him in the open. He sent McClernand's corps along three routes toward Vicksburg, with McPherson's following along the northern route. Sherman remained in Jackson to protect the rear of Grant's army. Pemberton sortied out of Vicksburg; however, rather than trying to link up with Johnston, Pemberton headed south, hoping to cut Grant's lines of communication. Unfortunately, Pemberton's army was not up to the task and, after a series of command and supply issues, found itself scattered along Champion Hill. Grant seized this opportunity and struck quickly, with McPherson's and McClernand's corps converging on the Confederates. Pemberton's men put up a determined fight but eventually were overcome and forced to retreat off the hill. The victory at Champion Hill enhanced Grant's situation as he pursued Pemberton's army.

Pemberton next hoped to halt, or at least delay, Grant until he could reach Vicksburg at a crossing on the Big Black River. On May 17, as McClernand formed two of his divisions to attack the dug-in Confederates, one of his brigade commanders found a covered route up to the Confederate positions. Rather than waiting for orders, Brigadier General Michael K. Lawler immediately formed his regiments and attacked. His brigade quickly rolled up the enemy position. The rest of the Confederates retreated across the bridge, setting it on fire after they cleared it. Pemberton led his demoralized army back to Vicksburg to begin the final phase of the battle.

Grant hoped to take Vicksburg quickly and avoid a prolonged siege. His first move was to occupy Snyders Bluff to open up a line of supply along the Mississippi. Then on May 19, he launched an attack directly at Vicksburg at the Stockade Redan. Unfortunately for Grant, along with its well-prepared defense, the terrain also favored the Confederates. Grant's men were repulsed, with heavy losses. Grant tried again on May 22, with all three corps attacking separate parts of the Confederate line. Sherman attacked the Stockade Redan, McClernand the Railroad redoubt in the south, and McPherson the Great Redoubt in the center. All three attacks failed, and Grant and his army settled in for a long siege.

For six weeks, Union artillery, supported by Porter's ships on the Mississippi, continuously shelled the city of Vicksburg. On land, Grant turned to centuries-old

A contemporary photograph of the aftermath of the great Siege of Vicksburg showing captured Confederate equipment in July 1863. (Kean Collection/Archive Photos/Getty Images)

siege techniques. Union sappers dug saps (covered trenches) to bring artillery and soldiers closer to the Southern lines. The engineers also dug mines under the Confederate lines to pack with explosives in order to blow an opening in their defenses. All the while, the conditions in Vicksburg itself were deteriorating. Pemberton believed that he had sufficient provisions to hold out; however, as the siege wore on, morale among both the soldiers and the civilians declined as disease and malnutrition spread. At the end of June, Pemberton received an anonymous letter suggesting that he surrender the city. On July 3, he sent word to Grant that he was ready to negotiate a surrender. The next day, the weary, ragged Confederates marched out of Vicksburg. The Mississippi was under Union control.

CONCLUSION

In July 1863, the Confederacy suffered two defeats in two days from which it would never recover. On July 3, Robert E. Lee and the Army of Northern Virginia was defeated at Gettysburg, and on July 4, Pemberton surrendered Vicksburg. Lee's defeat was a great political victory for the north; however, the fall of Vicksburg had a greater military effect. Not only was the South now a divided nation, but the capture of the Mississippi opened up more operational possibilities for the North in the west.

Following his victory, Grant was called back to Washington to take command of the entire Union army. His campaign plan for 1864 capitalized on the operational opportunities that his victory at Vicksburg helped make possible. As for the Confederacy, it would be on the strategic defensive for the rest of the war after Vicksburg.

John C. Pemberton (1814–1881)

John C. Pemberton, a native of Philadelphia, entered the U.S. Military Academy at West Point, New York, in 1833. Graduating twenty-seventh out of a class of fifty in 1837, Pemberton was commissioned a second lieutenant of artillery and assigned to the 4th Artillery Regiment. He saw action during the Second Seminole War and on the frontier before the Mexican-American War. During the latter war, Pemberton was promoted to brevet major for his actions at the Battle of Molino del Rey, and he was wounded during the assault on Chapultepec Castle. Following the war, he returned to frontier duty until the outbreak of the Civil War.

Pemberton resigned his commission in the U.S. army in April 1861 to serve with the Confederacy, and he rose quickly through the ranks despite concerns about his Northern origins. In October 1862, Pemberton was promoted to lieutenant general and given command of the Department of Mississippi and East Louisiana. His primary mission was to hold Vicksburg at all costs. However, after a lengthy siege, Pemberton surrendered the fortress to Ulysses S. Grant on July 4, 1863. That October, Pemberton returned to the Confederacy as part of a prisoner exchange. Nevertheless, no one wanted the discredited Pemberton, and he resigned his commission as a lieutenant general. He ended the war as a colonel, serving as an ordnance inspector. After the war, Pemberton lived on his farm in Warrenton, Virginia, before returning to Pennsylvania. He died on July 13, 1881.

Further Reading

Ballard, Michael. *Vicksburg: The Campaign That Opened the Mississippi.* Chapel Hill: University of North Carolina Press, 2004.

Groom, Winston. *Vicksburg, 1863.* New York: Alfred A. Knopf, 2009.

Smith, Timothy B. *The Decision Was Always My Own: Ulysses S. Grant and the Vicksburg Campaign.* Carbondale: Southern Illinois University Press, 2018.

Tomblin, Barbara Brooks. *The Civil War on the Mississippi: Union Sailors, Gunboat Captains, and the Campaign to Control the River.* Lexington: University Press of Kentucky, 2016.

53. Koeniggratz

Date: July 3, 1866
Location: Koeniggratz, Austrian Kingdom (near modern-day Chlum, Czech Republic)

OPPONENTS

1. Prussia

 Commanders: Helmuth von Moltke, chief of the General Staff

 1st Army: Prince Frederick Charles

 2nd Army: Crown Prince Frederick

 Elbe Army: Karl Eberhard Herwath von Bittenfield

2. Austrian Empire

 Commander: Ludwig August von Benedek

BACKGROUND

The Battle of Koeniggratz (also known as Sadowa) was the decisive battle of the Austro-Prussian War (June 14–July 26, 1866), which had the result of deciding which nation would unify Germany. In 1864, Austria and Prussia allied to wrest control of the duchies of Schleswig and Holstein from Denmark. Following the war, Prussia assumed sovereignty over Schleswig, and Austria over Holstein. However, not much time passed before Otto von Bismarck, the chancellor of Prussia, believed that it was in Prussia's interest to control both duchies. For the next two years, he began meddling in Austrian affairs and concluding alliances to isolate Austria if a war were to come to pass between Prussia and Austria.

For the Prussian army, the war with Denmark was an opportunity to test the reforms instituted by the chief of the General Staff, Helmuth von Moltke. First and foremost among these was the founding of the Great General Staff, an outgrowth of the Prussian experience during the Napoleonic Wars. Events on the battlefield and changes in technology required central planning and organization; the Great General Staff would provide that planning. The staff, composed of handpicked and specially educated officers, would provide the Prussian army with a synthetic genius in planning for war. Also, these officers would be the chiefs of staff, down to the corps level. In that role, the General Staff officer was almost a cocommander and provided advice and assistance to the commander, but he also had a direct line back to Berlin if he needed it.

In peacetime, the Great General Staff prepared estimates on potential enemies and developed contingency plans in case of war. This centralized planning became more critical as the size of armies continued to expand. However, it was the railroad expansion that caused the greatest reassessment. By 1864, von Moltke was already contemplating how to coordinate the rail movement of his corps in order to mass his army at the right time and place. The Danish War tested his ideas; however, von Moltke and his staff were already considering how best to use the railroads in a war with Austria.

In June 1866, Bismarck had maneuvered Austria diplomatically, including convincing Italy to join Prussia, into a position where war was inevitable. As the Prussian army mobilized, von Moltke directed that three armies would invade Austria from separate directions. All the staff work was paying off; von Moltke had five rail lines that led to Austria, while the Austrian army had only one to move its army. By the accepted strategies of the day, the Austrian commander, Ludwig von Benedek, with interior lines, should have been able to reposition his forces to meet any Prussian threat. However, the railroad negated the concept of interior lines, giving Prussia an operational maneuver advantage.

On June 21, von Moltke's three armies arrived at the Prussian/Austrian border and awaited further orders. That same day, war was officially declared, and on June 23, the 254,000 soldiers of combined Prussian armies crossed the border, planning on linking up at the town of Gitschin. Von Benedek had 320,000 of Austria's best troops to oppose the invasion. Fortunately for von Benedek, the Prussians were not moving as rapidly as von Moltke had intended and were making slow progress. But von Moltke sent orders to get the armies moving again.

At one point, von Moltke lost contact with the 1st Army for three days and, accompanied by the Kaiser and Bismarck, moved his headquarters from Berlin to Gitschin. After several days of skirmishing, the Austrians had lost 30,000 men, due mostly to the tactical advantages of the needle gun. Benedek, chosen to command because of his bravery and loyalty, suggested to the Austrian emperor, Franz Joseph, that he should consider opening negotiations. The emperor telegraphed back, asking if a battle had been fought yet. To von Benedek, the message was clear—he was to fight the Prussians.

Von Benedek considered retreating to a more defensive position behind the Elbe River. However, fearing he could not get his army across the river in time, he decided to defend along the Bistritz River instead. The river itself was not much of an obstacle, but the Austrians dug in on the hills overlooking it. Von Benedek hoped to break the Prussians' tactical advantages against his prepared emplacements.

Prince Frederick Charles, the commander of the 1st Army, decided on the evening of July 2 to attack the next day with his army and the Elbe Army on his right. Despite some misgivings, von Moltke let the prince's orders stand. However, as a precaution, fearing the frontal attack might fail, he ordered the 2nd Army to attack into the right flank of the Austrians. Then von Moltke left the battle in the hands of his subordinates. A cold rain greeted both armies on the morning of July 3.

THE BATTLE

The battle opened around 7:30 a.m. with an artillery duel, followed shortly by an advanced by four of the 1st Army's divisions. Three of the divisions were quickly pinned down by Austrian artillery fire along the Bistritz River, where they would remain for the rest of the day. The 7th Infantry Division, on the left of the Prussian line, occupied the Swiep Forest. Seven Austrian infantry battalions attempted to push the Prussians out of the woods. The Austrians' rifled muskets had range and accuracy over the needle gun–armed Prussians, but the needle gun gave the Prussians two overpowering advantages: They could remain behind cover as they worked the bolts of their rifles, whereas the Austrians had to stand to reload; and the speed with which the Prussians could reload gave them a higher rate of fire. The deadly fire of the Prussian needle guns quickly decimated the Austrians. Before the battle was over, the Austrians would commit forty-nine more battalions to driving the Prussians out of Swiep Forest. Nonetheless, the Prussians also suffered heavy casualties and were barely holding on.

On the Austrian side, von Benedek, based on the reports he was receiving, believed the battle was going well. It appeared that his troops were holding the line along the Bistritz. On his left flank, his soldiers were delaying the advance of the Elbe Army. However, he was unaware that his reserves were being frittered away in senseless attacks in Swiep Forest. Then, around 3 p.m., the situation began to change. On von Benedek's left flank, the Elbe Army routed the Saxon Corps and was advancing eastward. At the same time, von Benedek became aware that the 2nd Army was closing in on his right flank. His assessment quickly went from optimistic to desperate, as he realized he was facing a double envelopment.

The battle was reaching its conclusion. It was not until von Benedek attempted to organize counterattacks that he realized that he had lost most of his reserves in the Swiep Forest. Facing the reality of the situation, von Benedek decided that it would be best to save what he could of his army by retreating across the Elbe. He launched several successful counterattacks to keep the Prussians away from the crossing sites. Despite the success of these attacks, poor staff work eventually defeated the Austrian army. Without proper planning and coordination, it was the scene of chaos at the crossing sites along the Elbe, and the Austrian army was rendered combat ineffective.

Fortunately for the Austrians, the Prussians did not immediately pursue the retreating Austrians. It is not clear why the Prussians did not push their pursuit, but more than likely, it was the result of the three Prussian armies coming together at the crossing sites. Even the best staff work cannot compensate entirely for the natural friction of the battlefield, and von Moltke realized that he would need some time to sort out the traffic jam and get the armies reorganized.

CONCLUSION

The Austrian army lost 24,000 killed, with another 20,000 taken prisoner, compared to the Prussians' 9,000 total casualties. After such a devastating victory, the Prussian army expected a triumphant march into Vienna. They would be disappointed. Bismarck, ever the politician, preferred to offer Austria generous peace terms rather than humiliate it. Other than Holstein and Venice, Austria lost no other territory; however, it had to agree to exclude itself from German affairs. This concession set in motion a series of events that would eventually lead to German unification, which was always the chancellor's ultimate goal.

Further Reading

Craig, Gordon. *The Battle of Koeniggratz: Prussia's Victory over Austria, 1866.* Westport, CT: Greenwood Press, 2003.

Rothenburg, Gunther. *The Army of Francis Joseph.* West Lafayette, IN: Purdue University Press, 1976.

Wawro, Geoffrey. *The Austro-Prussian War: Austria's War with Prussia and Italy in 1866.* Cambridge: Cambridge University Press, 1997.

54. Sedan

Date: September 1–2, 1870
Location: Sedan, France

OPPONENTS

1. North German Confederation

   Commanders: Kaiser Wilhelm I and Field Marshal Helmut von Moltke

2. Second French Empire

   Commanders: Napoleon III, Marshal Patrice de MacMahon, and General Emmanuel Felix de Wimpeffen

BACKGROUND

The Battle of Sedan was the pivotal battle of the Franco-Prussian War, which had its roots in the aftermath of the Austro-Prussian War. After Prussia defeated Austria-Hungary in 1866, it became more of a threat to the balance of power in Europe. France was particularly concerned that Prussia would become a direct threat. On the other hand, many in Prussia, including Otto von Bismarck, the chancellor, believed that war with France was not only inevitable but necessary to achieve the goal of German unification.

Bismarck maneuvered the French into declaring war in July 1860 over the selection of a Prussian prince, Leopold of Hohenzollern-Sigmarigen, to the Spanish throne. Leopold withdrew his candidacy, but Bismarck leaked a letter describing the situation to the French public in misleading terms. Incensed by the letter, the French people, supported by the press, began clamoring for a declaration of war. Bismarck wanted to paint France as the aggressor, and events played out as he desired when France declared war on Prussia on July 16, 1870.

Prussia could field an army of approximately one million men. Most of these were conscripts because Prussia had instituted universal compulsory service as part

of its reforms following the Napoleonic Wars. Each soldier carried the Dreyse needle gun that had proved so devasting during the Austro-Prussian War in 1866. The
Dreyse was the first operational breech-loading rifle. It had an effective range of
only 600 yards, but it had a higher rate of fire than the conventional muzzle-loading
rifled musket, and it allowed the shooter to fire and reload from behind cover. However, the French Chassepot rifle outclassed the twenty-five-year-old Prussian Dreyse.
The other vital piece of technology for the Prussians was the breech-loading Krupp
80-mm field gun, which outclassed the French muzzle-loading artillery in all areas.
However, the biggest advantage the Prussian army possessed was the Great General
Staff, which was devoted to planning and preparing the army for war and had proved
its worth in 1866. No other army in the world had such an organization.

The French army could field almost 300,000 regulars, which could be augmented
by nearly 800,000 more reservists upon mobilization. It had the edge in rifles with
its Chassepot breech-loading rifle. A newer design, the Chassepot fixed some of
the flaws in the Dreyse, such as a rubber seal for the bolt, and had a range of 1,600
yards—nearly three times that of the Dreyse. However, in artillery, the French were
far outranged by the Prussian Krupp guns. Additionally, the French army, unlike
the Prussians, did not possess a central staff to organize and control a large army.

The French were also counting on the southern German states, Bavaria, Wur-
temberg, Hesse, and Baden, joining them in stemming Prussian overreach. But they
did not join the French; instead, they sided with Prussia. Neither did the support
that France was hoping to receive from Austria-Hungary materialize. Nonetheless,
Napoleon III was pressured to launch an offensive, and on July 19, the French
invaded German territory. After a series of battles, the largest being at Gravelotte,
where the French were defeated, the remaining French units retreated into the fortress at Metz. The Prussians surrounded Metz, and on August 17, a relief force
under the command of Napoleon III was intercepted on August 30 and forced to
retreat to Sedan.

THE BATTLE

Marshal Patrice de MacMahon, commanding the Army of Chalons, deployed
his corps along the ridgelines around Sedan. By holding the high ground and the
Meuse River to his rear and south flank, MacMahon believed that he was in a commanding defensive position. In any case, he planned to occupy Sedan only long
enough to resupply before resuming his attack.

Meanwhile, Helmut von Moltke, commanding the Prussian army, left the First
and Second Prussian Armies to continue the siege of Metz and followed the French
to Sedan with the Third and Fourth Prussian Armies. He deployed one force to
hold the French in place and another to cross the Meuse and prevent the French
from retreating, while a smaller force would hold the riverbank.

The battle opened on Septemeber 1 with a French attempt to break out of the
encirclement. MacMahon hoped to penetrate the Prussian lines at a point opposite
the Prussian XII Corps, near the village of La Moncelle. The Prussians anticipated
that this was the most likely place for the French to break out, and they launched
an attack on La Moncelle, along with an attack on the French right in the vicinity

of Bazeille. The Bavarians crossed the Meuse and quickly entered Bazeille, but the French held, and reinforcements were moving south to aid the defenders. However, around 8 a.m., the Bavarian commander, General Ludwig Freiherr von der Tann-Rathsamhausen, received reinforcements of his own in the form of a Prussian infantry division. With this fresh division, Von der Tann ordered one last push, supported by artillery firing from the other side of the Meuse River, and eventually secured Bazeille.

MacMahon was wounded early in the fighting around La Moncelle and placed General Auguste-Alexnadre Ducrot in command. At 7 a.m., Ducrot ordered a retreat but was overruled by General Emmanuel Felix de Wimpeffen, MacMahon's designated replacement. Rather than retreat, Wimpeffen launched a counterattack. Catching the Prussians off guard, the French briefly pushed the Prussians back. However, after securing Bazeille, Prussian reinforcements were making their way northward toward La Moncelle.

Meanwhile, the Prussian V and XI Corps were in a position to the north of the French I and VII Corps, and Prussian artillery began firing on the French infantry. Nonetheless, the French VII Corps kept the Prussian XI Corps pinned down near the village of Floing. The Prussian infantry and artillery defeated several counterattacks by the French cavalry. By early afternoon, the weight of numbers was beginning to tell, and the tables were slowly turning against the French.

The Prussians were now pressing in from all sides, and those French units that had not been routed or had surrendered retreated to Sedan. The French were barely holding on, and Napoleon III, realizing that he could not break out and no French units were going to break in, decided to surrender. After running up a white flag, he sent a letter to the Prussian headquarters. After reading the letter, Bismarck and the Kaiser accepted Napoleon's surrender. Napoleon III signed the official surrender documents the next day.

CONCLUSION

The battle cost the Prussians nearly 10,000 killed and wounded, and the French suffered over 3,000 killed, nearly 15,000 wounded, and over 100,000 prisoners. However, the capture of Napoleon III did not end the war. After his surrender, the legislators in Paris formed a Government of National Defense, and the fighting continued for another five months before the Prussians laid siege to Paris. Eventually, Prussia would win the Franco-Prussian War, but it was the Battle of Sedan that assured that victory—a victory that would lead to the unification of Germany.

Further Reading

Barry, Quintin. *Moltke and His Generals: A Study in Leadership.* Solihull, UK: Helion, 2015.

Howard, Michael. *The Franco-Prussian War: The German Invasion of France, 1870–1871.* London: Rupert Hart-Davis, 1961.

Wawro, Geoffrey. *The Franco-Prussian War: The German Conquest of France in 1870–1871.* Cambridge: Cambridge University Press, 2005.

Wetzel, David. *A Duel of Giants: Bismarck, Napoleon III, and the Origins of the Franco-Prussian War.* Madison: University of Wisconsin Press, 2001.

55. Battle of the Little Bighorn

Date: June 25–27, 1876
Location: Little Bighorn River, Wyoming

OPPONENTS

1. Sioux, Cheyenne, and Arapaho
   Commanders: Sitting Bull, Crazy Horse, and Gall
2. United States, 7th Cavalry
   Commnanders: Lieutenant Colonel George Armstrong Custer, Major Marcus
   Reno, and Captain Frederick Benteen

BACKGROUND

The Battle of the Little Bighorn (or the Battle of the Greasy Grass, as it is known to Native Americans) was the most significant battle of the Great Sioux War of 1876. The war was the result of settlers and speculators flooding into the Black Hills after gold was discovered there in 1874. Unable to keep the settlers out, the U.S. government tried to negotiate a transfer of the lands. However, the Black Hills were sacred lands to the Sioux and Cheyenne, and they refused to negotiate. In the fall of 1875, the Bureau of Indian Affairs gave the Native Americans until January 31, 1876 to be back on their reservations or be considered hostiles. The deadline passed, and many bands refused to return, so the U.S. army was permitted to commence operations.

The first battle took place on March 17, 1876 when six companies of cavalry under the command of Colonel Joseph Reynolds located a Lakota village of sixty-five lodges. After a brief fight, the cavalry occupied and destroyed the village, but they were driven off by a Lakota counterattack. This battle set the stage for a more extensive spring campaign under the command of Brigadier General Alfred Terry.

THE PLAN

General Terry's plan was for three columns to converge on the Native Americans in the vicinity of their hunting grounds. One column would march east from Fort Ellis with six companies from the 7th Infantry Regiment and four companies from the 2nd Cavalry Regiment. Another column of ten companies from the 3rd Cavalry Regiment, five from the 2nd Cavalry Regiment, two from the 4th Infantry Regiment, and three from the 9th Infantry regiment would march north from Fort Fetterman under the command of Brigadier General George Crook. The main body, under the command of General Terry, would march west from Fort Abraham Lincoln. This force included twelve companies of the 7th Cavalry under Lieutenant Colonel George Armstrong Custer, as well as a battery of Gatling guns.

On June 17, Crook's column engaged the significant force of Native Americans in a ferocious battle along the Rosebud Creek. Following the battle, Crook sent a message to General Phillip Henry Sheridan informing him of this fight and the tenacity of the Native Americans. This report reached Sheridan on June 19. He immediately forwarded it on to Terry; unfortunately, it did not reach Terry until June 30, five days after the battle along the Bighorn River. Based on reconnaissance reports, Terry formulated a plan to trap the Native Americans between Custer and Colonel John Gibbon. Terry went with Gibbon west along the Yellowstone River before turning south along the Bighorn River. He sent Custer south along the Rosebud from there; Custer was to turn north along the Little Bighorn, driving the Native Americans toward Gibbon. On June 21, both forces broke camp and marched off, setting the stage for the Battle of the Little Bighorn.

George Armstrong Custer in his general's uniform at the end of the American Civil War, 1865. His permanent rank at the time of Little Bighorn was lieutenant colonel. (Universal History Archive/Getty Images)

THE BATTLE

On the evening of June 24, Custer's scouts arrived at the Crow's Nest at dawn; the next day, they claimed they could see a huge pony herd. The American officers with them could not see it, and neither could Custer after he joined them. Custer planned to take the village by surprise the next morning, June 26; however, his scouts reported that the Native Americans were aware of the 7th Infantry Regiment's presence. Custer decided to attack the village immediately. Concerned that the camp would break up and scatter, Custer divided his twelve companies into three battalions: Companies A, G, and M under Major Marcus Reno; H, D, and K under Captain Frederick Benteen; and C, E, F, I, and L with Custer; while Company B, under Captain Thomas McDougall, was assigned to escort the slower pack trains. Reno's men would charge the front of the village to fix the Native Americans, while Custer took his five companies north to get in behind the village to prevent the women and children from slipping out the back. Benteen took his three companies to scout to the south. What Custer did not or could not know was that on this day, the Native Americans were going to stand and fight.

The battle opened with Major Reno and his troops crossing the Little Bighorn around 3 p.m. Reno's companies moved toward the village, masked by the brush along the creek. This brush also masked the village from Reno, and he was not sure of the exact size of the encampment. As his force came around a bend, he realized that the Native Americans were not fleeing, but rather were coming out to engage him. Reno halted his force and formed a skirmish line to accept the Native Americans' attack.

Both sides exchanged long-range rifle fire for about twenty minutes when Reno realized that the Native American warriors were massing on his exposed left flank. Reno ordered his command to take cover in the trees along the Little Bighorn River. The warriors continued to push Reno's men and eventually set fire to the woods, forcing the troops out. A confused Reno gave orders to mount, dismount, and mount before finally ordering his men to cross the river and seek cover on the bluffs on the other side. Trying to make it to the bluffs, Reno lost three officers and twenty-nine troops; approximately sixteen others were left behind in the woods. Those who made it to the bluffs began digging in, using knives, spoons, and anything else at hand.

There is much debate on the exact details of Custer's fight; however, it can be described in general terms. After leaving Reno, Custer took his five companies and continued north along the high ground overlooking the Little Bighorn. In all likelihood, he was trying to get to the flank or rear of the village to prevent the women and children from escaping and exploit Reno's charge.

From what is today called Reno Hill, Custer could see how large the village was. He sent a messenger back to hurry along the pack trains with the extra ammunition. From this position, Custer could also observe Reno's charge along the Little Bighorn, and he realized that he needed to attack the flank of the village to support Reno. Custer moved his forces off the high ground and continued north, looking for a place to attack the flank of the village. Halting in a coulee, Custer and his scouts rode up to some high ground to assess the situation again. He saw Reno forming his skirmish line and knew he had to act quickly to support him. In all likelihood, Custer formulated a plan to move toward Medicine Tail Coulee and use that route to attack the village.

At this point, Custer sent bugler John Martin (born Giovanni Martini), a recent immigrant from Italy who barely spoke English, back to give Benteen a message: "Come on. Big Village. Be quick, Bring packs. PS Bring packs." Along the trail, Martin passed Custer's younger brother, Boston, on his way to link up with his brother. Martin found Benteen and gave him the note. After reading the message, Benteen questioned the bugler, but Martin could not communicate any more details. At first Benteen waited for the trains, but eventually he took off with his command to find Custer. Instead of Custer, though, Benteen found Reno's men digging in on the bluff. Some accounts have Reno pleading with Benteen to help him rather than pushing on to find Custer. Regardless of the reason, Benteen elected to aid Reno. Eventually, the pack trains arrived and further reinforced the defenders.

Reaching Medicine Tail Coulee, and unaware of Reno's situation, Custer sent Captain George Yates with Companies E and F down the coulee. Custer, along with the other three companies under the command of Captain Myles Keogh, moved to the high ground overlooking the coulee to support Yates. Yates's attack took that portion of the village by surprise, but the warriors quickly recovered and began to push the troopers back.

Custer's command reunited on Calhoun Hill. From this point, Custer may have decided to continue north to try to capture some of the fleeing women and children. To do this, he left Keogh's three companies as a rearguard as he continued with the remaining two companies. However, on this day, the warriors decided to press their attack. Possibly, realizing that his force was insufficient for the task, Custer pulled back to join Keogh and wait for Benteen. The Native Americans began pressing from all sides as more warriors shifted from Reno Hill to attack Custer. The cohesion of the defenders began to break down, and the battle became a series of small stands. Some tried to flee but were cut down. Eventually, Custer and those with him on Last Stand Hill were overwhelmed and killed.

From Reno Hill, Reno's and Benteen's men could hear rifle fire that could only be coming from the direction of Custer's command. Around 5 p.m., it became too much for Captain Thomas Weir, one of Benteen's subordinates. He took his company, Company D, and moved out toward the sound of the guns. A mile out, Weir halted on what is today called Weir Point. He observed Native American warriors riding around and firing at the ground. Benteen and Reno, with the rest of the command, joined Weir at about the same time the warriors started moving toward the men on Weir Point. Benteen ordered the troopers back to the more easily defensible terrain on the bluffs. As night fell, the attacks tapered off, but the troopers could hear the sounds of celebration coming from the village.

About 2:30 a.m. on June 26, the attacks began again and lasted until late afternoon. Around 5 p.m., the troopers watched as a massive cloud of dust signaled the departure of the village. The next day, Generals Terry and Gibbon arrived to relieve the beleaguered force. Benteen and Reno asked about Custer and were shocked when Terry told them that he was dead, along with his command.

CONCLUSION

Exact casualty figures for the Native Americans are difficult to assess; however, thirty-one warriors has become the accepted number. Reno's initial charge on the village killed six women and four children. The 7th Cavalry lost sixteen officers and 242 troops, for a total of 258. Of that number, 210 fell with Custer along with his brothers, Tom and Boston; his brother-in-law, James Calhoun; and his nephew, Henry Reed.

Despite their success, the battle sealed the fate of the Native Americans. When word of the defeat reached back east, the nation was shocked and horrified, with many demanding that something had to be done to settle the "Indian question." It would take fourteen more years, but the road that led to the Little Bighorn would eventually end at Wounded Knee.

Further Reading

Donovan, James. *A Terrible Glory: Custer and the Little Bighorn—The Last Great Battle of the American West.* New York: Little, Brown and Company, 2008.

Miller, David. *Custer's Fall: The Native American Side of the Story.* New York: Penguin Putnam, 1992.

Philbrick, Nathaniel. *The Last Stand: Custer, Sitting Bull, and the Battle of the Little Big-horn.* New York: Viking, 2010.

Wagner, Frederic C. *The Strategy of Defeat at the Little Big Horn: A Military and Timing Analysis of the Battle.* Jefferson, SC: McFarland & Company, Inc., 2014.

56. Isandlwana

Date: January 22, 1879
Location: Isandlwana, South Africa

OPPONENTS

1. Brtish Empire

   Commanders: Lieutenant General Lord Chelmsford, Lieutenant Colonel Henry Pulleine, and Lieutenant Colonel Anthony Durnford

2. Zulu Kingdom

   Commanders: Ntshingwayo kaMahole Khoza, Vumindaba kaNthati, and Mavumengwana kaNdlela

BACKGROUND

The British government did not seek a war with the Zulus, but it came about nonetheless due to the machinations of the High Commissioner for South Africa, Sir Henry Bartle Fere. Fere was sent to South Africa to pull together the various groups in South Africa into the Condeferation of South Africa. A major obstacle to forming this confederation would be the fiercely independent Zulu Kingdom, under King Cetshwayo. Fere passed on his concerns to Great Britain, but the government denied him permission to invade Zululand. Undeterred, Fere took matters into his own hands and issued an ultimatum to Cetshwayo that he knew would be unacceptable. When the Zulu king inevitably rejected it, Fere ordered the local army commander, Frederic A. Thesiger, Lord Chelmsford, to invade Zululand.

Chelmsford had over 15,000 British soldiers, Native Natal Contingent (NNC), and other colonial troops at his disposal. The heart of his command lay in the four regular Britsih battalions from the 24th and 90th Regiments. Battalions from several other regiments augmented these. He formed his forces into five columns: Three of them, with approximately 7,800 soldiers, would form the main body, with the others in reserve. Each British soldier carried the breech-loading Martini-Henry rifle and seventy rounds of ammunition. The NNC, on the other hand, was not uniformly armed or as well trained as the British regulars.

Facing Chelmsford was a Zulu Impi (roughly the equivalent of a regiment) of 20,000 warriors armed with the assegai thrusting spear and a cowhide shield. A few had old muskets, but the Zulus were not very proficient in their use and so this was not of much concern to the British. Despite being outnumbered, Chelmsford was confident that as always, the steadfast discipline of the British soldier could overcome any numerical inferiority when it came to fighting indigenous peoples. With his army in high spirits, Chelmsford crossed the Buffalo River on January 11 near an outpost called Rorke's Drift to begin his invasion of Zululand. Unfortunately, his columns were making slow progress and had only advanced eleven miles in nine days. On January 20, Chelmsford decided to make camp near Isandlwana Hill. Underestimating the fighting abilities of the Zulus, he did not order the necessary defensive precautions for a British force on campaign.

On January 17, 24,000 Zulu warriors under the command of Ntshingwayo kaMahole Khoza departed from Ulundi, the Zulu capital. Moving in two columns, the Zulus moved quickly, covering fifty miles in five days. After detaching 4,000 warriors to cover the British lines of communication, the remainder of Khoza's force moved into the Ngwebeni Valley on January 21 and took up a position only five miles from Chelmsford's forces. He intended to attack the British on January 23.

THE BATTLE

Based on reconnaissance and some minor skirmishes, Chelmsford believed that the Zulus were to the southeast. On January 22, he planned to take a portion of his forces, including half of the British regulars, to seek out the Zulus and defeat them. Chelmsford left the defense of the camp to Lieutenant Colonel Henry Pulleine. Under his command, Pulleine had six companies of British regulars along with NNC contingents. Chelmsford also left him the two three-inch mountain guns from the 7th Brigade of the Royal Artillery. Around 8 a.m., Pulleine began receiving reports of Zulus on the nearby hills. Pulleine sent word to Chelmsford who, still convinced he was on the trail of the main Zulu forces, ignored the reports and continued his pursuit.

Around 10:30 a.m., Lieutenant Colonel Anthony Durnford, in command of five companies of the NNC, arrived at the camp. Durnford was senior to Pulleine and assumed command. Pulleine apprised him of the situation and his defensive preparations. Durnford concurred but surmised that the nearby Zulus might attack Chelmsford's force from the rear. Durnford recommended that he lead a party out to attack the Zulus; however, before this could happen, the Zulus struck.

A scouting party had chased a group of Zulus into a valley, but it ran into 20,000 warriors sitting quietly in the grass. All the Zulus rose up as one man and began charging the British scouts, who beat a hasty retreat out of the valley. Without orders, the Zulu warriors pursued the scouts back to the British camp and began organizing a hasty attack on the fly.

The Zulus typically attacked in a "buffalo horns" formation. The main body would be the "chest," and the forces on the flanks would be the "horns" in order to envelop the enemy. A reserve, or the "loins," would follow. The Zulu warriors instinctively organized themselves into this formation as they approached Isandlwana.

Hoping to stop the Zulus with firepower, Pulleine sent his six British regular companies forward to meet the Zulus in an extended firing line. Durnford's forces met the Zulus on the right of the camp and retreated along a dried-out gulley to form another defensive line. For a while, the discipline and firepower of the British held the Zulus at bay. However, the disparity in numbers began to tell, and the "horns" were gradually outflanking Pulleine and his command.

Under increasing pressure on the right, Durnford began to pull back, exposing Pulleine's right flank. Next, the Zulus quickly overran Company G of the 2nd Battalion of the 24th Foot. Seeing the threat to his flank, Pulleine began a fighting withdrawal back to the camp. Once again, the discipline and training of the British soldiers prevented this defeat from turning into a rout. Nevertheless, training and discipline could not compensate for lack of ammunition, as the soldiers' ammo pouches began to run empty.

Around noon, another messenger informed Chelmsford that his base camp was under attack. Chelmsford still could not (or would not) believe that the undisciplined and poorly armed Zulus could overrun the better-equipped and -trained British soldiers, so he dismissed the warnings as a false alarm. Missing his last chance to save the camp, Chelmsford continued his fruitless search for the Zulus.

Back at the camp, the fighting was becoming more desperate, but the steadfast British soldiers continued to hold off the Zulu warriors. However, firing on the line began to slacken as the soldiers ran increasingly low on ammo. Runners were sent back to retrieve more ammunition for the supply wagons, but in many cases, the position of the wagons did not align with the companies on the line. Many were hundreds of yards away from the company they supported. In the heat of the battle, the runners went to the nearest wagon, only to be turned away and sent farther on to their proper supply wagon. Adding to this dilemma was the fact that there were only two screwdrivers along the entire line to remove the nine screws that secured the lid to the ammunition boxes. To his credit, Chelmsford recognized this problem and had requested more screwdrivers, but the request was not acted upon before the campaign began.

The Zulus sensed that the British line was wavering and pressed in on them from all sides. Durnford's right flank began crumbling as some of his NNC soldiers slipped away. The rest were not equipped with bayonets, which made it difficult to hold off the Zulus with their assegais. The Zulus, now in the camp, were beginning to isolate the British companies. The fighting broke down in little stands of British soldiers as the Zulus wiped them out one by one. Durnford died with his remaining NNC soldiers in a depression near the supply wagons. Late in the battle, Pulleine handed the queen's colors of the 1st Battalion 24th Foot to Lieutenant Teignmouth Melvill for him to save them from capture. Pulleine then went to his tent and sat down to write a last note. As he was writing, a Zulu warrior entered. Pulleine shot first but only wounded the Zulu, who stabbed Pulleine in the chest with his assegai, killing him.

Melvill, aided by Lieutenant Nevill Coghill, eventually made it to the Buffalo River with the queen's colors. However, Melvill, succumbing to the many wounds he received during his escape, let the colors slip from his hand, and they fell into the river. The pursuing Zulus caught up with and killed both Melvill and Coghill. For their gallantry, both would receive posthumous Victoria Crosses in 1907. Later, some British soldiers found the colors downriver and returned them to the regiment.

By evening, the battle was over. Of the approximately 1,700 soldiers, British and NNC, that were present when the battle started, around 1,300 died in the fighting. Along with the two commanders, Durnford and Pulleine, fifty-two officers were killed. Most died fighting, but many others were run down and killed by the Zulus in what is known as Fugitives' Drift as they tried to flee. Zulu casualties are harder to assess, but sources put them between 1,500 and 2,000 killed and an unknown number of wounded.

CONCLUSION

Isandlwana was the single greatest defeat that the British army had suffered fighting indigenous peoples, and the news shocked the public back home. Blame for the defeat was placed squarely on the shoulders of Lord Chelmsford, despite his attempts to accuse Pulleine of disobeying his orders. Coincidentally, that same day, the 150-man force left behind at Rorke's Drift held off 3,000–4,000 Zulu warriors, and this gallant stand became the focus of the narrative in the British press. Nevertheless, the defeat at Isandlwana galvanized Parliament that something had to be done to avenge the loss and reestablish British dominance.

On July 4, 1879, with a larger force, Lord Chelmsford defeated the main Zulu army near the Zulu capital of Ulundi. The British then occupied and razed the

Frederic A. Thesiger, 2nd Baron Chelmsford (1827–1905)

Fredric A. Thesiger was born the eldest son of Frederic Thesiger, who later became Baron Chelmsford. In 1844, Thesiger, seeking a military career, was denied a commission in the Grenadier Guards and instead purchased a commission in the Rifle Brigade. He served with the Rifles before obtaining a transfer to the Grenadier Guards. In 1855, Captain Thesiger left with the Guards to fight in the Crimean War. After a brief stint with his unit, he served in several staff positions, including aide-de-camp to the 2nd Division commander. For his actions, Thesiger was promoted to brevet major and was mentioned in dispatches. He next served in India during the mutiny and was once again mentioned in dispatches. The up-and-coming Thesiger served as the adjutant general in the East Indies from 1869 to 19874.

In 1877, Thesiger, with the temporary rank of brigadier general, was given command of a brigade. The same year he was promoted to major general, and in 1878 he was given command of the forces in South Africa. In January 1879, Thesiger (now Lord Chelmsford) invaded Zululand; however, a major part of his command was annihilated at the Battle of Isandlwana. Following this debacle, Chelmsford was relieved of command. However, the irrepressible Chelmsford defeated the Zulus at the Battle of Ulundi before his replacement could arrive. Despite his tarnished reputation, he continued to serve, reaching the rank of lieutenant general in 1882. Chelmsford suffered a seizure while playing billiards and died in 1905.

village. They eventually captured King Cetshwayo, which broke the Zulus and ended the war. However, Lord Chelmsford would never clear his name from the defeat at Isandlwana, and he was recalled to Britain and never commanded British troops in the field again.

Further Reading

David, Saul. *Zulu: The Heroism and Tragedy of the Zulu War of 1879.* New York: Penguin Books, 2005.

Knight, Ian. *Zulu Rising: The Epic Story of Isandlwana and Rorke's Drift.* London: Pan Books, 2011.

Lock, Ron. *The Anglo Zulu War—Isandlwana: The Revelation of a Disaster.* London: Pen and Sword Books, 2017.

Morris, Donald R. *The Washing of the Spears: The Rise and Fall of the Zulu Nation.* New York: Da Capo Press, 1998.

57. The Yalu

Date: September 17, 1894
Location: Mouth of the Yalu River, on the Yellow Sea

OPPONENTS

1. Qing navy
    Commander: Admiral Ding Ju Chang
2. Imperial Japanese Navy
    Commander: Admirals Ito Yuko and Tsuboi Kozo

BACKGROUND

Korea served as the nexus for conflict in nineteenth-century Northeast Asia between the modernizing Japanese empire and the tottering Qing dynasty of China. After many European humiliations, the government in Beijing attempted to reform itself via a "self-strengthening effort." China's successful generals led this effort, which coincided with those of the Meiji oligarchs (former samurai lords) inside Japan. However, it had slowed considerably in China as the forces of reaction pushed back. Nonetheless, the Chinese military reforms continued, and the most capable and modernized forces—both army and navy—were under the control of the viceroy of North China, Li Hongzhang. By the 1890s, the Chinese had a respectable fleet, although it still had some way to go.

Japan's concerns, though, had to do more with Russia than with China. General Oritomo Yamagata feared that once the Russians completed the Trans-Siberian Railroad, they might use Korea as a springboard to invade Japan and subject her to the same treatment as the European powers had leveraged on an unwilling China in the Opium Wars. However, Japan's efforts to quietly build a buffer state in Korea against Russia brought them into conflict with the Qing. Chinese efforts had been somewhat successful in combating the encroachment of Russia and Japan. The occasion for the outbreak of war involved the appointment by the Qing court of a "resident" in Seoul to protect its special relationship with the Korean court. The Japanese used an outbreak of rebellion against the Korean king as an excuse to intervene in Korea to protect their interests.

A Japanese division landed at Inchon in July 1894 and on July 21, the Japanese seized the Korean royal palace and installed a regent loyal to them. Open hostilities broke out as the Chinese rushed troops across the Yellow Sea to Korea. Admiral Ito Yuko put to sea on July 23 with Japan's Combined Fleet. A "flying squadron," commanded by the American-trained admiral Tsuboi Kozo, stumbled on a lightly escorted Chinese troop convoy and sank a gunboat and a Chinese transport, causing the deaths of nearly 1,000 soldiers and sailors. It was with this surprise (read impromptu) naval attack that formal hostilities began.

THE PLANS AND BATTLE

The naval engagement at the Yalu River was not the result of a specific plan by either side, but rather a maritime meeting engagement by both fleets during an amphibious operation by the Chinese. The centerpiece of the new Chinese navy were its German-built battleships *Chen Yuen* and *Ting Yuen*, the latter being the flagship of Admiral Ding Ju Chang's Northern Fleet. The battle resulted when the Chinese Northern Fleet rendezvoused with a troop convoy at the mouth of the Yalu and then covered its troop disembarkation to protect against a possible attack by the Japanese fleet under Ito. On the night of September 16–17, the convoy arrived at the Yalu, and the transports, escorted by gunboats and torpedo boats, proceeded upriver to unload troops. According to Ding's second-in-command, an American naval officer in Chinese service named Philo McGiffen, Ding was restricted from even searching for the Japanese fleet.

Ito's fleet of twelve warships, none displacing more than 4,300 tons, arrived at the mouth of the Yalu around midday on September 17. McGiffen (1895) described them as follows:

> Monday . . . was a beautiful day, a light breeze gently ruffling the surface of the water. . . . [The] Japanese ships, forming apparently a single line and preserving station and speed throughout most beautifully, could not but excite a feeling of admiration.

The Chinese fleet also consisted of twelve ships, but it had the weight of tonnage and armor on its side, principally due to the two battleships (including McGiffen's *Chen Yuen*). Two of the Chinese ships, an armored cruiser and a torpedo cruiser, were at the mouth of the Yalu and would not join the fleet until after 2 p.m. The Japanese had audacity and initiative on their side. Almost immediately, the Chinese lost two of their warships as their captains fled in a cowardly manner to the safety of Port Arthur's protected harbor to the north. Meanwhile, the two fleets started to pound each other. The Chinese had the armor and balance of heavier guns, but the Japanese had the advantages of maneuverability and rapid-fire, smaller-caliber weapons and machine guns. Two older Chinese cruisers were obliterated at the end of the Chinese line by the Japanese soon after the engagement began.

The battle degenerated into a slugfest between the Japanese fleet and the two modern battleships *Chen Yuen* and *Ting Yuen,* with the Japanese ignoring the remaining smaller Chinese vessels. The range of the gunnery varied between 1,000 to 2,800 yards, and the carnage aboard the ships was incredible, although the armor belts kept the two battleships from receiving any damage below the waterline. With the arrival of night, Ito broke off the action as the remaining six Chinese ships, most of them badly damaged, retreated north to Port Arthur.

This battle is often touted as an overwhelming victory for the Japanese; however, the Japanese had received a punishing fire from the Chinese. Five Chinese ships had been sunk and four (including the battleships) heavily damaged, as compared to four seriously damaged Japanese warships (especially the cruiser *Hiei*). The Chinese suffered over 1,300 killed and wounded, compared to Japan's nearly 300. Most of the dead Chinese drowned.

CONCLUSION

McGiffen (1895) credited the Japanese victory to "better ships, more of them, better and larger supplies of ammunition, better officers, and as good men." The Imperial Japanese Navy had established itself as a force to be reckoned with. Admiral Ding, meanwhile, took his fleet to Weihaiwei, where it was bottled up by the Japanese in January 1895 and besieged from the land. This gave the Japanese command of the sea, allowing them complete freedom to prosecute the war aggressively against the Chinese armies, including an amphibious assault at Weihaiwei.

The war ended quickly, by April 1895, with the Japanese levying a humiliating peace on the Chinese that ceded them de facto control of Korea. The Sino-Japanese War accelerated the collapse of Qing China so that by the time of the Boxer Rebellion in 1900, it had become essentially a failed state on the verge of revolution and civil war.

Further Reading

Drea, Edward J. *Japan's Imperial Army: Its Rise and Fall, 1853–1945.* Lawrence: University Press of Kansas, 2009.

Evans, David C., and Peattie, Mark R. *Kaigun.* Annapolis: Naval Institute Press, 1997.

Mahan, A. T. "The Battle of the Yalu: An Interview with the Times," in Robert Seager II and Doris D. Maguire, eds., *Letters and Papers of Alfred Thayer Mahan, Volume 3:* 583–585. Annapolis, MD: Naval Institute Press, 1975.

McGiffin, Philo N. "The Battle of the Yalu: Personal Recollections by the Commander of the Chinese Ironclad 'Chen Yuen.'" *Century: A Popular Quarterly,* 50(4) (1895): 585–605.

58. Manila Bay

Date: May 1, 1898
Location: Luzon Island, Philippines

OPPONENTS

1. Spain
    Commander: Rear Admiral Patricio Montojo
2. United States
    Commander: Commodore George Dewey

BACKGROUND

The Battle of Manila Bay was the decisive battle in the Pacific during the Spanish-American War. The animosity between the United States and Spain had been building during the latter part of the nineteenth century and finally came to a head when the USS *Maine* blew up and sank in Havana Harbor on February 15, 1898. Despite Spain's protestations to the contrary, the American people believed that Spanish sab-oteurs had blown up the ship. Facing political and public pressure, President William McKinley sent Spain an ultimatum demanding their withdrawal from Cuba. In reply, Spain declared war on the United States on April 24, and the United States declared war on Spain the next day.

On April 26, Commodore George Dewey, commander of the U.S. navy's Asiatic Squadron, received orders to proceed to the Philippine Islands and engage the Spanish naval forces in the area. Dewey had been preparing his ships for this eventuality as soon as he received word of the U.S. declaration of war. His squadron consisted of four cruisers, *Olympia* (Dewey's flagship), *Baltimore*, *Boston,* and *Raleigh*; two gunboats, *Concord* and *Petrel*; a revenue cutter, *McCulloch,* and

Admiral George Dewey, hero of the Battle of Manila Bay. Dewey was later made admiral of the fleet by an Act of Congress and is the only U.S. officer to ever hold this rank and title. (The Print Collector/Getty Images)

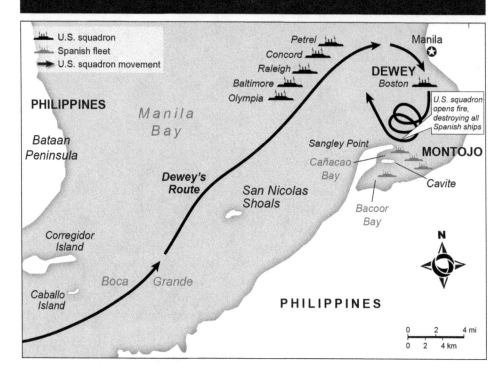

BATTLE OF MANILA BAY, MAY 1, 1898

two supply ships, *Nanshan* and *Zafiro*. On April 27, Dewey's ships weighed anchor and headed for the Philippines. Arriving off the coast of the islands on April 30, Dewey sent the *Boston* and *Concord* to scout Subic Bay for Spanish ships; they found none. Dewey proceeded to Manila Harbor, satisfied that he had the Spanish fleet bottled up.

The Spanish Philippine fleet consisted of seven obsolete (or nearly obsolete) ships. There were six cruisers: *Reina Cristina, Isla de Cuba, Isla de Luzon, Don Juan de Austria, Don Antonio de Ulloa,* and *Castilla*. And the *Castilla* was in such bad shape that it could not make to the battle under its own power. Rounding out this contingent was a gunboat, *Marques del Duero*. The fleet commander, Rear Admiral Patricio Montojo, had intended to fight the American ships in Subic Bay; however, after realizing that the Subic defenses would not be ready, he held a conference with his commanders. He elected to defend Manila Bay, hoping to take advantage of the superior shore defenses there. On April 29, the Spanish ships left Subic Bay for Manila, with the *Castilla* in tow.

Dewey's reconnaissance had missed Montojo's fleet by one day. Montojo, who had never held out any hope that he could defeat the Americans, positioned his ships in shallower water away from Manila in order to save the city from bombardment and give his crews a chance to swim to shore. On the night of April 30, he received word that Dewey's ships were in Subic Bay.

THE BATTLE

At midnight, the Asiatic Squadron, with Dewey's flagship in the lead, entered Manila Bay. After some ineffectual fire from a shore battery protecting the entrance, Dewey detached the cutter *McCulloch* and the two supply ships and sailed on with his four cruisers and two gunboats. Traveling in line formation, the Asiatic Squadron found the Spanish ships anchored off Sangley Point. Dewey turned his ships to bring their port guns to bear, and at 5:41 a.m., he issued the now famous "fire when ready" command to the captain of the *Olympia,* Charles Gridley. For whatever reason, and to Dewey's dismay, the first salvos from the American ships failed to score any hits. On the other hand, the smoke generated by their guns rendered the Spaniards' return fire ineffectual as well. Dewey turned his flotilla to bring the starboard guns to bear.

For the next two hours, Dewey's ships circled around the Spanish ships a total of five times. On the second pass, most of the American fire was directed at Montojo's flagship*, Reina Cristina,* wrecking it from bow to stern. Before abandoning the ship, approximately eighty Spanish sailors lost their lives. On each subsequent pass, the Americans inflicted more damage on the Spanish fleet. By the time the Asiatic Squadron completed its fifth pass, they had sunk two Spanish ships, and the rest were heavily damaged. In return, the Spanish landed one hit on the *Baltimore,* causing the only U.S. casualties during the battle.

Around 7:45 a.m., Dewey received word that the *Olympia* had only fifteen rounds of 5" ammunition per gun remaining. Coupled with this news was the fact that Dewey could not discern the exact condition of the Spanish fleet, so he elected to withdraw out of range. During the lull, Dewey held a conference aboard the *Olympia.* The reports from his commanders revealed that his ships had incurred very little damage and that the ammunition report was misinterpreted. The report should have been that *Olympia* had expended only fifteen rounds per gun. With this news, Dewey gave orders to reengage the Spanish ships.

The attack resumed at 11:16 a.m., when the Americans quickly sank *Don Antonio de Ulloa.* With all or most of the Spanish fleet sunk or ablaze, the U.S. ships turned their attention to the shore batteries. This result of this duel was a foregone conclusion, as the U.S. ships outranged the antiquated Spanish guns. The final act of the battle occurred when the *Petrel* fired on the colonial government building. Shortly afterward, the Spanish forces surrendered. The Battle of Manila Bay was over, and the U.S. navy had decisively won its first engagement since the American Civil War.

CONCLUSION

In this one-sided victory, the Spanish fleet lost eight ships and nearly 350 were killed or wounded. Admiral Montojo returned to Spain in disgrace to face a court-martial. On the U.S. side, the ships of the Asiatic Squadron suffered minor damage and the only casualties, eight wounded and one death due to a heart attack, were onboard the *Baltimore.* Once word of the victory reached the United States, Dewey became an instant national hero. He was promoted to admiral in 1899, and then, in 1903, an act of Congress promoted him to Admiral of the Navy. Dewey is the only officer ever to attain this rank. He served out the remainder of his career, and his life, as president of the General Board of the Navy.

Following the battle, Dewey set about consolidating his position in and around Manila. He sealed off the approaches to the bay and worked with the Filipino nationalists under Emilio Aguinaldo to keep the Spaniards off balance. Two weeks after the battle, Dewey received word that reinforcements were on the way, and in August, the combined American and Filipino forces entered Manila. Unfortunately, the Filipinos expected this to be the first step to independence, but the United States was not ready to grant them this status. Angered at this betrayal, Aguinaldo and his force slipped off into the jungle, setting off the Philippines Insurrection.

Further Reading

Anonymous. "Battle of Manila Bay, 1 May 1898," Naval History and Heritage Command, at https://www.history.navy.mil/research/library/online-reading-room/title-list-alpha betically/b/battle-of-manila-bay-1-may-1898.html (accessed September 12, 2019).

Leeke, Jim. *Manila and Santiago: The New Steel Navy in the Spanish-American War.* Annapolis, MD: Naval Institute Press, 2009.

Love, Robert W., Jr. *History of the U.S. Navy: Volume I, 1775–1941.* Harrisburg, PA: Stackpole Books, 1992.

Nofi, Albert A. *The Spanish-American War, 1898.* Boston: DaCapo Press, 1997.

PART VI

Recent Military Disasters

59. Tsushima Strait

Date: May 27–28, 1905
Location: Tsushima Strait, between Korea and Japan

OPPONENTS

1. Empire of Russia
   Commander: Admiral Z. P. Rozhestvensky
2. Empire of Japan
   Commander: Admiral Togo Heihachiro

BACKGROUND

The causes for the Russo-Japanese War can be found in the Empire of Japan's humiliation after the Treaty of Shimonoseki, which had led to Russian imperial gains in Manchuria and North China at Tokyo's expense. Russia signed a lease with the weak Qing court for Port Arthur's naval base on the Liaodong peninsula for twenty-five years, with rights to an extension. In 1903, matters came to a head when Russia, which had deployed troops to protect the rail trunk into Manchuria from the Trans-Siberian Railroad, kept those troops in place in violation of previous agreements. The Russians were also improving the Trans-Siberian by making it a double rail line to increase their ability to build up forces in the Far East—obviously with Japan in mind. Imperial Russia now posed a clear naval threat from Port Arthur and a land-based threat from southern Manchuria against the Korean buffer zone.

Japan's leaders, strengthened in 1902 by a naval defensive treaty with Great Britain, began to plan seriously for war. On the Russian side, Rear Admiral O. V. Stark commanded the Pacific Squadron for Russia. Neither Stark nor the overall commander, Vice Admiral E. I. Alekseev, had thought to take any extra precautions after the Japanese severed diplomatic relations on February 8, 1904.

The overall Japanese fleet commander, Admiral Togo, decided to open the war with a surprise torpedo attack by his lighter forces on the night of February 8–9. His caution prevented him from deploying the mass of his fleet closer to his destroyers delivering the initial blow. Somewhat like Pearl Harbor almost forty years later, the Japanese found their adversary's ships anchored in the roadstead, oblivious, with all their lights on. The Japanese surprise attack, unlike Pearl Harbor, did

BATTLE OF TSUSHIMA STRAIT

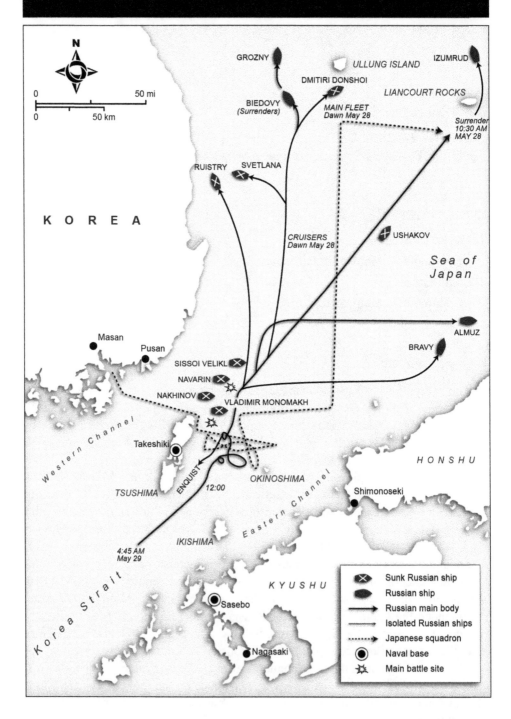

N

0 ————— 50 mi
0 ————— 50 km

GROZNY

ULLUNG ISLAND

IZUMRUD

DMITIRI DONSHOI

LIANCOURT ROCKS

BIEDOVY
(Surrenders)

MAIN FLEET
Dawn May 28

Surrender
10:30 AM
MAY 28

RUISTRY

SVETLANA

K O R E A

CRUISERS
Dawn May 28

USHAKOV

Sea of
Japan

Masan

Pusan

BRAVY

ALMUZ

SISSOI VELIKL

NAVARIN

NAKHINOV

VLADIMIR MONOMAKH

Takeshiki

Western Channel

ENQUIST

12:00

HONSHU

OKINOSHIMA

Eastern Channel

Shimonoseki

TSUSHIMA

IKISHIMA

4:45 AM
May 29

K Y U S H U

Korea Strait

Sasebo

Nagasaki

⊗	Sunk Russian ship
◆	Russian ship
→	Russian main body
—	Isolated Russian ships
⋯→	Japanese squadron
◉	Naval base
✹	Main battle site

not significantly damage the Russian fleet, but it did force the cautious Russian commander back into port. The following day Emperor Meiji, in his role as supreme warlord, formally declared war on Russia.

It was the fate of this fleet, the First Pacific Ocean Squadron, that resulted in the catastrophic destruction of a second Russian fleet at Togo's hands fifteen months later in the Tsushima Strait off southern Korea. Togo spend most of the next year trying to lure this fleet out to battle, fighting numerous engagements and even killing Russia's most talented admiral, S. O. Makarov, and his successor, Rear Admiral V. K. Vitgeft, in battle. However, the Russian fleet scurried back into the safety of Port Arthur's fortifications and guns every time. Accordingly, the Japanese army decided to simply capture the port and finally neutralize the fleet in this way. When it became apparent to the Russians that this would indeed happen, another fleet—the Second Pacific Ocean Squadron, sometimes mistakenly called the Baltic Fleet—was dispatched under Admiral Z. P. Rozhestvensky to rescue the first fleet.

After months of a bloody siege, the Japanese army under General Nogi Maresuki finally captured Port Arthur on January 2, 1905. None of the Russian fleet escaped. Nogi lost over 59,000 men but would go on to be lauded for this hollow so-called victory. Rozhestvensky's fleet was still five months from arriving in the theater, though no one thought to tell him to turn around. Togo wisely spent this period of reprieve giving his crews rest and his ships necessary maintenance.

THE PLAN

Togo and his Combined Fleet staff relentlessly prepared for battle, repairing their ships and putting in place intelligence collection and reconnaissance assets to track the Russians. He also decided to throw caution to the winds, changing his conservative battle tactics and deciding that he would close in to a range where his gunfire couldn't miss—3,000 meters or less. Togo and his planners also predicted that Rozhestvensky would go to Vladivostok when he finally appeared. Accordingly, he took up a position in the Tsushima Strait and awaited his prey.

Rozhestvensky soon obliged him. His squadron contained more than forty ships, but it was a "cats and dogs" force, with many outdated and obsolescent ships, including lumbering monitors that had been added at the last minute. After a lengthy stay at Can Ranh Bay in Indochina, Rozhestvensky pushed on in May with everything he had to attempt to slip through the Tsushima Strait to safety at Vladivostok. Beyond that, he had no plans. Togo's patience and intuition were rewarded on May 26 when his scouts sighted the Russians in the East China Sea, east of Shanghai.

THE BATTLE

Battle was joined between the two forces on May 27–28, 1905, and the results were predictable, given Togo's preparation and Rozhestvensky's grim fatalism. Upon sighting the Russian column, Togo sent a very Nelsonian signal to his crews: "[T]he existence of our Imperial country rests on this one action, and every man of you must do his utmost." Just like Nelson at Trafalgar, Togo was outnumbered in his total number of battleships, but he outnumbered the Russians overall, with his light motor torpedo boats and destroyers making up a large part of his fleet.

Straining to "cross the Russian T," Togo did not wait for the maneuver to begin to destroy his quarry and had his ship open fire as soon as the Russians were in range. His belief in the efficiency of his crews and gunnery was rewarded, and he crossed the T about 30 minutes after the gunplay started. The Japanese achieved a command and control kill when they knocked Rozhestvensky's *Suvorov* out of the fight early, with the wounded Russian commander avoiding death on his sinking ship only by transferring to a torpedo boat. The Russian fleet fell into the incompetent hands of Admiral N. I. Nebogatov.

Throughout the rest of the day and night, the Japanese pursued, sank, and captured Russian vessels, with Nebogatov surrendering two battleships, two coastal ships, and a cruiser on May 28. It was a confused and chaotic fight. The wounded Rozhestvensky was also captured when the vessel carrying him surrendered. Of the thirty-eight Russian ships that attempted passage, thirty-four had been scuttled, sunk, interned in foreign ports, or captured. Only four ships escaped.

CONCLUSION

Tsushima was among the most complete naval battles in history, and its impact now combined with the perceptions of Russian defeat on land, even though Russia's strong position in Manchuria had caused Japan to seek a diplomatic solution. Tsushima did two things: First, it contributed to the outbreak of antiwar demonstrations and revolution in Russia that threatened the survival of the ruling Romanov regime; and second, because of the magnitude of the defeat, it provided an opening

Alfred Thayer Mahan (1840–1914)

Alfred Thayer Mahan was born in West Point, New York, as the first son of Dennis Hart Mahan. The elder Mahan graduated first in his class at West Point and then went on to teach at West Point for most of the rest of his life. The younger Mahan was slated to become a churchman but cut short his studies at Columbia University and entered the U.S. Naval Academy as a second-year student in 1856. He graduated second in his class in 1859 and served in the Gulf Blockading Squadron during the Civil War and later cruised to Japan. After the war, he taught at the Naval Academy and became known as a naval reformer, joining the nascent U.S. Naval Institute and contributing regularly to its *Proceedings*.

His history of the Gulf Blockading Squadron gained the attention of Commodore Stephen Luce, president of the newly founded Naval War College. Luce had Mahan ordered to the college and when Mahan arrived, he found Luce gone, and he became the second president. While at the Naval War College, he published his lectures in 1890 as *The Influence of Sea Power upon History, 1660–1783*. After receiving rave reviews from people like Theodore Roosevelt, it became a best-seller and one of the most influential books in modern history. Mahan's views on sea power and grand strategy informed an entire generation of naval strategists, although by the time he died in 1914, he was more known for his views on political policy than on naval strategy.

for both parties to end the war. U.S. president Theodore Roosevelt offered to host peace talks at Portsmouth, New Hampshire, and the Russians and Japanese accepted. Russia stood firm on not paying Japan an indemnity but grudgingly ceded the southern half of Sakhalin Island in the Sea of Okhotsk to Japan, recognition of Japan's rights in Korea, and—most significantly—the railroad lines in southern Manchuria and the Liaodong concession with China. Neither side was happy with the peace, but it was clearly a military disaster for the Russians.

Further Reading

Evans, David C., and Peattie, Mark R. *Kaigun.* Annapolis: Naval Institute Press, 1997.

Mahan, A. T. "Reflections, Historic and Other, Suggested by the Battle of the Japan Sea," *U.S. Naval Institute Proceedings,* 32(118) (June 1906): 447–471.

Menning, Bruce W., and John W. Steinberg, David Schimmelpenninck Van Der Oye, David Wolff, and Shinji Yokote, eds. *The Russo-Japanese War in Global Perspective: World War Zero,* Volume 29 of the "History of Warfare" series, general editor Kelly DeVries. Boston: Brill Publishing, 2003.

Pleshakov, Constantine. *The Tsar's Last Armada: The Epic Voyage to the Battle of Tsushima.* New York: Basic Books, 2002.

60. Tannenberg

Date: August 26–30, 1914
Location: East Prussia (present-day Poland)

OPPONENTS

1. Germany
    Commanders: Generals Paul von Hindenburg and Erich Ludendorff
2. Russia
    Commanders:
    First Army: General Paul von Rennenkampf
    Second Army: General Alexander Samsonov

BACKGROUND

The Battle of Tannenberg, occurring in the opening weeks of World War I, was one of the most successful German offensives of the war. The Germans believed that any future in Europe would involve them fighting multiple opponents; the Germans developed a prewar strategy to deal with this contingency. Developed by the chief of the General Staff, Field Marshal Alfred von Schlieffen, the plan that bears his name was to address this problem. Schlieffen proposed that the main threat to Germany were the western allies, and they should be defeated first. The German staff estimated that it would take Russia at least six weeks to mobilize fully. By that time, they predicted that the war would be over in the west, and those German divisions then could be sent east to finish off Russia. Therefore, the plan called for one German army to defend East Prussia until reinforcements arrived from the west. But the German staff underestimated the time that Russia required for mobilization and two Russian armies were poised to invade East Prussia within two weeks of the start of the war.

The Russian First and Second Armies crossed into East Prussia on August 17. The First Army, under the command of General Paul von Rennenkampf, attacking from the northeast, was to hold the Germans while the Second Army, under the command of General Alexander Samsonov, encircled the German Eighth Army. The two Russian armies were slowly pushing the Germans back into East Prussia. To forestall any further Russian advances, General Maximillian von Prittwitz, the commander of the German Eighth Army, ordered a counterattack on August 20 near Gumbinnen. The Russian First Army was driven back but quickly recovered, and von Rennenkampf went back on the offensive. Caught off guard, the Germans began to break, and von Prittwitz informed Berlin that he was going to withdraw to the Vistula River, ceding all of East Prussia to the Russians. But Field Marshal Helmut von Moltke, chief of the General Staff, denied von Prittwitz permission to withdraw and recalled him and his chief of staff back to Berlin. Then von Moltke replaced them with Generals Paul von Hindenburg and Erich von Ludendorff.

Meanwhile, after his victory at Gumbinnen, von Rennenkampf decided to regroup rather than pursue the Germans. To the south, Samsonov continued to make progress, but the weaknesses in the Russian plan were beginning to show. The main weakness was the logistics system. Because of different rail gauges, Russian supplies were unloaded at the border and moved by wagon from there; as a result, Russian armies were beginning to outrun their supplies. A heavily wooded and swampy area around the Masurian Lakes separated the two armies, which would have made coordination difficult even if the Russian communications system had been up to the task. Also, the personal relationship between Rennekampf and Samsonov further complicated matters. Even though both men were highly regarded in the Russian army, they detested each other. They may have even come to blows in the past. As such, neither man was inclined to come to the assistance of the other.

Hindenburg and Ludendorff arrived on August 22 to take control of the Eighth Army and the situation in East Prussia. Colonel Max Hoffmann, the Eighth Arny's operations officer, briefed them on a plan that the staff was working on to encircle the Second Army. Hoffman pointed out that it would entail some risk on the German left flank, facing von Rennenkampf's First Army. Hindenburg considered the risk acceptable and ordered the planning to continue. Ludendorff wanted to launch the attack as early as August 25, but the corps commander responsible for the attack refused until all his artillery was in place. Ludendorff was incensed by the corps commander's response but eventually agreed.

In the meantime, the Germans intercepted two messages in the clear that would shape the battle to come. The first message confirmed that von Rennenkampf was not going to march southward to support Samsonov, meaning that a cavalry screen might be sufficient to fix the First Army, freeing more divisions to attack the right flank of the Second Army. The second message detailed the route that Samsonov planned to take to continue his pursuit of the Germans. With this information in hand, Hindenburg and Ludendorff refined Hoffmann's plan and set a date for the offensive to begin: August 26.

THE BATTLE

The German offensive did not get off to an auspicious start. On the right, the commander of I Corps, General Hermann von Francois, was still reluctant to attack until his entire corps was in position. Nevertheless, at 8 a.m., part of his 1st Division made a half-hearted attack on the Russians, which kept them occupied until the rest of the corps detrained at around noon. Later in the afternoon, after his corps was ready, von Francois's corps penetrated the Russian outposts. However, rather than exploit his success, Francois halted for the day to prepare for a larger attack the next day. But the XX Corps had more success and nearly destroyed a Russian division in its opening attack. On the left, Hindenburg and Ludendorff lost contact with their forces and knew little about the progress of the XVII or I Corps (Reserve) advancing on Samsonov's right flank. To compound matters, they received reports that von Rennenkampf's infantry was moving to support the Second Army. The evening of August 26 was a tense one at Eighth Army headquarters, but the steadfast Hindenburg was willing to let the plan unfold.

Meanwhile, Samsonov, because of Russian communication shortcomings, did not have a clear picture of the situation on either side of the front line. The grand duke and uncle to the tsar, Prince Nicholas, visited the Northwest Military District commander, General Yakov Zhlinsky, to assess the situation. After the briefing, he recommended that Zhlinsky send help from the First Army to support Samsonov. Zhilinsky relayed orders to von Rennenkampf to send two corps to link up with the Second Army. He received the orders but did not begin moving his cavalry until the next day and held up his infantry until they were resupplied. It was into this confused Russian situation that the Germans launched their attack.

On August 27, I Corps, following a devasting artillery barrage, attacked on the Second Army's left flank. The German infantry quickly seized the town of Usdau and pushed on. Meanwhile, the I Corps (R) and XVII Corps resumed their attack on the north flank of the Second Army, pushing Russians into the trap that was forming around the Second Army. Despite these setbacks, the Russians could claim some success in the center against the German XX Corps.

The next day, August 28, Hindenburg and Ludendorff one again received reports that Rennkampf's army was advancing, only this time the reports indicated the Russians were threatening the German rear areas. Fearing that the Eighth Army might be falling into a trap, Ludendorff wanted to call off the attack in order to face the new threat. Once more, Hindenburg calmed down his quartermaster general, and eventually it turned out that the first report was in error. The threat, real or imagined, passed, and the attack on the Second Army continued. Both of Samsonov's flank corps were now in full retreat, with the Germans in pursuit. Even the Russian center was weakening and was giving ground. The German Corps commander, Francois, defied his superiors—not for the first time—and advanced farther than called for in his orders. As it happened, by exceeding his orders, Francois trapped more Russians in the encirclement.

On August 29, the advancing units of the German army linked up, trapping three Russian Corps in what was to become a bloody cauldron. The Germans began to rain relentless artillery fire on the trapped men, as Hindenburg and Ludendorff watched from a hilltop. Those that tried to break out were cut down by German rifle and machine-gun fire. Most, however, surrendered, and long columns of prisoners headed west. The next day, the Russians launched an unsuccessful attack from the outside to break through and relieve those trapped inside. By the evening of August 30, the most successful German offensive of the war was over.

Of the nearly 200,000 soldiers in the Russian Second Army, approximately 78,000 were killed or wounded, and another 92,000 were taken prisoner. The total casualties for the Germans amounted to 12,000. More impressively, the Germans sent sixty trainloads of captured Russian equipment back to Germany.

CONCLUSION

Hindenburg reported his victory to the Kaiser and asked the battle be named Tannenberg, after the nearby site where the Poles defeated the Teutonic Knights in 1410. The scale of the German victory made it seem like poetic justice to Hindenburg. Ludendorff and Hindenburg would continue to make a name for themselves as a winning team in the east. As a result, both would be transferred to the west

Russian prisoners from the defeat at Tannenberg (1914) incarcerated by Germany's ally Austria-Hungary. (Hulton Archive/Getty Images)

after the debacle at Verdun about a year and a half later. Eventually, they would be de facto running both the war and the German economy. Later, Hindenburg would be the last president of the Weimar Republic before Adolf Hitler, and Ludendorff would be at Hitler's side during the failed Munich Putsch in 1923.

Rather than face the tsar, Samsonov slipped off into the woods to commit suicide. His body was recovered by the Germans the following year and returned to Russia. Meanwhile, Rennenkampf, following an investigation into the conduct of the battle, was exonerated and returned to command in Poland. He retired in 1916.

Further Reading

Hastings, Max. *Catastrophe 1914: Europe Goes to War.* London: Knopf, 2013.

Showalter, Dennis E. *Tannenberg: Clash of Empires, 1914.* Washington, DC: Brassey's, 2004.

Sweetman, John. *Tannenberg, 1914.* London: Cassell, 2002.

Tuchman, Barbara W. *The Guns of August: The Outbreak of World War I.* Reprint ed. New York: Random House, 2014 (orig. 1962).

61. The Gorlice-Tarnow Offensive

Date: May 1–September 30, 1915
Location: Eastern Front

OPPONENTS

1. Germans and Austro-Hungarians

   Commanders: August von Mackensen and Conrad von Hötzendorff

2. Russians

   Commanders: Overall Grand Duke Nicholas and, on the Southwestern Front, General N. Ivanov

BACKGROUND

The year 1914 brought a stalemate to the western front in World War I. However, on the eastern front, the Russians, while suffering defeat at the hands of the Germans in the north, had achieved great victories in the south against the Austrians, capturing Lemburg (Lvov) and placing the great fortress of Przemsyl under siege. By mid-March 1915, the Russians had captured the fortress, but their other offensive operations in the Carpathians ground to a halt in the bloody snow. However, German successes in the north at Tannenburg and Masurian Lakes had tempered victory in the south so that neither side had a clear edge. Also, the Russians continued to grind away in a late winter offensive in the Carpathian Mountains in the hope that the Austro-Hungarian forces would crack, opening the way to Budapest, and even Vienna.

Germany and her ally Austria were faced with a strategic dilemma. The chief of the German General Staff, Erich von Falkenhayn, realized that the war could be lost in the east due to the precarious situation of the Austrians. Surely in the late spring, after the rains stopped and the ground dried out, the Russians would try again to drive over the Carpathians into the Hungarian plain in order to end the war. Thus, the area most at risk was Galicia, in southern Poland. Falkenhayn had formed a new army—the Eleventh—from reserves and units on the western front to use in the east. Field Marshal Paul von Hindenburg believed that the best recipe would be to employ the army in an offensive farther north to tie down Russian reserves there, where he commanded. The Austrian commander-in-chief, Conrad von Hötzendorff, instead wanted an offensive, supported by the Germans, on his southern front, in the Carpathians. Falkenhayn wanted to take care of the problem of Serbia first, but he agreed to support Hötzendorff with an offensive against Russia. Serbia could wait.

THE PLANS

Planning for the Austro-German offensive was turned over to the talented chief of staff—Hans von Seeckt—serving under the Eleventh Army, commanded by August von Mackensen. Falkenhayn was also trying to create a foil to the increasing power and influence of Hindenburg by turning this operation over to Mackensen. At the strategic level, Falkenhayn used a limited offensive in the west near Ypres to cover the eastward movement of the Eleventh Army. He also had Hindenburg conduct an offensive to distract Russian attention farther north in Lithuania, sending strong reserves there as well. These offensives succeeded in their intent, pulling Russian attention and reserves north and blinding the Allies to the movement of the Eleventh Army to Galicia.

Next, von Seeckt and Mackensen deployed the Eleventh Army and the Fourth Austrian Army in absolute secrecy. They planned to use a short but massive artillery barrage by over 700 guns to disrupt and rupture the front from Tarnow down to the town of Gorlice, in the foothills of the northern Carpathians. Their target was the Russian Third Army, commanded by General Radko Radko-Dimitriev.

THE CAMPAIGN

The Germans knew that the opening battle hinged on artillery. The Russians opposite them had far fewer guns, and, worse, their ongoing offensive operations in April had depleted their stockpile of shells to as low as ten rounds per gun. The Germans also had heavier, longer-range guns. Their tactical plan went according to plan. On the night of May 1–2, they began intermittent artillery bombardments all along the front to disrupt and confuse the Russians. Then, at 6 a.m., all 700-plus guns opened up with a terrific bombardment that lasted until 10 a.m. Their intelligence had plotted Russian reserves, command centers, and strongpoints in the first Russian trench line accurately, and this line of defense was simply blown to smithereens. As the German infantry moved out, the artillery shifted fire to the second line of Russian defenses.

The Russian trench lines were shallow and thus afforded little protection. The main effort of the attack took place against the Russian 61st Division, which was obliterated in the attack that followed. The Russian artillery was ineffectual and soon ran out of ammunition. All along the front, the Germans and Austrians, who outnumbered the Russians two to one, advanced. By the end of the first day, the Russians' first line of defense had been captured, including the town of Gorlice. Radko-Dimitriev asked for the only reserve that Ivanov had, the III Caucasus Corps, to plug the gaping hole in his line at the juncture of his IX and X Corps. Mackensen responded by committing one of his divisions from the reserve to the breakthrough. The Russians managed to fall back slowly under Mackensen's hammer blows, but now three of their corps, still engaged south in the Carpathians, were in danger of being cut off.

On May 4, the battle climaxed with the near-annihilation of the Russian Xth Corps in an encirclement. Several Russian divisions were mauled, and by May 5, the entire Southwest Front began to withdraw as the scope of the disaster became clear. The Russians employed a scorched-earth policy familiar to anyone who had ever fought them, and that levied untold miseries on the civilians of this region. It denied the Germans further success and allowed the Russian army, despite heavy losses, to break contact and fall back. The Russians herded as many military-age men that they could along with them as they evacuated.

The result now meant that adjacent Russian armies also had to fall back. At the Russian High Command (Stavka), Grand Duke Nicholas ordered Ivanov to surrender no more ground. After an abortive counterattack, Radko-Dimitriev ordered his Third Army to retreat again on May 10 and recommended to Stavka that all the armies in that part of Poland pull back. Ivanov bowed to the inevitable and also ordered General A. A. Brusilov to also withdraw his Eighth Army from its gains to avoid its being cut off.

By now, the Germans had advanced farther and faster than in any offensive since 1914—almost fifty kilometers in some sectors—all the way to the San River. The Austrian Fourth Army was given the task of recapturing the fortress of Przemsyl. Meanwhile, Radko-Dimitriev had been ordered to maintain bridgeheads over the San. These proved lucrative targets for the German artillery, which pulverized them. The Germans crossed the river and established bridgeheads of their own, resulting in the Russians conducting another round of failed counterattacks.

Mackensen now paused, his army was 150 kilometers from its supply railheads, to resupply and reorganize, which gave the Russians a breather. The objective remained Przemsyl, and on May 23, the cycle of offensives began again, using the same artillery tactics that had proved so effective earlier. Also, the Germans misdirected the Russian defense by feinting their main effort toward Lemberg once in the open, but then driving on Przemsyl in the hope of enveloping its defenders. The Russians again withdrew, abandoning Przemsyl on June 2 and leaving a small group of 8,000 prisoners to the Austrians. On June 21, Mackensen's forces captured Lemberg, which the Russians abandoned rather than lose more troops in a hopeless defense.

The offensive in the south had completely exposed the flank of the Russian positions farther north. However, Italy had declared war on the Central Powers, on May 24, which changed the entire dynamic. Mackensen had captured over 120,000 prisoners by this point and inflicted roughly another 300,000 casualties on the Russians. Ironically, Falkenhayn decided to continue the offensive over concerns that if the offensive were halted to transfer troops to the Italian or Western front, the Austrians might lose everything just gained, given that the Russian army remained a cohesive (albeit weaker) force. Mackensen was given two new armies: the Austrian Third, which had not been heavily engaged to the south, and a new German force entitled the Bug Army (named after the Bug River).

Mackensen, using the same tactics, swung north against the Russian Northwestern Front, holding a now-exposed giant salient that included Warsaw and Lublin. Falkenhayn's conception of the operation was an attempt at a smaller encirclement that would include the German Twelfth Army driving in from the north and west, with Mackensen coming up from the south to cut off the Russian forces at Brest-Litovsk. At the same time, the offensive pressure was applied all along the front to prevent the Russians from transferring reserves, with Hindenburg attacking toward Riga and Hötzendorff's other Austrian armies attacking toward Tarnopol, Brody, and Rovno in the south.

The tactics and results were similar. The Warsaw salient was pinched off, although Hindenburg failed to capture Riga. On the other hand, the Russians managed to withdraw, despite heavy losses, and reestablished and stabilized the front by late summer. They had lost an immense amount of territory and as many as a million troops. They had also lost Poland, and the Germans were now deep iside Russian territory, although the Russian position at the hinge of neutral Romania remained favorable for future offensive operations against the Austrians should the Germans depart.

CONCLUSION

There is another element to this disaster: It was not disastrous enough to get the Russians to agree to a separate peace when such a thing was still possible. The Russian army held together just enough to enable it to do what it would do again in World War II—reconstitute and reenter the fray again the next year. And it gave the Germans hope that they could prevail. After all, one does not quit when one has just conducted the most successful offensive of the war (in terms of casualties and territory gained). The victory in this sense was pyrrhic—it led to a longer war, and Germany could not win a longer war. But neither could Russia, at least not in 1914–1917.

Further Reading

Esposito, Vincent, ed. *The Point Atlas of American Wars, Volume II, 1900–1953*. New York: Praeger, 1959.

Stone, David R. *The Russian Army in the Great War: The Eastern Front, 1914–1917*. Lawrence: University of Kansas Press, 2015.

62. Verdun

Date: February 21–December 18, 1916
Location: Verdun, France

OPPONENTS

1. Germany
   Commanders: General Erich von Falkenhayn
   Fifth Army: Crown Prince Wilhelm
2. France
   Commanders: Marshal Joseph Joffre
   Second Army: Marshal Phillipe Petain, General Robert Nivelle

BACKGROUND

The Battle of Verdun was one of the costliest and most brutal of World War I. By 1916, the western front has settled into a stalemate after the horrendous offensives

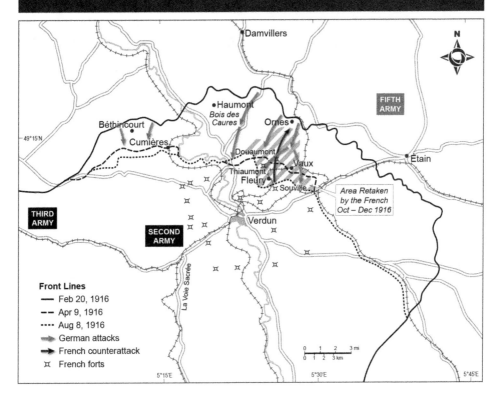

of the opening phase of the war. General Erich von Falkenhayn replaced Helmut von Moltke, the nephew of Helmut von Moltke, the elder who shaped the German army, as chief of the German General Staff. As von Falkenhayn assessed the situation, he believed that Great Britain was the greater threat to Germany. However, rather than fight the British directly, he surmised that the best chance for success was to attack them through their allies, primarily the French on the western front. Falkenhayn also deduced that at this point in the war, a single decisive battle was no longer possible. Therefore, the key to victory lay in fighting an attritional battle. To that end, his plan was no more subtle than that the Germans were to kill more French soldiers than they would lose German soldiers. All that remained was selecting the location for this bloodbath. Falkenhayn knew he had to choose a spot that the French would feel compelled to defend at all costs and, therefore, send more and more soldiers to the slaughter. He selected the ancient fortress of Verdun.

Verdun had been a critical part of France's eastern defenses throughout history. Verdun itself was the site of a seventeenth-century Vauban "star fort." Varying in distance between 1.5 and 5 miles from Verdun, twenty-eight smaller forts ringed the high ground around it. The forts, equipped with various calibers of guns, many of them in armored retractable turrets, were positioned to provide mutual support. However, since the beginning of the war, the Verdun sector had been relatively quiet, and the French removed many of the guns and sent them to other parts of the front. By the time of the German attack, the largest fort at Douaumont was no

French trench system around one of the many forts surrounding Verdun in 1916. Over one million soldiers were killed or wounded in this hellacious campaign. (Hulton-Deutsch Collection/Corbis via Getty Images)

more than a shell scheduled for demolition. All that remained of the once-formidable Douaumont fortress were the turreted guns and some machine guns. The German attack would not be a walkover, but the French preparations appeared to increase Falkenhayn's chances of success.

Verdun sat in a salient, and Falkenhayn's plan called for an attack from all three sides. The Germans also had cut the main rail line into the city, adding to its vulnerability. Falkenhayn selected the German Fifth Army, under the command of Crown Prince Wilhelm, to lead the German attack. The plan was for the Corps of the Fifth Army to seize the high ground around Verdun and then wait for the French to counterattack. From their commanding defensive positions, the Germans would be able to destroy the French as they tried to close on the German lines.

The Fifth Army was augmented with 1,200 artillery pieces to enhance the destruction of the French. The twelve days of preparatory fires that the plan called for would require over four million artillery shells. The battle would also see the Germans introduce the flamethrower to the growing list of weapons to come out of World War I. Wet weather postponed the opening of the battle from February 12 to February 21. In the meantime, French intelligence developed an accurate picture of Grman preparations for the battle. However, Marshal Joseph Joffre, the commanding general of the French army, dismissed these reports because he could not see any strategic advantage in an attack at Verdun. Unfortunately, he could not foresee a strategy based on anything other than killing.

THE BATTLE

At 7:15 a.m. on February 21, 800 German guns began a ten-hour bombardment of the French positions. During that time, the German artillery fired over one million rounds along a nineteen-mile front. When the fire lifted, three German corps began their attack. Led by the specially trained and equipped storm troops, the Germans made significant gains by the end of the day, even securing the fort at Bois d'Haumont. However, the French did not break. On February 22, the Germans continued their attacks, advancing three miles and capturing Bois des Caures. After repelling several French counterattacks, the Germans by February 24 had secured portions of the French second line and were in a position to seize the fort at Douaumont.

On the afternoon of February 25, two battalions of the 24th Brandenburg regiment launched an attack on Douaumont. They quickly swept away the French defenders and were within a few hundred meters of the fort when the German infantry came under machine-gun fire from the village. The Germans sought cover and called in artillery support. Early in the evening, after the machine-gun fire slackened, the Germans continued their attack. In the fading light, the French thought the Germans were French reinforcements, and the Germans secured a corner of the fort. The Germans cautiously cleared the fort, not realizing how few defenders were left. Eventually, a Fench prisoner led them to the remaining French soldiers in the lower level, who promptly surrendered. After several unsuccessful counterattacks, Marshal Petain ordered that there be no more attempts to retake Douaumont.

With the fall of Douaumont, the Battle of Verdun entered a new phase. The French had been feeding more reinforcements into the fighting, as Falkenhayn expected; however, the French were holding on dearly, and the Germans were not making much headway. In addition, the Germans got word of a pending Anglo-French attack along the Somme. Falkenhayn redoubled his efforts around Verdun in an attempt to draw off French forces from the planned Somme offensive. However, the Germans had been victims of their success. The infantry had outpaced the artillery, and the muddy ground was making it difficult to relocate the guns. At the same time, the Germans had advanced deeper into the range of the French artillery.

By the end of March, the Germans could, with heavy artillery support, make minor advances and, with these tactics, had captured the key fort at Vaux. However, the French used the same methods to retake any lost ground. The situation looked bleak for the Germans, and Falkenhayn considered calling off the offensive; however, the Fifth Army staff recommended another major attack, claiming that the French were near exhaustion. Falkenhayn acceded to their request; however, the French were far from exhausted, and the attack resulted in negligible gains by the Germans.

From April through June, the Battle of Verdun seesawed back and forth; one side would advance one day, only to be thrown back the next. For example, the village of Fleury changed hands sixteen times. In May, General Robert Neville was named to command the French Second Army and immediately launched an attack to retake Douaumont. After much effort, the French occupied the fort, only to be cut off and forced to surrender. After three days of fighting, the French suffered nearly 6,000 casualties, and the Germans lost 4,500 in defending the fort. Adding to the Germans' problems, in June, the Russians began an offensive in Ukraine as part of the allied plans for 1916, further distracting the Germans as they prepared for the anticipated Anglo-French Somme offensive.

With the start of the Battle of the Somme to the north on July 1, the Battle of Verdun entered its last phase. On July 11, the Germans launched an offensive to capture Fort Souville. After much hard fighting, on July 12, a handful of soldiers made it to the fort, from which they could see the spire of the cathedral in Verdun. However, the French quickly counterattacked, driving the Germans back to their starting line. For the remainder of the month, both sides conducted minor attacks for little or no gain. A surprise attack by the Germans on August 1 netted nearly 1,000 yards, which prompted another round of French counterattacks. By this time, the Germans were the ones nearing exhaustion, and the counterattacks reclaimed all the territory that the French had lost in July and August.

In October, the French began the final major offensive to recapture Fort Douaumont. In preparation, the French fired over 800,000 shells, and on October 24, the attack began. Moving behind a creeping barrage, the French drove the Germans out of the fort. In the process, the French captured over 6,000 Germans and fifteen artillery pieces. Next, the French launched an attack to recapture Vaux. Failing to take the fort on its first attempt, the French regrouped and bombarded the Germans for a week before attacking again. The Germans evacuated the fort, and the French occupied it on November 2. This final offensive brought the French back to their

February 24 starting positions in that sector. Preceded by a six-day bombardment, the French launched their last offensive on December 2. By the time the offensive was called off on December 17, the French had retaken all the ground that they had lost since February 21.

CONCLUSION

Before the Battle of Verdun was over, there would be major shake-ups in the senior levels on both sides. On August 29, Paul von Hindenburg replaced Falkenhayn as chief of the General Staff. General Joseph Joffre was promoted to marshal of France and became a military advisor. His replacement, Robert Neville, would lead a series of costly offensives in the spring of 1917. The result destroyed French morale and set the conditions for the French Mutiny in 1917. However, the relief of senior commanders does reflect the true tragedy of Verdun.

Falkenhayn began the offensive with an objective no more subtle than to inflict so many casualties on the French that they would surrender. In this, he failed—the French proved to be more resilient than he anticipated and were able to weather the initial assault, eventually winning back all the lost ground. Nevertheless, both the French and the Germans paid a high price. As is usually the case in dealing with large numbers in a sometimes confusing situation, the exact numbers of casualties are hard to determine. Estimates for French casualties range from a low of 351,000 to a high of 542,000 total casualties for the ten-month battle. The spread for the Germans is just as dramatic, ranging from 337,000 to 442,000. Regardless of the numbers, the scale of human suffering and sacrifice was the same on both sides, with no change in the front line, and the war would grind on for nearly two more years.

Further Reading

Axelrod, Alan. *The Battle of Verdun.* Guilford, CT: Lyons Press, 2016.

Buckingham, William F. *Verdun 1916: The Deadliest Battle of the First World War.* Stroud, UK: Amberly Publishing, 2016.

Holstein, Christina. *Fort Douaumont.* Havertown, PA: Pen and Sword, 2010.

Jankowski, Paul. *Verdun: The Longest Battle of the Great War.* New York: Oxford University Press, 2013.

63. Battle of the Somme

Date: July 1–November 18, 1916
Location: Northeastern France

OPPONENTS

1. Germany

Commanders: Crown Prince Ruprecht of Bavaria, General Max von Gallwitz, and General Fritz von Below

2. Great Britain: Field Marshal Sir Douglas Haig, General Henry Rawlinson, and General Hubert Gough

3. France: General Emile Fayolle

BACKGROUND

Involving more than three million men, the Battle of the Somme was one of the largest of World War I. A third of these soldiers would become casualties before the battle was over. It was part of an allied plan for a combined offensive in 1916. As originally conceived, the French army was to make the main effort, with the British Expeditionary Force (BEF) in a supporting role. However, the German offensive outside Verdun that began in February 1916 forced the French High Command to divert forces earmarked for the Somme offensive to halt the Germans at Verdun. It then fell to the BEF to take over the main effort.

The combined Franco-British offensive that would become the Battle of the Somme was conceived in December 1915. That month, the commanders of the Italian, Russian, French, and British armies met in Chantilly, France to decide Allied strategy for 1916. They decided to exert pressure on the Central Powers from three directions: by the Italians from the south, the Russians from the east, and the Franco-British armies from the west. The new commander of the BEF, Sir Douglas Haig, proposed an offensive in Flanders to clear the coast and hamper the German U-boat campaign on Allied ships. The staffs finally agreed that the offensive, with the French as the main effort and the British in support, would take place at the juncture between the two armies along the Somme River. However, in February 1916, the Germans launched an offensive at Verdun, with the sole objective of causing enough casualties that the French would surrender. Regardless of the objective, the German attack drew French divisions away from the planned Somme offensive. With the French decisively engaged at Verdun, Haig and the BEF would now be the main effort at the Somme. The reduction in available French divisions curtailed the goals of the Somme offensive. While a breakthrough might be possible, the primary objective was to relieve pressure on the French by diverting German forces from Verdun.

By the time of the Battle of the Somme, the BEF consisted of the remnants of the prewar professional army, the Territorial Forces, Kitchener's New Army, and the Pals battalions. Kitchener's Army was formed from the initial call-up of volunteers after the outbreak of World War I and was of varying quality in training and readiness. The Pals battalions were composed of mostly volunteers from the same areas who had joined up together and were promised that they would serve together. The Somme would be their first test; the result would bring an end to the program.

The plan called for the British Fourth Army, with eleven divisions under the command of General Henry Rawlinson, to attack north of the Somme River. The French Sixth Army, with five divisions, under the command of General Emile Fayolle, would attack south of the river. During the first phase, both armies were to occupy the German first and second trench lines in one attack. It was an ambitious plan, but the senior leaders hoped that five days of preparatory artillery fires

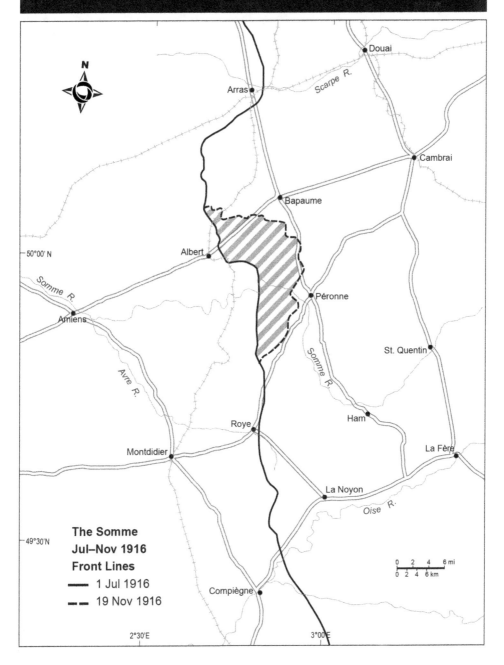

SOMME OFFENSIVE, 1916

Douai

Arras

Scarpe R.

Cambrai

Bapaume

50°00' N

Albert

Somme R.

Péronne

Amiens

St. Quentin

Avre R.

Somme R.

Roye

Ham

Montdidier

La Fère

La Noyon

Oise R.

49°30'N

**The Somme
Jul–Nov 1916
Front Lines**
—— 1 Jul 1916
— — 19 Nov 1916

0 2 4 6 mi
0 2 4 6 km

Compiègne

2°30'E

3°00'E

preceding the attack would make it feasible. Over those five days, the British gunners fired approximately 1.7 million shells, contributing to a growing sense of optimism among the British Tommies. Their commanders told them that after such a barrage, all they would have to do was cross "no man's land" and occupy the German trenches. However, the German trenches were more formidable than anticipated.

By the time of the battle, not only were the German trenches more formidable, but their doctrine was more flexible; rather than defending one strong line, the Somme front consisted of three trench lines. The first or outpost line was lightly manned and was more of a tripwire for the second line, which was the main line of defense and contained the bulk of the defending forces. The final line held the reserves, which could be brought forward as necessary. All three were connected by traverse trenches to aid the movement between lines. More important, local commanders were expected to conduct local counterattacks on their initiative to restore the frontline.

Additionally, they changed the depth of their dugouts from six to nine feet to twenty to thirty feet below ground. The result of this change meant that, despite the fear of being trapped underground, the German soldiers could ride out any artillery fire in relative safety and be ready to man their positions after the artillery fire lifted. This is the situation that the British and French soldiers faced on July 1, 1916.

THE BATTLE

At 7:30 a.m., whistles began blowing all along the line as the soldiers of the British Fourth Army clambered out of their trenches—not an easy task for a man burdened with over sixty pounds of equipment. Nonetheless, convinced that nothing could have survived the weeklong bombardment, the soldiers were in high spirits as they went over the top. One company commander had given each of his four platoons a soccer ball to kick into the German trenches. The officers and noncommissioned officers formed their soldiers into orderly lines before they began their measured walk across no man's land. At a pace of 100 yards a minute, the soldiers set off behind a creeping barrage of artillery. This artillery fire was to get the troops into the trenches. Unfortunately, the weeklong artillery preparation had not destroyed the Germans' defenses and only served to let the enemy know where the attack was coming. After the bombardment stopped, the Germans came out of their dugouts to take their positions.

It soon became apparent to the British soldiers that the past week of artillery bombardment did not have any effect, and neither did the detonation of the eight large mines painstakingly dug under the German position. Nevertheless, the Tommies pressed on, closing to 100 yards before the German machine guns opened fire. The exposed British soldiers were caught in the relatively intact obstacles and were mowed down by the hundreds. At the same time, the German artillery began landing among the massed soldiers, adding to the carnage. Officers continued to urge their men forward. However, with no way to communicate with their artillery, they could only watch as the creeping barrage that was to cover them up to the first German trench line continued moving on, and the German machine guns continued their deadly chatter.

In a matter of hours, nearly, 60,000 British soldiers were casualties that day with approximately 20,000 of those killed in action. One Newfoundland regiment began the day with 752 soldiers; by evening, 684 were dead. For the number of killed and wounded, the gains were negligible, and the first day of the Somme became the single worst day in the long and distinguished history of the British army.

However, the first day was not all bad news. The French Sixth Army succeeded in attacking along both banks of the Somme. On the north bank, the French XXXV Corps delayed its attack two hours as its artillery silenced the German guns. By the end of the day, the corps secured the German second line. On the south bank, the story was much the same. The 1st Colonial Corps reached its first-day objectives and then some. Despite several German counterattacks, the French had advanced almost 1.5 miles—quite an accomplishment in 1916. Unfortunately, General Haig did not reinforce this success.

Despite the first day's losses, and after conferring with his commanders on July 2, Haig decided to continue driving the Germans back, with the Fourth Army supported by the British Third Army on its left. From this point, the Battle of the Somme would drag on for four months. With the Allies launching deadly attacks and the Germans giving ground grudgingly or regaining ground by counterattacking. By November 18, the Somme offensive had run its course, and both sides prepared for the coming winter.

CONCLUSION

The Battle of the Somme fell short of its goals and did not sweep the Germans from their trenches or open up the front for a sustained offensive. The combined British and French armies advanced a total of six miles during the four months of the offensive. British casualties numbered nearly 420,000 total casualties with around 100,000 killed in action. The French committed fewer soldiers to the battle, but the percentage of killed to wounded matched the British, with 50,000 killed out of 200,000 total casualties (roughly 25 percent). Even the defenders did not fare

---

Sir Douglas Haig (1861–1928)

Douglas Haig, the son of a highly successful distiller, entered the Royal Military Academy at Sandhurst in 1884. One year later, Haig was commissioned a lieutenant in the 7th (Queen's Own) Hussars. He spent most of his early career in India before deploying to South Africa for the Second Boer War. Following the war, he returned to England to serve as the director of military training before returning to India as chief of staff of the Indian army. The outbreak of World War I found him in command of the 1st Corps of the British Expeditionary Force (BEF). The BEF was under the command of Sir John French; however, as the war bogged down, the British cast about for a replacement. Based on his performance as a corps commander, Haig was selected for the job. Despite numerous attempts to break the stalemate, Haig's armies could not break through the German defenses. The war would drag on until late 1918, when the exhausted Germans collapsed before the combined Allied offensive. Nonetheless, the horrendous casualties on the western front will be linked to Haig's name forever.

After the war, Haig was given command of the British Home Forces until his retirement in 1921. In retirement, Haig helped to found the Royal British Legion of wartime veterans, and he devoted the remainder of his life to veterans' causes. He died on January 28, 1928.

well in the outcome. The Germans suffered approximately 500,000 casualties, with 160,000 killed in action. Meanwhile, the war would drag on for another two years.

However, the battle was notable for the debut of the tank on September 13. However, the early tanks were subject to breakdowns and became bogged down in the mud of no man's land. Of the forty-nine tanks available, only twenty-five made it to the line of departure on September 13. And indeed, most of them broke down before they got into the fight. Nevertheless, one intrepid crew made an advance of 2,000 yards before their vehicle broke down, making it an easy target for German fire. Nonetheless, hopes for the new vehicle remained high, and their first use gave a glimpse into the future.

Further Reading

Duffy, Christopher. *Through German Eyes: The British and the Somme 1916*. London: Weidenfeld & Nicolson, 2006.

Philpott, William J. *Three Armies on the Somme: The First Battle of the Twentieth Century*. New York: Vintage Books, 2011.

Sebag-Montefiore, Hugh. *Somme: Into the Breach*. Cambridge, MA: The Belknap Press of Harvard University Press, 2016.

Stewart, William F. *The Canadians on the Somme, 1916: The Neglected Campaign*. Solihull, UK: Helion, 2017.

64. German U-Boat Offensive in World War I

Date: January 1917–November 1918
Location: North Atlantic, English Channel, and littoral waters around Great Britain and France

OPPONENTS

1. Imperial Germany
   Commander: Admiral Reinhardt Scheer
2. Allied powers (principally Great Britain and the United States)
   Commanders: Admirals Sir John Jellicoe and Sir David Beatty, and Vice Admiral William Sims (United States)

BACKGROUND

The German U-boat offensive of early 1917 was something of a disaster for all parties. It is often portrayed as showing the Royal Navy of Great Britain in a very negative light, unable to respond as German submarines tightened the noose around the neck of the British Isles. It was very nearly that. However, it was far more disastrous for the Germans—they may have won one decisive battle at sea, but it suffered the political effect of not winning the war against the Allies' sea lines of communication. The cost to the Germans was the breaking off of diplomatic relations with the United States and finally, as the Germans sought allies in Mexico and Japan against the Americans, outright war with the United States. This result, more than any other, guaranteed that Germany would lose its war with its enemies later, or as it turned out, sooner.

THE PLANS

When the Germans resumed unrestricted submarine warfare against the Allies (in hindsight, an incredible crapshoot), they had done something the British had not—they looked at the lessons learned during their first attempt at unrestricted methods in 1915. Unrestricted warfare by submarines was in violation of accepted international law, as codified most recently in London in 1909, which outlawed sinking a neutral or merchant ship without first boarding it and ensuring the safety of the crew. The Germans made crucial adjustments after their studies to make themselves more effective should they decide to try unrestricted warfare again. They prepared a new class of smaller UB submersibles that were easily prefabricated and assembled to operate out of a new base in Bruges, Belgium. This conferred the factor of strategic surprise on the Germans because to that point, they had been limited to their small coastline between the Netherlands and Denmark for U-boat sorties by the High Seas Fleet. Additionally, the Germans built reinforced concrete submarine pens in anticipation of an Allied naval counterattack on the source of the scourge. The German improved their torpedoes as well.

Significantly, 1916 was the year that saw the greatest production of U-boats during the entire war. Thus, when the Germans unleashed their submarines to sink any ship within a "war zone" around Great Britain, they achieved astounding success and caught the Royal Navy entirely flat-footed and unready to address the problem, even though submarine sinkings under legitimate rules had been going up throughout 1916 without any British effective countermeasures.

To understand the Germans' initial success, it is important to back up and realize that the Allies had adopted a ruinous strategy for combating the U-boat. This strategy was based on a long and comfortable naval tradition that esteemed the offensive, kinetic form of warfare that had characterized naval warfare for millennia. The Royal Navy, faced with the resumption of German U-boat warfare in February 1917, continued, in the finest tradition of the Royal Navy, to employ the supposedly effective tactic of patrolling the sea lanes hunting for the U-boats. After all, commerce warfare, or *guerre de course*, had never really succeeded in recent memory against a major naval power. Never before had the commerce raiders been able to achieve a decisive result in a sustained campaign of privateering and raiding against sea lines of communication. A. T. Mahan's histories were full of examples to support this position, and if that weren't enough, so were those of Sir Julian Corbett, the great British naval theorist—at least until the German submarines began to reap their horrible harvest.

THE CAMPAIGN

On the Allied side, though, it is worth mentioning how catastrophic this offensive nearly was for them as well. In the opening phases of the offensive, the British ambassador to Washington even characterized the war at sea in dire terms:

> At the present rate of destruction more than four million tons will be sunk before the summer is gone. Such is this dire submarine danger. The English thought that they controlled the sea. . . . The submarine is the most formidable thing the war has produced—by far . . .

These views were not just limited to British leaders. The Russians, Italians, and French made similar *cries de coeur*. In fact, President Woodrow Wilson became so alarmed about the German terror offensive against the sea lines of communication that he sent Herbert Hoover, a bright, number-crunching kind of person, to Europe to investigate the U-boat's real impact on his new allies—was the damage simply British propaganda? Hoover reported that bread riots were imminent if the carnage continued, not so much in Great Britain, but in Italy and France. The Germans had not only sunk record numbers of ships, they took out almost the entirety of the South American grain harvest bound for Europe.

Fortunately for the Allies, the British knew how to learn lessons, too, although applying them turned out to be much harder. The British already knew that they had serious problem in late 1916 with the barely more restrained ("restricted") U-boat campaign. These methods, moreover, had already led to over 355,000 tons of lost Allied shipping in December 1916. What makes this all the more amazing is how ill prepared the British were for the all-out campaign in February 1917. There was an air of hopelessness reflected in the words of war correspondent Charles à Court Repington, "it was at present a question whether our armies could win the war before our navies lost it." Nonetheless, the Royal Navy, under Admiral Sir John Jellicoe's direction, had instituted (at the last minute, one might say) an organizational response to the problem that had long been overdue when he established the Admiralty Anti-Submarine Division under Admiral A. L. Duff.

Setting up an antisubmarine warfare syndicate is one thing, but adopting the correct antisubmarine measures is an entirely different matter. The challenge was unprecedented; as historian John Terraine wryly noted, "there was no manual" for antisubmarine warfare. So the British Navy essentially adopted the policy already in place for commerce raiding: the use of frigate-type vessels to counter the U-boat, as discussed previously. Duff, meanwhile, through analysis, had discovered that the solution to the problem was escorted convoys, where the hunters could in turn be hunted. The Royal Navy had a useful warship type, the destroyer, ready for this job, but it had too few of them. Destroyers originally targeted torpedo boats, intended to screen the main bodies of fleets against the torpedo attack, itself a rather new development in warfare. There simply were precious few of them left after their assignment to the main fleet and troop convoys. The British knew they needed more and so attempted to build more, but the building of new destroyers as a priority only occurred at the eleventh hour.

The U.S. declaration of war in April 1917 came during the worst months of the U-boat terror campaign. This need not have happened. The antisubmarine division of the Admiralty had all the analytic data at its fingertips to indicate the wisdom of convoying. As early as February, Duff and his staff were arguing that the data seemed to indicate, given the low losses in escorted convoys, that the convoy was the best means to counter the U-boat. However, there were strong interests opposed to the convoy, and the biggest argument seemed to hinge on the numbers of escorts, that there simply weren't enough.

All these arguments proved to be flawed, but the issue of escorts was in part solved by the entry of the Americans and thirty U.S. Navy destroyers into the calculations for the needed escorts. Some have even argued that these ships provided the necessary margin for the tentative adoption of the convoy system as an experiment—almost a last gasp, if you will. The results were immediate; indeed, Terraine argues that the "convoy acted like a spell" in turning the naval war in the Allies' favor and against the Germans. Throughout the summer, the tonnage of ships went slowly down, then drastically down that fall—so much so the Germans shifted their patrol areas. By the end of the year, although much hard convoying remained, the Germans could see the writing on the wall.

What had happened? The Allies' navies had regained the initiative and the ability to move what they needed to sustain the war effort via the sea. Their key vulnerability was also their key strength. The Germans had to come to the convoys in the open ocean to be successful. Even without escorts, the sheer math of the convoy resulted in lower loss rates when pitted against individual submarines. Once escorts were in place, the U-boats became the hunted rather than the hunters. The addition of aircraft patrols further hindered the U-boats because finding where they were *not* was as important as finding where they were. Denied their prey, the U-boats

U-boat crew surrendering to U.S. naval warships in late 1917. By that time the U-boats had clearly lost in their gambit to win the war for Germany. (Library of Congress/ Interim Archives/Getty Images)

had to attack the convoys—a no-win situation in 1917 and 1918 once the escorts, weapons, and tactics were in place.

CONCLUSION

When it dawned on the Germans that they would not win the war with the U-boats alone, they were forced to adopt the strategy of trying to win on land—which had eluded them ever since 1914. The U-boat failure led the Germans to throw the dice in 1918 on a series of offensives that squandered the combat power of the German army and then ruined it altogether, which led to Germany's complete collapse in the fall of 1918.

Further Reading

Conrad, Dennis. "Were They Really So Unprepared? Josephus Daniels and the U.S. Navy's Entry into World War I." *U.S. Military History Review*, December 2016, 5–19.

Halpern, Paul W. *A Naval History of World War I.* Annapolis, MD: Naval Institute Press, 1995.

Terraine, John. *The U-Boat Wars, 1916–1945.* New York: G. P. Putnam's Sons, 1989.

65. Caporetto

Date: October 24–November 19, 1917
Location: Kobarid, Austria-Hungary (present-day Slovenia)

OPPONENTS

1. Austria-Hungary

    Commander: Field Marshal Svetozar Boroevic

2. Germany

    Commander: General Otto von Below

3. Italy

    Commander: General Luigi Capello

BACKGROUND

Italy entered World War I on the side of the Allies in May 1915, with visions of expanding its territorial sovereignty. It was with a sense of high optimism that the army, with the full support of the nation, went off to defeat the Austro-Hungarians. But two years later, the Austro-Hungarians were not defeated, and the Italian army and nation were becoming war-weary. Beginning that May, the Italian army had attacked along the Isonzo River eleven times, making little headway for the casualties they had suffered. The chief of staff of the Italian army, General Luigi

Cadorna, was planning a twelfth attack when aerial reconnaissance revealed a buildup of arms and supplies behind the Austro-Hungarian lines.

Despite holding the line against the Italian army for two years, the Austro-Hungarian army found itself in a desperate situation. Morale at the front and at home was sinking, and the Germans were concerned that their ally Austria might pull out of the war. The German High Command recommended that a successful combined offensive by the German and Austro-Hungarian armies would help keep Austria in the war. After reconnoitering the front, the Germans suggested a quiet sector near the town of Caporetto for the new offensive. It was also considered the weakest part of the Italian line. For the attack, a new army, the 14th, was created and placed under the command of General Otto von Below. The Austrians contributed nine divisions to complement the six German divisions of the 14th Arny. To add to the shock and surprise, the attack would be preceded by a barrage of chemical shells. The Germans also saw the offensive as another opportunity to test their new storm troop tactics. After a two-day delay due to bad weather, the offensive was set to open on October 24.

THE BATTLE

At 6 a.m., a mix of high-explosive and chemical shells signaled the beginning of the main artillery preparation. At 8 a.m., two mines that had been dug under the Italian flanks and packed with explosives were detonated. Soon after that, the Austrian and German infantry went over the top to attack the Italian positions. The main force attacked along the valley floor, supported by specially trained forces along the ridges. The storm troops, using their new infiltration tactics, bypassed the Italian strongpoints and quickly overcame the Italian defenders. The Germans continued advancing southward rapidly, covering twenty-five kilometers by the end of the day.

Stunned by the ferocity of the attack, the Italians were in full retreat. However, it was not all bad news for them. The units on the flanks of the main attack were holding, but to stem the Germans' main advance, some of these units were withdrawn from the flanks. The Italian 2nd army commander, General Luigi Capello, requested permission to withdraw to the Tagliamento River; the Italians next prepared the defense line. However, believing that the situation could be salvaged, Cardona denied Capello's request.

Nonetheless, over the next few days, the Germans continued to push the Italian 2nd Army back to the Taglimento River. By October 30, the Italian 2nd Army reached the river, and regrettably, it was not in very good condition by that time. The Italians had suffered many casualties, but more telling was the number of soldiers who were captured or had deserted. However, it still took four days to get the entire army across the river. Fortunately, for the Italian army, the Austrians and Germans were too successful—they had advanced so far that they were outrunning their supplies. Despite securing a bridgehead across the river on November 2, the Germans and Austrians needed time to regroup and refit before resuming their attack. The Italians took this time to bring in fresh units and prepare for the inevitable attack by the Austro-German forces.

With the Germans across the Tagliamento, Cardona intended to pull the 2nd Army farther back, to the Piave River. The Piave line was in more defensible terrain and would be shorter than the Tagliamneto, meaning that Capello could occupy it with fewer troops. This time the retreat was more organized, and they kept the Austrians and Germans at bay as they fell back to the Piave. On November 9, the 2nd Italian Army reached the Piave and established a defensive position that they would hold until October 1918.

The Austrians and Germans resumed their offensive on November 12, hoping to break through the Italians to reach Venice, approximately 15 miles behind the front. For six days, the Central Powers kept trying to penetrate the Italian line; however, the Italian army, better prepared and bolstered by the promise of French and British support, held the line. The poorly supplied and battered German and Austrian troops fought heroically, but in the end, the offensive was called off. At this point in the war, both sides were content to let the line stabilize, and it would remain unchanged until the last few weeks of the war.

CONCLUSION

On the German side, Caporetto was the final gasp for the underfed and poorly equipped armies on the Italian front. Combined, the Austrians and Germans suffered approximately 70,000 casualties of all types. From this point, on the Italian front, the exhausted troops of the Central Powers would stand on the defensive for the remainder of the war.

One historian called the Battle of Caporetto the greatest defeat in Italian military history. If it was not the greatest defeat, it surely seemed that way at the time. The hard-won success of the previous two-and-a-half years had been wiped out in a matter of weeks. The Italian army suffered 40,000 killed or wounded, more than 260,000 soldiers became prisoners of war, and approximately an equal number just disappeared; the majority of these more than likely were deserters. The Italian government cast about for a scapegoat to charge with this debacle. Cardona, the chief of staff, was the prime candidate, and he was subsequently relieved of duty. It would take time and effort to rebuild the morale of both the Italian army and people, but, like the Central Powers, the Italians were content to stay on the defensive and would remain so until the final weeks of the war.

Further Reading

Herwig, Holger H. *Germany and Austria-Hungary 1914–1918.* London: Bloomsbury Academic, 2014.

Macdonald, John, with Zeljko Cimpric. *Caporetto and the Isonzo Campaign: The Italian Front 1915–1918.* Barnsley, UK: Pen and Sword Books, 2011.

Stevenson, David. *1917: War, Peace, and Revolution.* Oxford: Oxford University Press, 2017.

Tucker, Spencer C. *Battles That Changed History: An Encyclopedia of World Conflict.* Santa Barbara, CA: ABC-CLIO, 2010.

66. Shanghai

Date: 1937
Location: Shanghai, China

OPPONENTS

1. Republic of China (Nationalists)
    Commanders: Generalissimo Chiang Kai-shek and General Zhang Zhizhong
2. Japanese
    Commanders: General Matsui Iwane and Rear Admiral Hasegawa Kiyoshi

BACKGROUND

On July 7, 1937, Nationalist Chinese (GMD) and Japanese troops exchanged gunfire at the key Marco Polo Bridge, some thirty miles north of Peking. These shots ushered in World War II in Asia. To understand why it all happened here, we must return to the policies of the Imperial Japanese Army (IJA) in North China. The official policy was not proactive, but rather "wait and see." By 1937, Japanese officers in the Kwantung Army (KTA) concluded that the resources of North China were not essential to their long-range goals. In fact, they felt that development in North China would retard growth in Manchuria. Accordingly, they recommended that the leadership of the North China Army (NCA) issue strict instructions to their troops to avoid incidents with the Nationalist Chinese troops. The Japanese were almost to the point where they were willing to exchange their North China buffer zone for a Sino-Japanese friendship treaty that included Chiang Kai-shek's recognition of Manchukuo. The chief of operations, General Ishiwara Kanji, finalized a new policy of integrated military, political, and economic synchronization. Ishiwara believed that the real enemy was the Soviet Union and wanted to avoid war with the Chinese Nationalists now that Manchuria was in hand. Nonetheless, the sustained Japanese policy of intervening and meddling in Chinese affairs now yielded a harvest of violence against the backdrop of what was probably an accident rather than a conspiracy.

On July 7, 1937, an incident occurred at the Marco Polo Bridge, which separated the Japanese and Chinese armies. While senior officers from both sides tried to determine what happened, a headstrong Japanese field grade officer escalated the incident into a much wider engagement. Before long, all efforts to control the situation had been overcome by events. The Nationalists deployed four divisions into North China in reaction, which was a violation of a 1935 agreement. Before long, the IJA was committed to a policy of reaction and reprisal. In Japan, with events spinning out of control, Ishiwara reluctantly ordered the mobilization of three divisions. Japan and China were at war.

Japan's task appeared formidable, the leader of Nationalist China, Generalissimo Chiang Kai-shek, had over 176 divisions. Also, the Nationalists and Communists now formed a united anti-Japanese front. The conflict led these uneasy allies to practice a form of resistance known as *compound warfare,* with Chiang and the Nationalists battling the IJA in conventional battles and Mao Zedong's forces employing guerilla warfare in the Japanese rear and behind the lines. Only thirty-three of Chiang's divisions were trained by German advisors, and they were dispersed over the entire country. The remainder were of uneven quality and sometimes insubordinate, answering to their generals and not to Chiang.

Japanese arms, close to their base of operations in Manchuria, at first succeeded brilliantly. Japan had complete control of the sea via the Imperial Japanese Navy (IJN), as well as air superiority. In these operations, the IJN's bombers were often employed as the interdiction and strategic bombing force of choice. On the ground, the NCA quickly overran Beijing and Tianjin. At this point, a split occurred inside Japan over how to proceed, now that the ostensible problem had been solved by the occupation of North China's five provinces. One group inside the War Ministry wanted to negotiate, but the General Staff advocated a more hawkish approach. The deliberate decision was made not to declare war in order to avoid international repercussions related to trade, and the policy became that of an undeclared war controlled by militarists at home, with generals executing "disciplined initiative" in the field. Command and control of the armies in the field became so tenuous that finally, in November 1937, the Imperial General Headquarters (IGHQ) was established, but it did not include the prime minister and civilian ministers.

The IJA's greatest weakness—logistics—came to the fore in China once the army began to operate away from the sea and its bases. The wisdom in the Nationalist Army soon spread that one need fight the Japanese for only ten days, and after that, they would run out of supplies. The IJA could accomplish much in those ten days, but its ability to consolidate gains would be limited to the cities (which it had to garrison) and the maintenance of the rail lines in order to connect its urban conquests with each other. The NCA became the North China Area Army and was reorganized into the First and Second Armies. It advanced south along two rail lines toward the lower Yangtze River Valley and the Shanghai-Nanjing area.

Chiang responded by opening a second front in Shanghai, attacking the lightly armed Japanese naval troops that had been stationed there since the troubles of 1932. The Japanese 3rd Fleet began evacuating Japanese citizens from Shanghai in August. Chiang hoped that this would force the Japanese to ease the pressure in their southern advance. This move precipitated one of the largest battles in Asia of the entire war.

THE PLANS

The Japanese IGHQ ignored the emperor's advice to send two divisions to the hard-pressed naval forces in the city. However, it soon reversed course and decided that the capture of Shanghai might be an ideal way to end the war via a decisive battle. Chiang also decided to take a stand at Shanghai, and he would eventually feed seventy Nationalist divisions into the fight to defend the city. Perhaps he could break the back of the Japanese army by employing the wisdom of Sun Tzu, which cautions invaders not to fight in cities. In any case, he had little choice because

Shanghai was only forty miles from the Nationalist capital at Nanjing. Chiang's initial plan was to try to have his local forces under General Zhang Zhizhong, a former aide, to attack the Japanese garrison and destroy it before the Japanese could bring forces to the area. Zhang would greatly outnumber the garrison, with almost 50,000 men, but his divisions were far less trained than those of the Japanese.

For the upcoming battle, the Japanese had improved somewhat on the firepower of their infantry divisions and generally were twice as big as the Chinese divisions, with double the number of mortars, machine guns, and artillery. Each Japanese division was also equipped with about twenty-four tanks. Their plan was to hold out with their garrison until forces could arrive from the north or by amphibious landing.

THE BATTLE

General Zhang opened the formal battle according to plan on August 14, 1937, but was unable to achieve surprise because the day before, his troops had alerted the Japanese garrison by unwisely attacking them early. The Japanese garrison was under the command of IJN Rear Admiral Hasegawa Kiyoshi, with mostly naval troops and a smattering of IJA forces. Zhang was initially repulsed by the prepared Japanese garrison, which used its superior firepower, including armored cars, to dominate the narrow streets. Zhang then made the critical decision to commit two of his precious German-trained divisions to try to break the back of the defense on August 17. Despite their use of infiltration tactics to initially penetrate the Japanese lines, the Japanese restored the situation with firepower, which their Chinese counterparts lacked. However, their situation was desperate. The Japanese had already decided to commit the Shanghai Expeditionary Force commanded by General Matsui Iwane, who came out from retirement to command; so now it entered the battle.

Most of the subsequent fighting did not take place inside the city because both sides wanted to avoid antagonizing the Western presence there. Instead, it took place in a World War I–style conflict northwest of the city, with trenches and position warfare. The result would be that Chiang's forces were sandwiched between Matsui's forces coming from the north (three divisions strong) and the garrison. Matsui also could land another two divisions in the south if he needed to, which belong to the IJA's amphibious forces (not to be confused with those of the IJN). Mastui's tactics employed massed banzai charges to try to penetrate the Nationalist lines. The assault stalled, predictably, with heavy Japanese casualties, but it wore the Chinese down and attrited their best-trained troops. More and more Japanese and Chinese troops were drawn into the maelstrom. It proved to be a battle of Japanese discipline and firepower—including naval gunfire by battleships and cruisers and complete command of the air by mostly naval aircraft—against Chinese infantry and courage.

The Chinese were now fighting on three fronts, and Chiang committed even more troops to the battle. Chiang had committed over a half million troops, and the casualties were immense. By September 18, the battle centered around the Shanghai suburb of Luodian, a "grinding mill of flesh and blood," as the Chinese now fought a defensive battle, retreating from a series of prepared defensive lines.

The Japanese goal was to cut off the bulk of the Chinese army in Shanghai, which would leave the way open to Nanjing and hopefully end the war altogether. By October 25, the Japanese had reached the town of Dachang, the hinge between the various Chinese army groups. Using a combined arms assault of artillery, tanks, infantry, and air attacks, they broke the back of Zhang's forces, and Chiang realized that he needed to extricate what combat power he could from the deadly trap that Shanghai had become.

Matsui doubled down and conducted an uncontested amphibious landing south of Shanghai with the 10th Army in early November to try to encircle Chiang's remaining troops. But Chiang pulled his men out of the trap. The Chinese could retreat faster than the Japanese could advance, and surprisingly, the retreat was conducted with skill, taking advantage of the difficult waterlogged terrain, despite the immense losses that the Nationalists had incurred.

CONCLUSION

The disaster that had befallen the Nationalist cause was immense—almost a quarter of a million troops became casualties, with equally large civilian losses— some estimates go as high as half a million. A total of 70 percent of Shanghai's industrial capacity was destroyed in the battle. The Japanese sustained over 40,000 casualties, and the shock of these unexpected losses stunned the people, who had

In one of the iconic images from the Sino-Japanese War, a Chinese baby cries in the rubble in Shanghai, the "Stalingrad of the Far East," 1937. (Keystone-France/Gamma-Keystone via Getty Images)

been assured by their government that only minor combat was taking place. The backlash within Japan against the IJA at these casualties caused protests and suicides, and the police had to be called out in Tokyo to deal with mobs angry at the army. However, these sunk costs in blood only hardened the attitude of the IJA, which saw itself engaged in a war of retribution and conquest.

The Nationalists' most significant loss at Shanghai became apparent soon afterward. Chiang's best divisions had been wrecked, and he now began a fighting retreat up the Yangtze in a campaign of sheer survival, banking that the Japanese would outrun their supply lines. The Japanese pressed to the capital at Nanjing, hoping that a rapid pursuit would capture the city quickly and bring Chiang to the table to end the conflict.

By December, the 10th Army, which was the freshest formation, arrived at the city—burning, looting, and living off the country during its rapid advance. The makings of an even larger humanitarian disaster were present, with indiscipline widespread during the campaign. Added to this were the Chinese army's stubborn resistance and the strain of constant combat. After three days of a confused defense, Chiang withdrew toward Wuhan, another couple hundred miles upriver.

Japanese naval air forces sank the U.S. gunboat *Panay,* causing American casualties during the general chaos. Japanese forces sacked Nanjing in an orgy of violence not seen since the Taiping Rebellion. Rape, murder, prisoner executions, arson—every crime imaginable was committed, and although accounts of the toll vary, it was certainly in the hundreds of thousands of civilians murdered. These actions, known collectively as the "Rape of Nanjing," only hardened the hearts of the Chinese and pushed Japan to the fore in international opinion as a pariah nation—yet no collective action was taken against it. Shanghai was thus a disaster not just for the losers, but for the winners, who found themselves trapped in a war that eventually led to the destruction of their empire.

Further Reading

Drea, Edward J. *Japan's Imperial Army: Its Rise and Fall, 1853–1945.* Lawrence: University of Kansas Press, 2009.

Macgregor, Douglas. "War Without End: The Battle of Shanghai, 1937," in *Margin of Victory,* 41–69. Annapolis, MD: Naval Institute Press, 2016.

67. Nomonhan

Date: 1939
Location: Eastern Outer Mongolia

OPPONENTS

1. Japanese Imperial Army (IJA)
    Commander: Lieutenant General Mitchitaro Komatsubaro
2. Soviet Far East Military District
    Commander: General G. K. Zhukov

BACKGROUND

While Japan became more and more involved in its undeclared war in China from 1937, incidents along the Soviet-Japanese border in Korea increased to regimental-size actions, causing the Imperial General Headquarters (IGHQ) of the Japanese military to halt a key offensive drive on Wuhan in China. The Soviets, meanwhile, increased their forces in the Far East to almost 500,000 troops, with plentiful artillery, armor, and over 3,000 aircraft. This modern force had been created by the recently purged Marshal M. N. Tukachevsky, and although Joseph Stalin continued his brutal purge of the Soviet officer corps, some of his most talented generals managed to escape (or rather avoid) political murder by being actively engaged in the Far East. Among these was General G. K. Zhukov, one of the greatest heroes of World War II.

Similarly, Japan's Kwantung Army (KTA) in Manchuria now numbered over 200,000 troops. The Japanese knew of the Soviet purges, and the Soviets had backed down from a confrontation on at least one occasion. This probably contributed the leadership of Japan's Imperial Army (IJA) miscalculating the threat from the Soviet Union. The Soviets struck at Changkuofeng in July 1938 along the border, occupying the high ground. Despite being ordered not to attack, a Japanese local commander exercised "[un]disciplined initiative," which had caused so many woes to the Japanese, and committed them to conflicts that wiser heads preferred to delay or not fight at all. The Soviets countered the Japanese attack with an all-out mechanized and air attack, pummeling units of the Japanese Korean army. Chastened, the Japanese and Soviets signed an armistice in August in Moscow. As it turned out, this would be only a temporary truce in the ongoing Japanese and Soviet confrontation and conflict in northeast Asia.

THE PLANS

Japan's China war settled into a stalemate—Japan's version of the later U.S. quagmire in Vietnam—except on a far more vast and hopeless scale. Things now went from bad to worse with the Soviets, whom the Japanese army leaders regarded as their real enemy. Interpreting Soviet willingness to cease operations in August 1938 as weakness, the KTA pushed forces forward on the Manchurian-Mongolian frontier in the spring of 1939 near the village of Nomonhan (also known as *Khalkin Gol*) in pursuit of Soviet proxy Mongolian cavalry forces. The cause of the outbreak of open hostilities was essentially Japanese-Soviet disagreement over the boundary line between the two empires in Outer Mongolia.

The Japanese appeared to have had no plan for a conflict in this region other than aggressively reacting with the forces at hand. The Soviets, on the other hand, were much better prepared, and they certainly intended to administer a powerful lesson should the opportunity offer itself. General Zhukov had over 100,000 troops in the vicinity, 844 tanks and armored cars, hundreds of artillery pieces, and hundreds of aircraft at his disposal. He would eventually employ over 50,000 troops in the upcoming battle. He would also have complete command of the air.

THE BATTLE

On May 11, 1939, the Japanese detected the Mongolian cavalry near Nomonhan and attempted to evict them with their own Manchurian proxy forces, but without success. Underestimating Soviet resolve, they sent a weakened infantry regiment from the 23rd Division, plus the division's reconnaissance element to finish the job. This force was led by Lieutenant Colonel Azuma Yaozo. On May 14, he advanced but was forced to withdraw across the Halha River when his Manchurian troops refused to fight. Azuma, unaware that the Soviets had substantially increased the numbers of their 57th Rifle Corps troops in the area, went back a week later, and his entire force was surrounded and annihilated.

The KTA leadership had no other plan than to continue to feed troops into the fight and ignored the warning sign when Azuma never returned. As they prepared their response with the rest of the 23rd Division, the Soviets continued to reinforce their forces around Nomonhan. On July 2, the Japanese 23rd Division crossed the Halha River in force. It was essentially an infantry with only limited artillery (compared to the Soviets) and two weak tank regiments (with probably no more than seventy tanks and armored cars) in support and massively outgunned and outnumbered by the opposing Soviets forces waiting in ambush. While the Japanese understood nothing about their enemy's disposition, the Soviets were much better informed. The Japanese also underestimated the ability of Zhukov to logistically build up supplies for his larger, more modern army. Zhukov did this by a massive use of over 1,000 trucks along the limited roads available to him.

When the 23rd Division attacked, Zhukov was still light in infantry to support his very strong armored forces, but he was concerned about the Japanese threat to his artillery. He thus committed the bulk of these forces to a counterattack on July 5. At the same time, the Japanese tried to counter this move with an attack by their two weak tank regiments on Soviet forces to the east of the river. In both cases—throwing the Japanese back in the north and repulsing the tank attack in the south—the Soviets were successful. They took losses in the armored counterattack, but their artillery was safe.

The Japanese antitank equipment and tactics proved woefully inadequate. The Japanese tank regiments were decimated and lost over half their number in ill-coordinated and fanatical attacks on the dug-in, prepared Soviet positions. The Japanese continued to press their attacks on orders from KTA headquarters, which seemed to not understand the reality on the ground. This offensive petered out by late July, with over 5,000 total casualties for the Japanese and about half that for the Soviets. The Japanese then went on the defensive, with the 23rd Division's position centered east of Nomonhan in a bend of terrain formed by the confluence of the Halha and Holstein rivers.

Zhukov rapidly built up his forces, which was missed by the Japanese. On August 20, in a signature operational approach that he would employ on a much vaster scale in World War II, Zhukov launched a two-pronged, all-arms offensive that surrounded the 23rd Division. The fighting proved savage, as one would expect, with the Japanese fighting fanatically, often to the death. The Soviet tanks quickly overran the Japanese artillery, a crucial loss for the Japanese, and this compromised the entire defensive scheme. The 23rd Division was effectively surrounded and annihilated, and what little remained of it retreated to the east across the Halha.

By mid-September, a cease-fire was signed. Japanese losses totaled over 17,000 (over 22,000 for the entire battle since May), and Soviet losses were only a little less. However, Japan's confidence in its ability to fight and win against a modern opponent was severely damaged, and this later contributed a great degree to the signing of a secret Japanese-Soviet nonaggression agreement prior to the start of the Pacific War, which was kept secret from Japan's nominal Axis ally, Germany.

CONCLUSION

The Soviets had won a great victory, and, as historian Edward Drea (1981) notes:

> The Nomonhan disaster was all the more traumatic because the army had employed its premier doctrine, tactics, and equipment that it specially designed to produce a lightning victory. Instead everything from nighttime bayonet assaults to vaunted spiritual power had failed. Rather than admit . . . disaster, the high command blamed the troops . . .

Prisoners who returned to the IJA were mistreated and their officers encouraged to commit suicide. Worse, the Germans—Japan's nominal anticommunist Axis allies—signed a nonaggression accord with the Soviets that was finalized just as the Nomonhan catastrophe was coming to its grim conclusion.

Further Reading

Coox, Alvin D. *Nomonhan: Japan Against Russia, 1939, Vols I and II*. Stanford, CA: Stanford University Press, 1985.

Drea, Edward J. *Nomonhan: Japanese-Soviet Tactical Combat 1939*. Leavenworth Paper No. 2. Fort Leavenworth, KS: Combat Studies Institute, U.S. Army Command and General Staff College, 1981.

68. France 1940

Date: May 10–June 25, 1940
Location: France, Belgium, Luxembourg, and Netherlands

OPPONENTS

1. France, United Kingdom, Belgium, Luxembourg, and Netherlands
   Commander: General Maurice Gamelin (French)
2. Germany
   Commander: Walther von Brauchitsch

BACKGROUND

On September 1 1939, German armies crashed over the Polish border in a blatant gambit to annex the entirety of Poland. Two days later, Great Britain and France,

Poland's allies, declared war on Germany. Adolf Hitler had successfully annexed Austria in 1938, followed by the Sudetenland, and then all of Czechoslovak in 1939, but in Poland, the gamble failed, and World War II began—a world war that the Germans were unprepared to wage, and one that the Allies did not wish to fight.

THE PLANS

The unexpected declaration of war by Great Britain and France placed Germany in the awkward position of fighting the world's strongest navy, as well as one of the best armies in the world. Technologically and numerically inferior, the Wehrmacht (armed forces) needed a novel solution to this intractable problem. Unfortunately, the first several operational plans put forward to Hitler looked strikingly similar to, albeit feeble imitations of, those used in the initial invasion of France in 1914.

Then, in what must have seemed the most catastrophic of all possible events, a plane carrying the invasion plans crashed in Belgium. The Allies, with the German invasion plans in hand, took prudent precautions and moved forces to counter the potential invasion. This is a classic example of how catastrophe can turn to good fortune. The Allies, of course, did not know whether the plans were true or false. Nevertheless, they had to react as any good general would, by taking judicious action. Thus, the Germans got a front-row seat to observe how the Allies would react to the invasion.

As a result, new plans were proposed, and General Erich von Manstein's "sickle cut" plan came to the forefront. Manstein's plan moved the main focus from Army Group B in the north (the German right flank) to Army Group A in the center. To support this, the bulk of Panzer and mechanized forces were moved to Army Group A. Army Group B would launch an invasion into the Netherlands and northern Belgium in order to draw Allied armies north. Army Group A would move through Luxembourg and across southern Belgium to Sedan. Once there, Army Group A would force a crossing at Sedan across the Meuse and then race for the channel coast. Allied armies to the north of the sickle cut would be effectively isolated and cut off.

THE CAMPAIGN

Operation Fall Gelb (Case Yellow) began on May 10, when German Fallschirmjägers (paratroopers) captured a key Belgian fortress to support of Army Group B's advance. As Army Group B advanced into the Netherlands and Belgium, French and British forces poised along the French-Belgian frontier rushed forward to meet the threat—and into the trap.

Army Group A advanced into the Ardennes with over 41,000 vehicles along four narrow roads. The Belgian army put up a scattered, though spirited, resistance that nevertheless slowed the progress of Army Group A. The greater problem for the Allies emanated from the lack of coordination between the Belgian and French forces in the region. The Germans exploited these errors, which accelerated their advance toward Sedan.

Allied reconnaissance had reported a strong buildup of German forces opposite Luxembourg in early May, but Marshal Maurice Gamelin (the overall Allied commander) assumed that these forces were secondary to the primary attack, expected to fall in the north. Furthermore, the restrictive terrain of the Ardennes and the formidable obstacle provided by the Meuse River would give France ample time to react to any attack in this sector. The French had assumed that it would take the Germans sixteen days in total to move through the Ardennes and cross the Meuse. Unfortunately for the French, the Germans accomplished both by the end of the third day.

Once across the Meuse, Hitler envisioned his armored forces expanding the bridgehead. But General Heinz Guderian and other Panzer commanders of Army Group A had other plans. Despite orders to the contrary, German armored forces rushed westward toward the channel coast. Allied forces launched several attacks to break through the thin German spearheads, but poor coordination resulted in failure. By June 4, Dunkirk had fallen, and the battle for northern France was over.

At dawn on June 5, the Germans wheeled south to begin Fall Rot (Case Red), the second phase of the operation to conquer central and southern France. The French had reconstituted a defensive line that traced the Somme and Aisne rivers. Now French forces had regained their balance from the surprise attack through the Ardennes and fought tenaciously. Army Group B made slow progress and sustained heavy losses as it moved down the coast. Nevertheless, the defeat of France was a forgone conclusion by this phase.

Many within the French government began to push for armistice talks. On June 10, the French government evacuated Paris, and to prevent damage to Paris, the French army departed as well. Meanwhile, Army Group A pushed southeast toward the Swiss border, and by June 19, Army Group A had encircled nearly 500,000 French soldiers. The Italians entered the campaign on June 21, lest they miss out on a chance to permanently loot French territory in the peace talks to follow. On June 22, France and Germany signed an armistice. An Italian armistice followed shortly afterward on June 25.

CONCLUSION

The success of this campaign largely pivoted on surprise, and achieving surprise rests on two separate, though related, premises. First, one must give the enemy what they expect—the logical move. In this case, Army Group B advanced along a similar path to that which was taken in World War I. The terrain along Army Group B's invasion route was understood by both sides to be the best for mobile warfare. In short, this invasion route made sense. Manstein's plan exploited these expectations.

The second premise requires that one violate logical expectations. Army Group A's invasion route through the Ardennes did not makes sense for several reasons. First, many Allied commanders, though not all, assumed the Ardennes terrain impenetrable to armored forces. Second, even if passable, they reasoned that the narrow roads and restricted terrain made the terrain highly unsuited for armor. Third, once through the Ardennes, the Germans' armored forces would then need to conduct a river crossing. Given these obstacles, and the prime maneuver terrain that existed to the north, it just didn't make sense to go through the Ardennes.

On the one hand, Manstein's operational plan delivered the expected blow to the north under Army Group B. And on the other, the fatal dagger was delivered by Army Group A, which required the cooperation of Allied commanders— cooperation that they unwittingly provided. The subterfuge was effective because it conformed to, rather than deviated from, the mental models of Allied generals.

The German invasion of France in 1940 demonstrates how a military force that is numerical and technologically inferior achieved one of the greatest victories in the annals of military history. Yet, the laurels of success are as much a product of planning as of disobedience. Time and again, German generals exceeded and frequently ignored orders to halt the advance. The momentum of the advance produced its own fortune. For all the focus that this campaign often receives in military history, the greatest, and perhaps most overlooked, lesson is this—the French were not so much outfought as outthought.

Further Reading
Frieser, Karl-Heinz, with John T. Greenwood. *The Blitzkrieg Legend.* Annapolis, MD: Naval Institute Press, 2005.

Horne, Alistair. *To Lose a Battle: France 1940.* New York: Penguin Books, 2007.

Murray, Williamson. "May 1940: Contingency and Fragility of the German RMA," in MacGregor Knox and Williamson Murray, eds., *The Dynamics of Military Revolution, 1300–2050,* 154–174. Cambridge University Press, 2001.

69. The Battle of Britain

Date: July 10–October 31, 1940
Location: Great Britain

OPPONENTS

1. Germany

   Commanders: Field Marshal Albert Kesselring, Field Marshal Hugo Sperrle, and Colonel-General Hans-Jurgen Stumpf

2. Great Britain

   Commander: Air Chief Marshal Hugh Dowding

BACKGROUND

Following a six-week campaign, the Battle of France was over and what Winston Churchill called in a speech on June 18 "the Battle of Britain" was about to begin.

Strategically, after the fall of France, Germany was in an ideal situation. Most of Europe was under the direct control of or allied with the Third Reich. A nonaggression pact with the Soviet Union ensured that Germany's eastern flank was

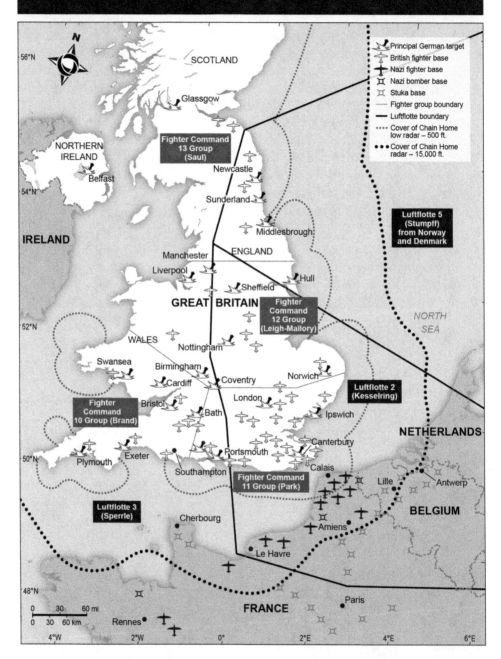

BATTLE OF BRITAIN, 1940

secure until Adolf Hitler was ready to move against Joseph Stalin. Operationally, the Wehrmacht (armed forces) was at its peak. The army and the Luftwaffe were battle-tested, having perfected their organizational and doctrinal concepts during the previous campaigns. There was only one country left to challenge Hitler's bid for hegemony in Europe: Great Britain.

Hitler hoped that the British people and politicians, realizing how perilous their situation was, would do the sensible thing and negotiate a peace. Despite some calls for a negotiated peace, Winston Churchill was determined to fight on. If he were going to force his will upon Great Britain, Hitler would have to invade England. All his advisors were in agreement that the number one precondition for a successful invasion was gaining air superiority over the landing sites. Gaining air superiority would require the Luftwaffe to destroy the Royal Air Force (RAF) and set up the first true air campaign in history.

OPPONENTS

The historical narrative portrays the battle as a "David and Goliath" match between a small but determined band of pilots in the RAF and the colossus of the invincible Luftwaffe. In reality, the difference in numbers was not that significant. In early August, just before the most intense phase of the battle, the RAF had 1,032 fighters on hand, with another 424 in reserve. At the same time, the Luftwaffe had 1,011 fighters available for operations.

Technologically, both sides possessed equally advanced modern fighters. Most of the British squadrons were equipped with Hawker Hurricanes and Supermarine Spitfires. The Spitfire was faster, but the slower Hurricane was a more stable gun platform. During the battle, Hurricane squadrons were directed to attack the bombers and the Spitfires to engage the escorting fighters. The mainstay of the Luftwaffe fighter force was the Bf 109E. A slightly older design than the British fighters, it could not turn as tightly, but the German pilots could outdive their opponents. The Bf 109's biggest shortcoming was its limited range. The German fighters could spend only ten minutes over London before they had to return to France. However, the RAF's most significant advantage was its integrated air defense system.

Under Air Chief Marshal Hugh Dowding, Fighter Command, the organization responsible for the air defense of Britain, had been working on a means of using radio waves to detect airborne aircraft since the mid-1930s. By the time of the battle, there was a continuous chain of these stations arrayed around the north, south, and east coasts of England. Called "Chain Home," some were designated "Chain Home Low" to detect low-level aircraft and "Chain Home High" for high-level aircraft. However, it was the integrated air defense system that Dowding developed that made radar truly effective.

Every element of Fighter Command was an integrated "system-of-systems." Along with the radar stations, Dowding had 1,000 observation posts manned by 30,000 observers arrayed along the coast. Fighter Command headquarters then collected the information from the radar and observer sites for further analysis. Each incoming raid was tracked on a massive plotting board so that the chain of command could make decisions on alerting fighter squadrons and antiaircraft batteries. This information was then relayed to the sector stations to scramble individual squadrons to intercept the incoming German bombers. Fortunately, for Great Britain, the Luftwaffe never understood how tightly integrated the RAF defense was and never set out to systematically destroy the induvial parts.

THE BATTLE

The Luftwaffe began nuisance raids over Great Britain almost immediately following the fall of France. However, it was not until the middle of July before it began intercepting shipping in the English Channel and probing the RAF's defenses. The Germans called this phase *Kanalkampf* (Channel Battle). The Luftwaffe's attacks on shipping were successful enough to force the British to call off sending convoys into the channel. During this phase, both sides were beginning to get the measure of the other, but the next phase would go to the RAF.

Luftwaffe planners, based on previous operations, assumed that it would take four days to defeat Fighter Command and another four weeks to eliminate the rest of the RAF and cripple aircraft production. For this phase, the Luftwaffe concentrated on attacking Fighter Command airfields. The Luftwaffe code-named this anticipated final blow to the RAF Adlerangriff (Eagle Attack), with August 13 slated as Eagle Day (*Adlertag*). However, for the Luftwaffe, Eagle Day got off to an inauspicious start. Rainy, windy weather forced the recall of the morning raids. Unfortunately, not all the bombers received the recall and continued their attack unescorted. They suffered significant losses. The afternoon raids fared better, but by the end of the day, the Luftwaffe had lost forty-five aircraft, and Fighter Command thirteen. It was going to take more than four days to defeat the RAF.

On August 15, the Luftwaffe launched its largest attacks. Throughout the day, German pilots flew over 2,000 sorties, and Fighter Command flew nearly 1,000. The pilots of 11 Group bore the brunt of the fighting, with many of its pilots flying up to three missions that day. August 15 was also significant because for the first and last time, Luftflotte 5 sent a raid from its bases in Norway. Believing that most of Fighter Command was in the south, Luftwaffe planners thought that the targets on northern England would be vulnerable. Thus 115 bombers escorted by 35 long-range fighters attacked various targets in the northeast. The fighters of 12 Group intercepted and destroyed sixteen bombers and seven fighters. Surprised by the ferocity of the defenders, the Luftwaffe never launched another daylight raid from Norway. In total, by the end of the day, the Luftwaffe had lost 161 aircraft of all types, and Fighter Command lost 34.

August 18 has been called the "hardest day." Once again, the Luftwaffe launched massive raids against the airfields and radar stations in southern England. One of the most significant attacks involved 109 Ju87 Stuka dive bombers, escorted by 150 Bf 109s, launched against the Poling radar station. During this raid, the Luftwaffe lost seventeen bombers and eight fighters. After this attack, the Luftwaffe quietly removed the Ju87s from future operations. Total losses for the day were sixty-nine for the Luftwaffe and twenty-nine for Fighter Command. Rainy weather gave each side rest for a few days before the battle of attrition began again.

The battle raged for three more weeks, with losses in pilots and planes mounting on both sides. The RAF was looking to be on the ropes, but the Germans were unaware of this, and the Luftwaffe switched its strategy from attacking the airfields to bombing London. On September 7, Hermann Goering personally watched from Pas-de-Calais as 400 bombers and 600 fighters crossed the channel on their way to bomb London. While the switch in strategy was detrimental to the citizens of London, these raids gave Fighter Command a much-needed respite.

The last major daylight raids took place on September 15. The Luftwaffe high command believed that the RAF was broken, telling their pilots that they would meet little resistance over London. Throughout the battle, Luftwaffe intelligence consistently overestimated the effect of their attacks and underestimated the strength and resilience of the RAF. In the morning, Spitfires and Hurricanes of 11 Group intercepted two attacks of over 100 bombers apiece. The British pilots forced the bombers to drop their bombs and turn back to France. Later that day, another force of bombers fought its way to London, but with minimal effect. Surprised by the large number of British fighters, the Luftwaffe ceased large-scale daylight operations over Great Britain. The Luftwaffe would continue nighttime raids on Great Britain for the remainder of the war. Nonetheless, the Battle of Britain was over.

CONCLUSION

By the end of the battle, the Luftwaffe had lost nearly 2,000 aircraft and more 2,500 crew. The RAF losses were over 1,000 aircraft and 544 aircrew. Over 40,000 civilians lost their lives during the battle and the subsequent nighttime raids. However, it was Germany that really lost, both strategically and politically.

Politically, this was Hitler's first major setback. The battle did not compel Great Britain to negotiate a peace, and he was forced to call off the invasion. Strategically, the outcome of the battle put Hitler in a quandary about what to do next. Not relishing a war on two fronts, he convinced himself that Great Britain was at least neutralized, and so he could turn his attention to the Soviet Union, laying the groundwork for an even greater strategic and political defeat.

Further Reading

Bergstrom, Christer. *The Battle of Britain: An Epic Conflict Revisited.* Havertown, PA: Casemate Publishers, 2014.

Bungay, Stephen. *The Most Dangerous Enemy: A History of the Battle of Britain.* London: Aurum Press, 2000.

Fisher, David. *A Summer Bright and Terrible: Winston Churchill, Lord Dowding, Radar, and the Impossible Triumph of the Battle of Britain.* Washington, DC: Shoemaker and Hoard, 2005.

Overy, Richard. *The Battle of Britain: The Myth and Reality.* New York: W. W. Norton, 2002.

70. Crete

Date: May 20–June 1, 1941
Location: Crete

OPPONENTS

1. German-Italian forces
   Commander: Major General Kurt Student
2. British Commonwealth and Greek forces
   Commander: Major General Bernard Freyberg

BACKGROUND

The Battle of Crete was an attempt to seize an island without a massive amphibious assault. However, the number of casualties sustained by the German airborne forces led the Wehrmacht (armed forces) to reconsider the use of airborne attacks. Crete would be the last major airborne operation for the German army during World War II.

Located between Greece and North Africa, Crete was strategically positioned to dominate the eastern Mediterranean Sea. Both the Allies and the Germans recognized that controlling Crete would be critical to any operations in North Africa. The British wanted Crete's ports for the Royal Navy's operations in the eastern Mediterranean Sea. Further, the airfields on Crete would put the Royal Air Force (RAF) bombers in range of the Romanian oil fields at Ploesti, Germany's main supply of oil. The Germans wanted Crete to support operations in North Africa, as well as to control the eastern Mediterranean. However, the Wehrmacht was deeply involved in planning for Operation Barbarossa, the invasion of Russia. However, concern over the Romanian oil fields caused Hitler to approve the invasion of Crete, so long as it did not interfere with Operation Barbarossa.

Major General Bernard Freyberg, a British–New Zealand officer, was in command of the Allied forces on Crete. Under his command, he had almost 40,000 British and Commonwealth soldiers. Approximately 25,000 of these had been evacuated from the mainland before Greece fell. Also, he had three battalions of the 5th Greek Division, which were augmented by survivors of the 12th and 20th Greek Divisions as well as the local Gendarmerie, at his disposal. There were three RAF and one Fleet Air Arm squadrons on the island; however, they had only twenty-four aircraft between them.

General Kurt Student, the father of the *Fallschirmjäger* (Airborne), had the 7th Flieger Division and the 5th Mountain Division. The 7th would parachute in and seize the airfields, and the 5th Mountain would then be airlifted onto the secure airfields. In support would be the fighters and bombers of the Fliegerkorps VIII. The paratroopers of the 7th were seasoned veterans of smaller operations during the invasion of France, and the Luftwaffe high command was anxious to prove what airborne troops could do en masse.

THE BATTLE

Operation Mercury (*Unternehmen Merkur*) called for the airborne and glider troops to seize the three airfields at Maleme, Heraklion, and Rethymno in order to airlift in the 5th Mountain Division. Maleme, the largest airfield, and the best situated to support the operation, was the main focus of the German efforts. However, the German intelligence had severely underestimated the strength of the defenses, and the attack ran into trouble from the outset.

At 8 a.m. on May 20, 1941, the first wave of German paratroopers began landing near Maleme. However, in the confusion of combat, many of the gliders and paratroopers missed their drop zones and set up defensive positions west of the airfield after landing rather than advancing on the airfield. Those who did land in the right location quickly organized and went on to Maleme. Meeting stiffer than anticipated resistance from the New Zealanders, they went to ground as well. Later that evening, the Germans regrouped and resumed the attack. They met with some success and began pushing the New Zealanders back, but they never seized the airfield.

Late in the afternoon of May 20, the next wave of paratroopers began dropping to seize the airfields at Rethymno and Heraklion. The paratroopers quickly formed up and moved toward their objectives. The fighting around Heraklion went back and forth, with key points changing hands between the paratroopers and the mixed Australian and Greek defenders. The Germans eventually prevailed but failed to capture the airfield.

By any measurement, the first day was a failure for the Germans. The Germans had not achieved any of their objectives. More troubling for the Wehrmacht was the horrendous casualties suffered by the paratroopers. For example, one parachute battalion at Maleme lost 400 men (out of 600) and one company lost 112 men (out of 126). However, they were on the island and would continue the attack the next day.

General Kurt Student elected to concentrate on Maleme airfield, where the Germans had had the most success the previous day. It was a fortuitous choice. During the night, due to poor communications, the British had withdrawn from both Maleme and the surrounding high ground, leaving the airfield undefended. The Germans quickly exploited this mistake and occupied Maleme. Throughout the day, British attempts to retake the airfield were unsuccessful, and elements of the 5th Mountain Division began landing in transport aircraft during the night.

The only British success of the day occurred when three light cruisers and four destroyers intercepted a German convoy of twenty light transports trying to land forces near Maleme. The British ships forced the convoy to turn back, sinking half the transports without loss to themselves. Nevertheless, one intrepid transport captain managed to put ashore three officers and 110 soldiers.

On May 22, due to more confused communications, a planned night counterattack on Maleme by the British turned into a daylight attack. An assault force of three New Zealand battalions and one Maori battalion were assigned to retake the airfield. By this time, the paratroopers and mountain troops were well dug in and, with the help of the Luftwaffe, were able to defeat the New Zealanders. Eventually, the New Zealanders retreated to their starting point. At sea, it was a different story. The Royal Navy continued to control the waters around Crete, preventing the Germans from bringing reinforcements. However, the Luftwaffe controlled the skies over Crete, and British ships were under continuous assault, losing two cruisers and one destroyer.

The action from May 23–27 was chaotic on both land and sea. The Royal Navy continued to face determined attacks from the Luftwaffe, and on May 23, it was ordered to cease daylight operations. On Crete, the Germans continued to consolidate their gains but were running short of supplies and were in dire need of reinforcements. The German navy, with support from the Italian navy, tried to force men and supplies through but was continually rebuffed. Both sides fought tenaciously, but neither could gain an advantage. On May 26, the Germans requested that the Italian prime minister Benito Mussolini provide Italian troops to support their forces. By the early evening of May 28, a total of 3,000 Italian troops from the 50th Infantry Division made an unopposed landing and moved westward to link up with the Germans. However, unknown to the Germans and Italians, the British had decided on May 27 that the battle was lost and began making plans for an evacuation.

The Commonwealth forces began a disciplined fighting withdrawal to their embarkation points, preventing the Germans from turning the loss into a rout. Beginning May 28, the British were evacuated to Egypt. The biggest lift came on the night of May 29–30, and the last troops left on the night of May 31–June 1. When the island surrendered on June 1, over 18,000 Commonwealth troops had been evacuated to bolster the forces in North Africa. Nonetheless, despite these heroic efforts by the Royal Navy, approximately 12,000 Allied soldiers were marched off into captivity.

The British Commonwealth forces suffered over 3,000 killed and nearly 2,000 wounded. Meanwhile, the Royal Navy lost three cruisers, five destroyers, and one aircraft carrier, with two battleships, five cruisers, two destroyers, and one submarine damaged. Losses during the battle reduced the Royal Navy's operational strength in the eastern Mediterranean to two battleships and three cruisers.

CONCLUSION

While the battle was an apparent German victory, it had come at an unacceptably high price. The Germans suffered a 30 percent loss rate among the ground forces. The losses to 7th Flieger Division were so high that Hitler forbade any more mass airborne operations. More important, the Luftwaffe lost more than 250 transport aircraft—aircraft that they needed for the upcoming Russian campaign. However, the immediate effect of the Battle of Crete was on the decision not to invade the more strategically important island of Malta. Sitting astride the sea lanes that led to North Africa, the Allied forces on Malta could interdict the flow of supplies to the Afrika Korps, which would determine the outcome of Erwin Rommel's campaigns in North Africa.

Further Reading

Beevor, Antony. *Crete: The Battle and the Resistance.* London: John Murray, 1991.

Davin, Daniel Marcus. *Crete: The Official History of New Zealand in the Second World War, 1939–1945.* Wellington: Historical Publications Branch, Department of Internal Affairs, Government of New Zealand, 1953.

Kurowski, Frank. *Jump into Hell: German Paratroopers in World War II.* Mechanicsburg, PA: Stackpole Books, 2010.

Palazzo, Albert. *Battle of Crete.* Canberra: Army History Unit, 2007.

Sadler, John. *Operation Mercury: The Battle for Crete 1941.* Barnsley, South Yorkshire, UK: Pen & Sword Military, 2007.

71. Pearl Harbor

Date: December 7, 1941
Location: Oahu, Hawaii

OPPONENTS

1. United States
    Commanders: Admiral Husband E. Kimmel and General Walter Short
2. Japan
    Commander: Admiral Nagumo Chuichi

BACKGROUND AND PLANS

In 1940, Admiral Yamamoto Isoroku, who had opposed his country's alliance with Germany, was reassigned from his post as vice naval minister to command of the Combined Fleet due to worries over assassination threats by radical young officers. By mid-1941, an impasse between Japan and the United States over its war of aggression in China against the Nationalists under Chiang Kai-Shek led to a U.S. embargo on Japanese oil exports. The military-dominated government now decided on war against the United States and occupied southern Indochina. It assigned Yamamoto the leading role in opening it; he reluctantly planned for war and conceived the brilliant idea of a surprise air and minisubmarine attack on the U.S. fleet—an attack only possible now that that fleet was in Hawaii. After working through technical problems with launching aerial torpedo attacks in shallow Pearl Harbor, the six big aircraft carriers of *Dai Ichi Kido Butai* (The First Mobile Strike Force), probably the finest naval aviators in the world at that time, departed from their anchorage at Takan Bay in the Kurile Islands in late November 1941, under the command of Vice Admiral Chuichi Nagumo, for a stealthy North Pacific transit.

Unbeknownst to the U.S. navy, *Kido Butai* was something new in warfare—a mobile naval air striking force with an operational capability not seen before in naval history. The closest thing to it in terms of firepower and innovation was the Germans' *Panzergruppe Kleist,* which had spearheaded the German Blitzkrieg against France the previous year. More than its German counterpart, *Kido Butai*'s air groups were almost entirely veterans of combat in China since 1937, and its deck crews were at a peak of perfection in getting their planes airborne. The idea for this concentration of naval air power had come from *Kido Butai*'s air operations officer, Commander Genda Minoru.

On November 27, Admiral Husband Kimmel, the intelligent and aggressive commander-in-chief of the U.S. Pacific Fleet, received a "war warning," which was in part based on decryption of the Japanese secret diplomatic code (Magic), indicating that war was imminent. Kimmel convened a meeting of his major commanders about preparations for war. At this meeting was his Pacific Fleet commander of aircraft carriers, Vice Admiral William "Bull" Halsey, and Lieutenant General Walter Short. The outcome was a heightened alert status for the forces in Pearl

ATTACK ON PEARL HARBOR, DEC. 7, 1941

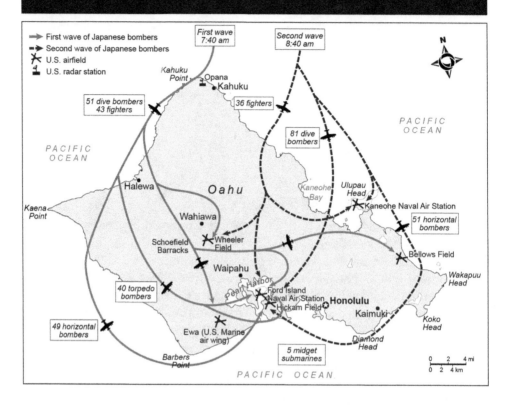

Harbor and a decision to send out the two aircraft carriers that were present to reinforce the islands. Halsey was to go to Wake aboard the carrier *Enterprise,* and *Lexington* was to reinforce Midway. The third Pacific fleet carrier, *Lexington's* sister ship *Saratoga*, was already en route to the West Coast of the United States for a scheduled yard period. Neither carrier took the slower battleships with them because speed was of the essence.

Back in Washington, D.C., on December 5, the initial excitement of the war warning seemed to have dulled everyone's senses. From mid-November to December 5, Op-20-G, the navy office tasked with the decryption of vital diplomatic signal intelligence with Japan, had been working overtime. The organization intercepted and decrypted signal intercepts smoothly and got them to the strategic intelligence consumers at the highest levels of the U.S. government rapidly. On December 6, this performance suffered its first real setback. Because of a series of failures and compromises, most of the key strategic decision-makers in Washington, D.C., went to bed that night without having been informed that the Japanese were sending their diplomatic entourage instructions that constituted a diplomatic break just short of war, and that a critical final section of the message had yet to be decrypted—before the Japanese delegation, as it turned out.

President Franklin Delano Roosevelt was aware that the situation was tense, but he had decided to leave the initiative for peace or war with the Japanese. The ongoing negotiations between Secretary of State Cordell Hull and Ambassador

Nomura Kichasaburo had shown little progress. At the end of a midday budget meeting, Roosevelt remarked to his budget director that "we might be at war with Japan, although no one knew." Later that night, just before he went to bed, Roosevelt received the packet from the Office of Naval Intelligence that included a number of dispatches, with the key diplomatic decrypt at the bottom of the pile. Roosevelt rapidly read all fifteen pages. When he was finished, he said, "This means war." However, he had little idea of where the first attack would occur, and after all, the war warnings had been sent and everyone had acknowledged them.

THE ATTACK

The United States has been criticized for not being ready for the coming war, yet in most respects, their strategic planners got it right. They expected attacks on the Philippines, Guam, and Wake, as well as the resource-rich British and Dutch colonial possessions. All these occurred on December 7–8 or shortly thereafter, but what was not foreseen was Admiral Yamamoto's bold attack on Hawaii. Militarily, the Pearl Harbor attack was nothing more than a spectacular and highly successful raid. However, had it never occurred, the United States would still have gone to war because of all the other assaults against its possessions in the Pacific.

Admiral Nagumo's naval aircraft—183 in the first wave alone—caught the U.S. Pacific Fleet and air forces completely unaware on December 7, 1941, at 7:40 a.m., shortly after sunrise.

A second wave of 178 planes hit Oahu at 8:54 a.m. The first attack was picked up on radar, but due to a peacetime attitude, the information arrived only after the attack occurred. A number of B-17s flying in that morning were savaged as well. All eight U.S. battleships were damaged, but of these, two would be repaired within

Smoke pours from the crippled battleship USS *Arizona* at Pearl Harbor, December 7, 1941. The bulk of the casualties at Pearl Harbor came from this one ship. (Library of Congress)

a week and another four eventually came back in service as well. Only the *Arizona* and the *Oklahoma* were never returned to service. The majority of the losses to the fleet came from these two ships.

In addition to the battleships present, the Japanese—perhaps more important—crippled the U.S. Army Air Forces (USAAF), destroying or damaging almost 350 aircraft. Over 3,200 military and civilian casualties were incurred. However, once sober minds evaluated the damage, it was realized that the critical repair facilities and fuel depots surrounding Pearl Harbor were virtually untouched.

A myth evolved after the war that Nagumo had planned a third strike but failed to launch, but this was never the case. The Japanese lost 29 aircraft in the attack but had approximately 111 damaged. The Japanese minisubmarine was almost a disaster in its own right, launching early and almost giving away the surprise, with all the minisubs lost (sunk or destroyed) and one captured.

CONCLUSION

The results of Pearl Harbor were strategically insignificant as far as the Japanese conquest of the "Southern Resource Area" was concerned, because the U.S. fleet had little chance of reaching American possessions in the Western Pacific in time to prevent the loss of these key support bases once hostilities broke out. It certainly ranked as a tactical disaster for the U.S. navy; however, once the reality of war set in, the navy did what it had planned to do all along—methodically island-hop across the Pacific after remaining on the defensive for the first six months of the war. More important, Pearl Harbor served not as a morale-destroying defeat, but rather as a rallying cry that motivated Americans to greater efforts and hardened their hearts. It was a far greater disaster for the Japanese, although that was not

---

War Plan Orange

Beginning in 1909, two planning organizations in the navy and War Department began working on a contingency plan for war with Japan—War Plan Orange. The navy's organization was the General Board and the army's was the War Plans Section of the General Staff; they coordinated via the mechanism of a Joint Army-Navy Board (Joint Board). The planning focused around a defense of the Philippine Islands. It relied heavily on a navy thrust across the Pacific to relieve the American garrison on the main island of Luzon. After the Washington Naval Treaty (1922), the thrusting option, which relied on the buildup of a base on Guam, looked much less feasible. By the early 1930s, both army and navy planners decided that a better course of action would be a cautionary one that involved a step-by-step advance across the Pacific, relying on seizing advanced based until the Western Pacific could be reached. In this plan, the Philippines would probably fall and have to be recaptured.

The mature War Plan Orange envisioned a major battle between the U.S. and Japanese fleets in the Philippine Sea, after which the United States would be able to invade and liberate the Philippines. Ironically, Japanese intelligence obtained the U.S. thrusting plan and prepared their war plan in a reciprocal fashion. Just before the outbreak of war with Japan in 1941, the United States ostensibly abandoned War Plan Orange for the Rainbow plans; however, after the bombing of Pearl Harbor and fall of the Philippines, it was essentially reimplemented by Admiral Chester Nimitz.

apparent at the time. It also spurred Adolf Hitler to declare war on the United States several days later, which solved Roosevelt's problem of how to get into the war against Germany. Winston Churchill reputedly said of that he "slept the sleep of the saved and thankful" after he learned of the attack because now he knew that the United States was in the war as a full-fledged military ally.

Further Reading

Lundstrom, John B. *Black Shoe Carrier Admiral: Frank Jack Fletcher at Coral Sea Midway, and Guadalcanal.* Annapolis, MD: Naval Institute Press, 2006.

Parshall, Jonathan B., and J. Michael Wenger. "Pearl Harbor's Overlooked Answer." *Naval History*, December 2011, 16–21.

Zimm, Alan D. *Attack on Pearl Harbor: Strategy, Combat, Myths, Deceptions.* Philadelphia: Casemate Books, 2011.

72. Wake Island

Date: December 8–11, 1941
Location: Wake Island Naval Air Station

OPPONENTS

1. United States

   Commanders: Commander Winfield S. Cunningham and Major James P. S. Devereux, U.S. Marine Corps

2. Japan

   Commander: Rear Admiral Sadamichi Kajioka

BACKGROUND

In the possession of the United States since the Spanish-American War, Wake Island is approximately 2,000 miles west of Hawaii. It is composed of three islets; Wake, Peale, and Wilkes. This insignificant triangle of coral was a refueling stop for the Pan American Airways Clipper Service, but it gained strategic importance as war loomed between the United States and Japan before World War II.

War Plan Orange, the American plan for a war with Japan, envisioned the U.S. Pacific Fleet sailing across the Pacific to destroy the Imperial Japanese Navy (IJN) in a decisive battle before blockading the Japanese islands. To counter War Plan Orange, the IJN planned to attrit the U.S. fleet to the point that it could be defeated before it reached Japanese home waters. Based on their respective plans, both sides recognized the value of islands like Wake as patrolling and support bases. However, due to treaty restrictions, the United States did not begin fortifying Wake Island until 1941.

In January of that year, the first of more than 1,000 contractors arrived to begin converting the island to a Naval Air Station. In August, a 500-man detachment of the U.S. Marine Corps' First Defense Battalion arrived, under the command of

Major James P. S. Devereux. This unit brought with them six 5" naval guns, twelve 3" antiaircraft guns, and numerous .30- and .50-caliber machine guns to defend Wake Island. On November 28, Commander Winfield S. Cunningham arrived to assume command of the island. A week later, on December 4, twelve F4F-3 Wildcats of VMF 211 lifted off the USS *Enterprise,* landing on the partially completed airstrip to round out the defensive posture of Wake Island.

However, defenses were incomplete when the war broke out. Many of the gun positions needed improvement, and the Wildcats still needed hardened revetments for protection. Devereux worked his men hard to get the job done, but digging into the coral was backbreaking work. In recognition of their hard work over the previous months, he gave his Marines Sunday, December 7, off to rest. (Wake Island is west of the International Date Line and is a day ahead of Hawaii.)

THE BATTLE

Early on December 8 (December 7 Hawaiian time), Cunningham received word of the Japanese attack on Pearl Harbor. The island went on full alert. The Marines manned their guns as VMF 211 launched four fighters to patrol over the island. Cunningham recalled the Pan American clipper that departed earlier. Meanwhile, the Pan American workers prepared for evacuation. Early warning and detection of inbound Japanese aircraft were a concern for Cunningham and Devereux. With no radar, they would have to rely on visual observation; however, the island's water tower was the highest point, at only fifty feet. Nonetheless, it would have to do. One by one, the batteries reported ready, and the defenders waited for the Japanese.

Despite being on alert, the Japanese attack caught the Marines off guard. Around noon, land-based bombers from the Marshall Islands struck. The Wildcats on patrol could not find the enemy because of cloudy weather, and the attack came too fast for the antiaircraft gunners to have any effect. Most of the bombers focused on the airfield, destroying the eight Wildcats on the ground. The other bombers attacked the heavy guns, causing damage to the 3" batteries and fire control equipment of one 5" battery. Miraculously, the Pan Am clipper survived the attack and left that afternoon, for Pearl Harbor. On board were all the passengers and Pan Am personnel except for forty-five Chamarros. The island faced two more days of air attacks, each one leaving the defenses a little more diminished.

The Japanese assumed three days of aerial bombardment was enough to prepare the island for an invasion. Reports from the bomber crews supported this assumption. An invasion force assembled near Kwajalein, under the command of Rear Admiral Sadamichi Kajioka, to seize the island. Kajioka's force of three light cruisers, six destroyers, four transports, and 450 troops of the Special Naval Landing Force (SNLF), the equivalent of U.S. Marines, arrived off the southwest shore of Wake in the early-morning hours of December 11. After softening up the island with fire from the cruisers and destroyers, 150 SNLF soldiers landed on Wilkes, with the rest landing on Wake.

Lookouts on Wake spotted the ships looming on the horizon, and the alert went out. It is unclear who decided to hold fire; both Cunningham and Devereux claim credit for the decision. Regardless, as his force approached the darkened island, Kajioka believed that the previous day's attacks were more effective than reported. Emboldened, he decided to move in closer before opening fire. All the while, the Marine gunners on the 5" guns were tracking the Japanese ships, getting nervous as they came closer. At 6 a.m., the flagship, *Yubari,* turned west roughly 5,000 yards from Battery A, and, at long last, the batteries were permitted to open fire.

Battery A's first salvo struck the *Yubari,* and the captain withdrew his ship. The Marines' next salvo damaged a destroyer trying to cover the *Yubari*'s retreat. At the same time, Battery L engaged three destroyers and a transport approaching Wilkes. Their first salvo hit the destroyer *Hayate,* sinking it with all hands. The gunners with support from Battery B would hit several more ships before the battle was over. Shocked by the ferocity of the Marines' response, Kajioka decided to disengage and retire back to Kwajalein. However, the Marines were not finished with Kajioka's task force. By this time, the Wildcats from VMF 211, armed with 100-pound bombs, were in the air looking for Kajioka's task force. Spotting the retreating ships, the pilots dove in to attack. They hit several ships and sunk another destroyer before returning to Wake. A chastened Kajioka led his ships back to port. With his retreat, for the only time in World War II, shore defenses successfully repelled an amphibious invasion.

CONCLUSION

The first attempt to seize Wake Island was the only blotch on imperial Japan's record in the opening days of the war. To avenge this humiliating disaster, the Japanese returned on December 23 with a larger invasion and support force that included the carriers *Hiryu* and *Soryu,* which were returning from the Pearl Harbor raid. This time, superior numbers overwhelmed the defenders before a relief force, slowly making its way from Pearl Harbor, could arrive. Still, the defenders held out for eleven hours before Cunningham gave the word to Devereux to surrender the Island. After several days, the majority of the defenders boarded a ship bound for prisoner-of-war camps in China.

Despite both sides' prewar plans, the war bypassed Wake Island. The Americans never returned to reclaim it until the war was over. The U.S. navy used raids on Wake Island as train-ups for its carrier task forces. Nevertheless, the Japanese, expecting the Americans to attempt to retake the island, selected 100 civilian contractors to remain there to help improve its defenses—until they were executed in 1943.

Further Reading

Gilbert, Bonita. *Building for War: The Epic Saga of the Civilian Contractors and Marines of Wake Island in World War II.* Haverton, PA: Casemate Publishers, 2012.

Kuehn, John T., with D. M. Giangreco. *Eyewitness Pacific Theater.* New York: Sterling Press, 2008.

Lundstrom, John B. *The First Team: Pacific Naval Air Combatt from Pearl Harbor to Midway.* Annapolis, MD: Naval Institute Press, 1990.

Urwin, Gregory J. *Facing Fearful Odds: The Seige of Wake Island,* Lincoln: University of Nebraska Press, 2002.

73. Singapore

Date: February 7–15, 1942
Location: Island of Singapore, at the tip of the Malayan Peninsula

OPPONENTS

1. British Empire
   Commander: General Sir A. E. Percival
2. Japan
   Commander: General Yamashita Tomoyuki

BACKGROUND

The Japanese began planning in earnest to strike at the British Commonwealth, the Netherlands, and the United States shortly after these nations imposed a comprehensive oil embargo on Japan after it had occupied southern Indochina in the summer of 1941. Not long after, the government of Prime Minister Tojo Hideki received the emperor's grudging approval for the war, given that Japan could not continue her war in China without raw materials, especially the oil. To get to those raw materials, Japan had to neutralize the huge British base at Singapore, sometimes known as the "Gibraltar of the Far East." On December 8, 1941, in concert with a series of surprise attacks around the Pacific—including on Pearl Harbor, Hawaii, on December 7, on the other side of the International Date Line—the Japanese began a series of landings violating the neutrality of Siam (modern-day Thailand) to seize a lodgment from which to advance down the Malay Peninsula against Singapore. In overall command of the Twenty-Fifth Army for this operation was General Yamashita Tomoyuki. His key initial goals, after securing his landing beaches, involved seizing key airfields and ports, especially Patani and Singora. Yamashita also landed farther down the eastern side of the peninsula, in Malay territory at Kota Bharu, as a diversion for his main landings farther north. This landing had the most difficulty due to opposition and weather, yet it too managed to secure all its D-Day objectives. Yamashita's plan worked beyond his expectations. He seized the initiative on land as the British struggled to respond.

On sea and in the air, the Japanese quickly asserted their superiority. The Allied bombers and fighters—Hudsons and Brewster Buffalos—were outclassed by the Japanese Zero fighters and Betty class bombers. By day two of the invasion, Yamashita had effective air superiority. At sea, the British had deployed the battleship *Prince of Wales* and the battle cruiser *Repulse* as the centerpiece of Force Z, under Admiral Tom Phillips, to deter Japanese aggression. It had left its aircraft carrier in the Atlantic after that ship had run aground in Jamaica, and the Royal Navy authorities had oddly not detached the one aircraft carrier in the Indian Ocean to join Phillips. On December 9, Phillips took Force Z north to interdict a reported landing farther down the Malay Peninsula. On December 10, the Japanese naval aviators of the Nagoya strike group found the ships, without air cover (which Phillips had not planned for), and sank both capital ships. At one stroke, the Japanese gained complete command of the sea.

With the sky and seas safe for the advance, Yamashita's troops moved swiftly down the supposedly impassable jungles of Malaya, bypassing or bum-rushing every British attempt to set up a defensive line that would hold. By the first week of February, Yamashita's troops were clearing out Johore across the channel for Singapore, and General Sir A. E. Percival evacuated what was left of his army to Singapore proper.

THE PLAN

The British defense plan was compromised by the loss of sea and air control during the early days of the campaign. Singapore had been designed to repel an assault from the sea, with many of its big guns facing out into the South China Sea and the Malacca Strait. It had been assumed that the jungles of the Malay Peninsula, and a last-ditch defense of Johore, would protect the rear. Now the British had to protect an extended front against what would resemble an opposed river crossing across the strait between Johore and the island of Singapore. Nonetheless, Percival was hopeful that the still-substantial number of soldiers under his command could do just that, similar to what the Americans were doing in Bataan in the Philippines. But unlike Bataan, Singapore contained hundreds of thousands of civilians. Like Bataan, the authorities and Percival had not had time to prepare for an extended siege. Also like Bataan, there was no help on the way. Percival divided his defending groups into two forces known as *Western* and *Eastern Groups.* By far, the larger force consisted of the two divisions of Eastern Group, with the Australian 8th division comprising the Western Group.

Yamashita, however, was on a strict timetable. He had to secure Singapore so that the forces of imperial Japan could advance to the second phase of the campaign plan and conquer the resources of the Dutch East Indies, especially its oil and rubber resources. Also, his military success convinced him that a *coup de main* against the British defenses was all that was needed to crack the British will to resist. Why conduct a lengthy siege when he could end the campaign more quickly with an assault? He was also being badgered by his higher headquarters to do the assault, and his own supply situation was becoming difficult, if not critical. Like with most blitzkrieg-type operations, he had outrun his supply lines and the Imperial Navy had not opened up new ones yet.

With all these factors driving him, he put together a comprehensive plan to cross the strait. He was fortunate that his air power continued to pound Singapore, distracting the British from the more dangerous threat his soldiers represented. Victorious soldiers create their own success, often when things are most difficult. His plan included traditional elements of a cross-water assault, as well as a deception component. Yamashita would tantalize the British defenders with an initial assault using the Imperial Guard division against Palau Ubin Island in the eastern entrance to the strait. This would attract British attention and possibly convince them that Yamashita then intended to land on the Singapore shore immediately opposite of the island, which made sense because the crossing there would cross less open water and leave his troops exposed for less time. He also transported some of his other assault troops to that sector, but then moved them surreptitiously back to the west under cover of night. In addition, his artillery focused on this sector, a World War I–type tactic, as a means to misdirect British attention. At the same time, his main effort, with an assault force of 4,000 of his best troops—veterans of the Chinese war—prepared for assaults farther west. These troops rehearsed their landing drills relentlessly, out of sight of the British, who were still unable to discern where the main attack would come from.

THE ASSAULT

Yamashita opened his artillery bombardment as planned in the east on February 5. Combined with the constant air assaults, these continued the next day and caused much damage, including two airfields located in Easter Group's sector. On Feburary 7, Nisamura's guards executed their feint. With the British now looking for the major landings in the east, the artillery switched to the west and focused especially on communications lines and centers. The result was that the already-poor British communications became almost nonexistent. On the night of February 8, the first wave of the assault took place in the far west, against the Australians. The fighting was fierce, but the Japanese managed get ashore in strong numbers, in part due to the failure of the defenders to activate the searchlights covering the strait. The order never came down to illuminate the strait with searchlights because the lines had been cut and the top-down British command approach prevented initiative by local commanders.

Now, with Percival and the Australian tied down trying to contain the 5th Japanese Division's lodgment in the far west, another Japanese force crossed the strait on February 9 and threatened the flank of the Australian defense. Also, the guard division moved from east to west and also started to cross the strait, following in support of the other two divisions. The overall theater commander, Field Marshal Archibald Wavell, arrived on the following day in the midst of the chaos of the collapsing defenses. He wrote Prime Minister Winston Churchill afterward, "Battle for Singapore is not going well." He bluntly assessed that the Japanese were better trained and better fighters, but he assured Churchill that he had given orders for Percival to fight "to the end."

Meanwhile, Yamashita had brought up his medium tanks and began ferrying them across the now-uncontested strait on February 10. Yamashita had 30,000 undefeated troops across the strait; although outnumbered, he held all the cards. Percival frantically tried to pull his troops back into a tight perimeter in the Singapore City proper as his more extensive defenses unraveled. By February 15, his remaining troops, now down to 85,000, were packed into the city along with over half a million refugees, as well as the residents of the city itself. The Japanese were now threatening to seize the one water-processing facility left to the British, and food was already running out. Wavell continued to urge Percival to hold out, but he allowed him to make the judgment about when to capitulate.

Three days earlier, Yamashita had decided that the time was ripe to halt hostilities and send over an emissary for negotiating a surrender. He appealed to Percival's sense of humanity and the increasingly dire situation of the civilian population. On Sunday, February 15, Percival met with Yamashita and capitulated, surrendering the garrison and city into Japanese hands.

CONCLUSION

The fall of Singapore was one of the great catastrophes of World War II. It basically eliminated Great Britain's ability to affect any Japanese military operations east of Burma and India. In turn, it released Japanese forces to carry out further operations against Burma, and then India, threatening the very basis of British power itself, as well as the tenuous supply lines to the Nationalist Chinese. Further, it opened the Dutch East Indies to invasion. Without Singapore on their flank, the Japanese swiftly advanced south, and within three months, they had conquered a huge area rich in oil and other resources that Japan needed to fight a war with its enemies.

Worse, the civilians and soldiers who fell into Japanese hands might have done better to have kept on fighting. Japanese occupation, despite Yamashita's promises, proved extremely cruel, and many of these people, soldiers and civilians alike, ended up dying of neglect, brutality, and disease in the north as slave laborers constructing the infamous Thai-Burma Railroad. Churchill characterized the scope of the debacle best: "I speak to you all under the shadow of a heavy and far-reaching military defeat. It is a British and Imperial defeat. Singapore has fallen. . . ."

Further Reading
Churchill, Winston. *The Hinge of Fate*. London: Cassell, 1951.

Spector, Ronald. *Eagle Against the Sun: The American War with Japan*. New York: Vintage Books, 1985.

Swinson, Arthur. *Defeat in Malaya: The Fall of Singapore*. Introduction by Sir B. H. Liddell Hart. London: Ballantine Books, 1969.

74. Bataan

Date: 1942
Location: Luzon, Philippine Islands

OPPONENTS

1. United States and the Philippines
    Commander: Generals Douglas MacArthur and Jonathan Wainwright
2. Japan
    Commander: General Homma

BACKGROUND

When Japan attacked Pearl Harbor in 1941, it attacked the Philippines with its air forces only hours later, on the other side of the International Date Line on December 8. Mitsubishi "Betty" medium bombers, Japanese aircraft from Formosa, struck at Clark Field and Cavite Naval Base in the Philippines. Initially General Douglas MacArthur, in overall command of the Philippines, had his air forces ready, but fogged-in airfields in Japan had prevented his bombers from attacking and kept the Japanese strike grounded when U.S. fighters were airborne. The Japanese attack on Clark hit just after these aircraft landed to refuel, and at one stroke, the bulk of MacArthur's air forces were destroyed or damaged. The navy plan to contest the Philippines by withdrawing to the south had already begun, but the hope that torpedo boats and submarines might help cripple a Japanese invasion force had always been overly optimistic, and the navy's commander, Admiral Thomas Hart, knew it. After the attack on Cavite, he made the decision to join what few ships he had to the Australian, British, and Dutch naval forces forming up farther south to contest Japan's attacks on the Dutch East Indies, where the oil it craved was located.

THE PLANS

The Japanese plan was simple: They decided to invade the main Island, Luzon, via the best beaches at Lingayen Gulf with General Homma Masaharu's Fourteenth Army. With Hart's naval forces withdrawing south and de facto command of the air established by the disaster at Clark Field, the Japanese expected a lightly contested landing from air and sea. The original plan for the Philippines involved a bastion defense in the Bataan Peninsula to hold off the Japanese army for as long as possible, possibly until a relief force could be landed to contest the Japanese attack. Accordingly the plan was to position all the supplies for a lengthy siege in Bataan and for the American-Philippine army to fall back into prepared positions. However, this plan did not suit the temperament of MacArthur, who wanted to take the fight to the enemy with his new B-17 bombers. Because of this, he decided not to abandon Manila and the bulk of the Luzon to the Japanese and planned a cordon defense, redistributing his supply dumps throughout the Philippines.

As previously shown, without the ability to interdict Japanese invasion forces by either land or sea, it was only a matter of time before the Japanese successfully established themselves on the main island of Luzon. With his air force destroyed and most of the small naval forces being evacuated to the south, MacArthur was holding a very poor hand of cards. Accordingly, he scuttled his plan to defend Luzon on a broad front. Instead of opposing the Japanese landings in the Lingayen Gulf, which is where MacArthur's intelligence predicted they would land, MacArthur decided to challenge the Japanese in the broad plain south of Lingayen. He also delayed the order to reposition his supplies to Bataan in the hope that he would be victorious.

In the largest of their amphibious operations to date, the Japanese landed over 50,000 troops of General Homma Masaharu's Fourteenth Army at Lingayen Gulf, on the northwestern side of the main Philippine island of Luzon, on December 22, 1941. After the first contact with the well-coordinated air-sea-ground Japanese assault, MacArthur ditched his modified plan and decided to pull back into a fortified line of defenses on the peninsula of Bataan, located between Subic and Manila bays. Here, he would defend until relieved by the navy's Pacific Fleet, and yet any hope of executing this course of action had gone up in the pall of smoke rising over Pearl Harbor on December 7. Nevertheless, MacArthur had little choice other than to try to hold out, or at the very least tie down Japanese forces and prevent their use elsewhere.

THE SIEGE OF BATAAN

Fortunately for Major General Jonathan Wainwright (the commander of MacArthur's ground forces), Homma was more interested in capturing Manila than destroying his opponent, and Wainwright's withdrawal into the Bataan Peninsula was accomplished without much enemy interference. Bataan was simply not prepared for the 80,000 troops (including 20,000 Americans) who retreated into it, to say nothing of the civilian populace who also fled there. Large stockpiles of food did exist, but they were scattered across Luzon to support MacArthur's original defense scheme, and MacAthur's prevarications prevented any realistic chance that most of these stores could be transshipped into Bataan. In the confusion of the retreat, most of these supplies fell into the hands of the Japanese. After only one week in their new defenses, the "battling bastards of Bataan" were already on half-rations. The first Japanese skirmished with an American delaying force in the approaches to Bataan in early January.

Despite all these misfortunes, MacArthur's troops did their best to accomplish their new mission of delaying the Japanese timetable for conquest of the Philippines. The fight now settled into a siege, with disease and hunger afflicting both the Japanese and the Filipino-American forces. The Japanese began formal attacks against Wainwright's main defense line in mid-January, and by January 26, they had forced Wainwright's forces down almost one-third of the peninsula and seized the key town of Balanga.

Meanwhile, President Franklin Delano Roosevelt and General George C. Marshall, the army chief of staff, realized that it might be a catastrophe for American morale to have MacArthur captured, and perhaps executed, by the Japanese. They ordered MacArthur to escape through the loose Japanese blockade and go to Australia. He delayed his departure until March 11, when he finally boarded a PT boat with his family and staff for a 600-mile run to an airfield on Mindanao. Upon MacArthur's arrival in Australia, he announced, "I shall return."

In the meantime, the horrors in Bataan continued to their inevitable conclusion. In April, General Edward P. King ordered his famished and disease-ridden troops, now under considerable pressure by the Japanese and running low on ammunition—some 78,000 Americans and Filipinos—to surrender, with Wainwright's concurrence. It was the largest surrender of American-led troops in the history of the United States.

Homma had expected to capture supplies along with these troops and were dismayed to find little food at all. Not only were their troops on lower rations, but they

After the surrender of Bataan in April 1942, American and Filipino prisoners were brutalized by their Japanese captors during the Bataan Death March. (Corbis via Getty Images)

would take out their disappointment on their prisoners. In a horror of logistics incompetence and maltreatment, they marched their emaciated prisoners some sixty miles to a processing camp, with over 10,000 dying en route in an event known to history as the Bataan Death March. Most of the dead were Filipino. Wainwright and a forlorn group of 14,000 men held on into May on the island of Corregidor, at the mouth of Manila Bay. In the final analysis, however, these heroic sacrifices achieved very little—the stubborn defense of Bataan and Corregidor did not prevent, nor did it even slow, the Japanese conquest of Malaysia, Burma, and the Dutch Indies.

CONCLUSION

MacArthur's mistakes in generalship in this campaign nearly resulted in his removal. However, with him now setting up for the defense of Australia, President Roosevelt, advised by Generals Marshall and Dwight Eisenhower, decided that the blow to Allied morale would be too great to remove such a famous general. Instead, they awarded him the Medal of Honor and left him in command of the Southwest Pacific theater of operations, where MacArthur managed to salve his damaged reputation with his brilliant campaign in New Guinea, which resulted in his return to the Philippines a mere two and half years later in October 1944—a promise fulfilled.

Further Reading

Burton, John. *Fortnight of Infamy: The Collapse of Allied Airpower West of Pearl Harbor.* Annapolis, MD: Naval Institute Press, 2006.

Morton, Louis. *The Fall of the Philippines.* Washington, DC: Center of Military History, 1952.

Spector, Ronald H. *Eagle Against the Sun: The American War with Japan.* New York: Vintage Books, 1985.

75. Midway

Date: June 3–6, 1942
Location: Pacific Ocean, around the Hawaiian island of Midway

OPPONENTS

1. United States

   Commanders: Admiral Chester Nimitz and Rear Admirals F. Jack Fletcher and Raymond A. Spruance

2. Japan

   Commanders: Admiral Yamamoto Isoroku and Vice Admiral Nagumo Chuichi

BACKGROUND

Admiral Yamamoto Isoroku's Combined Fleet had achieved everything expected of it after its unlikely victory at Pearl Harbor that crippled the U.S. battleship fleet. His forces had gone from victory to victory. Yet his opponent, Admiral Chester Nimitz, the new commander of the Pacific Fleet, had unexpectedly adopted a defense strategy of raiding, both in the southwest Pacific and (more famously) in the North Pacific. In the south raiding, American carriers, aided by Nimitz's code-breakers under Lieutenant Commander Joe Rochefort at Pearl Harbor, had savaged several Japanese air raids, inflicting unheard-of casualties on Japanese military aviation forces. More spectacularly, in the north, TF-16's raid on Japan itself, with carrier-launched U.S. Army Air Force B-25s commanded by Lieutenant Colonel James "Jimmy" Doolittle, came at a critical moment. Yamamoto was arguing with the overall strategic command that the U.S. Pacific Fleet was still dangerous and must be eliminated once and for all, with an invasion either of Oahu, or, if that were not approved, of the westernmost island in the chain, Midway, where a large air base was located. The shame of the Doolittle attack finally got him the key support to launch Operation MI. However, MI's approval did not cancel existing plans of the Imperial Japanese Naval General Staff. These plans included Operation MO in the south and Operation AL in the north. *MO* stood for the objective of the next phase of the advance in the southwest Pacific—Port Moresby—by the Japanese army and navy against the Solomons and New Guinea. Additionally, naval General Staff planners saddled Yamamoto's Combined Fleet with the additional mission of

BATTLE OF MIDWAY, 1942

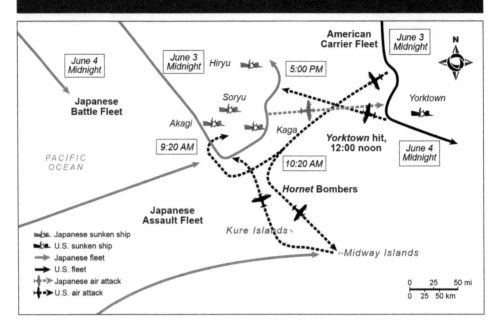

seizing the westernmost islands in the Aleutian chain (AL) because Doolittle's raid might have originated from there as well. All this led to a fatal watering down of the striking forces that Yamamoto had available for the operation against Midway—especially aircraft carriers.

Operation MO involved a two-pronged assault with two objectives: the seizure of the island of Tulagi, in the southern Solomons; and the capture of Port Moresby, on the southeastern tip of New Guinea on the Coral Sea. Tulagi's anchorage was ideal for ships and seaplanes. Port Moresby's capture would cap the conquest of Papua New Guinea. With New Guinea and the southern Solomons in hand, the Japanese would be poised—with sufficient air and sea coverage from new bases at these locations—to push into the Coral Sea and sever Australia's lifeline to the United States across the South Pacific.

To support this operation, Yamamoto was forced to send two large fleet carriers, *Zuikaku* and *Shokaku*, from his First Carrier Striking Force. Rochefort's codebreakers duly intercepted the Japanese plans, and Nimitz dispatched two carrier task forces built around *Lexington* and *Yorktown* to attack the Japanese invasion fleet in the Coral Sea. During the first week of May, during a confused series of air attacks in which neither the Japanese nor the American fleets actually saw each other, the Japanese invasion flotilla was turned back from Port Moresby—the first Allied operational victory of the Pacific War. The Americans did lose their fine aircraft carrier *Lexington*, but *Yorktown*, although damaged, made it back to Pearl Harbor. On the Japanese side, a light carrier was sunk and *Shokaku* badly damaged. They also sank an American oiler, which they misidentified as an aircraft carrier.

Despite this setback, the Japanese mood remained dangerously optimistic. They believed that they had sunk two, if not three, of the American carriers. That left at best two, and probably only one, aircraft carrier to defend Midway. In fact, the Americans, due to the incredible efforts of the sailors aboard *Yorktown* and the dockworkers at Pearl Harbor, had three big aircraft carriers potentially available to oppose Yamamoto's fleet. To Nimitz's credit, he decided to risk them all on another defensive battle to whittle down the Japanese fleet.

For the Japanese, the badly damaged *Shokaku* was no longer available for the Midway operation. As for *Zuikaku*, the punishing air battles over the Coral Sea reduced its air groups to dangerously low levels. Instead, pilots from *Zuikaku*, and some from *Shokaku*, beefed up the air groups of the remaining four carriers of Vice Admiral Nagumo Chuichi's *Dai Ichi Kido Butai* (hereafter *Kido Butai*). As it turned out, this would be a major error because the Japanese would find that they needed every one of their carrier decks at Midway. Yamamoto also dangerously diluted his naval air-striking power by agreeing to the AL operation, which subtracted the air groups of the medium carriers *Junyo* and *Ryujo* from the forces available for the main effort at Midway. Thus, the results of Coral Sea were twofold: It stopped the Japanese advance in the south, and it compromised the chances for success for the operation at Midway—fatally, as it turned out.

THE PLANS

Both Yamamoto and Admiral Nagano Osami of the Imperial Naval General Staff believed that the weight of the Combined Fleet, especially its battleships, must prevail. They misunderstood that the weight of naval power now lay in naval aviation. The losses from Coral Sea and the dilution due to the AL operation greatly weakened that power for Operation MI. Preparations continued apace with a plan that included six separate, and as it turned out mutually nonsupporting, naval forces for both the invasion and the subsequent naval battle that Midway's seizure was anticipated to provoke. Yamamoto's plan relied on surprise. He must capture Midway before the Pacific Fleet could deploy. Then, with Midway in hand and its air base neutralized as a factor (and possibly in use by Japanese planes), he would smash the Americans when they came to take it back.

Yamamoto's plan violated the principle of concentration and was too rigid. First, a screen of Japanese submarines would deploy in advance to report the movements of the Pacific Fleet from Pearl Harbor. Second, *Kido Butai*, alerted by the subs, would ambush any American naval forces coming out to meet the Japanese fleet. It was composed of the most veteran carriers and air groups in the Imperial Japanese Navy—*Kaga, Akagi, Soryu*, and *Hiryu*, as well as two escorting battleships.

A main force of seven battleships was under Yamamoto's personal command from the new superbattleship *Yamato*. This force also included the old, small carrier *Hosho*. The main force's role would be to engage any U.S. naval forces remaining after Nagumo's carriers neutralized or destroyed the American air from Midway and any aircraft carriers. The Midway Invasion Force, with escorts, was to seize and occupy Midway after its air force had been neutralized. An independent cruiser covering force supported it. Just to the north of these forces, but still some distance from Yamamoto and Nagumo, was Admiral Kondo's Second Fleet main body of cruisers, two fast battleships, and the new light carrier *Zuiho*. In addition to scattering his carriers among four widely separated forces, Yamamoto's confidence led him to scatter his battleships among three forces. His intent was to unite all the battleships at Midway for the final showdown. The carriers involved in the AL operation were hopelessly far away if things went wrong at Midway.

Yamamoto assumed that he could strike at Midway undetected, while at the same time receiving accurate and timely intelligence from his subs on the size and location of the U.S. fleet. In both cases, he was calamitously disappointed. Rochefort were already reading the traffic; to determine the target for the big attack, they had the garrison at Midway transmit in the clear that their water distillation unit was broken. The Japanese duly intercepted this message, and soon the Americans were reading that the target of the big upcoming naval operation had a problem with fresh water. Nimitz reacted decisively to this cryptographic intelligence. He decided to sortie all of his carriers into a position northeast of Midway and ambush his would-be ambushers. By doing this, he neutralized the Japanese submarine scheme in one stroke. When the Japanese were in position, Nimitz's carrier groups were already beyond the screening line.

Unlike the Japanese carriers, the American task forces were geographically separated into two groups—the *Yorktown* TF-17, under Admiral Fletcher; and a second carrier TF-16, composed of *Enterprise* and *Hornet* (of Doolittle raid fame) under Admiral Raymond Spruance.

Fletcher, the victor of Coral Sea, was the overall officer in tactical command but gave Spruance considerable latitude in conducting their operations in the upcoming battle. Nimitz chose his commanders well because both Fletcher and Spruance were cautious men who would not take undue risks with the valuable carriers of the Pacific Fleet. By this point, Fletcher was among the most experienced admirals in the fleet. Fletcher had the unsinkable "aircraft carrier" of the island of Midway, with its Marine, Navy, and Army Air Corps aircraft available to attack the Japanese once they were located. Given his three carriers and island airfield, Nimitz could put approximately the same number of aircraft into the air as the Japanese.

THE BATTLE

The Japanese lost their strategic surprise due to the codebreakers; they soon learned of this on the morning of June 3, 1942, when a PBY-5 CATALINA flying boat sighted the main Japanese armada (but not Nagumo) 700 miles west of Midway. Despite this, Yamamoto pressed on without a change to his plans. Aircraft from Midway struck the Japanese first on the afternoon of June 3 by launching B-17s to attack a group of enemy transports. The B-17s hit nothing, but the attack did focus the Japanese's attention on the danger posed by Midway and distracted them from the real danger undetected to their northeast—Fletcher's three aircraft carriers. That night, the Americans launched four radar-equipped PBYs on a night strike against the Midway Occupation Force, which attacked the Japanese invasion fleet with their defective aerial torpedoes shortly after 1 a.m. on June 4. Miraculously, one of the torpedoes exploded and damaged the Japanese oiler *Akebono Maru*.

The Japanese steamed on in radio silence as their plan unraveled. Nagumo still had no idea that the American carriers were present and decided to pummel Midway with the air power of *Kido Butai*, launching a heavy strike against Midway shortly after daybreak on June 4. Not long after the launch, Nagumo's carriers were located by a PBY. The news of Nagumo's location was passed to the American carriers, which altered course to come within range of the Japanese carriers (American carrier aircraft were shorter in range than their Japanese counterparts). Nagumo's strike found Midway's defenders prepared for them, but it easily sloughed off the obsolete Marine fighters. The Japanese lost more than thirty-eight aircraft to Midway's defenses, and probably another thirty damaged planes could not be used again that day. The Japanese strike commander radioed to Nagumo that a second air strike was necessary.

Around 7 a.m., Nagumo experienced the first of a constant series of air attacks that day, primarily from Midway. So long as the fighters launched and recovered from *each* carrier, they delayed operations like launching strikes. In addition, sufficient fighters must get airborne prior to recovery of the returning strike. All of Nagumo's decisions regarding the arming of aircraft for a second Midway strike and then rearming them once American carriers were located took a backseat to the fighter coverage. It is a myth that Japanese carrier decks were loaded with strike aircraft ready to launch when disaster struck later that morning. Most planes on deck were fighter aircraft, either just landed or spotted for launching to deal with seemingly endless U.S. air attacks.

As Nagumo was rearming his aircraft for a second strike on Midway and dodging its air attacks, he received a report on the location of an American carrier (*Yorktown*), but first he had to recover his Midway strike force and rearm them, as well as rearming those torpedo bombers already carrying bombs instead with ship-killing torpedoes. In the meantime, the Japanese were desperately scrambling to rejuvenate their fighter coverage. The bombers stayed below in their hangars in various stages of rearmament. However, the Japanese doom was now airborne, albeit heading to various locations. Only the combined air group launched by *Yorktown* was headed to the right location. In addition, Fletcher did not launch every plane but held back a reserve in case his first strike did not find the quarry where it was supposed to be. He also waited until after the first reports until he felt sure he was sending his three squadrons to the correct location.

Spruance, on the other hand, launched everything he had, including the very inexperienced air group from the *Hornet*. There was no coordination between the *Hornet* and *Enterprise* groups, and most of *Hornet*'s aviators never found the Japanese. *Enterprise*'s bombing group showed up over an empty ocean, and it was only due to perseverance and luck that her strike leader, Lieutenant Commander Wade McClusky, managed to find the Japanese carriers. In the meantime, the torpedo squadrons of *Yorktown* and *Hornet*, which were slower and were the first to launch, arrived to attack the Japanese carriers. In some of the bravest flying of the war, they pressed home suicidal attacks in their obsolescent Devastator aircraft. VT-8, most famously, lost all her aircraft, with only one survivor, Ensign George Gay, who watched the climax of the battle from his tiny liferaft.

At 10:20 a.m., time ran out for Nagumo's carriers. Dive bombers from the *Yorktown* and *Enterprise* arrived overhead of the four Japanese carriers, with virtually no Japanese fighters to oppose them. Most of the fighters were still down low, finishing off the torpedo bombers that arrived with the *Yorktown* group. Others became involved in deadly dogfights with *Yorktown*'s fighters, led by Lieutenant Commander Jimmy Thach. Japanese surface antiaircraft fire was almost useless against dive bombing. In a few minutes, *Yorktown*'s bombers lit up the carrier *Soryu* and McCluky's *Enterprise* dive bombers scored multiple hits on the *Kaga* and *Akagi*.

The Japanese were also caught with most of their strike aircraft in their below-deck hangars armed, and in some cases fueled, but they were nowhere ready to launch. Blazing infernos that the American bombs created in these hangar bays quickly overwhelmed Japanese damage control systems, which were inferior to those on the U.S. ships. Before long, all three carriers were blazing from end to end as secondary and tertiary explosions of bombs, torpedoes, and aviation gasoline ensued. Eventually, all three would sink or be torpedoed by their own escorts to prevent capture by the Americans.

The battle was not over. American dive bombers missed one Japanese carrier, the *Hiryu*. *Yorktown*'s torpedo planes attacked *Hiryu*, which easily evaded them. The *Hiryu*'s admiral immediately launched everything he had at the carrier *Yorktown*. These aircraft pressed home their attack with courage borne of desperation and set *Yorktown* ablaze with three bombs and two torpedoes. However, only twelve of these aircraft returned to *Hiryu*.

Forced to abandon the *Yorktown*, Fletcher radioed to Spruance that he now had control of the battle. In addition, many of his aircraft escaped the inferno by relocating to the other two American carriers (recall that Fletcher had not sent all his planes into the morning attack). Later that afternoon, Spruance found the *Hiryu* and administered the same treatment meted out to the other three carriers of *Kido Butai*. Even with the loss of *Hiryu*, the Japanese pressed on after dark with their remaining surface ships, but soon they realized that Spruance was withdrawing to the east to avoid contact.

By early morning on June 5, Yamamoto made the decision, much as at Coral Sea, to abandon the invasion and return to Japan, despite having a preponderance of naval surface power at his disposal. He was beaten and he knew it. U.S. naval aircraft managed to catch up to two of his tardy cruisers, *Mikuma* and *Mogami*— the two collided while evading a submarine—and heavily damaged both. By June 7, the Japanese were no longer in the range of U.S. aircraft, and Spruance decided not to pursue the enemy but to quit while he was ahead. As for the *Yorktown*, two days after first being damaged by the Japanese submarine *I-168*, she sank on her way back to port.

CONCLUSION

Midway proved a tactical disaster for the Japanese navy. It highlights how commanders must fight the enemy, and not the plan. Unlike most of the disasters discussed in this book, it had almost no effect on the losers politically. However, the odds were now even rather than in Japan's favor. The commander of the U.S. fleet,

The Japanese heavy cruiser *Mikuma*, sunk in the final phase of the Battle of Midway by U.S. carrier aircraft after a collision with the heavy cruiser *Mogami*, July 6, 1942. (Bettmann/Getty Images)

Ernest King, used the disaster to argue for a change in policy on the Allied side in the Pacific in order to resume offensive operations. The choice of location was in the South Pacific at a remote island named Guadalcanal.

Further Reading

Lundstrom, John B. *Black Shoe Carrier Admiral.* Annapolis, MD: Naval Institute Press, 2006.

Parshall, Jonathan, and Anthony Tully. *Shattered Sword: The Untold Story of the Battle of Midway.* Washington, DC: Potomac Books, 2005.

76. The Destruction of PQ-17

Date: July 1942
Location: Barents and White seas

OPPONENTS

1. Allied navies

    Commander: First Sealord Admiral Dudley Pound

2. German *Kriegsmarine* [navy] and Luftwaffe

    Commanders: Admiral Hermann Boehm Raeder and Luftwaffe General Hans-Jürgen Stumpf

BACKGROUND

The genesis for the disaster that befell the Arctic Convoy PQ-17 in the waters around the North Cape of Norway in July 1942 began with the German invasion of the Soviet Union in June 1941. In one of the most significant decisions of the war, and against the advice of his military advisors, U.S. president Franklin Delano Roosevelt decided to extend the lend-lease program to the Soviet Union to keep it in the fight with Great Britain against the Axis powers in Europe, led by Nazi Germany. From this decision flowed the convoy operations that led disaster in the summer of 1942 during crises both in the Soviet Union (at Stalingrad) and in Africa (at El Alamein, Egypt). One must understand how completely stretched Allied shipping resources were at the time, especially in the spring of 1942, with the Allies on the defensive in almost every theater from Hawaii to Leningrad (later St. Petersburg) to Stalingrad to Great Britain in order to understand why these convoys were so important. Sir Winston Churchill and Roosevelt considered them critical to keeping the Soviets in the war and preventing Joseph Stalin from making a separate peace with Hitler.

THE PLANS

The decision to send Roosevelt's lend-lease material to the embattled Soviets via the quick northern route to the Soviet ports of Archangel and Murmansk was made by Churchill. It was also the most dangerous route, not only passing through submarine-infested waters, but also being threatened by Luftwaffe bombers based in Norway and the most powerful German surface vessels, also based in Norwegian waters, especially the superbattleship *Tirpitz*, sister ship to the ill-fated *Bismarck*. The late spring and summer months were the best time to push convoys through before ice made the route almost impassable; although Murmansk could be reached year round, the ice meant that the convoys had to sail much closer to Norway. But the long summer days in the Arctic also made for happy hunting by subs, warships, and especially aircraft.

The first convoy had sailed for the Soviet Union (Operation DERVISH) in August 1941, only two months after the Germans invaded Russia. All these ships reached their destination at Archangel. It was decided to give the convoys the designation of *PQ* for those heading east to the Soviet Union and *QP* for those returning to Allied ports in the west. Not surprisingly, the British Royal Navy leadership—First Sea Lord Admiral Sir Dudley Pound and his fleet commander, Admiral Sir John Tovey, who would be tasked with protecting these convoys—were both opposed to this dangerous course of action, especially in the summer of 1942. Stalin, however, was desperate. The Germans made a resurgence after their defeats in the winter of 1941–1942 and now threatened to cut off the Soviet Union from its resources in the Caucasus flowing through Persia into the Caspian Sea up the Volga River to Soviet factories and armies. He was losing equipment at an astonishing rate to the Nazi war machine, but he fought for every last inch of territory. If Stalingrad fell, who knew what might happen? Thus, Roosevelt and Churchill prevailed, committing most of the Royal Navy to protecting these convoys, a fleet that already was overstretched trying to protect the sea lines against U-boats in the North Atlantic and the Mediterranean.

The spring and summer of 1942 had already seen several convoys sail (alas, weakly defended). However by the time that PQ-16 sailed, the convoys were escorted by much stronger forces but still did not have enough destroyers as was considered optimal for convoy protection. Also, the Royal Navy often included a covering force of several battleships, cruisers, and even an aircraft carrier (if it could afford it) to sail and screen the convoys during the long Arctic days. The navy also occasionally included submarines in its escort forces as a countermeasure to German surface ships.

PQ-16 had to sail much closer to Norway than preferred because the ice shelf from the winter was farther south that spring than in previous years. This put it much closer to the German surface raiders and the Luftwaffe's bases in Norway. It was the experience of PQ-16 that set the conditions for the disaster that followed. PQ-16 consisted of thirty-five merchant ships and left Reykjavik, Iceland, on May 21, bound for Soviet ports. It had a strong escort and an even stronger covering force of two battleships, an aircraft carrier, two cruisers, and thirteen destroyers. Even with these strong forces, though, PQ-16 was much battered and only twenty-eight of the ships reached their destination. Only the heavy antiaircraft fire by the strong escort prevented much higher losses.

Admiral Sir John Tovey knew about the presences of strong surface forces centered on Tirpitz, and supported by Pound, they recommended that P-17, forming up in Iceland, should be delayed or cancelled. The convoy contained the fuel and equipment for an entire mechanized corps to reequip Soviet forces reeling from the German summer offensives, and Churchill, supported by Roosevelt, refused to cancel or delay the operations.

The Germans, almost as well apprised of Allied activities by their electronic eavesdropping as the Allies were of theirs, decided to commit the *Tirpitz* in an operation known as Knight's Move (*Roesselsprung*). Their plan involved using *Tirpitz* and the heavy cruiser *Hipper* in concert with a second raiding group composed of the battleships *Lutzow and Admiral Scheer,* both with their escorting destroyers to attack the convoy and its escorts and covering forces. These forces would be under the command of Rear Admiral Otto Schniewind and would operate in concert with U-boats and aircraft. If the convoy stayed together, it risked being destroyed en masse by the surface ships, but if it scattered, it risked being destroyed in detail by roving aircraft and submarines. It was this plan that served as the mechanism for the disaster that followed. The British plan was to simply fight the convoy through as had been done with PQ-16, but if the *Tirpitz* group sortied, Pound and Tovey had always had it in mind to order the convoy to scatter, including the escorts.

THE BATTLE

PQ-17 at first consisted of thirty-nine merchant ships, and it departed Iceland on June 27, 1942. It was escorted by a long-range escort group of six destroyers and two submarines commanded by Commander John Broome, with a close escort group consisting of eight smaller corvettes and antisubmarine trawlers, as well as two minesweepers and two small antiaircraft vessels. The covering force was powerful and consisted of two battleships, six cruisers, one aircraft carrier, and numerous destroyers; it got underway on June 29. At this point, the cryptographers of both navies came to play a decisive role in subsequent events. The German signals service *B-Dienst* accurately informed Grand Admiral Erich Raeder of PQ-17's departure, as well as that of a powerful fleet covering and escort forces, although direct knowledge of the battleship force eluded detection.

Now the supreme amateur when it came to sea power inserted himself into the dynamic—Adolf Hitler. Hitler had given his chief of the *Kriegsmarine*, Grand Admiral Erich Raeder, strict instructions not to risk the surface fleet against the British battle fleet. Raeder had already given the go-ahead for Knight's Move, and instead of having it out with Hitler, he delayed the surface groups' sortie to Admirals Boehm and Schniewind. The *Tirpitz* and her colleagues were to remain in port for much of the most important naval battle of the summer in the Arctic.

British intelligence picked up on the movement and sortie orders, but not their cancellation. When Pound and Tovey were informed that a crisis approached, they faced a decision: Should they scatter the convoy to make them a less lucrative target for the German warships? If they did, it would mean their loss of escorts and easier pickings for the Luftwaffe and submarines. But Tovey, spurred on by Pound, and against Churchill's inclinations, instructed the convoy to scatter and for the covering force to prepare to intercept the *Tirpitz* and its companions. The British seemed to have no confidence that they could both fight off Schniewind's warships and keep it from the convoy and its escorts. By this time, the convoy was down to thirty-six vessels, after some had turned around due to ice damage and one had run aground. At the same time, a dummy convoy that was supposed to distract the Germans was completely missed by German reconnaissance aircraft.

As Pound and Tovey wrestled with the decision, PQ-17 was located by a U-boat (*U-255*) on July 1, and its position was reported. It first came under attack on July 3 by a single torpedo bomber, which hit one U.S. merchantman. Subsequently, on July 4, Luftwaffe bombers were driven off by antiaircraft fire and scored no hits early in the day. Things seemed to be going reasonably well. Then that evening—during the long Arctic days, it was still light—Heinkel torpedo bombers attacked and managed to sink two ships and damage a third. At about the same time, the intelligence referred to earlier caused the British Admiralty to panic and issue the infamous "scatter order," which was received by Broome, the screen commander, on the morning of July 5. He was incredulous, but obeyed the orders and passed on the information to the commander of the convoy. Despite these orders, some members of the close screen (the corvettes and trawlers) subsequently reformed and escorted some of the ships, hiding out for several days near the island of Nova Zemyla. In the meantime, the Luftwaffe and U-boat screen had a field day.

It proved to be a horrendous massacre. Only eleven of the thirty-five ships in the convoy made it to the Russian ports, the last one arriving on July 22. Twenty-two ships had been sunk in total. Most of the fuel and war materials—210 bombers, 430 tanks, and 3,350 other vehicles—went down in these ships. Over 153 seamen died in the icy waters—a remarkably low human casualty toll that reflected the efficacy of rescue efforts. In most cases, the Luftwaffe had initially damaged the ships, leaving them for the U-boats to finish off. Had *Tirpitz* sortied, there is no telling how many more might have perished. The German losses were light—five aircraft total.

CONCLUSION

The first result of this disaster was Churchill's notification to Stalin that all Arctic convoys were henceforth cancelled. He was supported in this by Roosevelt and Admiral Ernst King, who reluctantly agreed that the Artic convoys must cease for the time being. This information infuriated the Soviet leader, who became even more incensed when he learned that the Allied promise to open a second front in Europe that year had also been put off to the next year (1943).

The unity of the alliance was at a breaking point. Churchill took the drastic measure of traveling to Moscow with his advisors for direct talks with Stalin, arriving on August 12. Churchill managed to smooth things over and promised to renew the convoys in September, escorted by the entire Royal Navy's Home Fleet if necessary. Stalin was mollified, and the alliance was shorn up. In September 1942, PQ-18 fought its way through to Russian ports, still losing one-third of its merchant ships (thirteen), but proving that the British would keep their promises, no matter how grim the cost. No Allied convoys ever scattered again in World War II.

Further Reading

Dimbleby, Jonathan. *The Battle of the Atlantic: How the Allies Won the War.* Oxford: Oxford University Press, 2016.

Vego, Milan. "The Destruction of Convoy PQ-17: 27 June–10 July 1942." *Naval War College Review* 69(3) (2016), Article 7.

77. The Dieppe Raid

Date: August 19, 1942
Location: Dieppe, France

OPPONENTS

1. Germany
    Commnander: Lieutenant General Konrad Hasse
2. Allies
    Commander: Major General John H. Roberts

BACKGROUND

The Dieppe Raid, code-named "Operation Rutter" during the planning stages and eventually "Operation Jubilee," came about to address three issues facing Great

Britain following the Battle of Britain. First, the Royal Air Force (RAF) was try-ing to engage the Luftwaffe; however, the Luftwaffe refused combat along the chan-nel coast, forcing the RAF to fly deeper into France. To the RAF, a raid on a coastal town might convince the Germans that a full invasion was under way and the Luftwaffe would have to come up and fight. Second, Great Britain needed to reassure the Soviet Union that it was serious about opening a second front, and a raid such as this would be a preliminary step. The final reason, tied to the second, was that a raid would be a good test to find out the problems and issues that a cross-channel invasion would face.

THE PLAN

Built on a cliff overlooking the English Channel, Dieppe had two things going for it. From the Allies' perspective, it had a suitable harbor to supply forces once ashore, and it was in the range of the RAF. Germans understood that the Allies would eventually conduct a cross-channel invasion, and in 1942, they began forti-fying Dieppe. The first units to arrive were two artillery batteries to cover the beaches.

Operation Jubilee would involve 5,000 Canadian soldiers, 1,000 British soldiers, and 50 U.S. Rangers. The plan called for them to land on six beaches along a ten-mile front. The main force would land on four beaches, code-named "Blue," "Red," "White," and "Green," in front of Dieppe. Two more landings, designated as "Yel-low" and "Orange" beaches, would take place on the flanks to destroy the artillery batteries. The Royal Navy would provide 237 ships for fire support and transport. The RAF allocated seventy-four squadrons of fighters and bombers to support the landings. Also, fifty-eight Churchill tanks from the 14th Army Tank Regiment would support the main landing.

Assigned to the Dieppe sector was the German 302nd Static Infantry Division, arrayed along the beaches and nearby towns around Dieppe. Reinforcing the 302nd was an artillery battalion, a reconnaissance battalion, an antitank battalion, and engineer and signal support. The subordinate units of the 302nd deployed to overwatch likely landing places. Also, the ground forces could call on two nearby Luftwaffe fighter groups and three bomber groups.

THE BATTLE

At 4:50 a.m. on August 19, the initial landings took place on the Yellow and Orange beaches. No. 3 Commando, on the Yellow beach, was tasked with destroy-ing the artillery battery near Berneval. The ships carrying No. 3 Commando ran into a German convoy as they approached the Berneval beach. To the British dis-may, the convoy included an escort of several German S-boats. The S-boats turned on the British transports, sinking a few ships before being driven off by the British escorts.

Nevertheless, the landing force was now widely scattered, and the German defenses were alerted. Even though a small group of commandos eventually got ashore and maneuvered close enough to the German position to suppress the battery with small arms fire, they never put it out of action completely. By the end of the battle, most of the commandos that reached the beach had surrendered.

The story on the Orange beach was completely different; it would be one of the few successes during Operation Jubilee. No. 4 Commando, augmented with fifty U.S. Army Rangers, landed unopposed near Varengeville. After organizing on the beach, its commander, Lieutenant Colonel Lord Lovat, led his men toward their objective. Tasked to destroy the artillery battery located on the cliffs, the commandos quickly scaled the high ground and neutralized the battery. With their mission accomplished, the commandos withdrew at 7:30 a.m. and returned to England.

The attacks on the Blue and Green beaches, on the flanks of the main landings, did not go very well either. The 1st Battalion of South Saskatchewan Regiment made it to Green Beach, near Pourville, undetected, but most of the craft landed on the wrong side of the Scie River. Tasked to secure the hills east of the town, they would have to cross the only bridge in the Pourville to reach their goal. By now, the Germans were on high alert and covered the bridge with machine guns and antitank guns. Pinned down by the German defenses, the Canadians never reached their objective. Evacuation awaited those that made it back to the beach, while the rest surrendered.

However, the results at the Blue beach were even worse. A delay in the landing of the Royal Regiment of Canada and elements of the Black Watch of Canada got the effort off to a bad start. Unfortunately, the smoke screen that was to conceal their landing went in on time but dissipated before the Canadians arrived. Without the benefit of surprise or concealment, the Canadians who did reach the beach were pinned down behind the seawall and could not advance any farther. The Royal Regiment of Canada came ashore with 556 men, and by the end of the day, 200 were killed and 264 captured.

The main landings took place on the Red and White beaches. Four destroyers supported by five Hurricane squadrons began the attack by suppressing the beach defenses. The initial landings by the Essex Scottish and Royal Hamilton Light Infantry were to be supported by Churchill tanks from the 14th Tank Regiment. The tanks were late in arriving, but the infantry still went ashore. They were quickly pinned down behind the seawall and were taking significant casualties.

The tanks finally arrived, briefly bolstering the infantry's morale, but, in the end, this was another tale of disaster. Only half of the fifty-eight tanks made to the beach. Two sank in deep water, and twelve more became mired in the soft sand. The remaining tanks eventually cleared the seawall but were prevented from going farther by a series of tank obstacles. The tanks returned to the beach to cover the retreating infantry. None of the tanks or crews made it back to England.

At 7 a.m., the commander, Major General John Roberts, still offshore and unable to communicate with his units, sent in his reserves: the Fusiliers Mont-Royal and elements of the Royal Marines. The first ashore was the Fusiliers. Once again, the Germans laid down deadly machine gun and artillery fire, costing the landing force in both men and material. Unable to reach the town, the survivors moved down the beach and were eventually pinned down along the cliffs. The Royal Marines were sent in to support the Fusiliers, only to meet the same fate. However, the commander of the Marines, seeing the devastation, ordered the remainder to turn back.

Along the beaches, the survivors tenaciously held on as their numbers dwindled. General Roberts reluctantly concluded that the attack had failed, and the evacuations began at 9:40 a.m. By 2 p.m., the last soldier had been evacuated and the force turned back to England.

CONCLUSION

Operation Jubilee was an unmitigated disaster for the Allies. Nearly 5,000 Canadians landed that day; over 900 were killed and 1,874 taken prisoner. The British Commandos lost 247 men out of 1,000, and of the 50 U.S. Army Rangers, 17 were killed, wounded, or captured. The Royal Navy lost 1 destroyer, and the RAF lost more than 100 aircraft. The Germans suffered nearly 600 casualties of all types and lost 48 aircraft. Despite these figures, the Allies gained valuable insights into conducting amphibious operations against fortified beaches—lessons that would serve them well two years later, at Normandy.

Further Reading

Atkin, Ronald. *Dieppe 1942: The Jubilee Disaster.* London: Thistle Publishing, 2015.

Copp, Terry, and Mike Bechthold. *The Canadian Battlefields in Northern France: Dieppe and the Channel Ports.* Waterloo, Canada: Wilfrid Laurier University Press, 2011.

O'Keefe, David. *One Day in August: The Untold Story Behind Canada's Tragedy at Dieppe.* Toronto: Knopf Canada, 2013.

Zuehlke, Mark. *Tragedy at Dieppe: Operation Jubilee, August 19, 1942.* Vancouver, BC, Canada: Douglas and McIntyre, 2012.

78. El Alamein

Date: July 1–November 11, 1942
Location: Egypt

OPPONENTS

1. German-Italian forces

   Commanders: General Georg von Stumme and Field Marshal Erwin Rommel

2. British Commonwealth forces

   Commanders: General Sir Claude Auchinleck and Lieutenant General Bernard Montgomery

BACKGROUND

From late 1940, when the Italian army launched an attack eastward across the Libyan Desert, the Axis and Allied forces had fought a series of back-and-forth

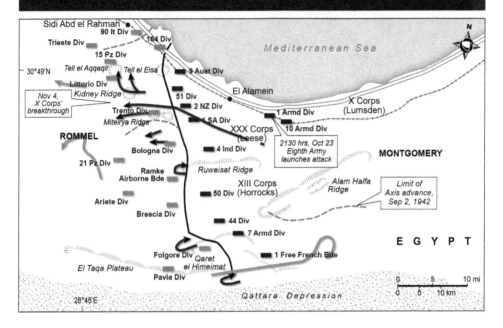

BATTLE OF EL ALAMEIN, 1942

campaigns through the spring of 1942. Neither side could achieve decisive results before the attacks bogged down, generally due to a lack of supplies. However, in May 1942, Panzerarmee Afrika, under the command of Erwin Rommel launched what would be the last Axis offensive in Libya. After a series of intense and costly battles, the vital port of Tobruk fell on June 21, 1942. Rommel, with only forty-four tanks, chased the British 8th Army back toward Alexandria. The British established a defensive line near El Alamein, sixty miles from Alexandria, setting the stage for the battle that would turn the tide of the war in North Africa.

After the fall of Tobruk and the subsequent retreat, General Sir Claude Auchinleck, commander of the Allied forces in North Africa, took over personal command of the 8th Army. Summoning reinforcements from throughout the Middle East, Auchinleck was able to scrape together 150 tanks, 60 of which were U.S. M3 Grants. At the end of June, Auchinleck halted the retreat at a forty-mile gap between the Mediterranean Sea and the Qattara Depression, an impassable stretch of desert. Even so, the 8th Army was stretched thin, but bolstered by these reinforcements and his defensive position, Auchinleck believed that he could halt Rommel and then go on the offensive.

After pursuing the 8th Army over 700 miles, Rommel and his Panzerarmee were in bad shape. The axis forces were down to twenty-six tanks and 1,500 motorized infantry. The remainder of his infantry had traveled in captured British trucks or walked across the Libyan desert. To compound matters, Panzerarmee Afrika was at the end of a very tenuous supply line. Whatever supplies that safely ran the gauntlet of the Royal Navy and RAF then had to be trucked hundreds of miles to reach the front. Besides, with the summer offensives in full swing on the Russian front, North Africa was a sideshow for Adolf Hitler and the Wehrmacht (armed forces). Nonetheless, Rommel intended to attack Auchinleck and the 8th Army immediately.

THE BATTLE

At dawn on July 1, 1942, Panzerarmee Afrika opened the first phase of the Battle of El Alamein. Rommel's plan was for one force to attack in the north and then turn toward the coast to cut off the British forces in El Alamein. At the same time, the Afrika Korps, along with the Italian 20th Corps, would swing south into the desert to envelop the remainder of the British forces. However, facing a new commander in Auchinleck, Rommel's plan ran into trouble from the outset.

For once, Rommel's intelligence let him down, and his main effort with the Afrika Korps ran into an Indian brigade. The Indians put up a stiff defense, stopping the Afrika Korps short of its objectives. In the north, Rommel's plan did not meet any more success. As the German/Italian forces struggled to penetrate the British lines and swing toward the coast, they were met by counterattacks by Auchinleck's South African troops. Pleased by his first day's success, Auchinleck directed his southern force to regroup and swing around Rommel's Afrika Korps. For his part, Rommel concentrated his forces in the north for another push toward the coast road. Both attacks failed, and for the next few weeks, the two sides went back and forth in swirling tank battles in the open desert. On July 27, Auchinleck tried one last attack along Miteirya Ridge; however, a counterattack by Rommel forced Auchinleck to call off the offensive. After nearly a month of grueling combat, both sides stood on the defensive and took time to rest and refit. Some considered the first phase of the Battle of El Alamein a British success, but the perception was different in London.

Shortly after the 8th Army stopped Rommel from reaching Alexandria, Churchill flew out to Cairo to review the situation; he ended up firing Auchinleck. General Sir Harold Alexander replaced him as the commander-in-chief of the Middle East. For the command of the 8th Army, Churchill initially chose one of the corps commanders, Lieutenant General W. H. "Strafer" Gott. Unfortunately, before he could take command, Gott was killed in an accident. The job then fell to Lieutenant General Bernard L. Montgomery. Montgomery was vain and arrogant, but perhaps as a result, he also possessed unwavering self-confidence in his abilities and in the ultimate success of the 8th Army over the Germans and Italians. He quickly imbued his command with this same faith.

Rommel opened the next phase of the battle on August 31, with an attack toward the Alam Halfa ridge. However, during the lull, the British received vast amounts of supplies and equipment—in particular, large numbers of the U.S.-made M4 Sherman tank, considered a good match for the German Mark IVs. On the other hand, with the Germans' summer offensive in full swing in Russia, Rommel had received very few supplies. Nonetheless, he believed that it would be better to strike now, before the British became even stronger.

Rommel's plan was his standard gambit: a wide sweep through the desert with the Afrika Korps to outflank the British. However, this time, his lack of fuel forced him to turn north before he wanted to, and his forces ran into the British 7th Armored Division and the dug-in 22nd Armored Brigade along Alam Halfa. With his forces nearly spent and his chances for success fading, Rommel ordered a retreat on September 2. Not wanting to fall into a trap, the British cautiously pursued the Axis forces, and by September 6, Rommel was back at his starting point. The stage was now set for the final and the most crucial phase of the battle.

Montgomery was not a bold, audacious commander, and after defeating Rommel, he chose to wait for more reinforcements and provide more training to his soldiers. Much to the chagrin of Churchill, Montgomery was not planning to attack until October 23. However, this late date would support the American landings along the coast of French North Africa, forcing Rommel to divide his attention.

For Operation Lightfoot, Montgomery had two infantry and one armored corps comprised of 220,000 soldiers and 1,100 tanks. Against this, Rommel could muster only 108,000 men, half of them Italian, and only 200 German tanks. Even more telling was the disparity in supplies, especially fuel. Rommel would not be able to take advantage of his tankers' tactical skill by outflanking his opponents; the best he could do was dig in along the El Alamein front.

Montgomery planned to make his main attack near the center of the line. In a very methodical fashion, his infantry and engineers were supposed to clear paths through the extensive minefields that the Germans and Italians had emplaced during the lull. The British tankers, expecting the German tanks to come to the rescue of the infantry, would defeat them in a great defensive battle before passing through their infantry to pursue the enemy. On the evening of October 23, over 1,000 British guns opened fire, and the attack was under way.

Every three minutes, the barrage crept forward as the infantry and engineers followed, laying down tape for the follow-on forces. However, the deeper they went, the stronger the defense became, and by morning, they were nowhere near clearing lanes for the tanks. Though badly outnumbered and outgunned, the German and Italian soldiers were putting up a stubborn defense. The offensive was beginning to bog down, and Montgomery was facing defeat.

It should be noted that, by the time of the attack, Rommel had been evacuated back to Germany, for health reasons. Unfortunately, his replacement, General Georg von Stumme, died of a heart attack, shortly after the British offensive started, while traveling to the front lines. Hitler ordered Rommel to return to take command.

True to form, Rommel decided the best way to redeem the situation was to attack. On the evening of October 27, the tanks of the 15th and 21st Panzer Divisions rolled into the British defenses. Unknown to Rommel, though, he was playing into Montgomery's hands by wasting his precious armor attacking into the British defense. The British line held, and Rommel's gamble failed. It was now Montgomery's time to redeem the situation.

After some tentative attacks, Montgomery decided that the time was right to execute his original plan. In the moonlit early morning of November 2, the 8th Army resumed its grand offensive. Once again, the beleaguered Germans and Italians prevented the British from attaining any of their first-day objectives. However, the Panzerarmee Afrika was only getting weaker and was able to hold out for long. Nonetheless, Rommel's and his tankers' prowess was on display once again. Through a series of skillful ripostes, Rommel's ninety remaining tanks were able to hold off 700 British tanks and give the bulk of his infantry time to withdraw. Contrary to Hitler's orders, Rommel continued a fighting withdrawal until he received word of the American landings on November 8. Realizing he would have to get back to Tunisia, he ordered Panzerarmee Afrika to begin its long retreat back to Tripoli.

CONCLUSION

The Battle of El Alamein was over. From July until November, the British fought the Germans and Italians to a standstill and saved Egypt, the Suez Canal, and the vital oil fields. The battle not only marked the high-water mark for Axis ambitions in North Africa, but it was the turning point for the Allied forces in the west. From El Alamein on, other than some operational attacks, the Axis was on the strategic defensive. There would be setbacks, but time and material were on the Allies side. As Churchill stated on Novemeber 10, 1942, in a speech before the House of Commons after the battle was over: "Now this is not the end. It is not even the beginning of the end. But it is, perhaps, the end of the beginning."

Further Reading

Ball, Simon. *Alamein (Great Battles)*. Oxford: Oxford University Press, 2016.
Bates, Peter. *Dance of War: The Story of the Battle of Egypt*. London: Leo Cooper, 1992.
Harper, Glyn. *The Battle for North Africa: El Alamein and the Turning Point for World War II*. Bloomington: Indiana University Press, 2017.

79. Operation Torch

Date: November 8–11, 1942
Location: Algerian and French Morrocan coasts

OPPONENTS

1. Allies (Great Britain and the United States)
     Commander: General Dwight D. Eisenhower
2. Vichy French and Axis sea and air forces
     Commander: Admiral Francois Darlan, German-Italian High Command Groups

BACKGROUND

Operation Torch—the Allied invasion of North Africa in November 1942—has little lodgment in popular memory. Yet it was a catastrophe for the Axis Powers, who until then had taken the war to their enemies on land, at sea, and in the air. However, it became the victim of a very busy period in military history. It occurred as the armies of Field Marshals Erwin Rommel and Friedrich von Paulus were being defeated at El Alamein and annihilated at Stalingrad, nearly simultaneously. It also occurred, not against the Axis per se, but against a former ally in the form of the Vichy French state. And what came after it—namely, the Allied campaign in Tunisia and the huge Allied amphibious landings in Sicily, Italy, and, especially Normandy—also tended to overshadow it. To make matters more confusing, amphibious warfare historians tend to focus on the great campaigns of the Pacific, such as Guadalcanal, which occurred before Torch and captured headlines concurrently with it. Subsequent broad-ranging Pacific amphibious operations against fierce Japanese beach defenses also tended to lessen and diminish the significance of what was accomplished at Torch.

Torch was the first successful step of a very long series of steps across beaches that finally led to victory in World War II. However, it was no cakewalk. The very idea of it—the war ostensibly still very much looking like a losing effort (other than Midway)—can still cause one to question its wisdom. Drive a huge armada across the Atlantic in the face of the fearsome Nazi U-boat threat that was raging at the time, and risk portions of that same armada in the enclosed waters of the Mediterranean in the face of German and Italian bombers, as well as the submarines of both nations? Also, why Africa, which was not the heart of the Nazi "center of gravity" in Europe? However, the Allies wanted to get U.S. troops into the fight against the Axis Powers, and this seemed the best means to do so.

THE PLAN

Torch was picked precisely because it promised success. It would get Allied forces on the ground in 1942, in answer to the repeated demands of the Soviet leadership, reeling from another year of bloody defeats on the Eastern front and in the Caucasus. The location, against the half-hearted Vichy French in Western North Africa, promised the British and U.S. troops low casualties and likely undefended beaches as well. Also, if handled properly, the Vichy French might choose to switch sides, especially if the French saw the invasion as primarily an American effort, not one by the British, who had attacked them less than two years earlier to prevent the French fleet from being handed over to the Nazis.

As for the Germans and Italians, Torch took them completely by surprise. They were completely focused on Russia and Egypt, respectively. The idea that the Allies might land 100,000 troops in their rear, at the other end of Africa, was simply something they did not plan for, nor even consider.

The Allied planning for the operation was extensive, involving moving over 100,000 troops, hundreds of ships, and hundreds of airplanes—although the air component was initially very small and restricted to what was aboard the limited number of Allied aircraft carriers. The bulk of the Allied landings would be beyond the Axis's ability to interdict with air power, although the naval forces of the Vichy French and Axis powers could, and would, present real challenges for the Allied effort once the landings occurred. Also, the Allies were unsure of the Spanish reaction—would Generalissimo Francisco Franco's fascists enter the war?

The Allies divided their invasion force into three large groups: a Western Group, focused on landing on beaches in the Atlantic north and south of Casablanca; a Central Group, landing at several sites near Oran in the Mediterranean; and an Eastern Group, which landed at three beaches around the city of Algiers. D-Day was set for November 8, 1942. The Western and Central groups were composed entirely of U.S. troops, while the Eastern one was a mixed British-American force that was expected to drive into Tunisia rapidly after securing Algiers.

THE LANDINGS

The massive Allied movements for the operation began in October. On October 22, the slowest convoy left England, followed five days later by a second invasion convoy. These two convoys rendezvoused at Gibraltar, where they reorganized into the Center and Eastern invasion groups. The Western Group, whose ground forces were commanded by Major General George S. Patton, left Bermuda on October 24 for the Atlantic crossing and had the most to fear from U-boats. It included over 100 ships of all types, including 3 battleships and 2 aircraft carriers with numerous escorts. However, the Germans were concentrating their efforts in the North Atlantic at this time, and this group made the arduous passage unmolested. The Germans regarded all the ship movements as simply more supply convoys going to Egypt to aid the British fighting Rommel there.

The Western Group embarked over 35,000 troops, and the landings did not go smoothly. The Vichy French, who Allied planners hoped would not resist, did. A major naval battle occurred off Casablanca, and one landing was delayed for two days by resistance. The fighting lasted until November 11, when the French here agreed to lay down their arms after being ordered to do so by Admiral Francois Darlan.

Similar problems plagued the other landings in the Mediterranean, but as at Casablanca, the French could not hope to prevail, and frankly their hearts were not in it. Around Oran, the Vichy French forces capitulated on November 10, and at Algiers, where Admiral Darlan, the overall commander, was located, hostilities ended by the evening of November 8. One historian has said of Torch that it was "a rushed, half-baked experiment in the art of war, full of untested ideas and amateur touches."

CONCLUSION

The landings and the quick capitulation of the Vichy French took the Axis high command completely by surprise. The reaction was not long in coming, with U-boat and air attacks sinking over two dozen ships in the subsequent weeks, including one escort aircraft carrier (the HMS *Avenger*). The Allies' long-term goal was to press on with subsequent operations to seize Tunisia. In this, they failed. The Germans immediately began to deploy airborne troops to secure Tunisian airfields, and once the Allied forces arrived in the vicinity of Tunis and Bizerte, they ran into determined resistance and got bogged down. Nonetheless, Rommel, in full retreat after his own catastrophe at El Alamein, had no choice but to retreat all the way into the Tunisian bridgehead.

Torch also synchronized with the Red Army battling for its life around Stalingrad and in the Caucasus at the same time, forcing the Germans to divert operational reserves and resources to try to hold Africa. The Axis reaction involved almost doubling the size of the German *Fliegerkorps II* in the Mediterranean. The nonavailability of all these fighters and bombers, which were much easier to deploy than ground forces, hurt the Wehrmacht (armed forces) in Russia. Additionally, we know that Adolf Hitler and Hermann Goering attempted to supply Stalingrad by air, but Torch gobbled up 673 German and Italian transport aircraft by November 10, and these aircraft remained in theater because of the tenuous supply lines by sea. Not only had Torch established a second strong Allied army on Hitler's flank, but it caused the Axis to make additional strategic mistakes that probably shortened the war.

The Allies paid a cost, though. Torch resulted in the denuding of convoy protection for the North Atlantic and resulted in November being the highest single month of sinkings by U-boats during the war—almost 1 million tons of shipping.

Further Reading

Atkinson, Rick. *An Army at Dawn.* Revised ed. New York: Holt Books, 2007.

O'Hara, Vincent P. *Torch: North Africa and the Allied Path to Victory.* Annapolis, MD: Naval Institute Press, 2015.

80. Guadalcanal

Date: August 7, 1942–February 1943
Location: The island of Guadalcanal and surrounding seas in the Solomon Islands

OPPONENTS

1. Allies

   Commanders: Vice Admiral Robert Ghormley and Vice Admiral William Halsey

2. Japan

   Commanders: Admirals Yamamoto Isoruku and Inoue Shigeyoshi, and General Hyakutaka Harukichi

BACKGROUND AND PLANS

The campaign that developed around the U.S. navy's seizure of Guadalcanal must be treated somewhat differently than the other disasters discussed in this book. It involved dozens of major engagements on the sea, in the air, and on the ground, and sometimes all three at once. None of it hinged on any single engagement, other than perhaps the U.S. Marines' initial landing on August 7, 1942, which seized the unfinished airfield in the first place. The decision to seize Guadalcanal was really an afterthought resulting from a decision by Admiral Ernest King to capitalize on the U.S. tactical victory over the Japanese navy at Midway in June 1942 by seizing the initiative from the Japanese somewhere in the Pacific. His choice for that was in the southern Solomon Island group, which was where the Japanese were advancing at the edge of their capabilities. The Japanese had seized the anchorage and developed a seaplane base at the protected harbor of Tulagi in May, just across the sound from Guadalcanal; then they decided to build an airfield on Guadalcanal to allow them to push farther south later that year.

When aerial photo-reconnaissance spotted the construction of this airfield, King issued a modification of his plan, known as WATCHTOWER TASK 1, to seize the Japanese airfield as well, using the reinforced 1st Marine Division under Major General Alexander Vandegrift. Initially, this offensive was to be done entirely with naval assets so as to avoid diverting from the strategy of "Europe First" agreed to by the Allies. The Marines were supported by the theater command known as the Southern Pacific Command under Vice Admiral Robert Ghormley, with fleet units assigned by Admiral Chester Nimitz, the overall Pacific Fleet commander.

For the Japanese, Guadalcanal was simply a continuation of the Imperial Japanese Naval General Staff's plan to advance to the southeast toward the New Hebrides and New Caledonia to cut the sea line of communications between the United States and Australia, where the Allies were building up combat power to go on the offensive in General Douglas MacArthur's Southwest Pacific theater. Until the Battle of the Coral Sea in May 1942, that advance was feebly contested by the weaker Allies, who had been giving up ground constantly.

THE CAMPAIGN

Guadalcanal proved to be a microcosm for the entire Pacific War—a campaign of amphibious assaults and fierce naval, air, and jungle battles. On August 7, the Marines seized Tulagi after a short, stiff fight. At Guadalcanal, they simply waded ashore as the Japanese construction workers ran off into the jungle. Upon landing, they found a pestilential, monsoon-swept hellhole. The airfield, with bonus Japanese bulldozers and earth rollers, was secured easily, and the Marines began to establish security perimeters, finish the airfield, and prepare for a Japanese counterattack. The Eleventh (Navy) Air Fleet in Rabaul, New Britain, had just the range to get its bombers to the southern Solomons. But once there, they had little time to deliver their attacks and did so without land-based fighter coverage. What was worse, Japanese carrier aviation, so reduced after the battles of Midway and Coral Sea, could provide only temporary air coverage before it had to withdraw to refuel its few carriers in safer waters. The American carriers, as Admiral Frank Jack Fletcher had already pointed out, were under the same constraints and particularly vulnerable to Japanese submarines and land-based aircraft.

The Japanese counterattacked savagely from air and sea, winning the lopsided night surface action off Savo Island on the night of August 8–9, sinking four Allied cruisers. However, the Japanese commander missed a golden opportunity after Savo to sink U.S. transport and supply shipping, which slipped away and left the Marines, who had offloaded several weeks of supplies, to their own devices.

However, the Japanese continued to make critical errors. Underestimating both the size and fighting prowess of the Marines, they landed the Ichiki Detachment (one battalion) in an attempt to quickly recapture the airstrip, now named Henderson Field. On August 21, these troops were wiped out at the Battle of the Ilu River. Additional Japanese reinforcements were turned back on August 24, thanks to the timely return of the U.S. navy.

Over the course of the next six months, there were six more major naval battles and at least nine more land battles—with attritional air combat occurring daily. The inspiring Vice Admiral William Halsey replaced the overwhelmed and sick Admiral Robert Ghormley in overall command that October. After a series of critical naval battles in mid-November, the back of the Japanese counteroffensive to take Guadalcanal was broken. The Japanese "Tokyo Express"—destroyers being used as supply ships and transports—could no longer logistically sustain the Japanese ground forces ashore that were trying to recapture Henderson Field. At the same time, the fierce air battles that raged during the carrier actions and around Henderson Field decimated both Japanese army and navy air arms, turning Guadalcanal into "a sink hole" that irreparably damaged its ability to contest the air.

Japanese prisoners during the half-year-long campaign on Guadalcanal. (Popperfoto via Getty Images)

The Marines, now reinforced with army divisions and under army command, resumed the offensive to push the Japanese off the island for good. By the time the campaign ended in early February 1943, Japan's land-based aviation was as decimated as its carrier counterparts. The Japanese losses exceeded 24,000 men killed or missing; however, it salvaged some of its troops from the defeat with a seaborne evacuation—but these types of retrograde soon become a rarity. American losses included over 7,000 killed and missing, almost 5,000 of them sailors, putting the lie to the myth that the U.S. navy left the Marines high and dry. The Americans, however, could afford these losses, while the Japanese could not.

CONCLUSION

Guadalcanal proved to be the "Stalingrad of the Pacific," with Japanese forces in the role of Hitler's Wehrmacht. It was a brutal, inelegant, six-month attritional slugging match. The Americans were able to both replace their losses and learn how to better fight the Japanese. The Japanese never recovered, so they remained on the defensive in the Pacific for the remainder of the war. Rear Admiral Tanaka Raizo, the commander of the Tokyo Express, expressed it best:

> The greatest pity was that every Japanese commander was aware of all these factors [that contributed to their defeat], yet no one seemed to do anything about any of them. . . . We stumbled along from one error to another while the enemy grew wise, profited by his wisdom, and advanced until our efforts at Guadalcanal reached their unquestionable and inevitable end—in failure. (Tanaka, 1956)

Further Reading

Frank, Richard B. *Guadalcanal.* New York: Random House, 1990.

Hornfischer, James D. *Neptune's Inferno: The U.S. Navy at Guadalcanal.* New York: Bantam Books, 2012.

Lundstrom, John B. *The First Team and the Guadalcanal Campaign: Naval Figher Combat from August to November 1942.* Annapolis, MD: Naval Institute Press, 1994.

Tanaka, Vice Admiral Raizo, with the assistance of Roger Pineau. "Japan's Losing Struggle for Guadalcanal, Parts I & II." *United States Naval Institute Proceedings* 82(7, 8) (July/August 1956), 687–699, 815–831.

81. Kursk (Operation Citadel)

Date: July 5–August 23, 1943
Location: Kursk, Russia

OPPONENTS

1. Germany

   Commnanders:

   Army Group Center, Field Marshal Gunther von Kluge

9th Army: Colonel General Walter Model

Army Group South: Field Marshal Erich von Manstein

4th Panzer Army: Colonel General Hermann Hoth

Army Detachment Kempf: General Werner Kempf

2. Soviet Union

Commanders: Marshal Georgy Zhukov, Deputy Supreme Commander

Central Front: General Konstantin Rokossovsky

Voronezh Front: General Nikolai Vatutin

Steppe Front: General Ivan Konev

BACKGROUND

After encircling the German 6th Army at Stalingrad in November 1942, the Red Army launched a winter offensive (Operation Uranus) that threatened the entire southern theater for the German army. Through expert maneuvering and limited but decisive counterattacks, Field Marshal Erich von Manstein was able to avoid catastrophe, and even recapture the key city of Kharkov. By March 1943, both sides were at the point of exhaustion, and the front stabilized as the *raputitsa* (spring rains) set in. However, both sides were attracted to a 160-mile-long by 99-mile-wide bulge in the front line, centered around the town of Kursk. This battle would decide the fate of the Soviet-German conflict.

For Operation Barbarossa in 1941, the German army managed to put together enough resources to conduct a general offensive all along the front. In 1942, they could put together enough assets for one major offensive. With Case Blue, Adolf Hitler gambled these resources on seizing the Caucusus oil fields. The gamble failed, and Germany was strategically worse off. Resources limited any offensive in 1943. However, Hitler believed that he had to conduct an offensive to demonstrate to his wavering allies that Germany could still win the war.

In mid-March 1943, Hitler directed his generals to study an offensive to cut off the Kursk salient. However, there was no consensus on when to take action. Manstein was in favor of continuing the offensive immediately before the Soviet army could recover, but other generals wanted to wait to refit and rest their own armies. Hitler was in favor of delaying until more of the PzKw VI Tiger heavy tanks and the new, but unproved, PzKw V Panther medium tanks came off the assembly line. After much deliberation and vacillation, July 5 was chosen as the date to begin Operation Citadel.

Meanwhile, on the Soviet side, there was much debate about a spring or summer offensive. Stalin was in favor of keeping the pressure on the Germans. However, Marshal Georgi Zhukov, the Deputy Commander of the Red Army, proposed standing on the defensive and letting the German army spend itself before going over to the offensive. Intelligence indicating that the Germans planned an offensive on the Kursk salient bolstered Zhukov's position. Stalin eventually concurred. Every German delay gave the Russians more time to improve the defenses awaiting the German forces.

BATTLE OF KURSK, JULY–AUGUST 1943

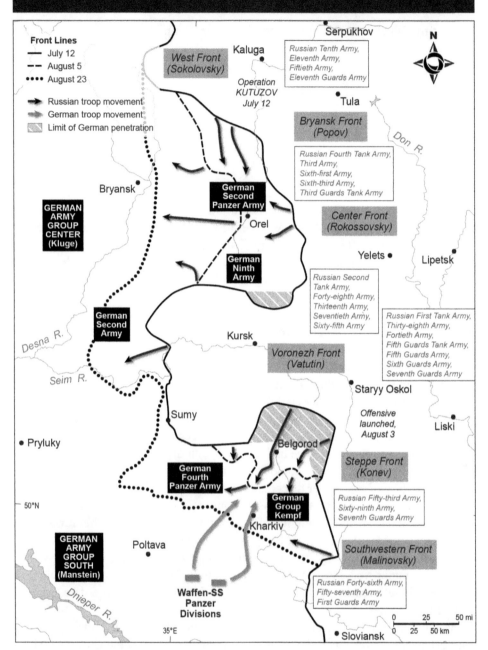

Front Lines
— July 12
-- August 5
•••• August 23

➡ Russian troop movement
➡ German troop movement
▨ Limit of German penetration

Serpukhov

West Front
(Sokolovsky)

Kaluga

Russian Tenth Army,
Eleventh Army,
Fiftieth Army,
Eleventh Guards Army

Operation
KUTUZOV
July 12

Tula

Don R.

Bryansk Front
(Popov)

Russian Fourth Tank Army,
Third Army,
Sixth-first Army,
Sixth-third Army,
Third Guards Tank Army

Bryansk

GERMAN
ARMY
GROUP
CENTER
(Kluge)

German
Second
Panzer Army

Orel

Center Front
(Rokossovsky)

Yelets

Lipetsk

German
Ninth
Army

Russian Second
Tank Army,
Forty-eighth Army,
Thirteenth Army,
Seventieth Army,
Sixty-fifth Army

Russian First Tank Army,
Thirty-eighth Army,
Fortieth Army,
Fifth Guards Tank Army,
Fifth Guards Army,
Sixth Guards Army,
Seventh Guards Army

Desna R.

German
Second
Army

Kursk

Voronezh Front
(Vatutin)

Staryy Oskol

Seim R.

Sumy

Offensive
launched,
August 3

Liski

Pryluky

Belgorod

Steppe Front
(Konev)

German
Fourth
Panzer Army

German
Group
Kempf

Russian Fifty-third Army,
Sixty-ninth Army,
Seventh Guards Army

50°N

Kharkiv

GERMAN
ARMY
GROUP
SOUTH
(Manstein)

Poltava

Southwestern Front
(Malinovsky)

Russian Forty-sixth Army,
Fifty-seventh Army,
First Guards Army

Dnieper R.

Waffen-SS
Panzer
Divisions

35°E

0   25   50 mi
0   25   50 km

Sloviansk

THE PLAN

The German plan called for simultaneous attacks from the north and south at the base of the Kursk salient. The forces would link up near the village of Kursk, shortening the front and cutting off the Soviet forces inside the pocket. The Ninth Army, led by Colonel General Walther Model, was to attack Kursk from the north.

With 658 tanks and 423 assault guns divided among fourteen infantry, one Panzer grenadier, and six Panzer divisions, the 9th Army was a formidable force. Model allocated eight infantry divisions and six Panzer divisions for the initial assault along a twenty-five-mile-wide section of the front. In the south, the 4th Panzer Army, commanded by Colonel General Hermann Hoth, consisted of the best of the German armored forces, including II SS Panzer Corps and the elite Grossdeutschland Panzer Grenadier division. The II SS Panzer Corps had nearly 600 armored vehicles, including 100 Tigers, and Grossdeutschland boasted over 500 tanks and most of the 4th's Panthers. Supporting the 4th Panzer Army's right flank was Army Detachment Kempf, commanded by General Walter Kempf. This force consisted of nine divisions over 300 tanks plus 48 Tigers.

The Red Army planned to attrit the German forces as they drove deeper into the salient. Once the Germans culminated, the Soviet forces would conduct a counterattack to drive them back. The Soviet high command assigned three Army fronts to the defense: the Central Front, the Voronezh Front, and the Steppe Front in reserve. Because of the German postponements, the Red Army, with the aid of 300,000 civilians, was able to establish a series of heavily fortified defensive belts that were up to seventy miles deep. Each belt consisted of trenches, camouflaged bunkers, and minefields. In some places, the density of mines was 3,000 per kilometer.

Opposite the 9th Army in the north was the Soviet Central Front. Commanded by General Konstantin Rokossovsky, the Central Front was organized into five rifle armies and possessed 711,500 soldiers, 11,322 guns, and 1,785 tanks. Defending the southern flank was the Voronezh Front, commanded by General Nikolai Vatutin. This front contained 625,600 soldiers, 8,718 guns, and 1,639 tanks divided among six field armies. Colonel General Ivan Konev commanded the Steppe Front, held in reserve to the east of Kursk, which had two missions. First, it was to provide forces where necessary to reinforce the other two fronts. Second, in case the Germans were successful, Konev was to establish defensive positions to block the Germans from driving farther east.

THE BATTLE

Operation Citadel was scheduled to begin at 5 a.m. on July 5, with simultaneous attacks from the north and the south. However, the battle unofficially began at 10:30 a.m. on July 4 when elements of the 48th Panzer Corps, in the south, seized the outposts of the first defensive belt. These attacks, along with information gained from German prisoners, indicated to the Red Army that the attack would begin on July 5. Around 2 a.m., in an attempt to disrupt the Germans' timetable, the Soviets launched a massive artillery barrage on the German assembly areas. These attacks caused some delays but failed to disrupt the Germans' plan, and the planned Wehrmacht bombardments began at the scheduled time.

NORTHERN FACE

At 5:30 a.m., as the artillery fire lifted, Model's 9th Army began its attack, supported by elements of the Luftwaffe. One Panzer division and nine infantry divisions, along with two companies of Tigers attached to the 6th Infantry Division, made slow progress through the dense minefields. At the end of the first day, after hours of hard fighting, the 9th Army had penetrated only up to six miles, at the loss of 7,000 total casualties and 213 tanks.

The next morning, the Red Army attempted a counterattack with two rifle corps and two tank armies. However, due to a lack of communication, the attack was not coordinated, and only one tank corps, the 16th, attacked on time. The 16th Tank Corps started the day with 200 tanks but ran into the Tigers of the 505th Heavy Tank Battalion. The 16th withdrew, but not before losing 69 tanks to the Tigers. Later that morning, the 9th Army resumed its attack toward the village of Olkhovatka in the second defensive belt. Once again, the attack stalled, with heavy losses.

Between July 7 and 10, the Model kept trying to force the Soviet defenses, but to no avail. The Red Army, deeply entrenched and reinforced by Konev's Steppe Front, could not be turned out of their positions. By July 9, it was becoming apparent that the attack in the north had failed, but Model was permitted to try again on July 10 to keep the pressure on the Russians. The Soviets stopped this final attack, and the offensive in the north was over.

SOUTHERN FACE

The Army Group South had greater success in the south. As in the north, the attack began with a 5 a.m. artillery preparation barrage. By dawn, elements of the 4th Panzer Army were engaged with the Soviet units in the first defensive belt, and as in the north, some units became mired in the dense minefields. Nonetheless, by the end of the day, the 48th Panzer Corps had penetrated the first defensive belt. The II SS Panzer Corps, east of the 48th Panzer Corps, destroyed a Soviet infantry division and penetrated nearly seven miles. Army Detachment Kempf, on the right flank of 4th Panzer Army, made slow progress against the 7th Guards Army. After fighting off several determined Soviet counterattacks, the divisions of Detachment Kempf cleared the first defensive belt. The 4th Panzer Army, along with Army Detachment Kempf, was in an excellent position to continue the attack the next day.

Hoth's 4th Panzer Army made slow but steady progress throughout July 6. Even though his forces had not achieved a breakthrough, they had forced the Voronezh Front commander to commit all his reserves. The Germans had only to penetrate the second defensive belt to create a breach in the Soviet lines. However, Zhukov quickly committed two armies from the strategic reserve and sealed off the penetration. The next day, the Soviets counterattacked into the II SS Panzer Corps in an attempt to expose the right flank of the 4th Panzer Army. Once again, poor coordination on the Soviet side led to a piecemeal attack that was handily defeated by the II SS Panzer Corps. The next few days were a continuation of determined German attacks and equally determined Soviet counterattacks. By July 11, the 4th Panzer Army had advanced nearly twenty miles and was a few miles from the vital road and rail junction at the village of Prokhorovka. Both sides understood the importance of Prokhorovka to the outcome of the battle, setting the stage for the largest tank battle of World War II.

The Battle of Prokhorovka was four separate battles, with the main engagement being between the II SS Panzer Corps and the 5th Guards Tank Army. The II SS

Corps had nearly 300 tanks and assault guns, and the 5th Guards had roughly 400 armored vehicles. The battle began on July 12 with a frontal attack by the 5th Guards' tanks to push the Germans back. The Soviet tanks charged headlong into the II SS positions. The fight quickly became a swirling mass of tanks, with engagement ranges down to point-blank. In one instance, four Tigers engaged a Soviet armored brigade for three hours. Suffering severe losses, the Soviet brigade eventually retired, leaving the four Tigers in control of the battlefield. At the end of the day, one Soviet Corps suffered 60 percent loses and another 30 percent, but the only thing that mattered was halting the Germans.

Events off the battlefield were happening that threatened to bring Operation Citadel to an end. As the battle wore on, Hitler was losing confidence in its ultimate success and was looking for a reason to terminate the battle. The Allies provided that pretext when they invaded Sicily on July 10. Hitler ordered the II SS Panzer Corps to prepare for redeployment to Sicily, bringing Operation Citadel to a close.

After the Soviets launched a series of counterattacks on both shoulders of the Kursk salient, the Germans were forced to withdraw or face being surrounded. The Germans withdrew under constant pressure from the Soviets. By September, the Soviets had recaptured Kharkov and pushed Army Group Center back behind the Dnieper River.

CONCLUSION

Operation Citadel was Hitler's last gamble to achieve some strategic success on the Eastern front; it failed. Instead, for the rest of the war, the German army, except for local counterattacks, was on the strategic and operational defensive. From this point on, the Red Army held the initiative, and in June 1944, Operation Bagration, the offensive that would take the Soviets to the gates of Berlin, would begin.

Further Reading

Clark, Lloyd. *The Battle of the Tanks: Kursk, 1943.* London: Headline Publishing Group, 2011.

Glantz, David M., and Jonathan M. House. *The Battle of Kursk.* Lawrence: University Press of Kansas, 1999.

Mulligan, Timothy P. "Spies, Ciphers and 'Zitadelle': Intelligence and the Battle of Kursk, 1943." *Journal of Contemporary History,* 22 (1987): 235–260.

82. Ploesti Raid (Operation Tidal Wave)

Date: August 1, 1943
Location: Ploesti, Romania

OPPONENTS

1. U.S. 8th and 9th Air Force
   Commander: Major General Lewis H. Brereton
2. Luftwaffe forces in Romania
   Commander: Lieutenant General Alfred Gerstenberg

BACKGROUND

Operation Tidal Wave was one of the costliest missions for the U.S. Army Air Forces (USAAF) in World War II. The intent was to knock out one of the primary sources of oil for the Third Reich: the oil fields and refineries around Ploesti, Romania. Ploesti was recognized early on by the Allies as a high-priority target because nearly 30 percent of Germany's oil and aviation fuel came from the refineries around Ploesti. A thirteen-bomber raid on June 12, 1942, caused limited damage but demonstrated the feasibility of a more significant raid. However, it also alerted the Germans to the vulnerability of this vital resource.

General Alfred Gerstenberg, overall commander of the Ploesti defenses, used the June 12 attack to request a greater allocation of German antiaircraft assets. By the time of Operation Tidal Wave, Gerstenberg had organized one of the most efficient and effective air defense systems in the Third Reich. His organization included several hundred 88-mm and 105-mm heavy antiaircraft guns, along with hundreds more smaller-caliber batteries. Gersgtenberg also built a special train, armed with even more antiaircraft guns that he could move to reinforce the local defenses. He could also call upon several nearby fighter groups of Messerschmitt Bf 109s and Messerschmitt Bf 110s, flown by both German and Romanian pilots, to help defend Ploesti. However, the key to the defense was the radar stations and signal interception units along the coast. Unknown to the USAAF planners, their planes would be tracked by the Germans almost as soon as they took off.

Planning for Operation Tidal Wave began in early 1943, following the Casablanca conference, where the Americans and British established the parameters of the Combined Bomber Offensive. The Ploesti oil refineries were a primary target. Planning for the operation fell to Colonel Jacob E. Smart, a skilled prewar pilot. Smart began with the supposition that a high-altitude attack would require more bombers that were on hand. However, a low-level attack would not only improve accuracy, but also would an element of surprise if the planes came in under the German radar. Even so, the number of bombers on hand remained an issue, and the 9th Air Force (9th AF) had to borrow three bomb groups from the 8th Air Force (8th AF) in England. These additions brought the total to five groups (the 98th and 378th from the 9th AF and the 44th, 93rd, and 389th from the 8th AF), consisting of 178 Consolidated B24 bombers. The plan called for the groups to fly to Romania together, and after reaching the release point, they would separate to attack their assigned targets simultaneously before returning to their respective airfields around Benghazi. To make the 2,300-mile round trip, the addition of special bomb-bay fuel tanks brought the total fuel load of each plane to 3,100 gallons.

Operation Tidal Wave was a complex mission, and the 9th AF spared no effort in preparing and training the crews. Detailed sand tables and low-angle photos helped the crews prepare for the mission. The USAAF even produced a training film specifically for this operation. At the same time, the crews practiced low-level formation flying—not a particular strength of the B24. As a final touch, engineers built scale replicas of the refineries in the Libyan desert. On July 28 and 29, all the groups ran full dress rehearsals on these replicas. The July 29 practice run was declared a resounding success, and everything was deemed ready for the upcoming mission.

THE BATTLE

Early in the morning of August 1, 178 B24s began lifting off from their airfields around Benghazi. As the heavily laden bombers struggled to get airborne, one of them crashed on takeoff. There would be many more losses before this day was over. The remaining 177 linked up and flew across the Adriatic Sea. En route, a plane from the lead group began flying erratically, rapidly climbing and diving before it finally crashed into the sea. Another plane dropped out of formation to look for survivors. The crew found none and turned to rejoin the formation, but it was too far behind to catch up.

Ten planes aborted and returned to Libya before the flight reached the Pindus Mountains. Climbing to 11,000 feet, the five groups passed over the 9,000-foot mountains. Unfortunately, the lead groups (93rd and 376th) used higher power settings to climb, and the formation began to lose cohesion. Unaware that the Germans were already tracking the mission, the crews refused to break radio silence to restore formation integrity. As the groups cleared the mountains, they descended back down to low altitude. The strung-out formation reached the town of Pitesti, and, as planned, the 389th turned toward its target. On the way to the final checkpoint, the lead group commander mistook the town of Targoviste for the checkpoint town of Floresti and inadvertently turned his group toward Bucharest. Compounding the error, the following group, the 93rd, turned with them. The crews now broke radio silence to alert the commanders to the error. Belatedly, the commander of the 93rd realized his mistake and turned back toward Ploesti.

Approaching their target, the Columbia Aquila refinery, the crews of the 93rd ran into the alerted and manned defense of General Gerstenberg. So many shells hit the lead plane that the pilot, Lieutenant Colonel Addison Baker, jettisoned his bombs in order to maintain formation and continued to lead his group over the target. Once clear of the target, Baker began to climb so that his crew could bail out. Unfortunately, no one survived, but Baker and his copilot, Major John L. Jerstad, were awarded the Medal of Honor posthumously for their actions. In total, the 93rd lost eleven aircraft over Ploesti.

Colonel Keith K. Thompson, the 376th commander, eventually realized his navigation error and turned his group toward its assigned target, the Romana Americana refinery. The flak over the target was so heavy that the mission commander, Brigadier General Uzal Ent, directed the 376th to break up and attack targets of opportunity. Most of the bombers lined up on the 389th's target, the Steaua Romana refinery. Despite the rocky flight to Ploesti, the 376th's crews fought through the intense flak to attack the refinery. Close behind the 376th was the 389th, the group assigned to attack the refinery. The 389th lost four planes from the intense ground fire over Ploesti. The pilot of one plane, Lieutenant Lloyd H. Hughes, would be awarded the Medal of Honor posthumously for continuing to the target despite his bomber being on fire. The combined attacks by the 376th and 389th knocked out production at the refinery for the duration of the war.

By the time the 44th and 98th Bomb Groups arrived over their targets, the German defenders were fully manned and ready. Also, their flight path would take them over Gertsenberg's special flak train. Despite the ferocity of the flak in front of them, the group commanders (Colonel Leon W. Johnson, of the 44th, and Colonel John R. Kane, of the 98th) led their groups into the fire and smoke billowing up over Ploesti. Coming in behind the 93rd Group, both Johnson and Kane's crews not only faced the German flak, but also had to fly through the explosions from the 93rd's delayed action fuse bombs. Despite planes falling all around, both commanders were determined to hit their primary target and flew on into the maelstrom. Johnson and Kane would be awarded the Meda of Honor for their heroism. The one bright spot was the attack by a portion of the 44th on the Credit Minier refinery. Twenty-one planes attacked the refinery without loss.

CONCLUSION

As the badly mauled groups turned back to Libya, over half of the surviving planes were damaged with many wounded on board. Forty-one planes were lost over Ploesti, and another thirteen lost en route or on the return flight. Over 1,700 airmen set off that August morning, and nearly 550 were killed, captured, or missing. With a 30 percent loss rate, Operation Tidal Wave was the greatest single mission loss for the USAAF during World War II. Five airmen were awarded Medals of Honor for their actions that day. Nevertheless, despite knocking out one refinery, most of the damage was repaired within a few weeks. Eventually, production would exceed preraid levels, and the Allies would have to return to Ploesti; however, that would not happen until 1944, when the 15th Air Force could fly, with fighter escorts, from bases in Italy.

Further Reading

Bradle, William R. *The Daring World War II Raid on Ploesti.* Gretna, LA: Pelican Publishing Company, 2017.

Newby, Leroy. *Target Ploesti: View from a Bombsight.* Novato, CA: Presidio, 1983.

Schultz, Duane. *Into the Fire: Ploesti, the Most Fateful Mission of World War II.* Yardley, PA: Westholme Publishing, 2007.

Stout, Jay A. *Fortress Ploesti: The Campaign to Destroy Hitler's Oil Supply.* Haverton, PA: Casemate, 2003.

83. The Second Schweinfurt Raid

Date: October 14, 1943
Location: Schweinfurt, Germany

OPPONENTS

1. Germany
    Commander: Generalmajor Adolf Galland
2. United States
    Commander: Lieutenant General Ira C. Eaker

BACKGROUND

During the interwar period, the U.S. Army Air Corps, later the U.S. Army Air Forces (USAAF), had staked its future and reputation on the concept of high-altitude, precision daylight bombing. Not even the wartime experience of Great Britain and Germany, indicating that unescorted bombers could not survive in daylight, which forced both to turn to the cover of night to protect their bombers, could deter the USAAF planners. Despite this evidence, the USAAF planners believed that their heavily armed bombers would be able to fight their way to the target while incurring acceptable losses. The U.S. entry into World War II provided the USAAF the opportunity to test this theory.

On August 17, 1942, the 8th Air Force (8th AF) opened the strategic bombing campaign against the Third Reich with a twelve-plane raid on the marshaling yards at Rouen, France. The raid, with General Ira Eaker along as an observer, was an auspicious start. The marshaling yards were damaged, and all the bombers returned without losses.

One year later, on the anniversary of this first raid, the 8th AF launched its most ambitious mission to date, when 127 bombers set out to bomb the Messerschmitt factory at Regensburg and another 183 were tasked to attack the ball bearing plants at Schweinfurt. The Regensburg force continued to North Africa, while the Schweinfurt group fought its way back to England. At the end of the day, the 8th AF lost sixty bombers and reduced ball bearing production at Schweinfurt by 30 percent. The Third Reich's armament minister, Albert Speer, was worried that the Americans would quickly follow up with another raid before the factories had time to recover. But Speer did not recognize the fact that the 8th AF considered those losses unacceptable for a prolonged campaign and could not follow up with another raid before rebuilding its forces. Two months later, the 8th AF was ready to return to Schweinfurt to finish the job; however, Mission 115 would go down in Air Force history as "Black Thursday."

THE PLAN

For the October 14 mission, unlike the August 17 raid, Eaker would mass both the 1st and 3rd Air Divisions (ADs) on Schweinfurt. The 1st AD would lead the air armada, with the 3rd AD on a parallel course ten miles to the south. Sixty B24s from the 2nd AD would fly a diversionary attack toward Emden and link up with the other divisions when they reached Schweinfurt. A total of nearly 380 bombers, over twice the number of the first raid, would target the ball bearing factories.

The Luftwaffe had not been idle in the interim. Herman Goering authorized the transfer of more fighters from the Eastern front to protect the Reich. In August, the 8th AF faced approximately 300 fighters, but this time, the Luftwaffe could put nearly 800 fighters in the air. Additionally, 300 flak guns had been moved from other cities to reinforce the air defenses around Schweinfurt, not to mention the antiaircraft fire that the bombers would encounter over other cities en route to the target. The Luftwaffe's air defense systems would be at their peak for the second Schweinfurt raid.

308   The 100 Worst Military Disasters in History

THE BATTLE

October 14 began in England with dense fog and low overcast, putting the mission in jeopardy. As the morning wore on, the overcast began to lift, and a reconnaissance plane reported that the continent was clear. At 10:15 a.m., the lead B17 from the 92nd Bomb Group, with the mission commander, Colonel Budd J. Peaslee, on board, took off from Bovington. However, the weather continued to affect the mission, disrupting the linkup among the various groups and forcing some groups to fly with the nearest division that they could find. Also, the weather delayed the linkup with the escort fighters.

Meanwhile, the 2nd AD had its problems. Only twenty-one of its sixty B24s were able to link up. Rather than send this much-diminished force to Emden, the planes flew to a secondary target on the Frisian Islands in the North Sea. After accounting for mechanical failures, 291 B17s of the 1st and 3rd ADs turned east and headed for the English Channel.

German operators watched in anticipation as this air armada was struggling to form up. They could not know the target, but they knew that it was a major raid, and the alert warning went out to the Jagdgeschwaders (Fighter Groups). As the bombers came closer, the ground controllers began scrambling the fighters so they would be at the proper altitude to meet the Americans. Me 109s from the veteran JG3 Udet opened the battle as the bombers crossed the coastline, but they were driven off by the P47 escorts. The remainder of the German fighters, knowing that the escort fighters limited range, waited for the P47s to turn around before they attacked. As the P47s turned for home, fighters from JG1 Oesau and JG26 Schlageter rolled in to attack the bombers. From this point on, the bombers would be under constant attack until they reached Schweinfurt.

The Luftwaffe employed every weapon in its arsenal in its attempt to stop the massed American bombers. That day, the 8th AF bombers were attacked by fighters trailing cables behind them to snag bombers, other aircraft dropped bombs with delayed action fuses set to explode in the middle of the formations, and still others stood off and launched air-to-air missiles. None of these were especially effective, and in the end, it was the traditional method of getting in close and shooting down the bombers with fixed cannon and machine guns that brought down the majority of the bombers.

Being in the lead, the 1st AD bore the brunt of the initial assault, as the fighters made head-on attacks with a closing speed of over 500 miles per hour. B17s began to fall as the formation relentlessly continued on its way to Schweinfurt. By the time the division reached Schweinfurt, around 2:40 p.m., it had lost thirty-seven bombers. As the bombers approached the target, the enemy fighters withdrew to avoid being hit by their flak. It took six minutes for the nine bomb groups of the 1st AD to drop their bombs before turning for home.

The 3rd AD had a relatively uneventful mission on the way in; however, more than 160 fighters were waiting for them to come off the target. As the division headed for home, they were subject to the same fury that the 1st AD faced on the way to Schweinfurt. It would be two hours of constant slashing attacks by the German fighters before the division reached the safety of the waiting fighters;

however, those two hours would cost the 3rd AD fifteen bombers. By 6 p.m., the last bombers reached their bases in England.

The 8th AF began totaling up the cost. A total of 291 bombers had set out for Schweinfurt, and 229 bombed the ball bearing factories, while the remainder dropped their bombs on the city proper. Sixty bombers failed to return, a further seventeen were damaged beyond repair after returning, and another 121 suffered varying degrees of lesser damage. The gunners claimed 186 enemy fighters; the actual losses were closer to 35. However, the most telling statistic was the 26 percent loss rate that the 8th AF suffered on this one mission. Coupled with the losses from the previous missions, the 8th AF lost 152 bombers over Germany in October alone. It would have to reassess its ability to continue strategic daylight bombing.

CONCLUSION

The immediate results of the raid were multifaceted. Ball bearing production went down 60 percent; however, that was only temporary. Within six weeks, the Schweinfurt factories were back in operation. This temporary setback was due in no small part to the efforts of Speer. Following the first raid, he began decentralizing production and seeking adequate substitutes made of ceramic. Also, Germany had built up a substantial surplus from outside sources, such as Sweden.

For the Luftwaffe, the results were ephemeral. Between the fighters and the anti-aircraft guns, sixty bombers had been brought down, for minimal losses. However, despite this massive effort by the Luftwaffe, the bombers were still able to get through and inflict considerable damage on their targets. The Luftwaffe could not know that the losses would prevent the 8th AF from mounting a follow-up raid on Schweinfurt, nor could they know the effect that their effort was having on the USAAF's strategic bombing campaign.

Mission 115 had an immediate effect on the USAAF in general, and the 8th AF in particular. It was now painfully obvious that unescorted bombers could not fight their way across Germany and back without sustaining prohibitive losses. No air force could sustain a 20 percent loss rate and remain viable. Following Schweinfurt, the 8th AF ceased all deep penetration raids into Germany until a long-range fighter became available. Long-range daylight attacks on Germany did not resume until February 1944, giving the Germans four months to rebuild and replenish its forces in anticipation of the coming offensive.

Further Reading

Caidin, Martin. *Black Thursday: The Story of the Schweinfurt Raid.* New York: Dutton, 1960.

Coffey, Thomas M. *Decision over Schweinfurt: The U.S. 8th Air Force Battle for Daylight Bombing.* New York: McKay, 1977.

Emerson, William R. "Operation POINTBLANK: A Tale of Bombers and Fighters," in Liutenant Colonel Harry R. Borowski, ed., *The Harmon Memorial Lectures in Military History, 1959–1987,* 441–472. Washington, DC: Office of U.S. Air Force History, 1988.

Kuhl, George C. *Wrong Place, Wrong Time: The 305th Bomb Group and the 2nd Schweinfurt Raid.* Westchester, PA: Schiffer Publishing, 1993.

84. Normandy Landings

Date: June 6, 1944
Location: Normandy, France

OPPONENTS

1. Allies

    Overall Commander: General Dwight D. Eisenhower

    American Commanders: Lieutenant General Omar N. Bradley

    British Commonwealth Force Commander: General Bernard L. Montgomery

2. Germany

    Commanders: Field Marshal Gerd von Rundstedt and Field Marshal Erwin Rommel

BACKGROUND

The Normandy landing, code-named "Operation Neptune," was the largest amphibious assault in history. It was also the opening phase of Operation Overlord, the Allies' plan to enter the continent of Europe and defeat the Third Reich in the west. The Allies (particularly the Americans) were anxious to invade Europe as soon as possible. However, the British wanted to wait for a bigger buildup of men and equipment. At the same time, Joseph Stalin was clamoring for the British and Americans to open a second front in Europe. British prime minister Winston Churchill and U.S. president Franklin Delano Roosevelt assured him that the long-awaited invasion would take place in May 1944. For a variety of reasons, including updates to the plan, the Western Allies postponed the invasion by one month, to June.

The planners chose Normandy for the landings because it allowed a landing on a broad front and provided room for the buildup and eventual breakout into the interior of France. The plan called for nearly 160,000 soldiers to cross the English Channel by ship and air on the first day. Over 7,000 ships, 5,000 landing craft, and over 13,000 aircraft of all types would transport these soldiers to their planned locations. The seaborne force would be put ashore on five sites along the Norman coast. The British and Canadian beaches were named (from west to east) Gold, Juno, and Sword. The other two beaches were for the U.S. army and were named Utah and Omaha.

The British 50th Infantry Division (ID) was assigned to Gold Beach, and the British 3rd ID would land at Sword Beach. In between the 50th and 3rd IDs, the Canadian 3rd ID would land at Juno Beach. On the flank, the British 6th Airborne Division (ABN) was tasked to capture two key bridges—one over the Caen Canal and the other over the Orne River. To the west, the American 1st and 29th IDs would land on Omaha Beach and the 4th ID on Utah Beach. To the flank and behind the beaches, 13,000 paratroopers from the 82nd and 101st ABN divisions would disrupt any German attempts to counterattack at the beaches.

A classic shot of a landing craft as it unloads at one of the Normandy beaches during Operation Overlord. Note the German beach obstacles exposed by the low tide. (National Archives)

Adolf Hitler knew that an invasion was inevitable and ordered the Wehrmacht (armed forces) to begin fortifying the coast of France. The Pas de Calais was the shortest point between France and England. Assuming this was the most likely place for the Allies to land, the Germans focused their fortification efforts there. Farther down the coast, the fortification effort was not nearly as extensive as at Calais. However, one of Hitler's favorite generals, Field Marshal Erwin Rommel, commanded Army Group B and was responsible for the defense of Normandy.

Along the beaches, Rommel had two static infantry divisions, the 709th and 716th. In March, Rommel moved the 352nd ID between the two static divisions in the general area of Omaha Beach. All the infantry divisions were dug into bunkers and reinforced with machine guns, mortars, and artillery. Rommel also had the 21st Panzer Division, located near Caen, at his disposal.

Nevertheless, the Germans differed on how to defeat the landings. The traditionalists wanted to let the Allies land and then defeat them in a battle of maneuver. Rommel, having experienced Allied air superiority firsthand in North Africa, believed that it would be nearly impossible to move any units during the day. He wanted to repel the invasion right on the beaches and wanted the Panzer divisions located nearer them. The commanders never resolved the debate, but the point as

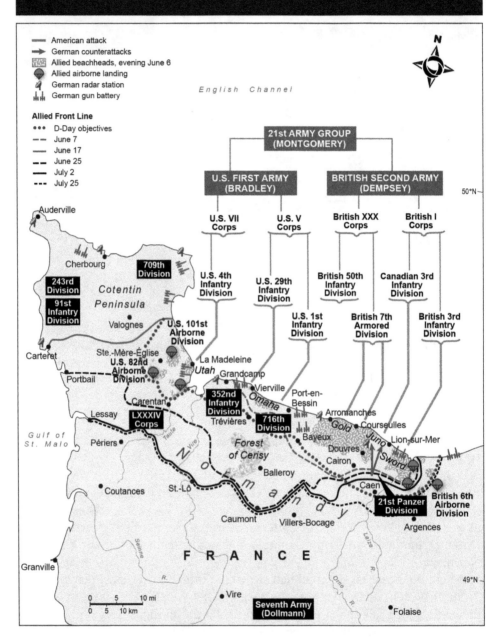

NORMANDY INVASION, 1944

moot because Hitler held release authority for the Panzer divisions himself. Also, the Allied bombing of Germany forced the Luftwaffe to pull back more fighters for the defense of the Reich, leaving few aircraft in France to contest the invasion. The Luftwaffe planned to move the fighters back after the invasion. Unfortunately for Rommel and Army Group B, there would be very little Luftwaffe support on the day the Allies landed.

General Dwight D. Eisenhower selected June 5 for the day of the invasion, and all over England, the massive Allied force was in motion, but bad weather rolled in. So Eisenhower elected to delay the landing for one day. To his chagrin, the weather did not look any better for June 6. However, his meteorologist told him that there might be a brief slackening in the weather. Eisenhower now faced the most important decision of his career: Risk a landing on June 6 or delay it for another week when the light and tide conditions would be right again. After weighing the pros and cons, Eisenhower decided to go on June 6 rather than wait another week and go through the deployment process all over again. On the other side of the channel, the Germans looked at the weather reports and were sure that the Allies would never attempt the landing in other than optimal conditions. They felt secure for a few more days—so much so that Rommel went on leave to celebrate his wife's birthday. They were wrong.

THE BATTLE

Shortly after midnight on June 6, the first U.S. pathfinders began landing to mark the drop zones for the 82nd and 101st ABN divisions. However, the low overcast made navigation difficult, and only a handful of the drop zones were marked properly. Nevertheless, the paratroopers from the 101st began dropping around 1:30 a.m., followed an hour later by the 82nd ABN. On the way in, because of the overcast, the pilots not only had trouble navigating, they also could not fly in close formation. Some planes came in low to get under the overcast and came under enemy fire. The result was the paratroopers from both divisions were scattered all over the Norman countryside. Many paratroopers drowned in fields that the Germans flooded before-hand. Despite these setbacks, many of the junior leaders took the initiative and gathered whatever troops they could find and set off to accomplish their missions. These ad hoc formations were not always successful, but they did create confusion among the Germans. The single biggest success for the U.S. paratroopers that night was securing the key crossroads at Saint Mere Eglise, behind Utah Beach.

Despite some formations being blown off course by the weather, things went somewhat smoother for the British 6th ABN division on the east flank. The British paratroopers quickly seized the bridges over the Orne River and the Caen Canal. Despite determined counterattacks by the 716th division, the paratroopers held the bridges until the British 3rd ID relieved them. They also managed to destroy an artillery battery that could have disrupted the landings on Sword Beach.

At the same time, the paratroopers were going in; the Allied air forces were bombing the beach defenses and the areas behind the beaches. However, due to the overcast, many of the bombers dropped late and missed their targets along the beach because they were afraid that they might hit their soldiers or ships. The errant bombing left many of the obstacles intact. Then, at 5:45 a.m., the sky lit up as the guns from the naval task forces opened fire. The Western Task Force supporting Utah and Omaha included three battleships and eight cruisers. Two battleships and twelve cruisers supported the British beaches.

The 352nd ID defended the ten-mile stretch of beach designated as Omaha; this would be the costliest beach for the Americans to secure. At 6:30 a.m., the lead units of the 1st and 29th IDs began exiting their landing craft. Blown off course by high winds, many of the landing craft missed their designated sites. Others ran aground on a sand bar, and the soldiers had to wade in water up to their necks to reach the shore—all the while under the murderous fire from the cliffs that dominated the beach. Specially outfitted tanks called Dual Drive (DD) tanks, from the 741st Tank Battalion, were supposed to provide armor support for the infantry. Unfortunately, twenty-seven of the battalions' thirty-two DD tanks were swamped and sunk by the rough seas.

Nevertheless, the soldiers bravely crossed the open beach to seek cover behind the seawall. The landing stalled at this point, and there were discussions over pulling them off the beach. However, by midday, through the determined efforts of the soldiers and junior leaders, a breach was made, and the units began moving slowly inland.

On Utah Beach, the weather worked to the 4th ID's advantage. Strong currents had driven the landing craft south of their landing zone. Nonetheless, the soldiers came ashore and quickly overcame the defenses. The assistant division commander, Brigadier General Theodore Roosevelt, Jr., surveyed the situation and elected to keep landing at this spot rather than shift to the correct site. Engineers began blowing gaps in the seawall, and by 9 a.m., the first troops, supported by twenty-eight DD tanks, began moving inland to link up with the 82nd ABN.

Because of the difference in tides, the British and Canadians landed an hour later than the Americans. Even though this gave them an extra hour of bombardment by the navy, their task was not made any easier. Before they came to grips with the Germans, they had to face the same miserable weather conditions as their ally. The biggest issues once again concerned the DD tanks. On Gold and Juno beaches, many of the tanks were lost in the rough seas. However, on Sword Beach, twenty-one of the tanks made it ashore to support the 3rd ID. The now-alerted Germans put up a determined defense as the British, Canadians, and a Free French unit on Sword began clearing obstacles and fortified houses along the beach before moving inland. By the end of the day, the British 50th ID and the Canadian 3rd ID had linked up. However, the fighting around Caen was harder, slowing the advance of the British 3rd ID and denying the Allies their first day's objective of establishing themselves on Caen.

Initially, the German reaction was slow due to a variety of reasons, not the least of which was a successful deception plan that the Allies ran leading up to the invasion. The Allies created a fictitious Army Group around the flamboyant American general George S. Patton. Radio traffic, decoys, and double agents fed the German belief that the invasion would come at Pas de Calais. The plan was so successful that the Germans were convinced that Normandy was a deception and held the Panzer divisions in reserve, waiting for the real invasion. Also, the Luftwaffe posed no threat to the mass of ships off the coast or the packed soldiers on the beach. On June 6, the Luftwaffe flew a few hundred sorties, as opposed to the thousands flown by the Allies. Complete mastery of the air over the beaches belonged to the Royal Air Force and the U.S. Army Air Forces.

Nonetheless, late on the afternoon of June 6, the 21st Panzer Division, located near Caen, counterattacked along the seam between Juno and Sword beaches. The

21st initially met little resistance and almost broke through to the beach before the British and Canadians blocked their advance. However, without any reinforcements to exploit the Panzers' success, the 21st withdrew that evening back to Caen rather than risk being cut off. That was the Germans' last chance to throw the Allies off the beach on June 6.

CONCLUSION

The Allies did not meet any of their D-Day objectives. By the end of June 6, the forces on Omaha, Gold, Juno, and Sword beaches were supposed to have linked up and moved up to ten miles inland, capturing Bayeux and Caen along the way. In actuality, the 1st and 29th U.S. divisions held a small section of Omaha Beach, while Gold and Juno beaches were still cut off from Sword. The first day's objectives, Bayeux and Caen, were still in German hands. The 4th ID, while more successful, failed to seize Carentan, the division's primary objective. It would be another week before the five beaches were linked.

On the other hand, despite 10,000 total casualties, over 100,000 soldiers were on the continent, and two of the Allies' main strengths, manpower and logistics, could now come into play. The U.S. army alone planned to have 1.3 million soldiers and over 250,000 vehicles in Europe by September. The Allies also anticipated that it would take ninety days to reach Paris; however, once the breakout began, the German retreat accelerated, and by D+90, the Allies were approaching the West Wall. All this began with the events of June 6. After that date, the defeat of Germany was inevitable.

Further Reading

Beevor, Antony. *D-Day: The Battle for Normandy*. New York: Viking, 2009.

Caddick-Adams, Peter. *Sand and Steel: The D-Day Invasion and the Liberation of France*. New York: Oxford University Press, 2019.

Howarth, David. *Dawn of D-Day: These Men Were There, June 6, 1944*. New York: Skyhorse Publishing, 2008.

Wilmot, Chester. *The Struggle for Europe*. Ware, UK: Wordsworth Editions, 1997.

85. The Philippine Sea

Date: June 19–20, 1944
Location: Philippine Sea, in the Pacific Ocean

OPPONENTS

1. United States
   Commander: Admiral Raymond Spruance
2. Imperial Japan
   Commander: Vice Admiral Ozawa Jisaburo

BACKGROUND

June 1944 was a very bad month for the Axis Powers. On June 6, the largest amphibious operation to that date occurred at Normandy, France, sounding the death knell for the Nazi reign of terror in Europe. Meanwhile, the greatest land offensive of the war began that June on the Eastern front. Starting on June 10 and then continuing for the remainder of the month and then into July, successive Soviet offensives exploded against Germany's hard-pressed Wehrmacht (armed forces). The front collapsed, and the Soviets literally destroyed the Germans' Army Group Center, which had been holding Belorussia (White Russia). In the Pacific, also in June, General Douglas MacArthur's forces had seized Biak, which opened the possibility of an early invasion of the Philippines—a move that would cut Japan's lines of communication to its critical fuel resources in the Indies. The final disaster for the Japanese occurred in the Philippine Sea, where Admiral Raymond Spruance, the covictor of the Battle of Midway, arrived with a juggernaut of his own.

For almost eighteen months, the Japanese had been attempting to rebuild their carrier force to a level that they felt might be able to challenge the naval air machine that the commander-in-chief of the Pacific, Admiral Chester Nimitz, had created. Operation A-Go, for the defense of the Mariana Islands, was believed to provide the ideal opportunity for the Japanese to turn the tables on the overconfident Americans and not only repulse their amphibious forces, but also regain command of the sea in one great naval battle. The Americans gave the Japanese little time to prepare, though, bypassing the Japanese base at Truk Island in the Caroline Islands—"island hopping"—and advancing their operational timetable to conduct an amphibious seizure of Saipan, Tinian, and Guam beginning in the second half of June 1944. Once these islands were secured, the Americans intended to use them to begin a strategic bombing campaign against the Japanese home islands.

Admiral Ozawa Jisaburo commanded a new operational entity, the Mobile Fleet, consisting of most of Japan's large, medium, and light carriers, including the new supercarrier *Taiho*. Japan had been carefully husbanding its naval aviators and managed to gather up almost 425 carrier-qualified pilots for the upcoming battle. Not since the Battle of Midway had the Japanese gathered a carrier force of such power. However, TF-58, under Vice Admiral Marc A. Mitscher, Spruance's carrier commander, had over 950 aircraft embarked on fifteen aircraft carriers. They were supported by seven new "fast" battleships that could keep up with the speedy flat tops. The American pilots were mostly veterans with recent combat experience, whereas the Japanese pilots had—at most—six months training in the carrier environment, and most of them had little or no combat experience.

THE PLAN

The Japanese plan was simple in concept. They intended to rely on their submarines, as they had at Midway, to provide them the latest intelligence on U.S. movements, as well as to whittle down the American carrier and amphibious task forces through attrition by setting up a screening line well east of the Marianas. They also deployed the cream of their army and navy land-based air power to Guam, Saipan, and Tinian—over 200 aircraft. These were to be augmented to over 500 by flying in additional aircraft from other bases. These planes would attack Spruance's carriers and sap their strength even further. Admiral Kakuta Kakuji commanded this effort, and it was imperative that he relay to Ozawa the success of his forces in accomplishing this mission before the Mobile Fleet was committed.

Finally, Ozawa would move in with his carriers for the kill, using his longer-range aircraft to strike the Americans while remaining beyond the range of their aircraft. In part, he would do this by launching at extreme range, recovering his aircraft in Guam, and refueling them there before bringing them back. They could make strikes both coming and going. Once the American carriers had been neutralized, the big battleships and cruisers would move in to help finish off the stragglers, sink amphibious and logistics ships, and help the defenders ashore. The Japanese land defenses had not been neglected either; there was a complex defensive system in place, especially on Saipan. In addition to defending at the beaches, the Japanese had a second line of fortifications in the mountainous interior of these volcanic islands that, it was hoped, would allow them to wipe out the Americans beyond the visual supporting range of the naval gunnery if the beach positions collapsed. Unfortunately, many of the reinforcements for this strategy, especially the artillery, had been sunk by U.S. submarines prior to the invasion. The Japanese preparations were not nearly as complete as they had planned.

THE BATTLE

Everything that could go wrong did go wrong for the Japanese defense of the islands. First, they did not expect Spruance to strike the Marianas until late June or July, at the earliest. On June 14, Admiral Nagumo Chuichi—the overall commander of the infamous Midway disaster—was still predicting that the attack was weeks away. In part, this was due to the Japanese fixation on Truk, which the Americans had continued to pound with army bombers flying out of new bases in the Marshalls and Bougainville. Not until June 11 did the Japanese even have an inkling that Spruance was on his way when Mitscher's aviators began their first raids on Kakuta's airfields. However, they interpreted this strike as another of the many American raids occurring from Wake all the way to Truk. Thus, they were shocked when on June 15, 1944, Spruance's ships, carrying 127,000 troops under the command of Vice Admiral Richmond K. Turner, arrived and began the invasion by landing at Saipan.

Mitscher's TF-58 ravaged the local air bases, as well as those farther away at Iwo Jima and Chichi Jima. Additionally, Spruance employed an aggressive hunter-killer antisubmarine effort against the Japanese submarine screen that not only protected his fleet, but also denied the Japanese critical intelligence about his offensive. Finally, it was a U.S. submarine that picked up Ozawa's main forces in the San Bernadino Strait as they transited the Philippines en route to the Marianas. The Americans had achieved strategic surprise, and the Japanese, who had hoped for a surprise of their own, were now known to be coming.

Admiral Kakuta compromised the Japanese plan by deliberately lying to Ozawa about the course of the air battle, leading him to believe that Kakuta had crippled Spruance's air forces. In fact, the situation was reversed. Kakuta barely had an air force left because Mitscher's fighter sweeps had destroyed 150 to 200 of his planes in the preinvasion air battles. Spruance, a cautious and careful commander, decided to stay close to the Marianas and conduct a close defense against the Japanese just west of Guam with Mitscher's TF-58, leaving several cruisers and old battleships to guard Turner's ships supporting the troops ashore.

On June 18, the Japanese carrier forces suffered their first loss from U.S. submarines that sank the large carrier *Taiho*. It was a harbinger of things to come. The next day (June 19) saw Ozawa launch long-range strikes against U.S. naval forces that resulted in the so-called Marianas Turkey Shoot. Between them, American aviators and the antiaircraft guns of the battleships, cruisers, and destroyers annihilated Ozawa's inexperienced pilots. Barely fifty remained.

While the fierce air battle was underway, the American submarines struck another blow, sinking the Pearl Harbor veteran carrier *Shokaku*. Spruance allowed a long-distance strike against the Japanese carrier force late that afternoon, at the very edge of their operational range. Mitscher launched his aviators, and they managed to sink another Japanese carrier, the *Hiyo*. Ozawa remained combative until he learned of his aircraft losses; he sent his surface forces for two hours toward the Americans after dark, but then he recalled them and withdrew. The cost to the Americans had been heavy, though, because of all the planes that ran out of fuel on the way back or crashed trying to land at night, something they had not trained for—the final total was eighty aircraft, although most of the air crew were recovered.

CONCLUSION

The Americans had won a great victory but seemed not to realize it. There was much criticism of Spruance after the battle for not destroying more of the Japanese fleet. It was not realized that this battle had been the death knell for Japanese naval aviation. Never again would it pose a credible threat to a U.S. fleet. However, the leadership of the U.S. navy did not realize this, and the Japanese were able to decoy the Americans with their impotent carrier forces in the fall during the invasion of the Philippines at Leyte Gulf, although it won them no victories.

Emperor Hirohito fully understood the results of the battle once the losses became known, especially the loss of the Saipan and Tinian, which had belonged to Japan before the war started. Prime Minister Tojo Hideki had promised a decisive victory and he got it—but for the Americans, not Japan. He offered his resignation to the emperor, and it was accepted. From now on, the militarists began to wield less and less power in Japan as a more moderate government took power and began to consider a negotiated end to the war on Allied terms.

Further Reading

Lacey, Sharon Tosi. *Pacific Blitzkrieg: World War II in the Central Pacific*. Denton: University of North Texas Press, 2013.

Miller, Donald L. *D-Days in the Pacific*. New York: Simon and Schuster, 2005.

Morison, Samuel Eliot. *The Two-Ocean War: A Short History of the United States Navy in the Second World War*. Boston: Little, Brown & Co., 1963.

86. Imphal and Kohima

Date: March-April 1944
Location: Eastern India and North Burma

OPPONENTS

1. Allied forces
   Commander: General Sir William J. Slim
2. Japan
   Commander: General Mutaguchi Renya

BACKGROUND

The China-Burma-India (CBI) theater was a result of the disastrous first days of Japan's expanded war begun in December 1941. It was not long after that the forces of Imperial Japan turned north to attack British possessions in Burma and secure the flank of its newly gained resources area to the south. The Japanese Fifteenth Army was assigned this task after it had easily conquered Thailand after the American debacle at Pearl Harbor. Burma was also important to the Japanese strategically because it was the last lifeline of Generalissimo Chiang Kai-Shek's regime to aid from the United States. If Japan could cut the Burma Road from Rangoon over the Himalayas to South China, it might bring an end to Japan's interminable war with Chiang's Nationalists.

After the fall of Singapore and the dissolution of the Australian, British, Dutch, and American coalition, the defense of Burma fell back to the India Command. Burma served one strategic purpose for the British—to protect India. To lose India was to lose the war in British eyes. In Burma, more than any other theater of the conflict, the Pacific War and the Japanese war in mainland Asia came together. However, before Singapore had even fallen, the Japanese Fifteenth Army, under General Shojiro Iida, began its offensive into Burma on January 20 1941. Iida captured Rangoon, the port terminus of Chiang's lifeline, in March 1942.

President Franklin Delano Roosevelt sent General Joseph Stillwell as his personal representative to Chiang's government, and to coordinate with the British for combined operations against the Japanese. The British resisted Chinese offers of military support, but the pace of Japanese operations caused them to relent. Chiang sent his best divisions to help protect his lines of communication through Burma. However, the combination of a divided command structure, the inferiority of the British, Burmese, and Chinese troops, and Japanese air and sea domination resulted in catastrophe. Although Stillwell had been placed nominally in charge by Chiang, he found it very difficult to control his Chinese subordinates. By May 1942, the British, Stillwell, and the Chinese had been run out of Burma— withdrawing on three axes. In Stillwell's words, "we got a hell of a beating." However, the Japanese, just like the Germans later that year, had strategically culminated—they could neither retreat nor advance. General Sir William J. Slim, the British commander of the Fourteenth Army, noted that despite the defeat, his army was still "recognizable as fighting units."

The Chinese, British, and Americans, along with indigenous allied Karen and Kachin tribesmen in Burma, now primarily focused on defending what they still had left. For most of 1943, Stillwell, Slim, and other commanders focused on training and protecting the construction of a new road through Ledo, in British India, across North Burma into China, while conducting a dangerous airlift across "The Hump" (a nickname for the Himalayas) to south China. Meanwhile, the Japanese satisfied themselves with limited operations against the airlift and Ledo Road construction efforts.

THE PLANS

Allied plans in 1944 revolved around the thorny problem of supplying the Nationalist Chinese. There were three points of vulnerability: British ports, such as Chittagong in the west; the route from these ports to Ledo along the Burma-India border; and the Ledo Road itself. Slim and the Fourteenth Army were responsible for the first two, and Stillwell and the Chinese for the last. At the First Quebec Conference, code-named QUADRANT, in August 1943, the Allies decided to clear North Burma once and for all to solve these problems. Accordingly three offensives were scheduled: two in Slim's area of operations and one in Stillwell's, to seize the airfield at Myitkyina that would secure both the air route and the Ledo Road. For Slim, this meant advancing to the Chindwin River with one of his corps, and along the coast against Akyab with the other. The Akyab offensive was conducted first, beginning in late 1943 against the Japanese Twenty-Eighth Army, and it succeeded even though it had to defend against a furious counterattack. On Slim's front, the Japanese Thirty-Third Army defended Myitkyina and held the town but lost the airfield.

Both of these operations on the flanks meant that the Japanese Fifteenth Army, commanded now by Mutaguchi Renya, would receive little help if it ran into trouble. The Japanese were aware that Slim was building up combat power to attack them, so they decided to preempt his offensive with one of their own. Slim learned about the Japanese plans and decided to dispose of his force to defend against this attack and then conduct a counteroffensive to seize his objectives. He stated in his memoir, "I was tired of fighting the Japanese when they had a good line of communications behind them and I had an execrable one. This time I would reverse the procedure."

Mutaguchi, on the other hand, famously declaimed to his theater commander, General Kawabe Masakazu, "We started this war, so we may as well finish it!" Mutaguchi's force was strong, composed of the veteran 15th, 31st, and 33rd divisions, with the attached division-size Indian National Army and an independent tank regiment. However, his command relationships with his three principal Japanese division commanders went from ambivalent to outright hostile. Additionally, the Japanese had no logistics plan in place to support their army should it fall short of capturing British supply dumps or be defeated. Additionally, the British now controlled the skies, the Japanese air forces having been slowly bled to death to the east and southeast against the forces of Admiral Chester Nimitz and General Douglas MacArthur. Slim also prepared his troops to fight surrounded and to use air drops to supply them, as had been demonstrated the year before in operations by the famous "Chindits" (the name was a combination of the words *Chindwin* and *bandits*) behind Japanese lines.

THE CAMPAIGN

Slim had expected the Japanese offensive to start about a week later than it actually did, so he was caught by surprise when the southern Japanese 33rd division attacked elements of the British 17th Division on March 6, north of the town of Tiddim. The division had already mapped out a route of withdrawal toward Slim's central position at Imphal, where he intended for the main battle to occur, but the Japanese cut its retreat off and then blocked another unit sent to its relief. As Slim was rushing reinforcements to rescue these forces, elements of the northernmost Japanese 31st Division attacked in eight columns along two axes—one toward Imphal and the other toward Kohima. If they Japanese captured Kohima, they might win the campaign in one fell swoop by capturing the rail line through Dimapur, through which Slim's troops could be supplied and reinforced. Slim made up his mind to commit his reserve to confronting the trouble to his south.

However, the real crisis of the battle occurred around Kohima, where the Japanese violently attacked the outnumbered defenders. Luckily, the commander, General Sato Kotoku, did not mask Kohima or push on to Dimapur. The Japanese pushed the regiment-sized defending force into a small area around Garrison Hill at Kohima, as Slim scrambled to use airlift assets to supply them and to move troops to relieve them. He used major portions of his XXXIII Corps to do this, moving some elements more than 200 kilometers. The Japanese logistical plan finally caught up with them around Kohima, and their attack culminated. The final battle occurred as the Japanese 15th Division attacked Imphal directly from the east, essentially blocking its defenders from the road to Kohima (which itself was surrounded). Here, Slim's plan worked to perfection; despite waging some very tough and bloody fighting, the Japanese petered out by mid April.

The Japanese were now in a bind—they had the equivalent of four divisions on the far side of the Chindwin, closely engaged with their enemy at all points, with no means to supply them in order to hold the ground that they had captured against Slim. Desperate to achieve something before the monsoons arrived, the Japanese resorted to irregular warfare, intermixing Indian National units with their units to try to infiltrate and unhinge Slim's defenders. Slim now implemented his campaign plan to grind the Japanese survivors down by attrition.

Mutaguchi's generals now lost control of the battle, and the Japanese Fifteenth Army started to melt away into the jungle as Slim counterattacked to link all his various surrounded forces. The Japanese broke contact and began to retreat to and beyond the Chindwin, through some of the most inhospitable terrain in the world, as the monsoons intensified. The food situation for these Japanese troops was so precarious that many of them resorted to cannibalism of their dead comrades to survive the trek through the jungle and across the Chindwin. The Fifteenth Army was effectively annihilated, and Slim followed up aggressively.

A general offensive ensued, and the Japanese position in North Burma collapsed so much so that by December 1944, the Irrawaddy River had been reached. In the fighting from March to June 1944, the Japanese lost over 53,000 troops, compared to only about 16,000 for Slim's troops. These casualties testify to the bitterness of the fighting. However, Slim's troops were victorious and in good order, and the Japanese were defeated and broken.

CONCLUSION

The Japanese offensive against Slim at Imphal and Kohima was a desperate military gamble from which the Japanese never recovered. Mutaguchi had been right—his offensive essentially heralded the end of the war in this theater. He probably knew as much, although his troops had given Slim and his troops months of fierce combat and anxiety to contend with. However, now all of Burma lay open to the Allies, and for the first time in World War II, an entire Japanese army had been defeated and destroyed in open battle. And, equally as important, the line of the Ledo Road to the Burma Road was now open through North Burma, saving China from strangulation by the Japanese.

Further Reading

Kolakowski, Christopher. "The Coming of Modern War: The Coalition War in North Burma, 1944." *Army History Magazine*, no. 107 (Spring 2018): 6–29.

Slim, Field Marshal Viscount William. *Defeat into Victory*. London: Cassell, 1956.

87. Operation Bagration

Date: June 22–August 19, 1944
Location: Belarus, Ukraine, and Poland

OPPONENTS

1. Soviet Union

Overall Commander: Marshal G. K. Zhukov

2. Germany

Overall Commander: Field Marshal Ernst Busch and (later) Field Marshal Walter Model

BACKGROUND

In April 1944, the series of Soviet offensives that began after the German failure at Kursk (Operation Citadel) had ground to a halt, as the Soviet army outran its logistics. The pause gave the Germans time to regroup and stabilize their defense on the Eastern front. However, they knew that the Soviets would resume their push westward sometime in the summer of 1944. Also, U.S. president Franklin Delano Roosevelt and British prime minister Winston Churchill informed Russian leader Joseph Stalin that the long-anticipated invasion of France would take place in May. Based on this information, Stalin decided that the Soviet summer offensive would begin in June. The question was: Where?

Stavka, the Soviet High Command, looked at the map and weighed their options. They could continue their southward advance through the Balkans, building on their previous success. However, this option would expose the northern flank to German counterattacks as the Soviet forces advanced through Romania and Hungary. The next option was an offensive through the Ukraine northwest to the Baltic Sea. This option opened the possibility of trapping Army Groups North and Center. Nonetheless, that plan was rejected as being too ambitious and again would expose the flanks of the Soviet forces. The last option was to attack westward through a bulge in the lines that was called the "Belorussian Balcony." For Stavka, this option would liberate parts of western Russia and place the Soviet army in position to strike Poland and East Prussia. The operation was code-named "Bagration," after the Georgian general and prince Pyotr Bagration, killed at Borodino during the Napoleonic Wars.

The Germans assessed the situation much as the Russians had, except for where the next blow would fall. The Oberkommando der Wehrmacht (OKW) believed that the best course of action for the Red Army would be to follow up on their success in Ukraine and retake the Balkans. Confident of their assumption, the OKW began shifting more units to Army Group Ukraine North, commanded by one of Adolf Hitler's favorite generals, Walter Model. Most of these reinforcements came from Army Group Center, the command that lay astride the area of the planned Soviet offensive.

Soviet intelligence surmised that the Germans were preparing for the next Russian offensive to come through Ukraine. With this knowledge, the Stavka set in motion an elaborate deception plan to convince the Germans that their assumption was correct. The key to successful deception operations is to make them support what the enemy wants to believe. The Soviets made sure that the Germans believed that there were at least four tank armies in the southern sector. With local command of the air, the Red Air Force could ensure that the Luftwaffe's reconnaissance flights saw what the Russians wanted them to see. Their efforts were so successful that a week before the attack, the OKW held a meeting of the chiefs of staff of the army groups and assured Army Group Center that the Red Army had every intention of attacking through Ukraine. Also, operations in the north distracted OKW as Finland negotitated an armistice with the Soviets that led to German-Finnish fighting on that front.

The deception in the south was so effective that by the time of the attack, Army Group Center could muster only 500,000 soldiers, barely 500 armored vehicles of all types, a little over 3,000 artillery pieces, and roughly 1,000 aircraft. These were grouped into four armies, arrayed from north to south along the front; the Third Panzer and the Fourth, Second, and Ninth armies were under the command of Field

Marshal Ernst Busch. Busch was given command of Army Group Center less because of his abilities and more because of his unwavering loyalty to Hitler.

On the Soviet side, their deception allowed them to mass over 1.5 million men, with another 1.2 million in reserve right in front of Army Group Center. Also, they could muster nearly 6,000 armored vehicles and over 30,000 artillery guns and rocket launchers. The Red Air Force could put up almost 5,000 aircraft (mostly fighters and ground-attack types). The ground force was organized into four fronts (the equivalent of a German Army Group), arrayed from north to south: First Baltic, Third Belorussian, Second Belorussian, and First Belorussian.

Kursk would be the largest operation of the war for the Red Army, and Stavka added another layer of control by assigning Marshals Aleksander Vasilevsky and G. K. Zhukov to coordinate the actions of the four fronts. All was in place, and Operation Bagration began on June 22, three years to the day after the Germans invaded the Soviet Union in 1941.

THE BATTLE

Bagration began with partisan attacks on the German lines of communication. Between June 19 and 23, partisans hindered the Germans by destroying rail lines and generally disrupting all movement behind the German lines. On June 22, the Soviet Front Armies began limited attacks against Army Group Center, putting their force in a better position for the main attack the next day.

At 5 a.m. on June 23, the artillery of the Red Army opened fire along the entire front and, supported by the 5,000 aircraft of the Red Air Force (and some aircraft

The wreckage of German Army Group Center near Minsk during Operation Bagration, the most successful Allied ground offensive of World War II. (Sovfoto/ Universal Images Group via Getty Images)

from adjoining fronts), began suppressing the German positions. The infantry and tanks of the 1st Baltic and 3rd Belorussian quickly overran the front line of the Third Panzer Army and began racing to encircle the town of Vitebsk. The story was the same along the rest of the front: The 2nd and 3rd Belorussian fronts tore through the German lines and headed toward Orsha and Mogilev, threatening to surround elements of the Fourth and Ninth Armies. The Soviets could not have asked for a more successful opening.

General Busch rushed back to the front from a meeting in Berlin on June 22. After the events of June 23, Busch informed Berlin that he would need to withdraw or receive reinforcements if he was going to stabilize the situation, Hitler forbade either option because he, along with OKW, still believed that the main Soviet attack would come in Ukraine. Instead, Hitler declared Vitebsk to be a *feste platze*, or a fortified place to be held at all costs. For his part, Busch was unwilling to transfer units from the Second Army, on the Fourth Army's right flank, until the situation was clearer. The next day, the situation would come into clearer focus for both sides.

On June 24, the Red Army continued to push the forces of Army Group Center back. In the Third Panzer Army sector, the 3rd Belorussian Front had penetrated far enough to get behind the left flank of the Fourth Army. The Fourth Army requested permission to pull back west of the Dnepr River, but once again, Busch refused any withdrawal. The next day, the Fourth Army commander, General Kurt von Tippelskirch, took the initiative and pulled his forces back. That same day, June 25, the Ninth Army commander, General Hans Jordan, asked Busch for permission to pull back to prevent his army from being trapped between the Dnepr and Berezina rivers. Busch refused his request. By June 26, it was apparent that Army Group Center's defense was crumbling, and the higher commands vacillated on what to do next.

Often, orders were given to withdraw, but they were quickly rescinded. Plus, orders were given to pull back from fortified places after they had already fallen to the Soviets. Busch reported to OKW on June 28 that his command was collapsing, The Fourth and Ninth Armies were retreating, and the Third Panzer Army had only one corps left intact. Nonetheless, even as the Red Army continued to grind down Army Group Center, OKW still expected the main blow to fall on Army Group North Ukraine. However, it did propose to Hitler that Army Group North could shorten its lines and divert some divisions to Army Group Center. Hitler responded by firing Busch and placing Field Marshal Model in command of both Army Group Center and Army Group North Ukraine. No matter how good a tactical commander Model may have been, he could not change the force ratios, nor could he undo the tactical disasters that had already occurred all along the front.

Hitler ignored his pleas to allow Army Group North to pull back and release those divisions to Army Group Center. By June 30, the Fourth Army was in full retreat across the Berezina River but was trying desperately to hold the line before Minsk. Nevertheless, elements of the Fourth and Ninth armies were trapped in a pocket when elements of the 5th Guards Tank Army and 65th Army linked up at Minsk on July 4. Army Group Center was shattered. In two weeks of combat, it lost twenty-five divisions and 300,000 men. However, the Soviet offensive was not over.

Model and OKW assumed that the Russians would have to regroup and resupply at this point, as they had in the past. Model hoped to use this lull in the fighting to stabilize his defensive line and establish contact between Army Group Center and the Army Groups on its flanks. However, Model's proposal required some shortening of the lines across the entire front and some counterattacks to shore up the front. Hitler was still reluctant to let the Wehrmacht pull back, but he did authorize the counterattacks. The commander of Army Group North, Colonel General Georg Lindemann, found himself relieved when he told Hitler he could not conduct the attack. His replacement, Colonel General Johannes Friessner, could not conduct the attack either. All of this was of little matter, though, because the biggest problem Model faced was the fact that the Red Army did not halt to regroup but continued attacking the Germans.

The 1st Baltic and 3rd Belorussian fronts started driving northwestward toward the Baltic coast, threatening to cut off Army Group North near the port of Riga, while the 1st and 2nd Belorussian fronts drove westward to Bialystock and Brest. Then things went from bad to worse for the Wehrmacht. Stavka launched the much-anticipated attack in Ukraine on July 13. Within days, elements of the 1st Ukrainian Front encircled the German XIII Corps near Lvov before pushing on through the Balkans. For two more weeks, the Wehrmacht fought numerous desperate battles along the front from the Baltic to the Carpathians, hoping to stave off total defeat. By the beginning of August, it appeared that the Soviet offensive was finally running out of steam and the Germans might be able to stabilize the lines.

Model was able to secure the Soviet bridgeheads across the Vistula, but his most critical task was to maintain contact with Army Group North. The commander of Army Group North, Field Marshal Ferdinand Schoerner, who replaced Friessner in late July, was ordered to hold on until Model could assemble enough divisions to counterattack. He agreed but notified OKW that he would be forced to withdraw to save his men if Model's attack did not happen soon. On August 20, elements of the Third Panzer Army reached the Baltic coast and opened a corridor between Army Group Center and Army Group North. By the middle of August, the Red Army had outrun its logistics capability and began to occupy defensive positions. Fortunately for the Germans, Operation Bagration was stopped by a lack of supplies.

CONCLUSION

Operation Bagration was the largest and most ambitious Soviet offensive of the war. The Red Army had advanced nearly 300 kilometers and shattered Army Group Center. They were at the gates of Warsaw and poised along the Prussian border. For the Wehrmacht, the magnitude of the defeat dwarfed Stalingrad regarding men and material. Some estimates suggest that the German army lost a quarter of its fighting strength during the two months of Operation Bagration. The Wehrmacht never recovered from this defeat and the Soviets, once refitted, were in a position to carry the final offensive to Berlin.

Further Reading

Citino, Robert M. *The Wehrmacht's Last Stand: The German Campaigns of 1944–1945.* Lawrence: University Press of Kansas, 2017.

Dick, Charles. *From Defeat to Victory: The Eastern Front, Summer 1944, Volume 2.* Lawrence: University Press of Kansas, 2016.

Glantz, David M., and Jonathan House. *When Titans Clashed: How the Red Army Stopped Hitler.* Lawrence: University Press of Kansas, 1995.

Stone, David. "Operations on the Eastern Front, 1941–1945," in John Ferris and Evan Mawdsley, eds., *The Cambridge History of the Second World War, Volume 1,* 331–357. Cambridge: Cambridge University Press, 2015.

88. The Falaise Pocket

Date: August 12–21, 1944
Location: Normandy, France

OPPONENTS

1. Germany

   Commanders: Field Marshal Gunther von Kluge and Field Marshal Walter Model

2. Allies

   Supreme Commander: General Dwight D. Eisenhower

   United States

   12th Army Group: Lieutenant General Omar N. Bradley

       1st Army: Lieutenant General Courtney Hodges

       3rd Army: Lieutenant General George S. Patton

   United Kingdom

   21st Army Group: General Bernard Montgomery

       2nd Army: General Miles Dempsey

       1st Canadian Army: General Henry Crerar

BACKGROUND

The Allied invasion of Normandy on June 6 kicked off, in the words of General Dwight D. Eisenhower, the "Great Crusade" to liberate Europe. However, by mid-July, the Allies were still bogged down in Normandy. On July 18, the British opened Operation Goodwood to finish clearing out the Germans in and around Caen. Two days later, the offensive became bogged down, but it provided a sufficient distraction for the Germans to support the American 1st Army's Operation Cobra. Launched on July 25, Cobra was to open up the lines around Saint-Lô and open a way into Brittany.

To further complicate the Germans' strategic situation, the Red Army had opened its summer offensive in the east, Operation Bagration, on June 22, and by July was in the process of destroying Army Group Center. On August 1, General George S. Patton's Third Army became operational and began racing through Brittany before turning east toward the Seine River. Adolf Hitler recognized the danger and ordered the commander of Army Group B, Field Marshal Gunther von Kluge, to attack west toward Mortain in the hope of trapping the Allies on the Cotentin Peninsula. The attack failed, and Allied commanders saw a chance to encircle and destroy Army Group B west of Seine and open the way to Paris.

THE BATTLE

Before they could begin planning for the battle, the Allies had to decide if they were going to advance deeper into France before encircling the Germans, or cut them off sooner. These were called the long or short envelopments. Generals Patton and Bernard Montgomery supported the long envelopment, hoping to encircle as many Germans as possible. On the other hand, General Omar N. Bradley, along with General Dwight D. Eisenhower, advocated for the short envelopment, as otherwise Allies might overextend their lines and be cut off by a German counterattack. The short envelopment argument prevailed.

On August 12, the British began limited attacks down the Laize Valley in preparation for Operation Tractable, the attack to seize Falaise and set the northern pincer to encircle the Germans. The next day, Patton's Third Army reached the outskirts of Argentan, roughly ten miles southwest of Falaise. Patton directed his 5th Armored Division to continue north to link up with the Canadians to complete the encirclement and cut off the Germans. Once Bradley realized what Patton was doing, he countermanded this order due to fear of friendly-fire casualties between the Americans and Canadians. The 5th Armored withdrew from Argentan, with orders to be prepared to attack in a different direction.

Operation Tractable opened on August 14 with an attack by the 4th Canadian Armored Division toward Falaise and the 1st Polish Armored Division south toward Chambois. The attack got off to a less than auspicious start. Many of the units got lost in their covering smoke, and the 1st Canadian used the same color of smoke to mark their position that the strategic bombers used to mark targets. The confusion led to Allied aircraft to bomb some Canadian units. Overall, the progress of both divisions was slower than anticipated. The Canadians pushed on and entered Falaise on August 16. The next day, after clearing out isolated pockets of resistance, the Canadians reported that the town was secure.

The Allies may have been less than thrilled with the speed of their progress, but it was enough for Hitler to relieve von Kluge and order him back to Berlin. Hitler also suspected that von Kluge was a supporter of the assassination attempt on him that had occurred in July. On his way back to Berlin, von Kluge committed suicide. He was replaced by General Walter Model, one of the better generals in the Wehrmacht (armed forces) and one who had Hitler's confidence. After assessing the situation, Model ordered the withdrawal of the 5th Panzer Army and the

7th Army before the Allies could close the noose around Army Group B. To cover their withdrawal, II SS Panzer Corps would hold the northern shoulder against the Canadians and Poles, while 47th Panzer Corps would hold the southern shoulder open against the Americans.

The Canadians and Poles kept driving forward in the north, and on August 19, the 1st Polish Armored Division, along with elements of the 4th Canadian Armored division, secured the town of Chambois. After effecting a linkup with the U.S. 90th Infantry Division and the 2nd French Armored Division, the Poles took up positions on Mount Ormel (Hill 262). From this position, the Poles had an unobstructed view of the Germans' escape route. However, the encirclement was complete but not well organized. German counterattacks kept parts of the gap open long enough for many German units to slip through that night.

Model, realizing the commanding position that the Poles held, ordered the 2nd and 9th SS Panzer divisions to drive the Poles off Mount Ormel. For the next two days, there was intense fighting between the Poles and the Germans. At one point, the 8th and 9th Polish battalions had expended nearly all their ammunition in holding off the German attacks, but the Germans could not drive them off Mount Ormel, nor could the Poles keep all the Germans from escaping, By the time that units of the 1st Canadian Army linked up with the Poles and completed sealing the Falsie Pocket, 20,000–50,000 Germans soldiers had escaped to fight another day.

CONCLUSION

The Falaise Pocket was a decisive defeat for the German army. Despite some inept decisions by the German High Command, the tactical prowess of the German army salvaged much of its manpower trapped in the pocket. Some estimates place the number of German soldiers in the pocket as high as 100,000 and as low as 80,000. Casualties range from 10,000–15,000 killed and nearly three times that number taken prisoner. As noted, 20,000–50,000 escaped, but they left behind most of their heavy equipment and tanks. The battlefield was littered with so many dead bodies and wrecked equipment that it took until November to clear it.

In the aftermath, there was much finger-pointing on the Allied side as to who was responsible for letting so many Germans escape. Some historians fault the boundary line between the British and American armies for preventing the linkup. Others blame Bradley or Montgomery for being too cautious or too nationalistic in outlook. Regardless of the Allies' mistakes, though, there is no doubt that the Battle of the Falaise Pocket not only marked the end of the battle for Normandy, but it also sealed the fate of the German army in France.

Further Reading
D'Este, Carlo. *Decision in Normandy.* 50th anniversary ed. New York: HarperPerennial, 1994.

Hastings, Max. *Overlord: D-Day and the Battle for Normandy.* London: Pan, 1985.

Keegan, John. *Six Armies in Normandy: From D-Day to the Liberation of Paris.* New York: Penguin Books, 1994.

89. Battle of Arnhem

Date: September 17–26, 1944
Location: Arnhem, Netherlands

OPPONENTS

1. United Kingdom
    Commander, 1st Airborne Division: Major General Roy Urquhart
    Polish Armed Forces of the West
    Commander, 1st Parachute Brigade: Colonel Stanislaw Sosabowski
2. Germany
    Commanders:
    II SS Panzer Corps: General Wilhelm Bittrich
    9th SS Panzer Division: General Walter Harzer
    10th SS Panzer Division: General Heinz Harmel

BACKGROUND

The Battle of Arnhem was part of a larger operation named Operation Market Garden. By early September, the western Allies had pushed the Wehrmacht back to a line running roughly from Antwerp, Aachen, Metz, and Belfort. The Allies were on Germany's doorstep, and it looked like the war would be over soon. Unfortunately, the Allies were outrunning their supplies and could not sustain their advance. Neither could General Dwight D. Eisenhower, the Allied Supreme Commander, continue with his broad-front strategy. Field Marshal Bernard Montgomery, the 21st Army Group commander, recommended a narrow-front strategy to get across the Rhine before the Germans could regroup. Montgomery's proposal would become Operation Market Garden.

Market Garden was a bold and risky plan. Allied airborne forces were to seize a series of bridges in the Netherlands, over which the tanks and infantry of the British XXX Corps would pass to cross the Rhine and trap the German Fifteenth Army. The plan hinged on the paratroopers quickly seizing the bridges, and XXX Corps quickly making it up a two-lane road to link up with the airborne forces. The planners estimated that the XXX Corps would take no more than four days to reach the northernmost bridge at Arnhem. It would take near-flawless execution to make the plan work.

For "Market," the airborne part of the operation, the Allied First Airborne Corps employed over 40,000 soldiers. The majority of the troops were in the American 82nd and 101st Airborne divisions, the British 1st Airborne Division, and the 52nd (Lowland) Infantry Division. The 82nd Airborne was to seize the bridges around Eindhoven and Veghel. These bridges would be the first linkup for the XXX Corps, constituting the "Garden" part of the plan. The XXX Corps would then pass through the 101st Airborne assigned to seize the bridges at Nijmegen and Grave. The last leg for the XXX Corps would link up with the British 1st Airborne Division at Arnhem before continuing across the Rhine. The ultimate prize would be the bridges in and around Arnhem; seizing them would be the responsibility of the 1st Airborne Division.

To accomplish his mission, Major General Roy Urquhart had at his disposal the two airborne brigades and one glider brigade that were organic to the 1st Airborne. Also, the 1st Independent Polish Parachute Brigade and the Glider Pilot Regiment reinforced Urquhart's force. However, he had minimal influence over the deployment of his command. The sheer size of Market made it impossible for IX Troop Carrier Command to land all the airborne and glider troops in one day. It would take three days to get all of Urquhart's men on the ground. To further complicate matters, the drop zones (DZs) and landing zones (LZs) adjacent to Arnhem would bring the transport aircraft into the range of the flak around Deelen Airfield. For that reason, the commander of the IX Troop Carrier Command refused to let his pilots fly anywhere near Arnhem. Urquhart was forced to select sites up to eight miles away from his objective.

On September 16, British intelligence picked up indicators that elements of the II SS Panzer Corps had moved into the Nijmegen and Arnhem areas. When Royal Air Force (RAF) reconnaissance confirmed the presence of tanks near Arnhem, Lieutenant General Sir Frederick Browning dismissed the report and had the officer delivering it relieved for exhaustion. Nothing was going to prevent Operation Market Garden from being executed on September 17.

THE BATTLE

Elements of the 1st Airborne Division began landing at 1:30 p.m. on September 17. The first unit on the ground was the 21st Independent Parachute Company, to mark the DZs and LZs for the main body. The opposition was light, and the battalions of the 1st Parachute Brigade quickly assembled to begin moving toward Arnhem. Meanwhile, the jeeps from the reconnaissance squadron raced ahead, hoping to seize the bridges before the Germans could react. The glider-borne troops took defensive positions around the DZs and LZs to protect the follow-on forces. Unfortunately, because of the airlift limitations, they would not arrive until the next day.

The Germans, initially caught off guard, quickly recovered. Initially, Field Marshal Walter Model, the commander of Army Group B, assumed that the British were coming for him and fled his headquarters. After assessing the situation, General Wilhelm Bittrich, the commander of the II SS Panzer Corps, sent the 10th SS Panzer Division south to deal with the American landings and ordered the 9th SS Panzer Division to defend Arnhem. Both divisions were under strength and still in the process of refitting, but they would be able to cause enough trouble for the lightly armed airborne infantry. Also, many of the local commanders took the initiative by forming ad hoc units from disparate formations.

One such unit took up a defensive position to block the British from Arnhem. The British reconnaissance squadron ran into this line and withdrew after suffering heavy casualties. The 1st and 3rd Parachute Battalions were held up by the same defensive line and could not reach Arnhem. Of the three battalions, only the 2nd, under the command of Lieutenant Colonel John Frost, was able to bypass the defenses and make it into Arnhem.

Frost and his men reached Arnhem late in the day, only to find an incomplete pontoon bridge and that the Germans had blown the rail bridge. However, they found the road bridge intact, and Frost deployed his men to secure the north end. The Germans repulsed Frost's first two attempts to seize the south end of the bridge. Nevertheless, Frost and his men held the north end against probing attacks by elements of the 10th SS Reconnaissance Battalion.

The second day, September 18, did not bode well for the British. Overnight, the 9th SS Panzer Division continued to reinforce the German lines, and the 10th SS Reconnaissance Battalion surrounded the 2nd Parachute Battalion at the north end of the bridge. Twice during the day, the 1st and 3rd Parachute battalions attempted to link up with the 2nd Battalion but were turned back each time. Cut off from the rest of the division, both physically and electronically, the 2nd Battalion was on its own.

Around 9 a.m., the 9th SS Reconnaissance Battalion tried to force its way across the bridge from the south. In a two-hour battle, the paratroopers of the 2nd Battalion held off the Germans. The German reconnaissance battalion eventually withdrew after suffering heavy losses, including the loss of its commander. For the rest of the day, the Germans probed the British perimeter, looking for a weak spot.

At the LZs, the division was still awaiting the arrival of the 4th Parachute Brigade. Since landing, the division had been out of contact with their higher headquarters in England and did not know that fog had delayed the 4th Brigade's takeoff. Further, they also could not warn the pilots that the DZs were not completely in British hands. When the planes carrying the 4th Brigade arrived around 3 p.m., they came under intense fire, and several aircraft were shot down. Nonetheless, the majority of the brigade landed safely, and two battalions were dispatched to support the 1st and 3rd Battalions in breaking through to Frost and his men in Arnhem.

On the first day, Urquhart, the division commander, had gone forward with the 1st Brigade but had been cut off trying to return to his headquarters. Urquhart and the members of his staff with him were forced to hide until they could find a way back. For over 48 hours, command of the division fell to Brigadier Phillip Hicks, commander of the 1st Airlanding Brigade.

By the third day, Urquhart made it back to his headquarters and got his first briefing on the 1st Airborne's situation. At dawn, the 1st and 3rd battalions, reinforced by the 11th and South Staffords battalions, made another failed attempt to reach the 2nd Battalion at the Arnhem Bridge. The badly mauled survivors retreated to the defensive lines around Oosterbeek. Frost's 2nd Battalion, running low on supplies, stubbornly held on to the north end of the bridge. The German ceased attacking with infantry and began systematically destroying the buildings that the troops of the 2nd Battalion occupied.

Later in the day, fog once again delayed the day's reinforcements. Eventually, thirty-five gliders brought in portions of the Polish glider-borne troops, but the Polish parachute brigade did not make it that day. This day also saw the first major air resupply by the RAF. Unfortunately, the Germans had reinforced the air defense units, and ten aircraft were shot down. Worse yet for the RAF's sacrifice, the 1st Airborne could recover only a small portion of the supplies. The rest fell into the hands of the Germans who, unbeknownst to the RAF, controlled most of the supply DZs.

The fourth day, September 20, was a painful one for Urquhart. Badly weakened, only one of the 1st Airborne Division's nine battalions was still an organized unit. The rest formed into ad hoc formations. Urquhart also came to the unpalatable realization that he would have to abandon the 2nd Battalion in Arnhem. Urquhart pulled what was left of his division into a defensive perimeter around Oosterbeek, hoping to hold the Driel Ferry crossing on the Rhine until the XXX Corps could reach the 1st Airborne. To make matters worse, they recovered less than 15 percent of that day's supply drop.

At the bridge, Frost finally got through to the division headquarters and was apprised of the situation, including that no help would be coming for the 2nd Battalion. With the number of wounded increasing, including Frost himself, the British negotiated a two-hour truce to hand their wounded over to the Germans for care. At the end of the two hours, the fighting resumed.

At 5 a.m. of the fifth day, the last defenders at the Arnhem Bridge surrendered or attempted to break out of the bridgehead. The Germans spent the rest of the day reducing the pockets of British resistance and clearing the bridge so that their armor could head south to reinforce Nijmegen. Even though the 2nd Battalion did not seize the Arnhem Bridge, they held one end long enough for the other bridges of Market Garden to be seized.

The day also saw the arrival of the Polish Airborne Brigade; however, due to a mixup, nearly a third of the transport aircraft turned back. The rest of the brigade dropped into a contested DZ and sustained some casualties. The rest quickly formed up and moved out to their new objective, Heveadrop Ferry on the south side of the Rhine, only to find that the ferryman had destroyed it. Urquhart badly needed the Poles on his side of the river to bolster the defense, but he could not contact them by radio. A swimmer crossed later in the day, and a plan was made to bring the Poles across that night in rafts. The Poles waited, but the rafts never arrived. The one bright spot of the day was when the 1st Airborne made contact with the XXX Corps' artillery. From this point on, the paratroopers could count on indirect fire support.

Leading elements of the XXX Corps linked up with Colonel Stanislaw Sosabowski's paratroopers on the sixth day. Meanwhile, heavy fighting continued around Oosterbeek, but the British Airborne clung tenaciously to their defensive line. Nonetheless, later in the day, Urquhart was forced to contract the perimeter in places. That night, another attempt was made to bring the Poles across on rafts. This time the rafts arrived, but the line to pull then across broke, and only fifty-five made it to the other side.

On September 23, the seventh day, the Germans renewed their attacks to cut the British off from the Rhine and any hope of reinforcements. Even though the airborne troops were short men and supplies, they beat back the German attack. However, not only were they aided by XXX Corps artillery, but the weather improved, and the RAF and U.S. Army Air Forces were able to fly ground support missions. Nevertheless, the aerial resupply fell short of expectations.

On the eighth day, at a contentious meeting of the senior commanders, it was decided to make one more attempt to send reinforcements across to Urquhart, but plans were also being made to bring the 1st Airborne back across the Rhine. Meanwhile, the fighting Oosterbeek was becoming more ferocious, and plans were made to arrange another truce to evacuate the wounded. Between 3 p.m. and 5 p.m. on September 24, 450 wounded were evacuated to the hospital in Arnhem before the fighting resumed.

The crossing that night did not go as planned, once again. The 4th Battalion Dorset Regiment, along with the Polish 1st Parachute Battalion, was supposed to cross at 10 p.m., but many of the trucks bringing up the boats got lost en route and did not arrive until 1 a.m. At that point, the decision was made to send only the Dorsets across. However, because of the current, the boats landed too far downstream, and most of the Dorsets were captured.

Urquhart received and agreed to a plan to withdraw the 1st Airborne on the night of September 25, the ninth day. The Germans, supported by tanks, made their heaviest attacks that day, nearly cutting off the British from the river. However, aggressive counterattacks restored the lines. That night, the British executed a phased withdrawal to prevent the Germans from knowing what was going on. Supported by XXX Corps artillery and a fortuitous heavy rain, nearly 2,500 men were evacuated. In the morning, the Germans resumed their attacks but did not finish clearing out remnants of the pocket until noon.

CONCLUSION

Even though Field Marshal Montgomery declared that Operation Market Garden was 90 percent successful, it was the last 10 percent that was the most critical. The Allies failed to cross the Rhine and outflank the Siegfried Line, which would have set the conditions to encircle the German Fifteenth Army and open the way to Berlin, and perhaps end the war in the winter of 1944. Instead, the Allies found themselves at the end of a tenuous supply chain and were forced to halt in order to regroup and replenish. In a 1987 article entitled "The Last Disaster of the War," intelligence officer Brian Urquhart (no relation to Roy Urquhart) assessed the catastrophe as follows: "I was sickened by the disaster, the loss of so many good men, the idiocy of the enterprise, and my own complete failure to do anything about it."

Further Reading
Beevor, Antony. *The Battle of Arnhem: The Deadliest Airborne Operation of World War II.* New York: Viking, 2018.

Bennett, David. *A Magnificent Disaster: The Failure of Market Garden, the Arnhem Operation, September 1944.* Havertown, PA: Casemate, 2008.

Clark, Lloyd. *Crossing the Rhine: Breaking into Nazi Germany 1944 and 1945–The Greatest Airborne Battles in History.* New York: Atlantic Monthly Press, 2008.

Middlebrook, Martin. *Arnhem 1944: The Airborne Battle.* New York: Viking, 1994.

Urquhart, Brian, "The Last Disaster of the War," in *The New York Review of Books*, September 24, 1987, 27–30.

90. Operation Bodenplatte

Date: January 1, 1945
Location: Belgium, France, and the Netherlands

OPPONENTS

1. Germany

   Commander, II Jagdkorps: Major General Dietrich Peltz

2. Allies

   Great Britain:

   Commander, 2nd Tactical Air Force: Air Marshal Arthur Coningham

   United States:

   Commander, 8th Air Force: Lieutenant General James Doolittle

   Commander, 9th Air Force: Major General Hoyt Vandenberg

BACKGROUND

By the fall of 1944, despite the Allied setback after Operation Market Garden in September, Germany was in a desperate strategic situation. Soviet forces were steadily pushing westward, the Bomber Command and the 8th Air Force continued to devastate German cities, and it would be only a matter of time before the western Allies resumed their offensive. Nonetheless, Adolf Hitler saw this as an opportunity to strike the British and U.S. armies and, perhaps, reverse the situation in the West. He issued orders for the German High Command to begin planning for an offensive to begin sometime in December; code-named Wacht am Rhein (Watch on the Rhine), it would be better known in history as the Battle of the Bulge.

The Germans hoped that the winter weather would neutralize one of the Allies' most potent weapons: their tactical air force. Operation Bodenplatte (Operation Base Plate) was conceived to further cripple the Allied air power with a simultaneous strike on sixteen airbases in Belgium, France, and the Netherlands as the ground offensive began on December 16, 1944. To the pilots' chagrin, the same weather that grounded the Allied air forces also grounded the Luftwaffe, and Bodenplatte was postponed until January 1, 1945, when the weather conditions would be right. Unfortunately, by that time, the ground offensive had stalled, and the Allies were regaining the initiative. Nevertheless, the execution order for Operation Bodenplatte went out, setting the stage for the battle that would break the Luftwaffe.

THE PLAN

The planning for Operation Bodenplatte was given to the II Jagdkorps under the command of Generalmajor Dietrich Peltz, an experienced ground support specialist and the logical choice to plan it. To carry out his mission, Peltz had ten

Jagdgeschwaders (Fighter Wings), two *Kampfgeschwaders* (Bomber Wings), and elements of another *Jagdgeschwader* (Fighter Wing) totaling approximately 900 aircraft (mostly single-engine fighters). To put this force together, the Luftwaffe took units assigned to defend the Reich from Allied bomber attacks, and any losses would weaken their future ability to stop the bombers.

The attack called for precise timing and navigation—the former, in order to achieve surprise by simultaneously attacking the airfields, and the latter because of the low altitude that the planes would fly, allowing them to avoid their antiaircraft defenses. Each fighter wing would make their way to their assigned target along prearranged routes and return along different routes. Several of those routes took the planes over or near the heavy antiaircraft concentrations around the V1 and V2 sites. A breakdown in communications with these batteries would result in significant German losses. The whole attack was expected to take no longer than a couple of hours. Unfortunately, two factors came together to hamper both the timing and the navigation.

The first was the experience level of the pilots. Through no fault of their own, the pilots of 1944 were not the pilots of 1939 in all cases. No matter how brave they might have been, no amount of courage can make up for lack of training and experience. Throughout the war, the Luftwaffe had steadily lost its most capable pilots, and more important, its flight leaders. To compensate for these losses, the Luftwaffe was forced to shorten flight training. The planners for Bodenplatte acknowledged this fact by assigning units from two-night fighter wings to provide guide planes to lead the fighters to the targets.

The second was the secrecy surrounding the plan. To maintain the element of surprise, the Luftwaffe high command went to great lengths to maintain secrecy. Limiting the number of officers who were in on the planning meant there was less chance of the plan leaking out, but it also meant that the goals and objectives of the operation were unclear at the lower levels. Some measures made sense from an operational view, such as maintaining radio traffic at the fighter wings' old bases to mask their movement to forward airfields. However, other measures, such as not allowing the pilots to mark their charts with their flight path or preventing the commanders from briefing the pilots until the last minute, contributed to the scale of the Luftwaffe's defeat.

THE BATTLE

After the high command canceled the planned attack on December 16, the wing commanders assumed that Operation Bodenplatte was off altogether. Much to their chagrin, they received word on December 31 to execute the plan at 9:20 a.m. on January 1, 1945. A persistent myth is that the date was chosen in order to catch the enemy pilots still hung over from their late night New Year's celebrating. But the date was chosen solely based on weather reports; if the Allied pilots were still groggy on top of it, then so much the better, the planners assumed. The lucky pilots received quickly put together briefings on targets, routes, and timings. Many others were still unsure of the plan when they took off the next morning. Even if they bailed out or crash-landed, the pilots understood that strict radio silence was imperative to maintain the element of surprise. Nonetheless, the morale of the pilots was high, especially among the newer pilots who were eager to strike the unsuspecting Allied pilots.

Early-morning fog delayed some of the fighters, but by 9 a.m., ten of the Geschwader (with over 900 aircraft) were on their way to their targets. Unfortunately, many of the antiaircraft batteries failed to get the word about the delays, and when large formations of aircraft suddenly appeared over their positions, the gunners naturally opened fire. The radio silence order prevented the pilots from warning the gunners to hold their fire, and many German fighters were lost before they even crossed into enemy territory. Nonetheless, the survivors pressed on to their targets in silence.

Coming in at treetop level, the attackers achieved complete surprise over the airfields, catching the planes and pilots in various stages of readiness. Over Eindhoven, the most successful attack of the day, Jagdgeschwader 3 "Udet" (JG3) caught two Canadian squadrons taxiing out for an early-morning mission. The German fighters methodically strafed the planes and airfield facilities. Minutes later, the German fighters withdrew, leaving most of the Canadian planes either destroyed or severely damaged. However, the attack still cost JG3 fifteen of the eighty-one planes that started the attack.

One of the costliest raids was the attack by JG11. The wing was supposed to attack the airfield at Asch, the home of two fighter groups with the U.S. Army Air Forces. En route, JG11 lost four fighters to antiaircraft fire, while half of the force mistakenly attacked the airfield at Ophoven. By chance, the Americans had launched two combat patrols that morning, and a third was taking off. The U.S. fighters pounced on the unsuspecting Germans. In exchange for destroying a handful of Allied planes, JG11 lost twenty-one of the forty-three of its fighters that took off that morning. However, the biggest blow was the loss of the *Geschwader* commander, Major Gunther Specht, who was reported missing in action. With thirty-four victories, Specht was a seasoned pilot and leader that the Luftwaffe could not afford to lose.

Calculating the cost of the raid is difficult due to conflicting claims, poor record keeping, and the general confusion of combat. However, the tactical surprise that the Germans achieved cost the Allies between 200 and 300 aircraft destroyed and approximately 200 damaged. On the other hand, the Luftwaffe lost nearly one-third of the attacking force (300 aircraft). Adding insult to injury, many of these were shot down by German antiaircraft gunners. However, for the Luftwaffe, far more significant was the loss of 143 pilots killed and 70 captured after they were shot down.

CONCLUSION

Operation Bodenplatte was the death knell for the Luftwaffe. It can be considered a short-term success that did significant damage to the Allied air forces; however, these were losses the Allies could absorb and easily rebound from. Within a few weeks, all the Allied fighter wings were back up to full strength. But as it turned out, Bodenplatte was a long-term defeat for the Luftwaffe. Not only did the day fighters lose a third of the attacking force, but they also suffered irreplaceable losses in terms of pilots. The Luftwaffe lost some of its most experienced pilots, including two *Geschwader* commanders, six *Gruppe* commanders, and ten *Staffel* leaders. Following Operation Bodenplatte, the Luftwaffe was a spent force, incapable of mounting any effective defense of the Reich's airspace as the Allies continued their inexorable drive to Berlin.

Further Reading

Girbig, Werner. *Six Months to Oblivion: The Eclipse of the Luftwaffe Fighter Force.* New York: Hippocrene Books, 1975.

Manrho, John, and Ron Putz. *Bodenplatte: The Luftwaffe's Last Hope.* Mechanicsburg, PA: Stackpole Books, 2010.

Price, Alfred. *The Last Year of the Luftwaffe: May 1944 to May 1945.* Osceola, WI: Motorbooks International, 1991.

91. Battle of Osan

Date: July 5, 1950
Location: Osan, South Korea

OPPONENTS

1. Allies

    United States

    Commanders: Lieutenant Colonels Charles B. Smith and Miller O. Perry

2. Democratic People's Republic of Korea (North Korea)

    Commanders: Major General Lee Kwon Mu and Major General Ryu-Kyong Su

BACKGROUND

The Korean War began on June 25, 1950, when the North Korean People's Army (NKPA) launched a ten-division invasion of South Korea. Caught by surprise, the army of the Republic of Korea (ROK) attempted to halt the NKPA's advance, but, outnumbered nearly two to one, it was not up to the task. Within three days, the NKPA occupied Seoul, the ROK capital, and the NKPA relentlessly continued southward.

North Korea's invasion became a test for the new United Nations, and the body voted to use military force to halt the invasion. The initial response came from the United States and British navies. Nonetheless, blockading the Korean Peninsula and launching airstrikes did not deter the NKPA. It was becoming obvious that ground forces would be needed to prevent the collapse of the ROK government. U.S. president Harry S. Truman ordered the Joint Chiefs of Staff to prepare plans for U.S. ground forces to intervene. The Joint Chiefs selected the 24th Infantry Division, stationed in Japan, as one of the divisions to be employed. However, occupation duty in the Far East, along with postwar budget cuts, had dulled the edge of the division, and the undermanned 24th was in no shape to fight a war. Nonetheless, it prepared to send as many resources as it could.

The division commander, Major General William F. Dean, chose the 1st Battalion of the 21st Infantry Regiment to be the first unit to land in South Korea. The battalion commander, Lieutenant Colonel Charles B. Smith, was a seasoned World War II veteran of the Pacific War. However, his unit had only two of its authorized infantry companies and was short of other essential equipment, such as radios, recoil-less rifles, and mortars. Even then, very few of his officers and noncommissioned officers had combat experience. His enlisted men were eager, but generally they were recruits just out of basic training. An artillery battery of six 105-mm howitzers, under the command of Lieutenant Colonel Miller O. Perry, augmented Smith's command. With a basic load of 12,000 high-explosive (HE) rounds and six high-explosive antitank (HEAT) rounds. These six rounds were the heaviest antitank capability that the battalion possessed.

Five days after the DPRK's invasion, 540 men of the newly designated Task Force Smith (named after its commander, Lieutenant Colonel Brad Smith) met their transport aircraft at Itazuke Airbase in Japan. Each man had 120 rounds of ammunition and two days' rations. The division commander briefed Smith before he left. He was told to head to Taejon to block the NKPA as far north as possible. The division commander wished that he could tell the force more about the situation, but he did not know much himself. With that, Task Force Smith left Japan and headed for Korea.

After the last remnants of his command arrived in South Korea on July 1, Lieutenant Colonel Smith led his men along the road to Suwon to meet the enemy "as far north as possible." On July 4, Smith picked a spot on the north side of the village of Osan to establish his defense. He arrayed his force on a one-mile front on two hills on either side of the road into the village. Smith placed one company on each hill supported by five of the six howitzers, the sixth howitzer, with the HEAT rounds, was sited farther south to cover the road. All Task Force Smith could do now was wait for the NKPA. They would not have long to wait.

THE BATTLE

The next day, at 7:30 a.m., the Americans spotted eight T-34 tanks of the advance guard of the 105th Armored Division coming down the road. When the tanks closed to within 2 km of the Task Force Smith's main defensive line, the howitzers opened fire. The artillery scored several direct hits, but the HE rounds were mostly ineffective against the armor of the tanks as they rolled toward the waiting infantry. Once in range, the American infantrymen engaged the tanks with their recoil-less rifles and 2.36-inch bazookas. These were no more effective than the artillery, but the buttoned-up NKPA tankers could not identify the American infantry positions either. Assuming they were only facing a ROK roadblock, the T-34s crested the hill. The lone howitzer damaged the lead tanks with HEAT rounds. Out of HEAT rounds, the gunners continue to engage the tanks with HE rounds. The Americans damaged one more tank before the rest continued down the road. Task Force Smith had lost one howitzer in the exchange, but more important, the gunners were out of HEAT rounds. An hour later, twenty-five T-34s of the main body of the 107th Tank Regiment was spotted coming down the road. The result was much the same. A few tanks were damaged and, after destroying all of Task Force Smith's vehicles, the rest kept on rolling south.

Around 11 a.m., the next NKPA formation from the 4th Infantry Division was spotted. Three tanks were leading a column of trucks containing 5,000 infantry of two NKPA regiments. The Americans watched the column come closer, seemingly unaware of the force's presence. Smith let the column come within 1,000 yards before giving the order to fire. The initial volley caught the North Koreans by surprise, destroying several trucks before the formation scattered. The North Koreans quickly recovered, and under the covering fire of the three tanks, around 1,000 NKPA infantrymen formed up to outflank the eastern side of the line. The Americans defeated this attack, but another assault was forming on the west side.

About this time, Smith lost contact with the artillery battery, and he pulled his men back from the west side of the road. The next NKPA assault, supported by artillery and mortar fire, was better organized. Nonetheless, the beleaguered Americans were able to hold their position for three hours before running low on ammunition. Rather than let his command become surrounded, Smith elected to pull back.

Smith attempted to conduct an orderly withdrawal by alternating his companies; however, a breakdown in communications caused a platoon from B Company to be left behind. By the time the platoon realized it was alone, it was too late, and it was forced to abandon not only its equipment, but also its wounded soldiers. The retreat continued until the survivors reached Osan and found their transport vehicles intact. Getting into the trucks, the remnants of Task Force Smith headed south to link up with the 24th Infantry Division. By nightfall, the Americans reached friendly lines. Task Force Smith suffered over 150 total casualties, in order to delay the NKPA advance for a mere seven hours.

CONCLUSION

The fate of Task Force Smith was an indicator of how far the U.S. army had fallen in preparedness since the end of World War II. It would take time for the army to regain its fighting edge; however, the NKPA was not going to give the Americans that time. Following the Battle of Osan, the U.S. and ROK forces were forced to retreat to a lodgment around the port of Pusan, where they held on until the Inchon landings in September turned the tide of the war in South Korea.

Further Reading

Fehrenbach, T. R. *This Kind of War: The Classic Korean War History.* Washington, DC: Brassey's, 1998.

Hanson, Thomas E. *Combat Ready? The Eighth Army on the Eve of the Korean War.* College Station: Texas A&M University Press, 2010.

Millett, Alan R. *The War for Korea, 1950–1951: They Came from the North*. Lawrence: University Press of Kansas, 2010.

Varhola, Michael J. *Fire and Ice: The Korean War, 1950–1953*. New York: Da Capo Press, 2000.

92. Chinese Intervention

Date: November 3, 1950–January 24, 1951
Location: Korean Penninsula

OPPONENTS

1. United Nations
    Overall Commander: General of the Army Douglas MacArthur
2. Republic of Korea (ROK)
    Major General Chung Il Kwon
3. People's Republic of China (PRC), People's Volunteer Army (PVA)
    General Peng Dehuai
4. North Korean People's Army (NKPA)
    General Kim Chaek

BACKGROUND

On June 25, 1950, soldiers from the North Korean People's Army (NKPA) crossed the 38th parallel to invade the Republic of Korea (ROK; South Korea). The NKPA quickly overcame the ROK army's counterattacks, capturing the ROK capital, Seoul, on June 27. That same day, the United Nations (UN) Security Council passed Resolution 83, recommending military assistance to the ROK. President Harry S. Truman mobilized the armed forces of the United States to help defend the people of South Korea.

General Douglas MacArthur was nominated to lead the UN forces and was permitted to commit U.S. land forces to South Korea. MacArthur alerted the 24th Infantry Division, on occupation duty in Japan at the time, for deployment to South Korea. Unfortunately, occupation duty, along with budget and manning cuts, had deteriorated the U.S. army's readiness. Nonetheless, the 24th Infantry Division sent an undermanned, underequipped, and undertrained task force to lead the way for the rest of the division. Named Task Force Smith, after its commander, Lieutenant Colonel Brad Smith, this unit was quickly overrun by the NKPA on July 5 at the Battle of Osan.

However, the defeat of Task Force Smith was only the beginning of the Eighth Army's problems. Throughout the rest of July, the NKPA pushed the U.S. forces back down the Korean Peninsula. Fortunately for the Eighth Army, the NKPA was almost at the end of its supply lines, allowing General Walton Walker to halt the

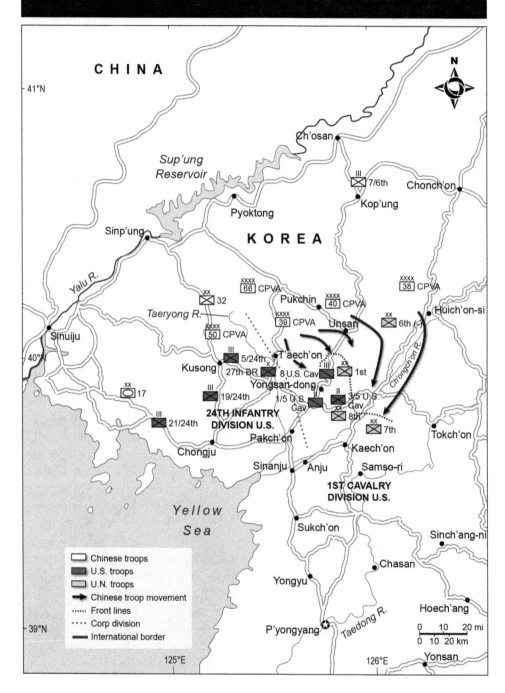

CHINESE INTERVENTION IN THE WEST

retreat and establish a defensive perimeter around the port of Pusan. For the next two months, the Eighth Army held off determined attacks by the NKPA, buying time for MacArthur to plan and execute one of the boldest operations of his military career.

MacArthur proposed an amphibious landing 100 miles behind the Pusan perimeter, at the port of Inchon. Despite misgivings by the Joint Chiefs of Staff, MacArthur was permitted to conduct the landing. On September 15, elements of the 7th Infantry Division, 1st Marine Division stormed ashore, along with several thousand ROK soldiers. Facing little opposition, they quickly advanced inland, and recaptured Seoul ten days later. Meanwhile, Walton's Eighth Army broke out of the Pusan perimeter to link up with MacArthur's force. Realizing they were in danger of being trapped in South Korea, the NKPA began retreating north. By the end of the month, UN forces were approaching the 38th parallel, changing the strategic situation in Korea.

The tactical and operational success of the UN forces appeared to offer an opportunity to reunite the Korean Peninsula. MacArthur was quietly permitted to cross the 38th parallel, with the caveat that he could do so provided that neither the Soviet Union nor the People's Republic of China (PRC) intervened. At the same time, the PRC, through back channels, gave warnings that they would intervene if UN forces crossed the 38th parallel. U.S. intelligence dismissed the idea of any Chinese intervention, believing that the PRC had missed its chance to support the NKPA directly. MacArthur advised President Truman that if the Chinese did become involved, then U.S. airpower would annihilate the Chinese forces. On October 1, assured that the PRC would not become involved, UN forces began advancing to the Yalu River.

The UN action set off an ongoing debate among Chinese leaders about sending soldiers into Korea. Mao Zedong was in favor of intervening; however, many opposed him and did not want to challenge the United States. Mao determined that it would be intolerable to have U.S. forces along a border with China, and planning began to send PRC soldiers to assist the Democratic People's Republic of Korea (DPRK; North Korea). At the same time, a delegation went to Moscow to secure help from the Soviet Union. Joseph Stalin refused to send ground forces but agreed to provide air support north of the Yalu. On October 25, the 200,000 Chinese troops, classified as volunteers and renamed the People's Volunteer Army (PVA), began crossing into Korea. To avoid detection, the soldiers moved only at night and hid during the day.

Meanwhile, MacArthur landed the U.S. X Corps at Wonsan, on the east coast of North Korea, and launched the U.S. Eighth Army directly across the 38th parallel in the direction of Pyongyang, the DPRK capital. Both forces drove steadily to the Yalu, with the U.S. Eighth Army on the west side of the Taebaek Mountains and the U.S. X Corps on the east side. In early November, as both commands approached the Yalu, it appeared that the assessments of Chinese intervention were proving correct. The soldiers were in high spirits, hoping that the offensives planned for later in the month would end the war by Christmas. Unfortunately, these hopes were misguided.

INTERVENTION

On November 1, elements of the PVA rushed out of the hills, blowing bugles as they attacked the U.S. 8th Cavalry Regiment and the ROK 15th Infantry Regiment. Caught by surprise and the ferocity of the attack, the PVA overran the ROK regiment, and the 8th Cavalry retreated in disarray. Over the next few days, the PVA launched more attacks against the Eighth Army, forcing a withdrawal back to the Ch'ongch'on River. However, by November 6, the PVA forces inexplicably disappeared back into the hills, and once again, all was quiet in the Eighth Army sector, leaving the UN commanders to ponder what the attack meant.

Most concluded that the limited PVA attack supported the belief that the Chinese did not have a significant force in Korea. With that in mind, Walker planned to resume his offensive on November 24, and Major General Edwin Almond, the commander of the X Corps, resumed his offensive three days later. Despite the PVA attacks, all along the front, everyone still believed that the war would be over by Christmas.

The Eighth Army met little opposition on November 24, and by the next day, all the units had reached their initial objectives. Things were looking up, and maybe the war really would be over by Christmas. However, on the night of November 25–26, the PVA came out of the hills once again, this time in force. They quickly overran or outflanked the dazed UN soldiers. The ROK II Corps, protecting the right flank of the Eighth Army, collapsed, exposing the entire flank. Walker sent the U.S. 1st Cavalry Division and the Turkish Brigade to salvage the situation on the right, but the Eighth Army was in full retreat by November 28. The retreating UN forces ran a gauntlet of PVA fire from the hills as they made their way along the narrow valley floors. Compounding their problem was Korean refugees trying to flee the approaching Chinese. On November 30, the battered Eighth Army finally halted along the Sunch'on River. However, most of its divisions were not in good enough shape to continue the fight without significant resupply.

On the other side of the Taebaek Mountains, late on November 27, the PVA launched a two-pronged attack on the UN forces on either side of the Changjin (also known as *Chosin*) Reservoir. For the next several days, the Marines on the west side of the reservoir and U.S. army soldiers on the east side fought a desperate delaying action as they tried to withdraw back to Hagaru-ri.

Through sheer courage and determination, the badly mauled soldiers and Marines made it back to Hagaru-ri to regroup. More important, their stubborn defense bought time for the rest of X Corps to escape being cut off by the rapidly advancing PVA. The newly arrived U.S. 3rd Infantry Division was arrayed in depth to cover the withdrawal of the X Corps back to the port of Hungnam. From there, on December 8, MacArthur authorized Almond to evacuate his corps to South Korea by sea. Over 100,000 soldiers and Marines, along with nearly 20,000 vehicles, made it back to the port of Ulsan. From there, they would reinforce the Eighth Army.

In the west, the Walker began pulling back the Eighth Army, hoping to form a defensive line near Pyongyang. However, believing that this was beyond the capability of his depleted forces, he ordered a retreat to the Imjin River on December 2. Fortunately for Walker, the PVA was not in any better condition to vigorously pursue the Eighth Army, and his units could conduct an orderly withdrawal. Three weeks later, the Eighth Army was in position along the Imjin River. On December 23, General Walton Walker was killed in an auto accident; it would be up to his replacement, Lieutenant General Matthew Ridgway, to conduct the next phase of the Korean War.

CONCLUSION

Despite warnings from the PRC, in September 1950, the UN forces crossed the 38th parallel full of confidence that they could reunify the Korean Peninsula in a matter of months and the war would be over soon. However, the overwhelming PRC intervention in late November drastically changed the strategic situation. Suddenly, the UN forces were faced with 200,000 Chinese so-called volunteers. Unprepared for this Chinese onslaught, the UN forces were pushed back across the 38th parallel. Only the courage and determination of the soldiers and junior leaders prevented the retreat from becoming a rout. Nonetheless, it would take several more months to stabilize the lines and over two years of stalemate before a cease-fire was in place. After December 1950, there would be no more talk of reunifying the Korean Peninsula, and the war ended almost where it began.

Further Reading

Barron, Leo. *High Tide in the Korean War: How an Outnumbered American Regiment Defeated the Chinese at the Battle of Chipyong-ni.* Mechanicsburg, PA: Stackpole Books, 2015.

Fehrenbach, T. R. *This Kind of War: A Study in Unpreparedness.* New York: Macmillan, 1963.

Sides, Hampton. *On Desperate Ground: The Marines at the Reservoir, the Korean War's Greatest Battle.* New York: Doubleday, 2018.

Taaffe, Stephen R. *MacArthur's Korean War Generals.* Lawrence: University Press of Kansas, 2016.

93. Battle of Dien Bien Phu

Date: March–May 1954
Location: Northern Vietnam, near the Laotian border

OPPONENTS

1. France

Commander: Colonel Christian de Castries

2. Viet Minh

Commander: General Vo Nguyen Giap

BACKGROUND

The Battle of Dien Bien Phu was the last major engagement of the First Indochina War. In 1953, the Viet Minh, fighting for independence, were pushing the French back and made gains throughout the region. The only thing that slowed the Viet Minh's advance was their tenuous supply lines. During one of the lulls while the Viet Minh regrouped, the French began fortifying hamlets and towns in the Hanoi delta. In May 1953, the French premier René Meyer appointed a new commander to the French forces in Indochina, Lieutenant General Henri Navarre. A veteran of World War II, the fifty-five-year-old Navarre would be the last commander of the Far East Expeditionary Corps.

Upon his arrival, Navarre found that a lackadaisical attitude permeated the command. There was no strategy, and the units were not proactive in engaging the Viet Minh. Navarre set about changing this attitude by establishing a fortified base in the enemy's rear. He hoped to simultaneously cut the Viet Minh's supply lines and draw them out to where French superiority in firepower could destroy them. That plan had worked in the fall of 1952 at Na San. Unfortunately for Navarre, Dien Bien Phu would prove less conducive to this strategy.

An airstrip built by the Japanese during World War II near Dien Bien Phu made it an ideal site for the French. The airstrip was going to be vital to resupplying the outpost. However, everything else about Dien Bien Phu gave the advantage to the Viet Minh. It was near their supply lines, and the Viet Minh would control the high ground around it. All of Navarre's subordinates pointed out these problems, but Navarre dismissed their concerns, and at a commanders' conference on November 17, he ordered the operation to begin three days later.

A Viet Minh assault on one of the French positions during the siege of Dien Bien Phu in March 1954. (Apic/Getty Images)

On November 20, Operation Castor began. By November 22, a total of 9,000 French soldiers had parachuted or were flown into Dien Bien Phu. Everything was going according to plan, and by the end of the month, the six airborne battalions on the ground continued to consolidate their gains. In December, the French in Dien Bien Phu, under the command of Colonel Christian de Castries, began expanding, establishing seven outposts (called Anne-Marie, Beatrice, Claudine, Dominique, Gabrielle, Huguette, and Isabelle) around the headquarters in their outpost, Eliane.

The Viet Minh watched the buildup as their commander, General Vo Nguyen Giap, formulated a plan to deal with this incursion. Giap, anticipating that the French wanted a major battle at Dien Bien Phu, launched a diversionary attack in another province to force the French to withdraw those forces. All the while, he would continue to reinforce his forces around Dien Bien Phu; in particular, he placed artillery on the hills overlooking the French outposts. His plan worked, and the French withdrew the units from Lai Chau province to Dien Bien Phu. The Viet Minh harassed the French all the way. Of the 2,100 soldiers who set out for Dien Bien Phu from Lai Chau on December 9, only 185 reached their destination thirteen days later.

By January 1954, the French at Dien Bien Phu were not only surrounded, but were outnumbered five to one in personnel and four to one in artillery. Throughout January and February, the Viet Minh actively probed the French defenses and kept them under sporadic artillery fire from their advantageous position in the hills. Satisfied that he understood the French defenses, Giap was ready to begin the siege in March.

THE BATTLE

From their positions in the surrounding hills, the Viet Minh could bombard all the French fortifications with artillery fire. Beginning with Beatrice, located northeast of the headquarters, the Viet Minh began assaulting the outposts one by one on March 13. Late in the day, the Viet Minh unleashed a devastating artillery barrage on the outpost. During the bombardment, the commander of the northern sector and his staff were killed. The Viet Minh's 312th Division followed the artillery prep with an infantry assault. The Viet Minh overran the badly shaken defenders, and Beatrice fell shortly after midnight, with a loss of 500 Legionnaires. A French counterattack the next morning was stopped short by intense artillery fire from the hills.

Emboldened by their success, the Viet Minh launched the next attack on Gabrielle, the northernmost outpost, on March 14. Around 5 p.m., the Viet Minh artillery began to soften up Gabrielle. Just as with the attack on Beatrice, the artillery fire stunned the defenders. The Viet Minh followed with a two-regiment assault. The French held on, and fierce fighting continued throughout the night. The next morning, Colonel de Castries ordered a counterattack to relieve the defenders. Some French units reached the defenders, but the accurate and intense Viet Minh artillery fire prevented the rescue of Gabrielle, and de Castries ordered a withdrawal, ceding the outpost to the Viet Minh. The loss of Gabrielle cost the French approximately 1,000 men. More important, now the Viet Minh could accurately target the airfield putting it out of action as a way to resupply the defenders.

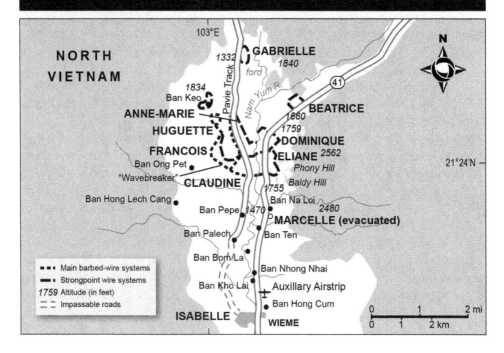

BATTLE OF DIEN BIEN PHU, MARCH 13, 1954

Anne-Marie was defended by troops consisting of the Tais, an ethnic Vietnam-ese minority. Giap had kept up an intense propaganda campaign against the Tais, warning them that this was not their fight. After the fall of Beatrice and Gabrielle, the Tais were ready to listen. On the morning of March 17, under cover of fog, the Tais left. The remaining French were forced to withdraw as well. Anne-Marie fell to the Viet Minh without a fight.

From March 17–30, there was a break in the action as the Viet Minh assessed the situation, but they continued to harass the remaining outposts. On the French side, morale continued to fall. The French high command in Hanoi lost faith in the ability of de Castries to command the situation. On March 17, General Cogny attempted to land at Dien Bien Phu to take command, but his plane could not get through the intense antiaircraft fire. Desperate to take over command of the gar-rison, Cogny briefly considered parachuting in until his staff talked him out of it. To compound matters, the French artillery commander, distressed at his inability to destroy the Viet Minh artillery dug into the mountains, committed suicide in his bunker.

On the evening of March 30, Giap resumed the assault, focusing on Eliane and Dominique. Using the same tactics that had worked previously, the Viet Minh opened with an artillery barrage followed by an infantry assault. This time, how-ever, the results were not the same, and for the next week, many of the smaller sub-sidiary outposts changed hands numerous times. After a week of bloody battles, the Viet Minh changed tactics and took a more deliberate approach to reducing the strongpoints. At the same time, fresh Viet Minh reinforcements were brought in from Laos. The French, on the other hand, despite receiving some reinforcements by airdrop, were not able to make up their losses.

For the rest of April, the Viet Minh continued to close the ring around the French defenders. On May 1, the final phase of the battle began. The Viet Minh quickly overran three smaller outposts, but the French beat back the attacks around Eliane 2. After spending several days of tunneling, the Viet Minh exploded a mine under Eliane 2 and seized the outpost. Giap set May 7 as the date for the final all-out assault to defeat the French. His 25,000 troops methodically overran the remaining outposts. The exhausted French defenders gave in to the inevitable and surrendered. The last strongpoint surrendered late in the evening, and the battle for Dien Bien Phu was over.

CONCLUSION

The fall of Dien Bien Phu reverberated across the world and shook the confidence of many nations about French credibility. The day after the defeat, a conference opened in Geneva to adjudicate the future of Vietnam. It was recommended to divide Vietnam temporarily along the 17th parallel until upcoming elections in 1956. Ho Chi Minh would administer North Vietnam, supported by the Soviet Union and the People's Republic of China (PRC). South Vietnam would be administered by Emperor Bao Dai and Premier Minister Ngo Dink Diem and supported by the United States. The elections were never held, and Vietnam remained divided, setting the stage for the Second Indochina War.

Further Reading

Davidson, Phillip. *Vietnam at War: The History, 1946–1975*. New York: Oxford University Press, 1988.

Fall, Bernard. *Hell in a Very Small Place: The Siege of Dien Bien Phu*. New York: Vintage Books, 1968.

Morgan, Ted. *Valley of Death: The Tragedy at Dien Bien Phu That Led America into the Vietnam War*. New York: Random House, 2010.

Windrow, Martin. *The Last Valley: Dien Bien Phu and the French Defeat in Vietnam*. Cambridge, MA: Da Capo Press, 2004.

94. Ap Bac

Date: January 2, 1963
Location: Dinh Tuong Province, South Vietnam

OPPONENTS

1. Army of the Republic of Vietnam (ARVN)

   Commanders: General Huynh Van Cao and Colonel Bui Dinh Dam (advised by Lieutenant Colonel John Paul Vann of the U.S. army)

2. People's Liberation Armed Forces (PLAF)

   Commander: unknown

BACKGROUND

Beginning in 1962, the United States restructured its effort to fight communist encroachment in South Vietnam. To that point, the Military Advisory Group (MAG) had executed its mission of training and assisting the Army of the Republic of Vietnam (ARVN) with a light touch and low footprint, but a deteriorating situation in the countryside with the North Vietnamese–supported National Liberation Front (NLF) insurgency led to new approaches. Ironically, setbacks for President Ngo Din Diem's regime in South Vietnam led Hanoi to push for more support for the NLF and the People's Liberation Armed Forces (PLAF, aka Viet Cong) in the south, including cadres of trainers and equipment of their own to support a more aggressive program against the south. Hanoi was becoming impatient with its long-stated goal of toppling the Diem regime and uniting the country under a Communist government in Hanoi.

The Americans responded to this slowly fragmenting situation by renaming their mission the "Military Assistance Command Vietnam (MACV)" and beefing up the numbers of military advisors, training, intelligence support, and supply of new equipment to the ARVN. The man in charge of all this activity was General Paul Harkins, who arrived in South Vietnam in February 1962. Harkins was a strong supporter of Diem, and he wanted to show Washington some return on its investment in the counterinsurgency fight in Vietnam. In 1962, his headquarters produced a dual military and political approach to be executed by the South Vietnamese. The political side of the equation was a restructured pacification effort known to history as the "Strategic Hamlet" program. Diem had tried to execute a similar program without strong American involvement and failed. Now in 1962 and into 1963, a fresh start was made, with much heavier involvement and monitoring by the Americans.

On the military side, the goal was to conduct offensive sweep operations by the newly trained ARVN to attack the PLAF in its base areas and sanctuaries in the countryside, which it controlled. The Battle of Ap Bac resulted from these operations in the heavily NLF-controlled area southwest of Saigon in the Mekong Delta. It was critical to achieve success in these heavily populated areas so near the capital. By Christmas 1962, MACV's signal intelligence assets had located an NLF radio transmitter near the hamlets of Tan Thoi and Bac (*Ap* means "hamlet" in Vietnamese) in the IV Corps area. Lieutenant Colonel John Paul Vann, the senior advisor to the new 7th Division commander, Colonel Bui Dinh Dam, lobbied MACV and the Vietnamese for an operation to seize the transmitter and any troops or NLF personnel near it. Initially, they had wanted to conduct the operation on January 1, 1963, but Dam moved the operation back a day in case the U.S. helicopter pilots had hangovers.

THE PLANS

The American/ARVN plan was to close in on Bac and Tan Thoi from three sides, using airmobile infantry in H-21 "flying banana" helicopters, followed up by M113 armored personnel carriers in support. Additionally, local militia, controlled by

General Huynh Van Cao, who had previously commanded the 7th Division prior to Dam, would cut off any attempt at escape to the rear by fleeing Viet Cong forces. Intelligence estimated that 120 fighters were protecting the transmitter. The Americans and ARVN expected no major problems for this operation and hoped to bag a considerable number of fighters and support their claim of this area as being "liberated" from the communists. They key challenge would be the airmobile assault of a battalion of 300 troops who would fix any defenders between the two hamlets as the M113s and provisional militia column moved in to close the trap.

The Vietnamese, on the other hand, had massed three times as many fighters in Tan Thoi and Bac. From previous engagements, they had learned how easy it was to shoot down helicopters and unhinge the ARVN leadership. They had practiced tactics against the M113, training to shoot through the driver slits as a way to neutralize these vehicles. Finally, they wanted to test their new tactics and equipment—mortars and captured American rifles and machine guns—against their opponent. If they were successful, they intended to stand and fight, and only withdraw if it looked like the ARVN gained the upper hand. Officers like Vann relished this sort of stand-up fight and were hoping for a major engagement, but they did not believe the PLAF would risk one yet.

THE BATTLE

On January 2, 1963, the operation began, with the Americans and ARVN nearly clueless about what waited for them. Vann monitored the course of the battle in the air overhead and on the radio in a light L-19 spotter aircraft. Neither Cao nor Dam was with the troops; rather, they were in the rear at their command posts, monitoring their radios.

The terrain favored the defense, with rice paddies to the south and west of Tan Toi and Bac, respectively, between which ran zigzagging dikes where the Viet Cong dug in amid heavy foliage provided by fruit trees. The American plan had been to land nearer to Tan Toi, where the transmitter was, but the assault became confused, undershot the planned landing zone, and debarked near the tree line in the rice paddies to the west of Bac. Several of the helicopters were shot down because they were too close, and flanking fire opened up from both Bac and Tan Toi, catching the force in a crossfire and pinning it down. Vann ordered the M113s forward in support, but the new Viet Cong tactics that targeted the drivers as well as the machine gunners, who were exposed while manning their weapons through hatches, succeeded. The M113 company ground to a standstill and refused to advance.

Vann struggled to get everyone moving, seeing that the enemy had given the ARVN a golden opportunity to destroy a considerable number of fighters. However, all the ARVN advantages were squandered, especially as more helicopters were brought down by the keen marksmanship of the Viet Cong. The provisional militia (civil guards) that was supposed to come up from the rear ended up getting hung up in the south in desultory fighting in a wood line south of Bac. An attempt to retrieve the situation with an airborne drop late in the day—which had been scheduled, but was delayed—also went wrong when the battalion jumped at the end of the drop zone and landed a half-mile away from the fight. By this time, some of the American advisors had been killed in the fighting and losses continued to mount, causing both Cao and Dam to panic. Meanwhile, the Viet Cong held their ground, although accounts of their losses will never be known. Reputedly, Cao gave the order that prevented the launching of night flares to facilitate attacking the PLAF battalion as it withdrew later that night.

CONCLUSION

Inside the MACV headquarters, the scope of the disaster was well known. The ARVN and Americans suffered almost 200 casualties, including three American advisors killed and eight wounded. Five helicopters were shot down, and the enemy battalion escaped in good order. Ap Bac became a propaganda triumph for the NLF/PLAF, on the scale of the American "victories" of Lexington and Concord in the Revolutionary War. They had stood, fought, and defeated a much larger force, advised by professional American officers, who had had all the advantages of fire-power, helicopters, and armor.

On the ARVN side, the façade that was the leadership of South Vietnam was exposed, although MACV and Cao publicly portrayed the engagement as a strategic victory that forced the enemy to leave the area. Even though the offensive by the ARVN continued into 1963, the overriding concern of ARVN officers was to *avoid* another Ap Bac. At the same time, the strategic hamlet program collapsed

---

Dau Tranh–*The Vietnamese Way of War*

The U.S. involvement in Vietnam has been characterized as an earlier form of what is today called *hybrid warfare*. It included warfare, in both the regular and irregular domains, with a politicized ideological opponent: the Communist regime in Hanoi. The Vietnamese approach to warfare—*dau tranh* (struggle)—evolved from classical Maoist people's revolutionary warfare, which consists of three phases: political, guerilla, and mobile warfare. In the first phase, the party builds the people's political consciousness and organizes; in the second, it engages in guerilla warfare to undermine the regime; and in the final phase, it moves to conventional military operations. In the Vietnamese version, the struggle is divided into two components: *dau tranh vu trang* (military operations and violence) and *dau tranh chinh tri* (political struggle). The military component is where both guerilla war and conventional operations reside, which often occurred at the same time during the Vietnam War, with guerillas of the People's Liberation Armed Forces (PLAF), aka the Viet Cong, fighting irregular war at the same time as North Vietnamese main-force units fought conventionally. The political component consists of actions among the enemy, among the people, and in the military. Included in these actions were political indoctrination and torture of American prisoners of war; programs against the American will to fight in the anti-war movement; and ensuring the political reliability of the North Vietnamese people, North Vietnamese Army (NVA), and Viet Cong. Finally, the NVA envisioned a final component of *dau tranh* involving a *khoi nghia* (general uprising), which was a spontaneous revolt by the Vietnamese people to throw off the shackles of colonial rule.

under the fiction that the government could challenge the Viet Cong and assert control over liberated areas. Ap Bac proved to be the beginning of a series of disasters that finally ended with the assassination of President Ngo Din Diem and his brother, Ngo Dinh Nhu, later that fall and almost led to the fall of South Vietnam. This in turn caused the Americans to intervene with major combat forces to try to snatch victory from the jaws of defeat in 1965.

Further Reading

Cosmas, Graham. *The United States Army in Vietnam, MACV: The Joint Command in the Years of Escalation, 1962–1967.* Washington, DC: U.S. Army Center for Military History, 2006.

Moyar, Mark. *Triumph Forsaken: The Vietnam War, 1954–1965.* Cambridge: Cambridge University Press, 2006.

Sheehan, Neil. *A Bright Shining Lie: John Paul Vann and America in Vietnam.* New York: Random House, 1988.

95. The Six-Day War (1967 Arab-Israeli War)

Date: June 5–10, 1967
Location: The Sinai Desert and Golan Heights

OPPONENTS

1. Arab forces

   Egypt:
   Commander: Field Marshal Abdel Hakim Amer
   Syria:
   Commander: General Ahmad Suwaydani
   Jordan:
   Commander: General Zaid ibn Shaker

2. Israel
   Commander: General Yitzhak Rabin

BACKGROUND

The Six-Day War was the third of the Arab-Israeli conflicts dating from 1948. After the second war in 1956, the Egyptian president Gamal Abdel Nasser agreed to keep the Straits of Tiran open and allowed a United Nations Emergency Force (UNEF) to occupy the Egyptian-Israeli border in the Sinai. The region was relatively calm until a series of border clashes and raids by Palestinian guerrillas broke out in the mid-1960s. The Israeli Defense Force (IDF) retaliated by striking Palestinian villages in Syria, Lebanon, and Jordan culminating with a deadly raid on Al_Samu that left eighteen killed and fifty-four wounded. In the air, the Israeli Air

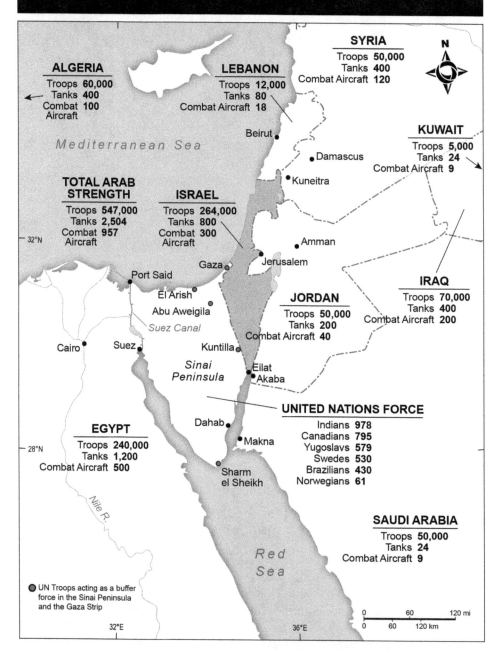

BALANCE OF FORCES, MAY 14–24, 1967

ALGERIA
Troops **60,000**
Tanks **400**
Combat **100**
Aircraft

LEBANON
Troops **12,000**
Tanks **80**
Combat Aircraft **18**

SYRIA
Troops **50,000**
Tanks **400**
Combat Aircraft **120**

N

Mediterranean Sea

Beirut

KUWAIT
Troops **5,000**
Tanks **24**
Combat Aircraft **9**

Damascus

Kuneitra

TOTAL ARAB STRENGTH
Troops **547,000**
Tanks **2,504**
Combat **957**
Aircraft

32°N

ISRAEL
Troops **264,000**
Tanks **800**
Combat **300**
Aircraft

Amman

IRAQ
Troops **70,000**
Tanks **400**
Combat Aircraft **200**

Gaza

Jerusalem

Port Said

El Arish

Abu Aweigila

Suez Canal

JORDAN
Troops **50,000**
Tanks **200**
Combat Aircraft **40**

Cairo   Suez

Kuntilla

Sinai Peninsula

Eilat
Akaba

Dahab

UNITED NATIONS FORCE
Indians **978**
Canadians **795**
Yugoslavs **579**
Swedes **530**
Brazilians **430**
Norwegians **61**

EGYPT
Troops **240,000**
Tanks **1,200**
Combat Aircraft **500**

28°N

Makna

Sharm
el Sheikh

Nile R.

SAUDI ARABIA
Troops **50,000**
Tanks **24**
Combat Aircraft **9**

Red Sea

● UN Troops acting as a buffer
force in the Sinai Peninsula
and the Gaza Strip

0   60   120 mi
0   60   120 km

32°E   36°E

Force (IAF) clashed with the Syrian air force, shooting down six Syrian fighters in April 1967 during one engagement. In May, events began to accelerate.

As the crisis unfolded, many Arabs accused Nasser of not doing enough to support Syria in its struggle with Israel. In response, Nasser mobilized the Egyptian forces in the Sinai on May 14. Four days later, he demanded the UNEF forces leave, and on May 22, he took his boldest step. Despite warnings from Israel that closing the Straits of Tiran would be considered an act of war, Nasser closed the straits to Israeli shipping on the same day he expelled the UNEF. On May 30, King Hussein of Jordan signed a defense pact with Egypt, and the next day, he invited Iraqi forces into his country. Contributing to Nasser's rush to action was faulty intelligence that he received from the Soviet Union that the IDF was massing on its northern border with Syria. By June 1, the Knesset began deliberating on how to respond. On June 4, Israel decided to preempt the Arabs by striking first.

Collectively, the Arab armies were well equipped but lacked training. Using mostly Soviet equipment, the Egyptian army was the largest of the Arab forces. The Egyptian air force alone possessed over 400 Soviet-built aircraft, including 30 Tu 16 bombers that could cover all of Israel. Nasser placed the bulk of his army in the Sinai, including two armored, one mechanized, and seven infantry divisions and four armored brigades and four infantry brigades. The entire Syrian army was deployed along the border with Israel, but the recent skirmishes, as well as internal turmoil, reduced its effectiveness. The Jordanian army only numbered 55,000 but was well equipped with 300 tanks, most of them U.S. made. On the other hand, with only 24 aircraft, the Jordanian air force would prove no match for the IAF. The Iraqis contributed 100 tanks and two squadrons of fighters to the effort as well.

The total strength of the Israeli army was 264,000 when fully mobilized. However, most of these soldiers were reservists and could not leave their jobs for long without affecting the Israeli economy. The IAF, using mostly French aircraft, was superior to the Arab forces in pilot skills and training, and the recent clashes had only made them better. Wishing to keep the war confined to Egypt, the IDF placed three armored divisions, with one infantry brigade, one mechanized brigade, and three airborne brigades for a total of 70,000 soldiers and 700 tanks, along the Sinai border for the coming attack. Five brigades faced Jordan, and another three were opposite Syria. With the IDF in position, the Knesset set June 5 as the start date for the war.

THE BATTLE

On the morning of June 5, 200 Israeli aircraft, which amounted to nearly all of the nation's combat air force, took off to attack the Egyptian airfields. The majority flew over the Mediterranean Sea, while the remainder came in from the Red Sea. Coming in low to avoid detection, the Israelis caught the Egyptian air defenders by surprise and attacked the airfields at will, destroying the parked aircraft and using special bombs to put the runways out of action. The IAF destroyed over 300 Egyptian aircraft, including all of their TU 16 heavy bombers, in the first attack. For good measure, the IAF also meted out the same punishment to the Syrian air force. For the loss of nineteen aircraft, the IAF gained air supremacy for the rest of the war.

The land battle in the Sinai began at 7:50 a.m. on June 5, when the advance of elements of two brigades from General Israel Tal's armored division crossed into the Gaza Strip. The 7th Armored Brigade was to attack along the coast, and

60th Armored Brigade would advance through the desert on the 7th's left flank. The Egyptians were caught by surprise, so initially resistance was light, but casualties mounted as the brigades advanced farther west. Nonetheless, after four hours of hard fighting, the Israelis seized the key rail junction at Khan Yunis by early afternoon. The division pushed on, taking more losses but inflicting more damage on the Egyptians, and by the end of the day, it was on the outskirts of Arish. Tal's left flank was supported by General Avraham Yoffe's armored division attacking through a lightly defended area that the Egyptians believed to be impassable. Yoffe's division also acted in support of the southernmost armored division commanded by Major General Ariel Sharon.

On June 6, Sharon's 38th Armored Division attacked the Egyptian 2nd Infantry Division, holding Kusseima and Umm Katef with 16,000 soldiers reinforced with an armored regiment. Sharon's soldiers made slow progress through the well-prepared Egyptian defenses. Later in the day, two brigades from Yoffe's division outflanked the Egyptians from the north and seized the key road junction at Abu Ageila, to the west of Um Katef ridge. Reinforced with artillery and additional soldiers, Sharon launched another assault at 10 p.m. The seizure of Abu Ageila helped, but the Egyptians continued to defend their positions fiercely as the Israelis bogged down in the dense minefields. Sharon pushed his soldiers harder, and after several hours of intense fighting, his division cleared Um Kagtef Ridge and was in position to continue their attack.

With the fall of Abu Ageila, Egyptian Field Marshal Abdel Akim Amer ordered a general retreat back to the Suez Canal. The three Israeli armored divisions seized the opportunity to occupy the key passes ahead of the retreating Egyptians. Harassed by the IAF as they retreated, the demoralized Egyptians were surprised to find Israeli tanks waiting for them in the passes. Many abandoned their equipment in their attempt to reach the Suez Canal. The same day, the Israeli navy landed elements at the southern tip of the Sinai at Sharm el-Sheikh to attack north along the coast. On June 8, the Israeli tankers reached the Suez Canal, and elements of Yoffe's division turned south to link up with the naval forces at Abu Zenima. The fight in the Sinai was over; however, the Israelis' desire to confine the war to the Sinai did not come to pass.

Encouraged by false reports from Nasser about Egyptian success on June 5, Jordan and Syria decided to enter the war that same day. After some sporadic skirmishes, both began shelling Israel. Disregarding Israeli warnings, the Jordanians shelled two kibbutzs and several sites in Tel Aviv, including a hospital. While the Knesset debated how to respond, the IAF attacked the Jordanian air bases, catching the planes refueling and rearming. The IAF destroyed all the Jordanian fighters, leaving the Jordanian air force ineffective for the rest of the war. Late on June 5, an Israeli infantry brigade attacked north to cut off Jerusalem, while an armored brigade attacked from the north near Meggido.

The Israelis made good progress in the face of inconsistent Jordanian defenses. As the IDF approached Jerusalem, Defense Minister Moshe Dayan forbade them to enter the Old City to protect the holy sites. By June 7, the IDF was in a position to occupy the West Bank, but the Jordanian army, fearing being cut off, began to withdraw across the Jordan. At this point, Dayan permitted the IDF to enter the Old City and to occupy the West Bank.

On the Golan Heights, the fighting unfolded much as it did with Jordan. On June 5, Syria began shelling Israeli settlements with artillery and air strikes. The IAF retaliated by destroying approximately two-thirds of the Syrian Air Force aircraft. The next day, a Syrian ground attack was easily repulsed, and the Syrians reverted to long-range artillery attacks. For the next two days, the Knesset debated attacking the Golan Heights. The IDF opposed the attack because it could mean costly casualties due to the enemy's well-prepared defenses. However, as the fighting in the Sinai and Jordan began to wind down and those forces became available, it was decided to attack the Golan Heights. On June 9, the offensive began with heavy attacks by the IAF. On the ground, the Syrians fought well on the confined terrain, and there were many point-blank engagements between tanks. However, by evening, the Israelis penetrated the Syrians' first line of defense and continued to the second line. The Israelis pushed on through the night, and by morning, the Syrians were withdrawing. By the end of the day on June 10, the Israelis occupied the heights; the next day, a cease-fire mandated by the United Nations went into effect.

CONCLUSION

After the cease-fire went into effect, Israel could claim a decisive victory over its Arab opponents. In six days, the IDF pushed Egypt back across the Suez Canal, occupied the West Bank, and seized the Golan Heights from Syria. Israeli casualties amounted to fewer than 1,000 killed and over 4,000 wounded. Estimates of Arab losses range from 10,000 to 18,000 total casualties. Materially, each of the Arab armies had lost approximately 80 percent of their fighting power. Nonetheless, for many Arabs, this defeat did not mean the end of the war with Israel; there would be a rematch before too long.

From the Israeli perspective, the victory meant that they had gained strategic depth in any future conflicts. The Suez Canal became a barrier with Egypt, and the Golan Heights gave Israel a defensive advantage over the Syrians. However, the occupation of the West Bank and the Old City was a huge psychological victory for the Israelis. The people took pride in the accomplishments of the IDF, and the IDF gained respect around the world. However, the IDF took too much pride in its victory and began to assume they would always be able to defeat any Arab army easily—an assumption that would be proven false in 1973.

Further Reading

Bowen, Jeremy. *Six Days: How the 1967 War Shaped the Middle East*. New York: Thomas Dunne Books, 2005.

Oren, Michael. *Six Days of War*. Oxford: Oxford University Press, 2002.

Pressfield, Steven. *The Lion's Gate: On the Front Lines of the Six-Day War*. New York: Sentinel, 2014.

Shlaim, Avi, and William Roger Louis, eds. *The 1967 Arab–Israeli War: Origins and Consequences*. Cambridge: Cambridge University Press, 2012.

96. The Tet Offensive

Date: January 30–April 8, 1968
Location: Republic of Vietnam (South Vietnam)

OPPONENTS

1. Communists

Democratic Republic of Vietnam (North Vietnam):
Commander: General Vo Nguyen Giap
People's Liberation Armed Forces (PLAF):
Commander: Colonel General Tran Van Tra

2. Allies

Republic of Vietnam (South Vietnam):
Commander: General Cao Van Vien
United States:
Commander: General William C. Westmoreland

BACKGROUND

Throughout 1967, U.S. involvement in Vietnam was facing increased criticism from within and without the government. To that end, the strategy came under scrutiny. The Military Assistance Command Vietnam (MACV) commander, General William C. Westmoreland, believed that a tipping point was coming when the enemy's casualties would exceed his ability to replace them. At that point, according to Westmoreland, the United States could declare victory. To quell criticism that the Vietnam War was incurring at home, President Lyndon Johnson recalled Westmoreland to testify before Congress on its progress. Westmoreland was also asked to speak at various venues throughout the country to enlighten the American people on the status of the war effort. Based on "body counts," pacified villages, and other metrics, Westmorland was sure the United States was winning the war. He assured Congress and the people, "We have reached an important point when the end begins to come into view."

North Vietnam was facing a crisis in 1967. The debate was among three factions about the strategy going forward. The centrists, led by Ho Chi Minh, wanted to resolve the conflict through negotiations. The moderates, including General Vo Nguyen Giap, wanted to keep up pressure on South Vietnam but also wanted to ensure the economic viability of North Vietnam before expanding the war. The last and most vocal group was the militants, who believed that the time was right for a major offensive in South Vietnam that would damage the legitimacy of President Nguyen Van Thieu's government in South Vietnam, as well as U.S. involvement. More important, the militants hoped their actions would lead to a general uprising among the people of South Vietnam. Following a crackdown on the moderates in

TET OFFENSIVE, 1968

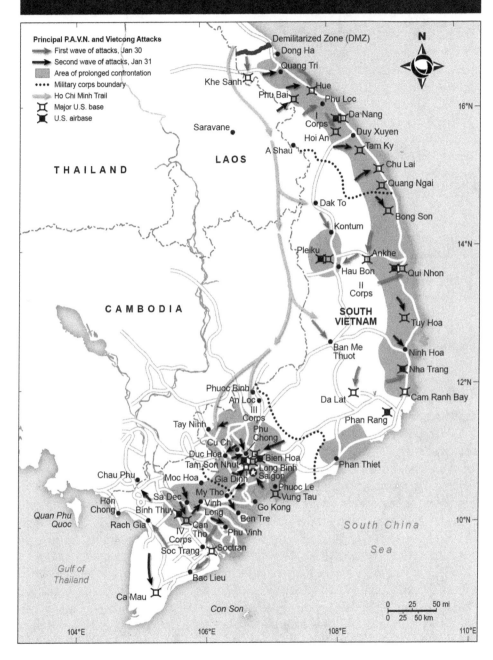

Principal P.A.V.N. and Vietcong Attacks
- First wave of attacks, Jan 30
- Second wave of attacks, Jan 31
- Area of prolonged confrontation
- Military corps boundary
- Ho Chi Minh Trail
- Major U.S. base
- U.S. airbase

July 1967, the militants won out. The planning for the "General Offensive, General Uprising" (as the North Vietnamese planners called it) began in earnest.

The plan called for a diversionary offensive near the Demilitarized Zone (DMZ) and along the border to draw U.S. forces away from the cities. The most famous of these actions was the siege of Khe Sanh, just south of the DMZ, which began on

January 21. Following these diversionary attacks, the main effort would begin, with simultaneous attacks on cities and provincial capitals throughout the Republic of Vietnam. The goal was to inflict as much damage to the Army of the Republic of Vietnam (ARVN) and MACV as possible and start a general revolt in the South. The planners settled on the Tet holiday as the best time to begin the attack.

The North's diversionary plan was working; the siege of Khe Sanh drew Westmoreland's focus despite intelligence reports of a major buildup of enemy forces in the south. In the days leading up to the battle, MACV was becoming concerned that the North was planning a significant attack throughout the countryside. The III Corps commander became very suspicious and was permitted to withdraw fifteen battalions to the outskirts of Saigon. Despite all the warning signs, however, the ARVN chief of staff refused to cancel leaves for the Tet holiday. Westmoreland even warned Washington that an enemy attack might be imminent; nonetheless, MACV was wholly surprised when the attack began.

THE BATTLE

The attack was scheduled to begin at midnight on January 31; however, due to a mixup, five provincial capitals were attacked at midnight on January 30. After the initial shock, the U.S. and ARVN forces pushed the Viet Cong and People's Army of Vietnam (PAVN) troops out of the affected cites by morning. The MACV intelligence chief warned Westmoreland to expect more attacks that night. Westmoreland wisely put all U.S. forces on alert, but not all the ARVN units were alerted, nor were all leaves canceled, as previously mentioned.

At 3 a.m. on January 31, a total of 84,000 Viet Cong and PAVN launched simultaneous attacks on key points, including U.S. bases, across South Vietnam, including the capital, Saigon. The North Vietnamese forces were initially successful, but the local ARVN forces quickly recovered, and within days, most of the cities were back under control of the South Vietnamese. However, several provincial capitals held out longer, including the ancient city of Hue. The battle for Hue, along with the battle for Saigon, would be the longest and bloodiest battles of the Tet Offensive.

Two battalions of the 6th PAVN regiment attacked Hue at 3:40 a.m. on January 31. Their objective was to occupy the Citadel, a nineteenth-century fortress and headquarters of the 1st ARVN Division. The PAVN forces occupied most of the Citadel, but the ARVN doggedly held their positions and did not relinquish full control. Once again, MACV underestimated the strength of the North forces, and Westmoreland believed that there were no more than a few enemy companies in the city. He ordered a Marine battalion to clear them out. It quickly became apparent that there were more than a few companies in Hue. Before the battle was over, the fight for Hue would last twenty-five days and involve elements of three U.S. divisions and one ARVN division, pitted against approximately six PAVN regiments.

The fighting in Hue was a new experience for both sides. Unlike fighting in the jungle, both sides had to adapt their tactics to an urban environment. The Marines and ARVN soldiers had to clear the streets house by house, each one a PAVN strongpoint. The toil was heavy, both physically and psychologically. After three weeks of intense urban combat, Hue was retaken on February 25, when the 1st ARVN Division occupied the Palace of Perfect Peace. The fight for Hue cost the United States 216 killed in action and nearly 1,600 wounded in action, and the ARVN lost 452 killed in action and over 2,000 wounded in action. PAVN losses are harder to ascertain; however, approximately 1,000–3,000 were killed in the city proper.

Outside of Hue, some of the heaviest fighting occurred in Saigon. While the North Vietnamese never intended to occupy all of Saigon, they did plan to attack six key targets, including the National Radio Station, the Tan Son Nhut Air Base, and the U.S. embassy. The attackers hope to seize the radio station long enough to play a recording of Ho Chi Minh calling for a general

Prisoners from the People's Army of Vietnam (PAVN or North Vietnamese Army) at Phu Bai near Hue during 1968's Tet Offensive, a disaster for both sides. (Nik Wheeler/Corbis via Getty Images)

uprising to overthrow the South Vietnamese government. The commandos quickly occupied the radio station, but a local ARVN commander cut the power lines before the broadcast could go out. The PAVN defenders held out for six hours before the last eight killed themselves with explosives before the ARVN could rush the building.

The attack on the U.S. embassy began at 2:45 a.m., when a nineteen-man sapper team blew a hole in the outer wall. Two American guards killed the first two sappers through the hole; however, more sappers poured through, killing the Americans. Once inside the compound, the sappers fired at the Chancery building, penetrating the walls with grenade launchers. However, early in the fighting, the sapper team's leaders were killed, and the remainder of the sappers were not sure what to do next.

In the confusion, there were reports of the sappers occupying the entire first floor of the embassy, causing more panic among the ARVN and MACV soldiers. The report was not true, but it was enough to make retaking the compound the number one effort in the fight for Saigon. Nonetheless, after a few hours of confused and intense fighting, along with more reinforcements, the MACV military police began getting the upper hand. By 9:20 a.m., inside the compound, all nineteen sappers had been killed and the embassy secured, at the loss of five American lives.

By the second week of February, the main fighting was over. The siege of Hue would continue until February 25, along with mop-up operations around Saigon. With the relief of Khe Sanh on April 8, the Tet Offensive was over. However, the PAVN forces initiated another offensive across South Vietnam in May that came to be known as "Mini Tet." This time, the U.S. and ARVN forces were better prepared, and that offensive was called off after eight days.

CONCLUSION

Tet had been North Vietnam's attempt to foment a general uprising among the people of South Vietnam and bring down Thieu's government. In that, they failed. They underestimated the resiliency and capabilities of the ARVN, and in the end, they suffered a significant tactical defeat. Some sources list PAVN/PLAF losses at 32,000–45,000 out of 84,000, the vast majority of which were among the Viet Cong, the local insurgents. It would be a long time before the Cong recovered. On the other side, the ARVN suffered nearly 11,000 total casualties and the United States over 9,000. However, despite suffering a tactical defeat, the North achieved an unintended strategic victory.

In the United States, the attack came as a shock. After months of reports on how well the war was going and that the end might be in sight, the American people could not understand how North Vietnam could pull off an offensive of this scale. While the Tet Offensive did not break American support, it did cause the people to begin questioning what the objective of the U.S. presence was.

President Johnson went on television on March 31 to announce that he was stopping the bombing of North Vietnam and that he would not seek reelection. On

William Westmoreland (March 26, 1914–July 18, 2005)

Westmoreland, a South Carolina native, spent one year at The Citadel before securing an appointment to the U.S. Military Academy at West Point, New York, in 1932. Graduating at the top of his class in 1936, Westmoreland was commissioned a second lieutenant of artillery. During World War II, Westmoreland saw combat as an artillery officer in Tunisia, Sicily, France, and Germany. He next saw action in Korea as a regimental commander. Following the Korean War, he served as a staff officer, commanded the 101st Airborne Division, and was the 45th superintendent for West Point.

In Vietnam, Westmoreland believed the United States could wear down North Vietnam with a strategy of attrition. He believed that his strategy was working, and in 1967, his positive comments before a joint session of Congress reassured the politicians that the war was going in favor of the United States. However, in January 1968, the North Vietnamese launched the Tet Offensive. The enormity of the offensive shocked the American people. Following Tet, Westmoreland was recalled to be the chief of staff of the army, a position he held until he retired in 1972.

In retirement, Westmoreland ran unsuccessfully for governor of South Carolina and published his memoirs. He also spent much of his time trying to clear his name. Westmoreland battled Alzheimer's in his later years, and he passed away on July 18, 2005 in Charleston, South Carolina. He is buried at West Point.

April 3, the government of North Vietnam announced that it would be willing to begin negotiations, setting the course for the eventual withdrawal of all U.S. troops from South Vietnam. Hanoi lost militarily but won politically, which ultimately meant more.

Further Reading

Karnow, Stanley. *Vietnam: A History*. New York: Penguin, 1991.

Schmitz, David F. *The Tet Offensive: Politics, War, and Public Opinion*. Westport, CT: Praeger, 2004.

Sorley, Lewis. *A Better War: The Unexamined Victories and Final Tragedy of America's Last Years in Vietnam*. New York: Harvest Books, 1999.

Willbanks, James H. *The Tet Offensive: A Concise History*. New York: Columbia University Press, 2008.

97. Lam Son 719

Date: February 8–March 25, 1971
Location: Laos

OPPONENTS

1. South Vietnam
    Commander: General Hoang Xuan Lam
2. United States
    Commander: General Creighton Abrams
3. North Vietnam
    Commander: Le Trong Tan

BACKGROUND

Lam Son 719 was the first major test of the U.S. Vietnamization policy. Elements of the 1st Army of the Republic of Vietnam (ARVN) Corps were supposed to interdict a portion of the Ho Chi Minh Trail, the supply route for the People's Army of Vietnam (PAVN) in southeastern Laos. Both sides claimed victory, but it is generally acknowledged that the PAVN won the battle.

The Cambodian Incursion (April 29–July 22, 1970) to disrupt PAVN supply operations in Cambodia, despite the domestic political fallout in the United States, was deemed a success by President Richard Nixon, as well as by the commander of Miltary Assitance Command Vietnam (MACV), General Creighton Abrams. In late 1970, a similar operation was proposed for southeastern Laos, near the DMZ. In December, President Nixon gave his consent to the operation, and planning began for a joint ARVN-MACV cross-border attack. However, the Cooper-Church Amendment passed and signed into law on December 22, forbid U.S. ground forces from operating in Laos and Cambodia, but it did allow the United States to provide air and indirect fire support to ARVN forces. The plan then became an ARVN operation backed by U.S. air and artillery support.

The plan called for the 1st ARVN Corps to attack along Route 9 to seize Base Area 604 near the abandoned village of Tchepone. After seizing Base Area 604, the ARVN forces would remain in the area until the start of the rainy season, interdicting the Ho Chi Minh Trail and destroying other PAVN supply bases in the area. To accomplish the mission, the 1st ARVN Corps would insert airborne and ranger units in a series of blocking positions to protect the right flank of the main armor force attacking along Route 9. At the same time, units from the ARVN 1st Infantry Division would be airlifted into blocking positions along an escarpment on the left flank of Route 9. Then the armored formation would drive directly to Tchepone, where the Corps would consolidate and continue operations in the area.

Even though U.S. ground forces could not enter Laos, Operation Dewey Canyon II called for a brigade from the U.S. 5th Infantry Division (ID) to clear routes up to the border and reoccupy the fire base at Khe Sanh to assist and provide indirect fire support to the 1st ARVN Corps units as they crossed the border. Also, the U.S. 101st Airborne Division would provide aviation support to the 1st ARVN Corps. The helicopters from the aviation brigade of the 101st were augmented by fixed-wing aircraft from the USAF and USN. Operation Dewey Canyon II began on January 30, and within a week, the 1st Brigade of the U.S. 1st ID seized Khe Sanh and cleared the routes to the Laotian border. The route was clear for the 1st ARVN Corps to begin Lam Son 719 on February 8.

After the success of the Cambodian Incursion the previous year, the PAVN anticipated that the U.S.-backed ARVN forces might try a similar operation on Laos. To counter any ARVN attack, the PAVN activated 70B Corps and assigned the 304th, 308th, and 320th divisions, augmented with armor, artillery, engineers, and antiaircraft units, to the vicinity of Base Area 604. These divisions would prove critical in the upcoming battle. However, when the battle commenced, there were only approximately 10,000 PAVN soldiers in the immediate area of Tchepone. Roughly half were combat soldiers, and the remainder were support troops operating the supply base.

THE BATTLE

The ARVN advance on February 8 was preceded by a massive artillery bombardment that included eleven B52 Stratofortresses bombing in the tactical role. After the fires lifted, the lead elements of the ARVN armored brigade crossed the Laotian border along Route 9. Simultaneously, the first units of ARVN Rangers were air-landed into their blocking positions north of Route 9, and units of the ARVN 1st Division were doing the same south of Route 9. Artillery was airlifted into position once the infantry had established their fire bases.

For the first few days, ground fighting had been relatively light as the PAVN took time to analyze the extent and direction of the ARVN attack. In the air, though, it was a different story. PAVN antiaircraft gunners brought down seven helicopters and damaged several more. Still, the ARVN and MACV commanders were pleased with the success of the 1st ARVN Corps on the first day. However, it did not take long for the situation to change.

For some reason, the advance of the armored column slowed, and the tankers did not link up with the paratroopers at Ban Dong, halfway to Tchepone, until February 10. At the time of the linkup, there were approximately 10,000 ARVN soldiers in Laos. Along with Ban Dong, the ARVN occupied ten blocking positions protecting Route 9. After the linkup, the armored column moved about 5 kilometers outside of Ban Dong and halted. The commander of the column was waiting for orders from General Lam before continuing, so they waited along Route 9 for orders that were not forthcoming. Unknown to the armored column, other intrigues were taking place behind the scenes.

Following a series of intense firefights between the ARVN and PAVN the previous days, the president of South Vietnam, Nguyen Van Thieu, flew out to the 1st Corps headquarters to confer with General Lam. Thieu, concerned that a large number of casualties could affect the upcoming election, warned Lam to be cautious. Before he left, he told Lam to call off the operation if his casualties exceeded 3,000. Meanwhile, in the United States, defense secretary Melvin Laird told reporters that the halt was merely a pause in order to assess the enemies' reaction to the incursion.

The PAVN reaction was slow as the 70B Corps commander evaluated whether the attack was the main effort or a diversion. However, after determining that Lam's attack was the main effort, the PAVN reacted quickly. Aided by the ARVN halt, the PAVN moved the 308th Division into the area from the north, and the 2nd Division moved to Tchepone from the south. More ominously, they moved more antiaircraft guns into the hills around the ARVN corps.

With the ARVN stalled and fresh reinforcements arriving, the initiative shifted to the PAVN. They began their counterattack by putting pressure on both flanks. In the north, the PAVN would isolate the individual fire bases from aerial support with antiaircraft fire. Then they would overwhelm the defenders with indirect fire before overrunning the ARVN outpost with ground forces. All the while, they maintained pressure on the southern flank. The ARVN's position in Laos was becoming tenuous.

On February 19, President Thieu revisited Lam. This time, Lam painted a bleak picture, emphasizing the continuous flow of PAVN reinforcements into the area. Lam warned the president that it would be risky to continue the advance toward Tchepone. Before he left, Thieu advised Lam that he should take his time and perhaps shift his effort to the southwest. Meanwhile, desperate fighting continued on the flanks of the 1st ARVN Corps.

By the end of February, the PAVN had overrun several of the fire bases and was heavily engaged with the 1st ARVN Corps when Thieu intervened once more. This time, he suggested that Lam conduct an airmobile operation to seize Tchepone. Thieu believed that seizing Tchepone would give him enough political cover to declare the operation a success before withdrawing Lam's corps back to South Vietnam. The plan called for elements of the 1st Division to be inserted into a series of landing zones (LZs), culminating in the occupation of Tchepone. The assault would be the largest airmobile operation for the U.S. army during the war.

The attack began on March 3 with the insertion of elements of the 3rd Battalion 1st Infantry Regiment into LZ Lolo. All went well with the first lift, but the second lift ran into the alerted PAVN air defenses. By the end of the day, LZ Lolo was secured, but the eleven helicopters were lost and forty-four damaged in the process. It was not an auspicious beginning to the operation. Two days later, elements of the 2nd Regiment were airlifted into LZ Sophia, 4.5 kilometers southeast of Tchepone. However, another nine helicopters were lost, and the remainder incurred varying degrees of damage. Despite the loss of so many helicopters, the ARVN was setting the stage for the final assault on Tchepone.

On March 6, another 5,000 ARVN soldiers from the 2nd Regiment landed on LZ Hope. The next day, the ARVN occupied Tchepone, inflicting significant casualties on the PAVN as well as disrupting their supply operations in the area. The 1st ARVN Corps had achieved its objective, and Thieu could claim the operation as a success. Thieu promptly ordered the withdrawal of Lam's corps. Unfortunately for the ARVN, the PAVN had moved over 60,000 soldiers, along with two tank regiments and nineteen antiaircraft battalions, into the area, hoping to cut off the 1st Corps' retreat.

A withdrawal under contact is one of the most challenging operations for an army to execute. There is always the risk that an orderly retreat will turn into a rout and an unmitigated disaster. On March 9, the units of 1st Corps began withdrawing from Laos. The PAVN kept up the pressure on the retreating South Vietnamese soldiers. On the flanks, the fire bases fell one by one. The PAVN overran some, while in others, the defenders were able to fight their way out and continue their retreat. Route 9 quickly became clogged with destroyed or abandoned vehicles as the battered corps found its way back to the border. Some units panicked, while others fought with distinction; regardless, the retreat from Laos could not be considered a bright spot for the South Vietnamese army. On March 25, the last 1st Corps unit left Laos, and Lam Son 719 was over.

CONCLUSION

Lam Son 719 lasted forty-five days, and both sides claimed victory. President Thieu called it "the biggest victory ever," while President Nixon used the battle to declare that "Vietnamization has succeeded." Neither president was correct. Some estimates claim that as much as half of the PAVN forces became casualties, and over 7,000 of the 1st ARVN Corps were killed, wounded, missing, or captured. The ARVN lost fifty-four tanks, ninety-six artillery pieces, and nearly 300 other vehicles. Nevertheless, the most significant figure was in rotary-wing aircraft losses: Combined, the U.S. army and ARVN lost 168 helicopters altogether and 618 were damaged, many beyond repair.

However, the biggest loser was the concept of Vietnamization (Nixon's optimism notwithstanding). Lam Son 719 made it evident that the ARVN was not ready to conduct operations on its own, without significant American support. Nonetheless, the United States was committed to withdrawing its forces from South Vietnam. Despite its losses, North Vietnam declared victory. For a time, the ARVN's operations disrupted the PAVN's supplies, but this only delayed their upcoming 1972 offensive. After Lam Son 719, the strategic initiative was in the hands of Hanoi.

Further Reading

Sander, Robert D. *Invasion of Laos, 1971: Lam Son 719.* Norman: University of Oklahoma Press, 2014.

West, Andrew A. *Vietnam's Forgotten Army: Heroism and Betrayal in the ARVN.* New York: New York University Press, 2008.

Willbanks, James H. *Abandoning Vietnam: How America Left and South Vietnam Lost Its War.* Lawrence: University Press of Kansas, 2004.

Willbanks, James H. *A Raid Too Far: Operation Lam Son 719 and Vietnamization in Laos.* College Station: Texas A&M University Press, 2014.

98. 1973 Arab-Israeli War–Sinai (Yom Kippur War)

Date: October 6–25, 1973
Location: Sinai Desert

OPPONENTS

1. Egypt

Commanders: President Anwar Sadat and General Ahmad Ismail Ali

2. Israel

Commanders: Prime Minister Golda Meir, Defense Minister Moshe Dayan, and

General David Elazar

BACKGROUND

In 1967, Israel defeated the combined forces of Egypt, Syria, and Jordan in six days. This stunning victory shocked the world and gave the Israelis an overweening sense of superiority. They believed that it would take a generation from the Arab armies to recover from their defeat. In the meantime, the Israeli Defense Force (IDF) would only improve and would handily defeat any Arab challenge.

Three pillars—intelligence, air power, and armor (i.e., tanks)—supported Israel's confidence. The Israeli intelligence community assured the politicians that they could provide forty-eight hours' notice of an impending Arab attack. By 1973, the Israelis had come to expect that the Israeli Air Force (IAF) could quickly gain air superiority and then turn to support the army. Finally, convinced that the tank was the decisive weapon in desert warfare; the Israeli army concentrated on its armor forces. Anwar Sadat and the Egyptian armed forces' preparations would undermine each of these pillars and exploit the Israelis' hubris.

Following Gamal Nasser's death in 1971, Anwar Sadat became the third president of Egypt. Sadat viewed the 1967 defeat as a temporary setback, but he also

OCTOBER WAR, 1973

Legend:
- ---- De-facto frontiers of Israel, June 11, 1967–Oct 6, 1973
- ⊔⊔⊔⊔ Deepest penetration of Arab forces, Oct 6–8
- ▨ Furthest limits of Israeli counterattacks, Oct 8–24
- ➡ Soviet arms supplies, Oct 8–24
- ➡ U.S. arms supplies, Oct 12–24
- ➡ Other Arab contributions
- ✸ Towns and ports bombarded by Israeli forces

TURKEY

SYRIA

Mint al Bayda
Latakia
Baniyas
Tartus
Homs

CYPRUS

15,000 Syrian Arabs leave area of new Israeli occupation

LEBANON

Mediterranean Sea

Beirut

Damascus

Jebel Baruch

Force from Iraq

Naifa

Token force of men and vehicles from Kuwait

Lod

Ashdod

Amman

Gaza

Token force of men and vehicles from Saudi Arabia

Dead Sea

Damietta

Port Said

Rosetta

Alexandria

El Arish

NEGEV

Suez Canal

Ismailia

JORDAN

1,500 troops

Algerian troops

Cairo

Nile R.

Akaba

EGYPT

Ras Zafarana

SINAI

SAUDI ARABIA

Forces from Iraq

Ras Gharib

0   30   60 mi
0   30   60 km

Red Sea

understood the weaknesses of the Egyptian armed forces. Distrusting the Soviet Union, Sadat hoped to draw closer to the United States, and he threw out the Soviet advisors in 1972. The United States, already involved in getting out of Vietnam, did not react to Sadat's move, and he returned to the Soviets for aid in 1973. At the same time, Sadat concluded that only a military operation would wake up not only the Israelis, but also both superpowers, to the problems in the Middle East. In early 1972, Sadat outlined his plans for a limited war.

The Egyptians sought asymmetrical responses to overcome the Israeli superiority. Sadat was aware that the Egyptian air force would not be able to challenge the IAF anytime soon, so he invested in a sophisticated Soviet air defense system to provide air protection to his ground forces. To overcome the IDF's armor superiority, the Egyptian army equipped its infantry with Soviet man-pack Sagger antitank guided missiles (ATGMs). Finally, to fool the Israeli intelligence community, the Egyptian army ran numerous exercises along the canal and portrayed an air of normalcy in the days leading up to the attack. He also negotiated with Hafez al-Assad, the president of Syria, to attack the Golan Heights at the same time to dilute the Israeli response further.

Along the Suez Canal, the Israelis built the Bar Lev Line, a formidable series of interlocking fortifications backed up by armor. In front of the fortifications, was a sixty- to eighty-foot-tall sand wall that ran the length of the canal. Israeli planners assumed that it would take the Egyptians twenty-four to forty-eight hours to breach this sand wall and establish their bridgeheads. Next was a series of forts to a depth of thirty to forty kilometers. A supporting armor division would seal off any penetration by the Egyptians. An added feature was an underwater pipe system to pump crude oil into the canal, to be set on fire. As in the Sinai, the IDF built a series of fortifications along the Golan Heights to thwart any Syrian attack. Backing up these forts was another armored division. These defenses were deemed adequate to thwart any Arab attack once they were fully manned, given a forty-eight-hour warning, as was expected.

The crossing of the Suez Canal by Israeli troops in 1973's Yom Kippur War, Israel's version of Pearl Harbor. (AFP/Getty Images)

The Egyptians planned to establish bridgeheads quickly along the east bank of the Suez Canal by using water cannon mounted on rafts to break down the sand wall. Egyptian testing found that this technique would cut the time needed to emplace the bridges to two hours, significantly reducing the time Israelis expected it would take. Then the Egyptian army would advance up to ten miles into the Sinai. The infantry, with their Sagger ATGMs, would ambush the expected Israeli counterattack with tanks. After four to five days, the Egyptians would decide whether to continue the attack to the key passes deeper in the Sinai. The initial limit of advance was set to keep the Egyptian forces under the Air Defense Artillery (ADA) umbrella of the fixed surface-to-air missile (SAM) sites on the Egyptian side of the canal.

The date for the attack was set for October 6, during the holiest of Jewish holidays, and that became the name of the war—Yom Kippur. In the weeks leading up to the war, the Egyptians and Syrians ran exercises along their respective fronts. They also called up reserves and began concentrating more forces near their borders with Israel. These moves concerned Israeli intelligence, but they informed the Israeli prime minister, Golda Meir, that neither country was ready to attack Israel. However, the indicators of an imminent Arab attack continued to build, and on the night of October 5–6, Israeli intelligence presented tangible evidence to the prime minister. Meir decided on a partial call-up of the reserves and approved moving another armored brigade to the Golan Heights. The call-up went into effect just hours before the war began.

THE BATTLE

On the west bank of the Suez Canal, the Egyptians amassed 100,000 soldiers, nearly 1,400 tanks, and 2,000 artillery pieces for the initial assault. Facing them was the 450 soldiers of the Jerusalem Brigade, manning the sixteen forts of the Bar Lev Line. At 2:05 p.m. on October 6, the attack began with numerous Egyptian airstrikes and a nearly hour-long artillery barrage along the Suez Canal. Under cover of the barrage, the initial invasion force began crossing the canal in rubber boats, along with the water cannon. Within two hours, the water cannon breached the sand wall, and the Egyptian engineers began emplacing ten bridges and another seven decoy bridges. The entire operation went so smoothly that by dusk 30,000 soldiers were on the west bank and by 10 p.m., the first tanks were crossing the bridges. It would take only twenty-four hours for the Egyptians to have all the bridges, along with fifty ferries, fully operational. By the end of the next day, the Egyptian army had penetrated the Bar Lev Line and advanced up to six miles into the Sinai. The only Egyptian failure was the commando operation to disrupt Israeli reinforcements; very few of the commando teams achieved their objectives.

Even though the speed of the Egyptian assault surprised the Israelis, they did not panic. They were sure that the IAF and the armored brigades would quickly turn the tide in the IDF's favor. The IAF launched a few successful attacks on Egyptian airfields; however, when they turned to support the ground forces, the pilots ran into the Egyptian SAM umbrella and suffered unacceptably heavy losses. The

IAF would not be able to provide the expected support until they could figure out how to neutralize the Egyptian air defenses. Meanwhile, on the ground, the armored brigades positioned behind the Bar Lev line moved forward, according to plan, to support the defenses. The confident Israeli tankers as they raced to the canal were unaware of the Egyptian ATGM teams waiting to ambush them. Without infantry support to clear out the ATGM teams, the tankers pulled back. Despite these setbacks, the Israeli political and military leaders were still confident in their ability to defeat the Egyptian within a matter of days.

By October 9, the front line had stabilized, and for the next few days, neither side made any large-scale attacks. The Egyptians tried to attack to the south; however, when the force left the protection of their air defenses, they were set upon by the IAF and suffered heavy losses before withdrawing. Still, Sadat's generals were pleased with the results so far and asked about advancing to the passes. Sadat was vehemently opposed to the idea. The amount of territory seized did not matter to him; his eyes were on a larger strategic prize. Also, he realized if the Egyptians left their ADA umbrella, the IAF would wreak havoc on his exposed soldiers. However, events on the Golan Heights were about to throw Sadat's plans into disarray.

After a few desperate days facing the Syrians on the Golan Heights, the IDF had stabilized the situation and were beginning to counterattack. The Israelis pushed the Syrian army off the Golan Heights and were threatening Damascus. Before they halted, the IDF was in artillery range of the Syrian capital. The Syrians called on Sadat to resume his offensive in order to relieve some of the pressure on them. Sadat understood he could not leave his ally in the lurch and still maintain credibility in the Arab world. Against his better judgment, Sadat reluctantly agreed to resume the attack.

However, by this time, Sadat's generals believed that the moment to drive to the passes had passed, so they cautioned against leaving their defensive positions. Sadat dismissed their concerns and ordered the attack for October 13. After further discussions among his advisors, Sadat agreed to postpone the attack until October 14. At 6:30 a.m., the Egyptian army attacked along four axes. This time it was the Israelis who were waiting, in defensive positions equipped with American-made tube-launched, optically tracked, and wire-guided antitank missiles. Within hours, the Egyptians lost 250 tanks and were pulling back to their defensive positions. Bolstered by their success, the Israelis saw an opportunity to turn the tables on the Egyptians.

The IDF planned to break through to the canal north of the Great Bitter Lake. Assisted by an airborne brigade, the 143rd Armored Division would seize both banks. Two more armored divisions would exploit the crossing to destroy the Egyptian ADA sites before turning south to encircle Egypt's Third Army. Despite the capability and aggressiveness, the Egyptians had demonstrated since October 6; the Israelis optimistically believed that the crossing would take no more than forty-eight hours. The fighting ability of the Egyptians would surprise the Israelis once more.

The attack began with a massive artillery barrage at 5 p.m. on October 15. The Israelis seized the crossing sites easily enough, but the Egyptians put up a stiffer defense than anticipated around the crossing sites. For several days, the Egyptian and Israeli tankers engaged in a bloody, close-quarters fight in an area known as Chinese Farm. One Israeli brigade lost fifty-six tanks in the first twelve hours. There was rising concern among the Israelis that the force on the west bank might be cut off. However, despite their heroic efforts, the fighting was wearing down the Egyptian army. In addition to the emotional drain, they were significantly down in tanks, so they began withdrawing from the Chinese Farm area.

Even though the Egyptians' stout defense threw off the IDF's timetable, they wasted little time exploiting this new opportunity; they rushed even more units across the canal. Some moved farther west to attack Egyptian ADA sites, creating a gap in the coverage by the IAF, while others turned south toward Suez City to encircle the Third Army. Despite the threat that the Israeli advance posed, Sadat, to the chagrin of his generals, refused to withdraw any troops from the east bank. Meanwhile, events behind the scenes were in motion that would affect the ultimate outcome.

On October 17, the oil-producing states not only raised the price of oil 70 percent, but they also instituted an oil embargo on the West. Nonetheless, the United States not only increased aid to Israel, but also began negotiations over putting a cease-fire in place. Sadat indicated to his subordinates that he would be amenable to a cease-fire.

Reluctantly, the Israelis accepted the cease-fire, which would go into effect on October 22. However, many of the Israeli commanders were disappointed that they had not completed the encirclement of the Third Army; they wanted to seize Suez City before the cease-fire took place. Looking for any excuse to resume their attack, they reported that the Egyptians had violated the cease-fire and received permission to advance. Nonetheless, the Egyptians continued to show their new mettle, and the Israelis failed to occupy Suez City.

At the same time, the Soviet Union alerted seven airborne divisions and took further actions to support their ally. The United States responded by going to DEFCON III for the first time since the Cuban Missile Crisis in 1962. The superpowers were on the brink of going to war. However, rather than escalate the situation, the Soviet Union backed down, easing the international crisis.

On October 25, the exhausted Egyptians and Israelis accepted the cease-fire. It would take many more months of negotiations before the Israelis withdrew and the Egyptian Third Army was relieved, but the fighting was finally over.

CONCLUSION

In the end, the Israelis won another brilliant tactical and operational victory over its Arab opponents. Nonetheless, the IDF came away feeling shocked at how close they had come to defeat. The Egyptian armed forces successfully undermined the three pillars upon which the Israeli defense rested. They spoofed the Israeli intelligence community through a series of ruses. The sophisticated air defense system that the Egyptians set up along the canal prevented the IAF from carrying out its air superiority mission. Armed with large numbers of inexpensive antitank missiles, the Egyptians blunted the centerpiece of the Israeli ground forces—their armored brigades. All three approaches set the IDF back on its heels until it recovered tactically and operationally, but nations do not win wars at those levels.

Strategically, Anwar Sadat achieved all his goals. His forces inflicted substantial damage on the IDF, the Egyptian army boosted Arab confidence by demonstrating that the Israelis were not invincible, and he forced the Western powers to reengage in the Middle East. The Yom Kippur War also energized the peace process, with the Egyptians negotiating from a position of strength and respect; they eventually won back the Sinai, but they also earned the enmity of the rest of the Arab world. For his actions, Anwar Sadat was assassinated by members of the Egyptian Islamic Jihad terrorist group, on October 6, 1981, during a parade commemorating the eighth anniversary of the crossing.

Further Reading

Blum, Howard. *The Eve of Destruction: The Untold Story of the Yom Kippur War*. New York: HarperCollins, 2003.

Daigle, Craig. *The Limits of Détente: The United States, the Soviet Union, the Arab-Israeli Conflict, 1969–1973*. New Haven, CT: Yale University Press, 2012.

Even, Jacob, and Simcha B. Maoz. *At the Decisive Point in the Sinai: Generalship in the Yom Kippur War*. Lexington: University Press of Kentucky, 2017.

Rabinovich, Abraham. *The Yom Kippur War: The Epic Encounter that Transformed the Middle East*. New York: Schocken Books, 2004.

99. Iran–Iraq War: The First Gulf War

Date: 1980–1988
Location: Iranian-Iraqi border

OPPONENTS

1. Iraq

Commander: Saddam Hussein

2. Iran

Commanders: Ayatollah Khomeini and various others

BACKGROUND

When President Saddam Hussein decided to invade Iran (also known as Persia) to seize territory in what he thought would be a short, cheap war, he had no intention of launching an eight-year conflict that threatened his very hold on power in Iraq and caused the deaths of millions. Iran's ongoing Islamic Revolution and impasse with the United States over the fate of American hostages seemed to offer an opportunity for an easy land grab. While Iran focused on "The Great Satan," Saddam reasoned, he could come in through the back door and gain some easy pickings from what he saw as Iran's military and economic weaknesses. Also, he figured that the chief supporters for his own military, France and the Soviet Union, would undoubtedly continue to support him in spite of what the world would

Iran–Iraq War, 1980–1988

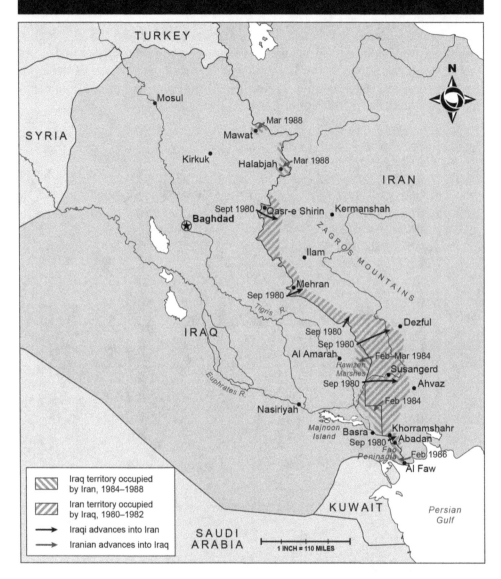

probably condemn as an unwarranted aggression. Saddam acted as the initial agent that caused the Iran–Iraq war in the 1980s to turn into a military disaster for both sides. Until the U.S. invasion of Iraq in 2003, this would prove to be the longest and most destructive Middle Eastern war in modern history.

The animus between the cultures of Iran and Iraq predated the actual conflict. Persian Iran had been less touched by European colonialism than Mesopotamian Iraq, which had long been a Turkish territory and then entered colonial status after World War I under the British Empire. Persia found itself between Britain and its threatening Russian neighbor to the north (which became the Soviet Union) and tended to align with Britain, but the fundamental racial and religious animosities between Sunni Arabs and Shi'a Persians remained. Nonetheless, the role of two outsized personalities contributed most to the outbreak of war—Saddam and Supreme Ayatollah Iman Ruhollah Khomeini.

The key geographic cause of the conflict was the longstanding insecurity of Iraq over the defensibility of its port of Basra, on the Shatt al-Arab waterway which gave it access to the sea and the closeness of Baghdad to the Iranian border, with no natural defenses. However, the navigation and control of the Shatt al-Arab were the primary *casus belli*. Saddam wanted to secure control of this waterway, as well as perhaps add the key ports that Iran used at Khorramshahr and Abadan to his own territory. Naturally, Iran had no intention of losing its key ports or ceding any control of the waterway to Iraq. Under the shah, Iran built up its navy and air force in the 1970s, with U.S. assistance, to resist the claims of Iran's new Ba'athist government under Saddam. However, with the loss of U.S. support after the fall of the shah and seizure of the U.S. embassy, it appeared to Saddam that the threat posed by Iran to resist its claims were weakened and would only become more so.

THE COURSE OF THE WAR

The border clashes that caused Saddam to invade began mostly in the north, where both Iraq and Iran were using the Kurds as proxies to attack each other, as well as a way to weaken the Kurds. Eventually, Iraqi warplanes attacked Iranian villages in June 1979. Both nations used proxies in each other's territories to try to destabilize the other, but Iran's Iraqi Shi'a allies in southern Iraq posed the more severe threat. To the Iraqi leadership, it appeared that Khomeini was trying to export his revolution to Iraq. They began to plan actively for a war that would eliminate this threat, seize the key oil province of Khuzestan from Iran, and replace the fanatical Shi'a regime in Tehran with a less-threatening secular government. Accomplishing these goals would make Iraq *the* regional power in the Persian Gulf and probably catapult it into the leadership of the Arab world that opposed Israel.

On September 22, 1980, Saddam launched his invasion of Iran with a surprise Pearl Harbor–style air attack intended to catch both Iranian aircraft and troops unprepared. It failed, doing minimal damage to both Iran's army and dispersed air forces. On land, Saddam's attacks occurred in two areas along the central border, primarily as a means to preempt an Iranian counterstrike at Baghdad and in the south. The southern invasion consisted of five divisions against one weak Iranian division, and initially, the Iraqis faced little opposition, seizing large chunks of Iranian territory. By the end of the first week of fighting, the Iraqis stood poised to seize both Abadan and Khorramshahr, but then they stopped to bring up their artillery and let their logistics catch up. That gave the Iranians enough time to contest further advances, and thus the first phase of the war, Iraq's conquest, came to a halt, and the war settled into the attritional contest that it would assume for the rest of the combat.

After Iraq's initial gambit, which some had believed would cause the regime in Tehran to collapse, the war settled into a grind. Saddam's thrust had failed much as the one made by Adolf Hitler had, almost forty years earlier in the Soviet Union. The war's second phase involved Iran's reclamation of its lost territory. With mobilized reserves and fanatical (albeit ill-trained) volunteers and Revolutionary Guards, Iran launched a series of counterattacks. Khorramshahr was effectively destroyed in the battle to push the Iraqis from their small footholds in the city. Khomeini turned the war into a holy crusade as a means to consolidate power and openly export his revolution to the rest of the Islamic world. Iraq had given him that opportunity. It also allowed him to unite Iranians in the cause, as had his earlier seizure of the U.S. embassy and hostages. Iran would punish Saddam Hussein and show him the vengeance of God, as administered by divine will through Ayatollah Khomeini.

Despite Iranian success elsewhere in reclaiming its lost territory, it was not until May 1982 that over 150,000 troops were concentrated around Khorramshahr. A monthlong battle occurred around the city and resulted in the defeat of the Iraqi forces, which retreated with heavy losses across the Shatt al-Arab into prewar Iraq territory. The second phase of the war had ended, but Khomeini, as discussed, had broadened the scope of the war and prepared to launch a new phase aimed at nothing less than the overthrow of Saddam's regime and "liberation" of Iraq. Even so, Iraq still controlled about 500 square kilometers of Iranian prewar territory farther north that protected the approaches to Baghdad. This too would have to be reconquered. While all this occurred, the Iranians and Iraqis attacked each other's oil assets and Iran achieved a notable diplomatic success when Syria cut the flow of Iraqi oil by pipeline through its territory. By 1982, most of the lost Iranian territory had been retaken.

Phase three of the war, which lasted until 1984, consisted of Iran's attempts to conquer Iraq. It might be considered among the most bloody and wasteful years of the war. It began in the summer of 1982 with the so-called Ramadan Offensive. Iran employed "human wave" tactics (i.e., mass assaults by infantry) to try to overwhelm Iraqi defenses due to its paucity of firepower and mechanized equipment. More and more, it was having difficulty with spare parts for its Western equipment, so it had to rely on sheer quantity, even using children in its wave attacks, sometimes through minefields. Iraq hung on, grimly determined to fight, although its chief problems were financial and economic.

Neither side seemed to have enough power to land a knockout blow against the other. Iraq was ready to accept a cease-fire, but the fanatics in Tehran refused to negotiate, and this drove the Gulf states into supporting Iraq. The United States and most Western powers tacitly supported the so-called unsavory regime in Baghdad as well. With the Gulf states throwing their financial support behind Saddam, the war shifted entirely to an attrition-based model that looked a lot like World War I, with trenches, stable fronts, and increasingly, attacks on neutrals and civilian populations. It also came to include chemical warfare, a form of war not in widespread use and considered to be obsolete or too illegitimate to use. Saddam in particular attacked Iranian cities with long-range missiles and used chemical weapons such as mustard gas at the front.

Iran did not employ chemical weapons (contrary to Saddam's claims), but it did expand the war to include attacks on third-party neutral shipping of the Gulf

Cooperation Council states supporting Saddam. This became the infamous "tanker war" in the Persian Gulf, in which oil tanker ships became targets. Iraq had been the first to employ this tactic in the war, although in a limited fashion. Now Iran employed this tactic on a wide scale and also began mining the Strait of Hormuz and other waters in the Gulf. Tit for tat occurred, and the United States entered the war in a limited fashion to protect the Kuwaiti ships, reflagging them with American identities and then engaging in limited naval operations to protect them. The broadening of the war by Iran backfired, causing the U.S. entry to support the Gulf Cooperation Council states, and this blunted the Iranian hope that it could put pressure on Iraq by attacking its supporters.

Iran turned again to land offensives in the final phase of the war, but the protracted fighting, over a million combat deaths, attacks on the cities, and failure to overthrow Saddam undermined support for the conflict. The only thing keeping the war going was the intransigence of Iran's supreme leaders, especially Khomeini. Iraq's attacks on the civilian population, and his use of poison gas, had shaken the resolve of even the hard-nosed Khomeini and his most intransigent supporters, such as Akbar Rafsanjani. The only holdouts were in the Iranian Revolutionary Guard, who were willing to fight to the last man, woman, and child. When they reported in 1988 that they needed at least another five years to overthrow Saddam, Khomeini finally responded to the various peace overtures, overruling the Revolutionary Guard's leadership.

THE COST

The war proved an unmitigated disaster for both sides. Between them, Iran and Iraq saw between 2 and 3 million in combat deaths, with Iran losing almost twice as many as Iraq. The wounded included another 1.5 to 2 million. Another 2.5 million became refugees (and most of these were Iranians). In terms of financial cost, both nations suffered heavily, but Iraq suffered more, with $160 billion, compared to $70 billion for Iran. The opportunity cost—the income that both nations may have generated via development in peacetime had there been no war—is incalculable.

The follow-on consequences are scarcely less disastrous. Saddam, emboldened after surviving this life-and-death struggle, turned on his erstwhile ally, Kuwait, thus drawing the United States further into the politics of the region in 1991 and causing a U.S. military commitment that has only grown over the years into the current, interminable "war on terror." The great irony is that in invading Kuwait, Saddam opened the door for the United States to eventually accomplish Khomeini's most fervent goal—the overthrow of Saddam's Ba'athist dictatorship and the installation of a pro-Iranian regime in Baghdad.

Further Reading

Cordesman, Anthony H., and Abraham R. Wagner. *The Lessons of Modern War, Volume II: The Iran-Iraq War.* San Francisco: Westview Press, 1980.

Takeyh, Ray. "The Iran-Iraq War: A Reassessment." *Middle East Journal*, 64(3) (Summer 2010): 365–383.

100. Iraqi Freedom

Date: March 2003–June 2014
Location: Iraq

OPPONENTS

1. American coalition/Iraqi National Security Forces (after 2004), including the Kurdish Peshmerga

   Commanders: General Tommy Franks and various others

2. Iraq/insurgents

   Commanders: Saddam Hussein and various others.

3. The Islamic State (ISIS, or *Daesh*)

   Commander: Abu Bakr al-Baghdadi

BACKGROUND

Readers may find it odd that this collection of military disasters closes with the U.S. invasion and subsequent lengthy involvement in Iraq. Many observers (although not this author) regard that conflict as a victory, if not in 2003, then certainly in the so-called postsurge period that resulted in the withdrawal of all but a token U.S. military presence in 2011 under President Barack Obama. However, history, and military history in particular, has a way of punishing premature declarations of victory and their close companion, national hubris, and such was the case in Iraq.

The causes of the U.S. invasion and change of the Iraqi regime of the ruthless dictator Saddam Hussein are not well known; they had their roots in the victory of the American-led coalition and the liberation of Kuwait in 1991. This victory became tarnished over time by continued U.S. involvement in the region with the goals of containing the regime of Saddam Hussein and the protection of the Kurdish minority in the north, as well as the imposition of no-fly zones in northern and southern Iraq to enforce ongoing sanctions by the United Nations. These sanctions were intended, above all, to constrain and ultimately eliminate Saddam's ability to build and use weapons of mass destruction (WMDs)—chemical, biological, and nuclear. By the time President George W. Bush occupied the White House, this U.S. air campaign had been going on for almost ten years as Operations NORTHERN and SOUTHERN WATCH, with occasional outbursts of violent strikes such as DESERT FOX (1998). Cracks had opened in the consolidated front that the United States was trying to maintain against Saddam rebuilding his capabilities, especially with France and Russia; and the United States found itself in a long-term commitment with seemingly no end. This changed with the 9/11 terror attacks on the United States in 2001 against the World Trade Center and Pentagon.

The iconic photograph of the toppling of the statue of Saddam Hussein in 2003, when many presumed the United States and its allies had achieved victory. The war continued another eight years and left Iraq unprepared to fight ISIS terrorists. (Trinity Mirror/Mirrorpix/Alamy Stock Photo)

THE INVASION

In the post-9/11 environment, a group of so-called neocon policymakers came to the fore, led ostensibly by two former U.S. secretaries of defense: Vice President Dick Cheney and Donald Rumsfeld, who had become secretary of defense for a second time. They were both well apprised of the Iraq "problem" and had become critics of George H. W. Bush administration's handling of the First Gulf War in 1991. They, and others, believed that the elder Bush and General Colin Powell had ended the war against Iraq too early, and that they should have pressed on to Baghdad to get rid of Saddam and his troublesome regime entirely. Now Osama bin Laden and his terrorist cadres in al-Qaeda had given them a *casus belli* to take care of their unfinished business in Iraq. Before Operation ENDURING FREEDOM, the campaign to destroy al-Qaeda, bin Laden, and its Taliban protectors in Afghanistan, had even been completed, they started planning for military operations against Iraq, with the purpose of overthrowing Saddam and solving that problem once and for all.

Rumsfeld, in particular, used his control of various intelligence reports and organizations to skew the intelligence to construct a threat—namely, that terrorists harbored by Iraq might leverage the nation's still-functioning WMD program to wage more attacks on the United States. At the same time, they took advantage of a credulous president and the warlike public mood to push a policy in the United Nations for the sanctioned use of force against Iraq, and a buildup began of ground and air forces in the Persian Gulf at the numerous U.S. bases there. At the same time, the air force commander in the Central Command region convinced his commander and Rumsfeld to begin a much broader air campaign against Iraq, especially against WMD and air defense targets. This campaign—SOUTHERN FOCUS—was opaque to the American public and to the world, and it managed to neutralize the feeble Iraqi air defenses in place, as well as to effectively ensure that Iraq's ability to build and employ WMD against U.S. ground forces was severely curtailed, if not eliminated. None of this was reported at the time—and certainly not to Secretary of State Colin Powell, who made a very public case for the invasion of Iraq on American television using incomplete intelligence.

By early 2003, the forces were in place, and by March, the air campaign was believed to have achieved all the objectives necessary to launch an offensive into Iraq with the purpose of destroying the Iraqi military, principally the Republican Guard, and then driving on Baghdad to displace Saddam. Operation IRAQI FREEDOM began on March 19, 2003, with attacks by both ground and air forces, including Tomahawk cruise missiles. It was hoped, in a reflection of the theories of air power evangelist John Warden, that Saddam might be killed at the outset by surgical air strikes, but these failed to kill him or any of the senior leadership.

In the meantime, Army general Tommy Franks sent the armored Vth Corps, commanded by Lieutenant General William S. Wallace and augmented by the First Marine Division under Major General Jim "Mad Dog" Mattis, straight toward Baghdad, principally through the Karbala gap, the historic invasion route to the city. This campaign was short, violent, and ultimately successful. By early April, U.S. mechanized forces had reached the center of Baghdad in the so-called Thunder Run, and the government effectively collapsed, although Saddam Hussein and his adult sons escaped.

At the last moment, another offensive from Turkey through northern Iraq, designed to link up with autonomous Kurdish forces in the north, was derailed when the government of Turkey refused to allow the 4th U.S. Infantry Division to pass through its territory. This division was rerouted through the Persian Gulf into the theater but arrived only after Saddam Hussein and his sons had fled Baghdad. Troubling signs emerged during the conventional military operations, with Saddam's irregular Fedayeen Saddam attacking the coalition's lines of communication, which prompted Wallace to state that the enemy he found most difficult were not "the enemy we war gamed against." Nonetheless, American and coalition casualties were relatively light in this phase of the war. On May 1, 2003, President Bush announced major combat operations to be complete (in the "Mission Accomplished" speech). As it turned out, the Americans had planned for everything except the peace.

THE INSURGENCY AND SURGE

With Saddam's flight, the American leadership proceeded to snatch defeat from the jaws of whatever victory it had attained over the regime. Although Saddam and his sons were all eventually killed, both Sunni and Shi'a militia insurgencies rose up against the foreign invaders. By 2004, American casualties began to rise in this insurgent warfare due to the use of terrorist tactics that used suicide bombings and improvised explosive devices against coalition troops and their allies, especially the new Iraqi army and security forces that the United States had created to support the fragile new Iraq government in Baghdad. The Ba'athist bureaucrats who had run Iraq were outlawed and the Iraqi army disbanded. Almost immediately, the Fedayeen Saddam, who were still fighting, found willing allies and adherents to its cause from the ranks of these disaffected Iraqis. Additionally, internecine fighting developed along ethnic, tribal, and religious grounds, making the insurgency both a civil war as well as an insurgency against the invaders. As the insurgency spread and gained strength in places like Fallujah, the leadership in Washington, D.C., denied that an insurgency even existed. This in turn framed the actions of Wallace's successors, like Lieutenant General Ricardo Sanchez, who implemented operational policies that arguably worsened the insurgency.

The full scale of the unfolding disaster was best represented by the Abu Ghraib prison scandal and the loss of Fallujah, both occurring in 2004. Fallujah was retaken in late 2004 by the Marines but took almost two years to pacify completely, in part because of the reaction of everyday Iraqis against the cruelty of foreign jihadists and home-grown extremists like Abu Musab al-Zarqawi, the leader of Al-Qaeda in Iraq, the entity that later transformed into today's Islamic State of Iraq and Syria (ISIS).

In the United States, politicians, such as senators Hillary Clinton and John Kerry, who had supported the invasion of Iraq, now turned against the war. By 2006, the situation seemed hopeless, and U.S. pundits and policymakers were in agreement that Iraq had become something of a quagmire along the lines of Vietnam, with no graceful way out.

Several subsequent events led to a turnaround. First, the United States and its coalition partners finally recognized the nature of the war they were in and took steps to implement a practical counterinsurgency doctrine in the army's Field Manual 3–24. At the same time, the driving force behind this doctrine, General David Petraeus, advocated for an increase in troops to Iraq (known as "the surge") to secure the population and undermine the various insurgent groups, both Shi'a and Sunni. Also, Iran realized that it was undermining the Shi'a-dominated government that it hoped to establish permanently in Baghdad, so it began to work with militia leaders like Muqtada al-Sadr to achieve a rapprochement with U.S. forces that might lead to their withdrawal. Furthermore, al-Sadr's forces were crushed by the surge in Baghdad. Finally, the brutal actions of the insurgents and an influx of foreign fighters who were as ruthless (if not more so) led to a reaction, especially in the broad Sunni province of Al Anbar, known now as the "Awakening."

The critical period came in 2007–2008, with Petraeus in command in Iraq. By the time Obama took office as president in early 2009, the situation in Iraq seemed to have created the space for a U.S. withdrawal. Obama finally withdrew all U.S. forces from Iraq in 2011, having failed to get an agreement with the Shi'a-dominated government for increased basing rights and certain status of forces protections for U.S. troops.

THE AFTERMATH—DISASTER

The U.S. narrative that emerged of Iraq in 2003–2011 as a U.S. victory was soon undermined. The Shi'a government antagonized its Sunni citizens and arrested Sunni leaders, particularly those in the west and north of Iraq. In 2013, as a result of the Syrian Civil War, a new force arose built around the remnants of Zarqawi's Al Qaeda in Iraq, which had rebranded itself as ISIS. It claimed the authority to conquer and declare a new caliphate, and with alarming speed, it began multiple offensives into Iraq.

The fiction that Iraq could defend itself against even a small dedicated band of fighters, especially in the Sunni areas it had neglected (other than Kurdistan, which relied on its own Pershmerga militia), was blown to bits as ISIS forces, under the leadership of Abu Bakr al-Baghdadi, overran multiple cities and towns. Fallujah fell to ISIS in January 2014, and in June that same year, Baghdadi's holy warriors seized the crown jewel of northern Iraq, the city of Mosul, where he declared the establishment of a new caliphate. In all these cases, the dispirited and poorly disciplined Iraqi troops (which U.S. advisors had trained) simply ran away and abandoned their equipment to ISIS forces. This happened so swiftly that the Americans and their partners were shocked and reluctantly had to reintervene with ground troops at the end of Obama's term in office to address the situation. Mosul was recaptured in 2018, but the city was destroyed in the process.

The shifting sands of Iraq had once again moved, upsetting the narrative of victory and exposing American efforts as only temporary. Furthermore, Iran was strengthened in the long run, and the Iraqi invasion did nothing to counterbalance Tehran or Damascus.

Further Reading

Bolger, Daniel P. *Why We Lost: A General's Inside Account of the Iraq and Afghanistan Wars.* New York: Houghton, Mifflin, and Harcourt, 2014.

Gordon, Michael R., and General Bernard E. Trainor. *Cobra II: The Inside Story of the Invasion and Occupation of Iraq.* New York: Pantheon Books, 2006.

Lambeth, Benjamin S. *The Unseen War: Allied Air Power and the Takedown of Saddam Hussein.* Annapolis, MD: Naval Institute Press, 2013.

Moten, Matthew Moten, ed. *Between War and Peace: How America Ends Its Wars.* Detroit: Free Press, 2012.

Index

Note: All disasters (i.e., battles, campaigns, wars, and operations) will give first page only unless reference to the event shows up later in another section.

About the Authors

John T. Kuehn, PhD (from Kansas State University), is professor of military history at the U.S. Army Command and General Staff College (CGSC). He retired from the U.S. Navy in 2004 at the rank of commander after twenty-three years. He has taught a variety of subjects, including military history, at CGSC since 2000. Dr. Kuehn has written several books, including *A Military History of Japan: From the Age of the Samurai to the 21st Century* (2014), *Napoleonic Warfare: The Operational Art of the Great Campaigns* (2015), and *A Short History of the Rise and Fall of the General Board of the Navy, 1900–1950* (2017).

David W. Holden, PhD, is an assistant professor of military history at the U.S. Army Command and General Staff College (CGSC). He retired from the U.S. army in 2005 at the rank of captain after being wounded in Iraq. He has taught a variety of courses, including "The Evolution of Military Thought" and "The Face of Battle." Dr. Holden earned his PhD in 2016 from the University of Kansas.